# Plotinus the Platonist

**Bloomsbury Studies in Ancient Philosophy**

*Also available from Bloomsbury*

*Happiness and Greek Ethical Thought*, M. Andrew Holowchak
*Ideas of Socrates*, Matthew S. Linck
*Socratic Method*, Rebecca Bensen Cain

# Plotinus the Platonist: A Comparative Account of Plato and Plotinus' Metaphysics

David J. Yount

*Bloomsbury Studies in Ancient Philosophy*

Bloomsbury Academic
An imprint of Bloomsbury Publishing Plc

B L O O M S B U R Y

LONDON • OXFORD • NEW YORK • NEW DELHI • SYDNEY

**Bloomsbury Academic**
An imprint of Bloomsbury Publishing Plc

50 Bedford Square
London
WC1B 3DP
UK

1385 Broadway
New York
NY 10018
USA

**www.bloomsbury.com**

**Bloomsbury is a registered trade mark of Bloomsbury Publishing Plc**

First published 2014
Paperback edition first published 2016



**British Library Cataloguing-in-Publication Data**
A catalogue record for this book is available from the British Library.

ISBN: HB: 978-1-4725-7521-0
PB: 978-1-4742-8368-7
ePDF: 978-1-4725-7522-7
ePub: 978-1-4725-7523-4

**Library of Congress Cataloging-in-Publication Data**
A catalog record for this book is available from the Library of Congress.

Typeset by Fakenham Prepress Solutions, Fakenham, Norfolk NR21 8NN

*To*
*Elaine*
*and*
*Bert*

# Contents

# Preface

When I first read Plotinus, I could not help but feel that there were many significant similarities between what Plotinus was claiming about the nature of reality, knowledge, and ethics on the one hand, and what Plato mentions in his dialogues on these philosophical studies on the other.[1] I do not believe that I was merely being misled by Plotinus himself, who frequently asserts that he is simply following Plato in what he says; one can show through the use of Plato and Plotinus' texts that they do not have essentially different views. After having read Plato and Plotinus, then, I assumed that there would be an entire tome that detailed the resemblance between the two philosophers. However, as I searched the major universities' library holdings, I was surprised that there was no work in English on their shelves whose main thesis argued either that their views were not essentially different or that they were essentially similar. That is, no scholar has shown that Plato and Plotinus (arguably) do not essentially differ on many significant metaphysical claims, as this project aims to show. Even more remarkable was the fact that not only was there no such book but that scholars (mainly in journal articles and in books on the interpretation of Plato's *Parmenides*, for instance) seemed to go out of their way to differentiate Plato's view from that of Plotinus. It is at this point that I decided to begin a project, of which the present project is a major portion, with the aim of showing that Plotinus' view does not essentially differ from Plato's view in the areas of mysticism, epistemology, ethics, or metaphysics. I chose to make the case for metaphysics in this work, because it contains the most controversial claims amongst Plato and Plotinus scholars. I hope to publish a work on the other three areas in the future.

Many years after I decided to write this book, I came upon an exception. John N. Findlay, in his *Plato and Platonism*, after explaining some of Plotinus' views, claims:

> There is nothing in all these Plotinian treatments which does not have abundant connections with the Platonic writings, and this is particularly so in the eschatological treatments of the life of the Soul after bodily death, its migration from one bodily form to another, and its final liberation.[2]

While I was pleased not to be the only person to see this strong connection between the two philosophers, I discovered that Findlay does not present his readers with anything resembling all of these "abundant connections" here, which thus leaves the present project worthy of pursuit. Moreover, I would (and will) argue that there are many more, and important, metaphysical issues, where there is no essential difference between the philosophers, besides ones merely related to the soul and its eschatology.[3]

Largely ignoring, and/or downplaying, the importance of Plotinus' thought and his interpretation of Plato's metaphysics not only does a great disservice in general to budding Platonic scholars but also erects a barrier to understanding Aristotle and Plato's thought. Whether or not Plotinus is wrong in what he holds, he, at the very least, offers another interpretation of Plato that merits investigation, just as Platonic scholars look to Aristotle, and other ancient, modern, and contemporary commentators, in an attempt to better understand Plato's views. At the most, Plotinus is the best interpreter of Plato, and he fills in the details left out of Plato's dialogues for whatever reason. At the least, his work is worth assessing and dealing with as a means of knowing more about the history of Platonism. As I hope to show, Plotinus' work is an excellent interpretation of Plato's metaphysics, and it is valuable for its own sake, as well as for the sake of understanding some of his predecessors.

Why is Plotinus' interpretation of, and adherence to, Plato's thought so superior? I would offer three reasons:

First, Plotinus questions almost nothing about what Plato says regarding metaphysical issues, and demonstrates his agreement with the claims in this book.[4] In contrast, almost every Platonic scholar or follower that I am aware of either questions to some extent or other Plato's views in some fundamental aspect, or, unfortunately, ignores what Plato is saying.[5] Examples of the former group (particularly with reference to contemporary scholars, but even Aristotle fits in this category) include those who ridicule or find implausible Plato's views, such as that reincarnation occurs, that learning is recollection of the Forms, that stars have souls; or his arguments for the immortality of the soul, his conception of the ideal state, or of the Forms.[6] Contemporary philosophers generally seem to refer to themselves as Platonists if they merely believe that Forms exist, but there are obviously many additional metaphysical claims that Plato makes (that the soul is immortal, that there is an All-Soul or World-Soul, God and gods, a Demiurge that created the visible universe, guardian spirits and that reincarnation occurs); hence, though one's commitment to the Forms may minimally qualify one as a Platonist, presumably one who is dedicated to more of what

Plato says is a Platonist to a greater degree than one who is not so committed. Not only does Plotinus never question any of the views just mentioned but also he argues strongly in favor of them. Examples of the latter group of scholars (who ignore what Plato says while endorsing some Platonic aspects) include St. Augustine (who rejected Neoplatonism in *The City of God*)[7] and Marsilio Ficino. According to Tigerstedt, in Ficino's "Exhortation to Those that Listen to or Read Plotinus," Ficino "solemnly advises them that they should consider themselves as listening to Plato himself. For, through the mouth of Plotinus, Plato speaks to us—a second Plato, as elevated as the first, and sometimes even deeper."[8] I thoroughly agree with Ficino's comment here, and indeed hope to move toward demonstrating its truth throughout the rest of this book, at least with respect to metaphysics. However, Ficino adds that, in his opinion, Platonism is second in correctness or divinity only to Christianity.[9]

The second reason for the superiority of Plotinus' interpretation of Plato's metaphysics is the fact that he is the only known man in history who was so convinced of the truth of Plato's work that he went to great lengths to procure some land and to attempt to create "Platonopolis"—Plato's ideal state—and to rule it according to Plato's laws.[10] I mention this only to demonstrate Plotinus' commitment to—at the very least—the views he believed Plato to hold, and I will argue throughout this work that what he believed was true.

The third reason is that, in the history of philosophy, there are only two men who to my knowledge personally attest to having had a vision and knowledge of the Platonic Good or the One: Plotinus and Porphyry. This distinguishes Plotinus and Porphyry from the other Neo-Platonists (Iamblichus, Syrianus, and Proclus), and later groups of Platonists (Cambridge and Thomas Taylor). In Porphyry's case, we do not have as many extant writings by which to compare his thought to Plato's on as many points as with Plotinus. Due to space constraints, moreover, I cannot examine evidence here for the claim that Plato is best interpreted as having had this very experience as well.

It should be apparent at this point that there is some evidence for the claim made in the title of this book: if anyone deserves to be called a metaphysical Platonist—though there are certainly many others, depending upon one's assumptions and interpretations—and not necessarily a "new Platonist," "recent Platonist," or "Neo-Platonist," it is Plotinus.[11] It is my aim to show, through a close reading of the texts, the overwhelming extent to which these two thinkers share not only compatible metaphysical views but also that they are not essentially different. I do not intend on, along the way, pitting Plotinus against any other philosophers (Platonists, Old Academicians, Middle Platonists, Neo-Platonists,

Cambridge Platonists, Aristotle, or Aristotelians), to argue who among them is the "best Platonist" or "more of a Platonist"—my object is simply to show no essential metaphysical disagreement between Plato and Plotinus.

It would be a great source of satisfaction to me if this book were to encourage many more philosophers to engage in trying to understand Plotinus' writings (let alone to engage my thesis that Plato and Plotinus share almost identical views).[12] The obvious problem is that most students of philosophy are not introduced to Plotinus, and—not being familiar with his work from the start—they seldom go on to study his work in graduate school. This sequence of "non-events" produces very few professors who have seriously studied his work, and so the cycle perpetuates. It will take a great shift in thinking to persuade scholars to focus more on Plotinus, but I think such a shift would pay many scholarly dividends.

It is in the interest of presenting as much evidence as possible in favor of the position that these philosophers do not essentially differ in their metaphysical views, to spur interest in examining Plotinus' reading of Plato further, and to increase awareness of Plotinus generally that I write this book.

I must acknowledge many who considerably improved this work. First of all, I would like to sincerely thank my students at Mesa Community College (especially my first two Plato classes), as well as the faculty and staff who have heard me discuss this book's contents for years. I would also like to thank Debi Campbell, Barry Vaughan, and Patrice Nango, colleagues who read parts of the manuscript and/or gave me invaluable comments. Russell Jones's comments on my APA paper, concerning the One of *Parmenides*' First Hypothesis and the Good of the *Republic*, allowed me to improve my argument in that section, for which I am grateful. I want to sincerely thank Arnold Hermann for discussing the relation between the One and the Good, and many other concepts related to Plato and Plotinus. I appreciate the moral support of Trina Hillery, Valerie Hill, Elizabeth Ursic, Keith Crudup, Tom Shoemaker, Nancy Ray, Kerry Leibowitz, Joan Price, Cathie Gagnon, Michael Yount and my parents, Richard and Pauline, throughout the project. Hackett Publishing graciously permitted my use of most of the Plato quotations and Princeton University Press has allowed me to use Barnes' translation of Aristotle and Cornford's translation of Plato's *Sophist*, for which I am also grateful. I would be remiss if I failed to mention Rosamund Louvel, Eliza Tutellier, and Jenn Neal for their invaluable assistance in the editing of this project. I would especially like to thank reviewers John Dillon, Michael Wagner, Lloyd Gerson and the anonymous reviewer, for their careful readings and insightful and encouraging comments. The standard caveat, that none of these scholars should be understood to agree with the contents, certainly applies. Finally, I would like to thank my wife Elaine and my sons, Alex, Elliot, and Holden for bearing with my fervor and long hours and years during this endeavor, as well as Robert Price, for spurring my interest in Plotinus in the first place and for helping me think about his philosophy much more deeply.

Dave Yount
Mesa Community College

# Introduction

There are a number of points to discuss before I lay out my argument that Plotinus does not essentially differ in his metaphysical views from Plato. First I will review and take stands on the authenticity or otherwise of Plato's dialogues and letters (section I). Second, I take up other interpretive issues in Plato's work, including the question of whether he has a doctrine at all (section II). Third, I discuss Plotinus' influence in the history of thought, and consider the way in which Plotinus' (and the Neo-Platonists') understanding of Plato's work has been characterized by commentators (section III). Lastly, I will explain the methodology and plan that I will use in my project in order to argue that there is no essential difference between the metaphysical philosophies of Plato and Plotinus (section IV).

## I. Plato's dialogues and letters: Authenticity issues

Let us now review the state of scholarship on the issue of authenticity of Plato's dialogues and letters. It should be noted that Plotinus takes the letters (especially *Letters* II, VI, VII, VIII) as being genuine, along with *Alcibiades* I[1] and the *Epinomis*.[2] As far as dialogues go, stylometric analysis by two scholars[3] shows that the *Epinomis* is genuine, but several others have questioned its authenticity, claiming that Philip of Opus is its author.[4] Stylometry also shows that the following works are inauthentic: *Alcibiades* I, *Alcibiades* II, *Amatores* (*Lovers*), *Axiochus*, *Clitopho*, *Definitions*, *Demodocus*, *Eryxias*, *Hipparchus*, *Justice*, *Minos*, *Sisyphus*, *Theages*, and *On Virtue*. However, based on Denyer's arguments in favor of the authenticity of *Alcibiades* I,[5] I will take it to be so. As for the rest of these works, they are Platonic in character and may have been written by Plato's students. In addition, I will assume that the *Epinomis* is inauthentic, but ask the reader to see which claims Plotinus may have taken from them, with a view to judging how Platonic they sound. For instance, the author of the *Epinomis* claims that, once initiated into her share of the singular true wisdom, the soul continues to observe the fairest things that sight can see; even if the *Epinomis* is inauthentic, this claim is certainly Platonic, so Plotinus would not have been misled in any serious way about Plato's view.

Concerning the authenticity of Plato's letters, stylometric analysis shows all of them to be genuine, but there is far from universal agreement on their authenticity: views range from all of the letters being genuine,[6] to none of them,[7] to the agnostic position,[8] with lots of variants in between.[9] I agree with Findlay[10] and Desjardins,[11] who (respectively) state that there is nothing inconsistent between what is said in *Letters* II and VII and the rest of Plato's corpus. In fact, I believe there may be much truth in Tigerstedt's statement: "If a Platonic text seemed to be opposed to their interpretation, it was simply declared spurious."[12]

In short, whatever Plotinus, or anyone, can find in the spurious dialogues or letters can, in spirit, if not in the letter (no pun intended), be found in Platonic writings that are universally accepted as being authentic. Hopefully the reader will witness the breadth of dialogues used—whether or not letters are adduced—to support what I take to be the Platonic view.

## II. Other interpretive issues in Plato

Tigerstedt, in his book, *Interpreting Plato*, has a fitting quotation about the interpretation of Plato, setting up just some of the pitfalls that await any Platonic commentator:

> The controversies about Plato are far more radical and fundamental. What some scholars regard as a faithful picture of Plato the man and his philosophy, is to other scholars an outrageous caricature or a pure invention… . Was Plato a dogmatist or a sceptic, an un-systematical questioner or a rigid system-builder, a fervid mystic or a cool dialectician, a noble extoller of the freedom of the human spirit or a sinister herald of the totalitarian state? Are his thoughts to be found in his writings, open to every fair-minded and careful reader, or are they hidden behind the written work, a secret doctrine, to be extracted painfully from hints in him and other authors?[13]

Thus, if Tigerstedt is correct, some scholars will take to be a pure invention my interpretation that Plotinus' view is significantly similar to Plato's, even though I believe that it is faithful to Plato's philosophy. Nonetheless, I will cover the following issues of Platonic interpretation: (1) the falsity of the "no doctrine" view of Plato; (2) the Unitarianism of the current project; (3) the systematization of the current project. First, then, how do we know that Plato had a doctrine?

*The No Doctrine View*: As beautiful and at times entertaining as Plato's dialogues are, they have led some commentators to read his work as being *nothing other than* fictional entertainment or literature, containing no real statements of any doctrine(s) or beliefs of his whatsoever.[14] Anderson gives us an example of this viewpoint:

> Plato's dialogues explore a number of possibilities. A variety of characters in those dialogues explicate, analyze, and argue for one solution or another. But there is no unified theory or doctrine that can be said to constitute a definitive solution.
>
> ... I think that Plato wrote his dialogues to lure his readers and listeners into the conversation. He wanted us to go beyond his text by examining the various possibilities and arguments presented by his characters and by formulating our own attempt at answering the profound questions they pose.[15]

Regarding the first paragraph, there is no question but that the dialogues explore possibilities. However, we can be relatively certain that, when the character, Socrates, espouses a consistent view across dialogues,[16] he represents Plato's view, especially when both of the characters in a given dialogue agree with it—instances include the immortality of the soul in the *Phaedo* and the program of the ideal state and tripartite nature of the soul in the *Republic*. If Anderson is correct about there not being one solution, then where, for instance, is the serious discussion *throughout* the dialogues that the soul may *not* be immortal? There is no such discussion; we do see, in the *Apology* (40c–41c), Socrates mention the possibility that perhaps we lose consciousness and that death is a dreamless sleep (while also mentioning the possibility of the soul's immortality), but, to my knowledge, there is no other questioning of that view elsewhere. In sum, there is ample evidence of a consistent teaching that can be extracted and reasonably inferred from the dialogues—the rest of this project is evidence thereof—along with Aristotle's statements and criticisms concerning Plato's doctrine, not to mention the oral tradition that assumes a Platonic position.

According to Anderson, there is some truth in my view that Plato wanted to lure his readers and listeners into the conversation to examine various possibilities. However, I believe this is truer in the "early", or aporetic, dialogues, where no conclusion is agreed upon or reached, but where Socrates refutes a proposed definition (or more). For instance, Athenians, or even contemporary believers in God, *mutatis mutandis*, would presumably be interested in determining what is wrong with the definition of piety as praying and sacrificing to the gods. So they read the early dialogues to discover how difficult it is, for instance, to define piety, courage, and temperance, and to learn about Socrates' life and death. In what are referred to as the middle and late dialogues, we find

Plato giving answers to philosophical questions generally—with the first section of the *Parmenides*, and the *Theaetetus*, being the obvious exceptions—even though he does consider other views along the way. We are welcome to form our own opinions about the issues raised, but that does not imply that Plato does not have a considered view. Besides the dialogues themselves, Aristotle lectured on Plato's observations on the soul, the Forms, and the Good in the *De Anima*, *Metaphysics*, and *Nicomachean Ethics*. Lastly, Anderson[17] does not address the fact that Aristotle prominently and explicitly attacks the existence of Plato's Forms (*Metaphysics* I.9), the existence of the Form of the Good and its relevance to ethics (*Nicomachean Ethics* I.6), and Plato's ideal state (*Politics* I and II). If Plato holds no view, why, in these cases, is Aristotle explicitly arguing against what he refers to as Plato's stance, which mostly matches what we see in the dialogues?

*The Unitarianism Approach*: I take the view that Plato basically held the same beliefs throughout the dialogues, even if we receive more details as we read the dialogues further—assuming a rough chronological order.[18] I agree with Gerson's approach here:

> I shall also require as a working hypothesis a qualified unitarianism in the treatment of the development of Plato's doctrines. I shall therefore not hesitate to draw on texts chronologically far apart. The justification for this is, of course, only to be found in the outcome.[19]

Whenever I see another issue raised or explained in more detail than before—that Forms not only exist but "blend," in the *Sophist*[20]—I refer to this phenomenon as a more detailed explanation of Plato's position, rather than a development: that he revised his view that Forms do not blend to the alternative that Forms do indeed blend.

So I agree with Shorey: "Plato on the whole belongs rather to the type of thinkers whose philosophy is fixed in early maturity (Schopenhauer, Herbert Spencer), rather than to the class of those who receive a new revelation every decade (Schelling)."[21]

Of course not everyone will agree with this approach. Note, however, that my view does not necessarily take a stand on the order of the dialogues.[22] Moreover, if Plato is actually best read as a developmentalist, it would presumably make my case easier, because I would only need to find Plotinian passages that agreed with either Plato's earlier or later view in order to defend my thesis. Thus, for the reader who disagrees with my thesis, it is more difficult for me to assume Unitarianism.

Tigerstedt posed the following challenge:

> The fact that Plato chose to express his philosophic thought indirectly, through the mouth of other persons, in dialogues, most of which are self-centred wholes, without any reference to other dialogues, means that the burden of proof lies with him who asserts the unity of Plato's thought.[23]

My response is that we find characters agreeing with one another about conclusions, such as the immortality of the soul, that Forms exist, and that we need to know the Good. If Plato did not believe that a given view was true, I assume that he would have had a character question that belief to the point where it was shown to be either problematic or false, given the attacks that are made against views found in the aporetic dialogues. We also see speakers (who a great majority of commentators agree represent Plato's view) espouse consistent and stable views, across the dialogues, about the Forms, All-Soul, and Demiurge, some of which, when raised, are explicitly mentioned as being Plato's and attacked by Aristotle, so we can reasonably assume that there are such views in the dialogues. My argument here is far from conclusive, but is intended more as an explanation of my approach toward the dialogues than as, say, a proof against developmentalists.

Before concluding, I should note that there are at least three different Unitarian positions: (i) The Shorey and Cherniss[24] Unitarianism: Plato has a unified view of entities such as Forms, but does not have an Unwritten Doctrine and does not contain the Plotinian Three Hypostases (The One or Good, Nous or Intellect, and Soul); (ii) The Tübingen[25] Unitarianism: Plato's Unwritten Teachings about the first principles is what unifies the dialogues; that is, the dialogues only hint at and express what Plato said to his preferred pupils about first principles, but are not inconsistent with the Unwritten Teachings; (iii) Plotinian[26] Unitarianism: Plato has a systematic, unified view throughout the dialogues that is also consistent with the Unwritten Teachings about first principles, including the Three Hypostases.

I do not subscribe to the Shorey and Cherniss position, because the Unwritten Doctrine is not implausible on the face of it, but more importantly because I do find Plotinus' Three Hypostases in Plato's view. I do not subscribe to the Tübingen position, because I believe that we have enough explicit evidence of Plato's view of his first principles in the dialogues (keeping in mind that, at the same time, I fully acknowledge Plato's claims concerning ineffability). I am more inclined to the Plotinian position here, fully endorsing the systematic Platonic dialogues and Platonic Three Hypostasis elements. However, while I realize that endorsing the Unwritten Teachings would aid my case, I intend to base my argument on what Plotinus and Plato's writings contain or imply, leaving the Unwritten Teachings as a friend who waits in the wings.[27]

Therefore, I have some plausible warrant to believe in the unity of Plato's thought and Plotinus' reading thereof for two reasons: both philosophers either directly (Plotinus) or indirectly (Plato) claim to have had an experience or vision of the Good, and Plato arguably does not change his mind across the dialogues—at least on the claims examined here.

*Systematizing Plato's Thought*: Several commentators, for instance, Katz and Tigerstedt,[28] argue that we cannot and should not attempt to systematize Plato. For instance, Katz[29] argues that Plotinus had a doctrine, but Plato wrote dialogues "in which philosophies are set against each other in living argument," so we cannot "distill a doctrine from the writings of Plato," because doing so "tends to neglect the context in which certain views are expressed and often naively tends to ascribe to Plato the views expressed by *one* of the speakers or in some argument of the dialogues—an approach analogous perhaps to an attempt to distill a philosophy of Shakespeare out of the speeches of, say, Polonius." My reply to Katz is as follows: Since Plato consistently and stably refers to many views in the dialogues—that Forms exist, or that the soul is immortal, among others—we are warranted in interpreting Plato as believing these to be true. There does seem to be a system of claims that can be culled and gleaned from the dialogues, and the reader should judge whether my systematizing approach is successful. For example, if I find every place in Plato's corpus where the All-Soul is mentioned explicitly or implicitly, analyze the texts for similarities and then summarize the results, I believe that the summary tells us what Plato's view of the All-Soul is. I have done the same with Plotinus' text in order to compare it with Plato's.

Moreover, there is certainly more to a Platonic dialogue than merely its conclusions and sub-conclusions,[30] and as a result I suggest reading every Platonic dialogue—authentic or not—and every *Ennead*;[31] there is no substitute for doing so in order to get a good sense of what these thinkers believe. Furthermore, in Plato's case, I suggest investigating every character in every dialogue,[32] the places mentioned, and the settings of the dialogues, in order to really understand what Plato was saying on every level.

In sum, I argue that there is a doctrine in Plato's work, one that we can reasonably infer from the agreed-upon conclusions, key premises, or key ideas that appear in the arguments across the dialogues. Further, I have a Unitarian approach toward Plato's work. Lastly, I have tried to justify my assumption that a system of Plato's thought occurs in the dialogues.

## III. Plotinus' influence on the history of thought

Very briefly, Plotinus (c. 204–70 CE)[33] was born in Egypt (perhaps in Lyco or Lycopolis), and died in Campania, Italy at the age of 66. See Porphyry's *On the Life of Plotinus and the Order of His Books* for more on Plotinus' life.[34]

Here, first, (a) as a counter to those who have not yet found Plotinus worthy of study, I want to show the great extent to which avid readers respect Plotinus' work, as well as lament how little his work has been studied. Further, (b) I will argue that Plotinus is best conceived of as a Platonist (as he thinks of himself), as opposed to (c) a Neo- (or new, original) Platonist. Moreover, (d) I will address the subject of the extent to which Plotinus was responding to his circumstances, as opposed to (my view) a Platonist who happened to live during that time period. I will finish by (e) examining and responding to criticisms that the Neo-Platonist, or Plotinian, reading of Plato is wrong.

### A. Plotinus' praises sung

I have discussed that, through Augustine's appreciation and adaptation of Plotinus' thought, Plotinus influenced Christian theology.[35] But Plotinian commentators in general also laud Plotinus highly:[36]

> Plotinus is incomparably the greatest of the Neo-Platonists and has had a far deeper and wider influence than any of his successors.[37]

> If anyone doubts that Plotinus was a man of genius, let him study the efforts of Plotinus' nearest predecessors and followers. Let him soak for a while in the theosophical maunderings of Philo and the Hermetists, in the venomous fanaticism of Tertullian, in the tea-table transcendentalism of Plutarch, in the cultured commonplaces of Maximus, in the amiable pieties of Porphyry, in the really unspeakable spiritualistic drivellings of the *de Mysteriis*—let him do that, and if ever he gets his head above water again, he will see Plotinus in his true historical perspective as the one man who still knew how to think clearly in an age which was beginning to forget what thinking meant.[38]

> Just as Aristotle overtopped so tremendously all the other pupils of Plato, so the disciples of Ammonius, the reviver of Plato, were all overtopped by Plotinus, the greatest thinker certainly between Aristotle and Spinoza, and by some critics regarded as an even greater metaphysician than Plato and Aristotle themselves.[39]

> [Plotinus] is the last great light of the Greek world.[40]

> Plotinus has been called by the modern critics Whittaker, Drews, and Réville (as quoted by Dean Inge) respectively, 'the greatest individual thinker between Aristotle and Descartes,' 'the greatest metaphysician of antiquity,' and 'one of the most vigorous thinkers humanity has produced.'[41]

It stands to reason, then, that, with accolades such as these, Plotinian scholars also lament that not much attention is paid to Plotinus by other philosophers and scholars. For instance, Davidson, in his introduction to Hadot,[42] states that Plotinus has "too often [been] consigned to the footnotes of philosophy." But Inge seems to lead the pack:

> If Plotinus had been studied with half the care that has been bestowed on Plato and Aristotle, the continuity of philosophical and religious thought in the early centuries of the Christian era would be far better understood, and the history of Greek philosophy would not be habitually deprived of its last chapter.[43]

## B. Plotinus *believes* he is a Platonist (whether or not he is in fact one)

Let us now examine the issue as to whether Plotinus is best seen generally as a Platonist, someone who does not essentially differ with Plato, as I contend, or as a Neo-Platonist—someone who essentially has a new philosophy with some Platonic elements but which goes beyond or differs from Plato in at least one major way.

First, many—including those who believe he is a Neo-Platonist—have acknowledged that Plotinus believed himself to be a Platonist (and minimizes any differences between his view and Plato's),[44] not a Neo-Platonist.[45] Emilsson actually argues for Plotinus' belief that he is a Platonist:

> In general, Plotinus' views must be seen in the light of the views of his predecessors. Plotinus was a Platonist. In fact he was so much of a Platonist that he thought that his most important doctrines contained nothing new, that he himself was merely an exegete who unfolds what lies implicit in the doctrines of Plato.[46]

Gatti puts the issue between Plato and Plotinus as follows:

> For this reason, the judgments of interpreters on such a question differ. For some scholars, the debt of Plotinus to Plato was absolute. Plato is beyond all criticism or polemic according to Plotinus, who considered himself nothing more than Plato's disciple (Zeller, Theiler, Schwyzer, [A. H.] Armstrong, Krämer). According to others, Plotinus is completely autonomous with respect

to the tradition, including Plato, availing himself of Platonic doctrines in an independent manner (Rist, Eon).[47]

I am inclined to the former view, but perhaps fall somewhere in between: I believe Plotinus had the same experience or vision of the Good that Plato did, and so their philosophies come out sounding, if not being, the same. However, it is not because Plato wrote what he did that Plotinus agrees with it; Plotinus agrees with it because he achieved knowledge of the Good; thus Plato wrote what he did because he also had the experience of the Good. These experiences made each philosopher agree with previous or current views, as they reflected reality as they had experienced it. This can be contrasted with Findlay's stance that it was "by a deep immersion in the writings of Plato and also of Aristotle that [Ammonius] Saccas and Plotinus came to create their Neoplatonic philosophy,"[48] although I agree with him that "Plotinus … understood Plato very deeply."[49]

Thus, Emilsson and I seem to be the only clear proponents of the view that Plotinus is best described as a Platonist (though Emilsson should certainly not be thought of as holding the rest of the views argued for here).

## C. Opposing view I: Plotinus is more accurately described as a Neo-Platonist because his view is significantly different from that of Plato

The standard view seems to be that Plotinus has a significantly different view from Plato; it is this view which motivates the present project. Perhaps one motivation for believing in at least one major difference between them is that Plotinus was responding to Stoic and Aristotelian concerns, and/or that one assumes Porphyry is correct when he says that, in Plotinus, we find the complete metaphysics of Aristotle (*Life*, Ch. 14.4–7). However, granting these considerations, I maintain that, as long as Plotinus is responding to these concerns from a Platonic perspective, and that whatever Aristotelian metaphysics is in Plotinus is also in Plato, we do not have an essential difference between Plato and Plotinus. For instance, Annas, in her *Ancient Philosophy: A Very Short Introduction*, states that Plotinus founded "an original new school … which revives some of Plato's ideas and is called 'Neoplatonism,'"[50] which rethought "Plato's ideas in a new and original synthesis."[51]

Anton is adamant that Plotinus is correctly called a Neo-Platonist, his reverential statements of Plato notwithstanding.[52] His main contentions of Plotinus' difference are that Plotinus is not as much of a political philosopher as Plato, and that he has a different aesthetic theory.

Gerson argues:

> Yet, when we study the *Enneads*, not only do we find claims that are made nowhere in the writings of Plato known to us, but we wonder how Plotinus himself could have thought that he was not advancing into new territory.[53]

I grant that Plotinus makes some claims that Plato does not;[54] however, my argument is that Plotinus has not significantly shifted into some other, new, metaphysics, but has all the markings of Platonism in his viewpoint.

Stace is the harshest:

> The word Neo-Platonism is a misnomer. It does not stand for a genuine revival of Platonism. The Neo-Platonists were no doubt the offspring of Plato, but they were the illegitimate offspring. The true greatness of Plato lay in his rationalistic idealism; his defects were mostly connected with his tendency to myth and mysticism.[55]

In Stace's view, not only is Plotinus not a Platonist, he is not any kind of legitimate Neo-Platonist, even though his thought is somehow an offshoot of Plato's.

I hope to show, however, that Plotinus' view of rationalistic idealism (assuming this is Plato's view as well), along with other metaphysical issues, is the legitimate offspring of Plato.

## D. Opposing view II: Plotinus' philosophy mainly results from his (or the readers') life circumstances

There are several commentators who emphasize the life and times of Plotinus as being the chief molder of his philosophy; moreover, one critic seems to state that we can only find out what Plotinus' view of reality is based on through our own thought and faith, which leaves his view subject to *your and my* life experience. However, since my position is that we can find Plotinus' view by directly reading his *Enneads* without bringing our own life experience to our interpretation—and that Plotinus maintains his stance as a result of his vision of the Good (and not of his culture)—I need to argue against these interpretations.

Of course Plotinus' culture influenced his thought to some extent. For example, he argues against the Gnostics and materialists—just as Plato argued against the sophists—presumably because their view held some sway in his day, and some of his writings were surely created in answer to questions posed by his students. However, it is equally clear that Plotinus claims to have had an experience of the Good, and so the commentators who believe that Plotinus is only reacting to the economic and social forces, for instance, need to account for this feature of Plotinus' thought.

Miles is an enthusiastic representative of this view:

> It is still the case that his thought was intimately shaped by the circumstances of his life, the conversations of his life, the conversations he shared with others, and the society in which he lived. Plotinus positioned his own proposals within the framework of ancient and contemporary philosophical discussion. He professed his allegiance to Plato and displayed a detailed knowledge of Aristotle. But it can be shown that, while early philosophers provided his tools, the philosophical problems he addressed primarily related to urgent contemporary concerns, to other attractive proposals of his own time, and to particular features of his personal and social situation. His teaching methods reflect his interest in immediate questions. He gave priority to the questions people asked him, not only in his classes but also in his writing.[56]

Granting the first two sentences mentioned above, I hope to show that Plotinus not only "professed allegiance" to Plato's view, but actually believed this (in metaphysics), even though he addressed contemporary concerns at his school and in his writings. Moreover, I fail to see why Plotinus holds that the Good is beyond being and the source of all things, that stars are gods, or that dialectic is the primary method to attain knowledge and that there is reincarnation—to name just a few instances—when Christianity was the predominant cultural view in his day. In addition, the fact that Plotinus answered questions in response to his students does not by itself imply that Plotinus' view—many metaphysical claims from which are represented here—was formed in response to those questions. I hold that Plotinus came to have knowledge of the Good, and then responded to people's questions in his time and place, but from the Platonic perspective, because his experience confirmed the truth of Plato's view.[57]

To examine the stance, "Plotinus' view mainly results from the readers' life circumstances"—which is implied by the claim that we cannot know what Plotinus' view of reality (of the vision of the One or Good) is without examining our own faith and reason—I quote A. H. Armstrong:

> *In the end he found a Reality the contemplation of which carried him beyond the bounds of that Platonic tradition to which he sought so devotedly to adhere. What that Reality was is a question which the readers of Plotinus must answer*

> *for themselves according to the faith and the reasons for which they have.* For myself, I have little doubt that Plotinus perceived however insecurely that Living Truth Whom he unknowingly sought, and though here I realize the theological difficulties involved, was touched, however lightly, by some gift of His grace of supernatural contemplation. No other explanation, whether [it is] inherited tradition or personal experience in development [of] thought, will, it seems to me, fit all the facts of Plotinus's doctrine of the One and the mystical union.[58]

Not surprisingly, I disagree with the claim that Plotinus went beyond the bounds of Platonic tradition. Both Plato and Plotinus discuss the knowledge that an individual can have of the One or Good, in addition to the vision (non-discursive, or non-knowledge, as it were) that a person can have of the One or Good, as paradoxical as that necessarily is and sounds.

## E. Views and objections that the Neo-Platonist, or Plotinian, reading of Plato is wrong (for various reasons), and my replies thereto

Many charges have been leveled against the Neo-Platonist interpretation of Plato in general,[59] and specifically against Plotinus' interpretation. I begin with Tigerstedt's hyperbolic claim that previous commentators had already declared this interpretive fight over. That is, according to Tigerstedt, it is an arguable fact that the Neo-Platonic interpretation of Plato has "fallen":

> At the beginning of the nineteenth century, the decline and fall of the Neoplatonic interpretation of Plato was an accomplished fact.[60]

One must decide whether the Plotinian, as opposed to the Neo-Platonic, interpretation of mine has fallen, or has been falsely declared so by Tigerstedt.

We need only make brief mentions of the remainder of the claims. First, I will briefly defend Plotinus against the charge that he did not focus on politics or political theory as much as Plato did.[61] Though Plotinus admittedly does not discuss politics as much as Plato, first, I have mentioned that he is the only person in history besides Plato to attempt to realize the ideal state on Earth (*Life*, Ch. 12). So Plotinus implicitly endorsed the laws of Plato, which are the laws of the ideal state, so we can infer that he endorsed the *Republic* model or something close to it, especially because Plotinus implicitly advocates for Platonic aristocracy (IV.4.17.19–35), explicitly endorses dialectic (I.3.1.1–4, I.3.3.1–10, I.3.4.1–23) and more specifically mathematical education for philosophers (I.3.3.1–10), and because he believes that philosophers are the best and happiest people (I.4.4.18–36).[62] It is thus plausible to suggest that Plotinus would believe that philosophers would make the best rulers.[63]

Second, according to Lewy, Plotinus systematically expressed the "transcendental tendency" of Plato which via "Porphyry became thereafter the principal feature of what is called Neoplatonism."[64] I have already argued that finding a system in Plato's philosophy is warranted; I will confirm that the "tendency" was indeed Plato's considered philosophy, and thus refute Lewy's charge.

Third, Rist[65] states that the view that "all, or almost all, the distinctive features of Neoplatonism are already to be found in Plato himself or in his immediate successors at the Academy, and that Plato clearly intended his works to be interpreted in a 'Neoplatonic' sense" is an extreme view. Though I grant that it is not clear upon one's first reading of Plato and Plotinus that the latter is correct in the details of the former's philosophy, I hope to convince that this view is ultimately not extreme but correct. Rist continues, describing "those who believe in a Neoplatonic Plato":

> Logical conclusions which Plato had not always made clear were brought out; furthermore it can then be shown that the developed form of these doctrines reveals certain inconsistencies in the Platonic originals. In these cases, by emphasizing the alternative that their Master had perhaps adumbrated but not followed up, the Neoplatonists were, in fact, formulating views which we may call 'unplatonic,' in the sense that they diverge from what is normally regarded as the Master's *conscious*, *positive* teaching.[66]

If I can show that almost every major metaphysical Plotinian claim appears in the dialogues and is Platonic, or is arguably Platonic (in the case of relatively few claims, see the conclusion for some), then Rist's claim here holds no water. I realize I am piling up promissory notes in the introduction, but I am asking the reader to honestly evaluate the evidence and to decide at the end of this journey.

Lastly, I believe Robinson[67] unfortunately begs the question when he claims that, though Plotinus merely "imagine[d]" himself only as an "interpreter" and a prophet but not as an inventor, Plotinus misinterpreted Plato. Robinson then apparently attempts to console the Plotinian enthusiast that, "Many of the great advances and novelties in human thought have arrived in the form of misinterpretations of the past."[68] I will defend Plotinus against this misinterpretation charge.

Plotinian interpreters are generally fortunate that he did *not* write in dialogue form—given that at present we only possess Plato's dialogues and not his lectures.[69] Had Plotinus written dialogues, interpreters of Plotinus might have done as some Platonic commentators, claiming that Plotinus is not presenting any doctrines or ideas in those works either. For instance, as we will see in Chapter 2.3, Plotinus explicitly says that he has had an experience or a vision of Beauty Itself,[70] and does his best, straining the Greek language like no other person before him—though Plato invented some Greek words as well—to tell us everything that he can about the way in which the intelligible and perceptible universe is laid out. Also, Porphyry tells us that Plotinus was united to the "God who is over all things" in "an unspeakable actuality."[71] Porphyry himself even avers: "I … declare that once I drew near and was united to him."[72]

I cannot show here that Plato's writings are sufficient to induce that his having had some experience of the Good similar to that of Plotinus' is the best explanation for his views as expressed in his dialogues. In any case, obviously, to question the veridicality of this experience that Plotinus and Porphyry describe is legitimate; but to deny that Plotinus and Porphyry *believed* that we can have such an experience, and their claims to have had one (or more) of these experiences, approaches intellectual dishonesty. Moreover, Plotinus and Porphyry tell us that Plato is correct about his main conclusions of metaphysics.

In sum, I have shown: that Plotinus is highly regarded by Plotinian (and some Christian) scholars; Plotinus thought of himself as a Platonist; a great many Plotinian commentators believe that Plotinus is a Neo-Platonist with views that are different from Plato's view (regardless of some similarities); the view that Plotinus developed his view *strictly* from his cultural or life experiences leaves much to be desired; replies can be given to objections to the view that Plotinus misinterprets Plato.

## IV. The methodology and plan of my argument

Since my project's thesis is to argue that the philosophies of Plato and Plotinus do not have essential differences, it is important for me to explain how I proceed to defend my view. First, I will use what I have dubbed The Compatibility Principle:

> *Plato and Plotinus' views are compatible or consistent in principle if Plotinus (or Plato) writes on some subject that does not appear in Plato (or Plotinus), unless there is written evidence in a particular case that one author writes something to the effect that 'A is true' and the other author writes that 'A is false.'*

The idea that, for instance, Plotinus writes against the Gnostics and fails to mention the sophists, or that Plato writes against the sophists but does not mention the Gnostics has nothing to do with whether or not these philosophers have the same metaphysical, epistemological, or ethical views. Another example is that Plotinus writes about there being Forms of individuals, such as a Form of Socrates, whereas Plato in the *Parmenides* is not quite sure if there is a Form of Man (in general). However, we do not find any statement by Plato that precludes there being Forms of individuals, and so we cannot say for certain that Plotinus' view of Forms of individuals is incompatible in principle with Plato's view.[73]

Furthermore, for the most part, I will not only ignore similarities between Plotinus' view and that of Aristotle, I will also ignore the similarities between Plotinus' view and the views of Pythagoreans, Stoics, and the Gnostics.[74] Why? I believe that Plotinus' central views on metaphysics (and epistemology and ethics) come to him as a result of having what will be termed here "the ultimate experience," and not primarily as a result of his culture, his place in history, or of his reading some or all of the Stoics', or Aristotle's, works. More simply, the idea is this: According to my reading of Plotinus, sometimes Aristotle and the Stoics got things right (as Plotinus saw it), and most of the time they did not; so, whatever philosophical view(s) coincides with Plotinus' view after he has had the ultimate experience is what Plotinus writes into the *Enneads*; and, whatever does not so coincide, he either does not write about or mentions the view only to show its falsity or to criticize it.[75] Hence, since Plotinus thinks he is only following the one whom he refers to as the Master (Plato), on my reading it is no surprise that Plotinus mentions Plato and his view most often, and that Plotinus never very directly criticizes Plato's view.

More specifically, regarding Plotinus' experience, it is my unprovable contention that Plotinus exited Plato's Cave, saw the Good and described it in as much detail as he and his listeners had time to question and investigate—everything from the shadows on the wall to the Good Itself. The fact that we find more details about his "furniture," as Mohr[76] calls it, does not in itself demonstrate that Plotinus' details are incompatible with Plato's views.

Obviously, my Compatibility Principle comes with some caveats: First, I am in no way claiming that this principle is sufficient in and of itself to show that Plato and Plotinus do not have essential differences in their views, or that they have *identical* views. This principle will merely show that the onus is on my opponent to show where the two philosophers essentially differ, where an essential difference amounts to a contradiction, as opposed to something one philosopher mentions while the other does not. Of course, many scholars have argued for essential differences. Thus, I will need to defend my view that these alleged essential differences either are apparent, non-essential, the result of a misinterpretation, not necessarily incompatible, or something along these lines. My opponent can view my project as asking, in effect: "Is Plotinus not warranted in reading or understanding Plato accurately, and is there textual evidence in Plato's corpus to justify Plotinus' statements of and arguments for his beliefs as beliefs that one can find in Plato?" I will answer these questions in the affirmative. Second, I am not intending that my principle covers that, say, quantum theory is compatible with Plato's view, since he does not claim that the former is untrue. I do not believe we find any view in Plotinus that is original in the same way, or to the same degree, as quantum theory such that we cannot also find that view—either directly stated, implied, or at least compatible with the view we find—in Plato.

Given that mere compatibility is not sufficient to prove my project, I must also attempt to demonstrate in the following chapters that Plato and Plotinus have passages with similar metaphysical views. In fact, keeping the aforementioned caveats in mind, I will try to show through lining up quotations from both philosophers, and sometimes arguing for a certain interpretation of either's writing, that there is no essential difference in their metaphysics.[77]

But what underlies this similar language that we find in Plato and Plotinus, regarding the Good (or One), Beauty, Nous, the Forms, the All-Soul and so on? They have shared philosophical principles (as I will show), such as holding that the Good or the One is the highest metaphysical entity and source of the intelligible region, the Forms, below which is the All-Soul, and so on. Underlying these claims, also, are philosophical principles such as anti-materialism, theism, realism, and ethical objectivism (and this because of their shared metaphysics). As I have argued above, and add here, for a systematic view of Plato, that neither Aristotle nor any of the other ancients thought that Plato changed his mind, the underlying unity in Plato (and, I will show via passages, in Plotinus) is the claim that there is an intelligible world that explains the sensible world, and that the intelligible world is an articulated world of essences (Forms). This common set of philosophical principles, together with my method of adducing passages that either avow these principles or seem to make essentially similar claims about, say, the nature of Nous, the Demiurge, and the All-Soul, makes my thesis that Plato and Plotinus' views do not have essential differences more and more likely.

In addition, I will be trying to address every commentator whom I have read in English who attempts to argue that there is an essential difference between these philosophers' metaphysics. My argument will only be as strong as the number and quality of my responses to opponents of my thesis. However, one can always propose more differences, so my thesis will presumably remain an open-ended challenge. In any case, hopefully, this feature of my method also explains why this work is as extensive as it is: to address as many actual (and possible future) objections as possible.

Lastly, I am trying to show that Plato and Plotinus do not have *essentially different* views, that is, differences on metaphysically significant matters. For instance, they do not disagree (but in fact agree) that dialectic is the most important part of philosophy, and not merely, as Aristotle would put it, that we should use our reason in order to be happy. To be *the*, as opposed to *a*, Platonist, is to hold many of the—if not the most—views that make one a Platonist, including the Good's existing and being the highest object of knowledge, the source of the Forms, the intelligible region's being eternal, Forms being immaterial, immutable, the immortality of the soul and so on. Indeed, in my view, to be *the* Platonist, one would also have to hold many other metaphysical claims, not the least of which is the mystical claim they each make (which will not be covered here) that the most important or ultimate experience a human can have is to see or know the Good or One. Allow me to stress once again that, by claiming that there are no essential differences between their views, I am not claiming that they have identical metaphysical views, since I admittedly cannot find every claim of each philosopher in the other's work. In sum, on my reading, the metaphysical views of Plato and Plotinus are so similar that I cannot find an essential difference between them. This project is challenging, given that I am arguing for a view that opposes many Platonic and Plotinian interpreters. Perhaps Glaucon is correct when he says in the *Republic*, "It doesn't look easy to me. Perhaps, Socrates, there's some truth in the old saying that everything fine is difficult" (*Republic* IV 435c7–8).

I have used the translations of Plato from Cooper's *Plato: Complete Works*, unless otherwise noted. Moreover, for the Platonic quotations, I have started them with the character or principal interlocutor who represents Plato—usually Socrates, but also the Athenian, the Stranger, Diotima, Parmenides—and put the responses second, unless otherwise noted. For Plotinus, I have used A. H. Armstrong's translation, unless otherwise noted. I will use the standard method of referencing the *Enneads*: Ennead, treatise, chapter and line (sans the chronological number of when a treatise was written), as follows: VI.9.1.12–13, which refers to the twelfth and thirteenth lines of the sixth Ennead, ninth treatise and first chapter. For secondary source quotations of both works, I have taken the liberty of italicizing the names of Plato's Dialogues and the word "Enneads," as well as converting Oxford English to American English ("colour" to "color," and so on), if necessary, to maintain continuity throughout the work.

In the next chapter, I will review Plato's and Plotinus' views of ontology, from the highest principle (the Good or the One), to Beauty, Intellect [Nous (including God or gods, the Demiurge, Forms, the Five Greatest Kinds)], the All-Soul or World-Soul, the Three Hypostases (more explicitly mentioned in Plotinus but shown in Plato), emanation, matter (and the Receptacle), and finally to evil, with the aim of showing that Plato and Plotinus do not essentially disagree in principle in their ontological views. Unfortunately, due to space constraints, the following metaphysical issues and entities will not be covered: eternity and time, the individual soul, reincarnation, guardian spirits, and eschatology. However, I have researched all of these issues and entities, and found that there are no essential differences between the philosophers on them, and that there are not as many (if any major) scholarly controversies over them as with the issues mentioned in this work.

I will then conclude, summarizing my argument, and considering several major objections that will not have been handled in earlier chapters.

# 1

# The One or the Good: The Source of All Things

The toughest connections to demonstrate between the views of Plato and Plotinus are undoubtedly those both between Plato's Good in the *Republic* and One in the *Parmenides* and other occurrences, and between Plato's Good and One on the one hand and Plotinus' One on the other. This is the heart of the thesis that Plato and Plotinus do not essentially differ on metaphysics, because they each claim that the Good (Plato) and the Good or the One (Plotinus) is the source of the Forms and knowledge, the Source of All Things.

Plato and Plotinus posit many parallel claims about the One or the Good. More specifically, I will show that each maintains the following claims about the One or Good:

1. The Good is beyond being, is the source of the Forms' existence, and of itself.
2. The Good is "in some sort" the cause of all things—seasons, years, the sun, earth, and so on.
3. The Good is the cause of all that is right and beautiful, the authentic source of truth and reason.
4. The Good is the source of ethical truth and goodness.
5. The One is interpretively equivalent to the Good [especially in Plato: The One of Parmenides' First Hypothesis (*Parmenides* 137c–142b) is the Form of the Good]; specifically:
   a) The One is without limits
   b) The One cannot be the same as itself or as another, nor other than itself or other than another
   c) The One cannot be like or unlike itself or another
   d) The One cannot have any other character distinct from being one
   e) The One will not be equal or unequal to itself or to another
   f) The One in no way has being, and in no sense is
   g) The One neither is one nor is at all
   h) The One cannot have a name or be spoken of
   i) There cannot be knowledge, perception, or opinion of the One[1]

## 1.1 The (Form of the) Good is beyond being and is the source of the Forms' existence

Plato and Plotinus both believe that the Good is beyond being (*epekeina ousias*), and that the Good is the source or cause of the Forms' existence. They also, inconveniently enough, claim that the Good is a being, and that the Good causes itself: this is a controversial section. I will specifically address Platonic commentators, who have inadequate interpretations of what "beyond being" means for Plato's view, who have inadequate interpretations of what the Good's being a source of Being, the Forms et al. means, who believe that the *Philebus* gives us a better sense of what the Good of the *Republic* is, and who have inapt interpretations of the Good in general.

I will also address Plotinian commentators who mistakenly argue that Plotinus and Plato have different views of "beyond being," have differing views of the One or Good qua source of Intellect or Forms, have a different view of the Good or One (for various reasons) and argue that the Good or One of the *Republic* and *Philebus* is not the Good or One of Plotinus.

Let us begin with Plato's view that the Good is beyond being and is the source of the Forms' existence.

**Plato**: Spanning the dialogues, Plato claims that the Good is a Form,[2] just as if it is a Form as all the other Forms; admittedly, as Inge has pointed out,[3] few of these passages give the Good the status of being the Source of All Things and only one *explicitly* states that the Good is beyond being. However, to interpret fairly Plato's view of the Good, one must concede that in some places he gives place of preference, metaphysically, to the Good.[4] In *Republic* VI and VII, and perhaps in the *Philebus*, as we shall see, Plato seems to emphasize the transcendence[5] and importance of the Good.

Plato says that the Form of the Good is responsible for the Forms' existence (or for Being and all Beings), and is beyond being. Here is what the character Socrates says to Glaucon about the Good:

> The sun, I think you would say, not only gives visible things the power to be seen but also provides for their coming-to-be, growth, and nourishment—although it is not itself coming-to-be.
>
> I would.
>
> Therefore, you should also say that not only do the objects of knowledge owe their being known to the Good, but their existence and being are also due to it; although *the Good is not being, but something yet beyond being, superior*

> *to it in rank and power* [*ouk ousias ontos tou agathou, all' eti epekeina tēs ousias presbeiai kai dunamei hyperechontos*]. (*Republic* VI 509b2–10; adapted from Reeve 2004; emphasis added)[6]

I interpret this argument from analogy as follows: The sun allows, supports, and sustains the generation of plants and all other living things, and creates them; analogously, the Good allows the generation of Forms and causes them to be. The sun makes it possible for visible things to be perceived, and for visible things to be created, to grow and to be nourished, but the sun itself is not creation (or created), growth (or growing), or nourishment (or being nourished) itself; analogously, the Good Itself not only makes it possible that the Forms—objects of knowledge—may be known by our minds, but also causes the Forms to exist and have the essences or characters that they do have. Lastly, the Good is not being but surpasses it by possessing more power and dignity than being.

Several points can be made in favor of the "not being but beyond being" reading of this passage. First, it is no interpretive stretch to argue that here Plato claims that the Good is beyond being, especially given that Plato states at 509b8 that the Forms receive from the Good their existence (*to einai*). After all, if the Good is the reason that eternal, immutable, immaterial objects (Forms) exist, it must have some special status apart from those objects to be able to create them.

Second, regarding the translation, I wish to underscore that the text states that the Good is "*not* being"—Plato does not merely say of the Good that it is "beyond being," which is the phrase that most commentators focus on, and which will become important as I examine what other commentators have said about this passage.

Third, in Plato's *Sophist*, the Athenian Stranger says that Being is one of the five greatest kinds (254d, 255b–d, 256a, d–e, 257a–b); if Plato believed that the Good Itself was Being Itself, he presumably would have stated that Being just *was* Goodness and that Goodness was the greatest kind. In fact, Plato does refer to the Form of the Good in dialogues after *Republic* VII—*Parmenides*,[7] *Theaetetus*[8] and *Philebus*[9]—and he does not equate Good with Being in any of those passages, so the *Sophist* is not an exception.

Nonetheless, in order to argue that Plotinus and Plato have compatible philosophies, it is not necessary to argue either that we *must* translate *ousias* as "being," or that we *must* think that Plato holds that the Good is beyond being. All that is necessary for compatibility is to show that the "beyond being" reading of the *Republic* VII 509b2–10 passage is plausible given the text and the context, which has been shown. As we will see, Plotinus interprets this key passage as claiming that the Good is beyond being.

Shorey[10] wonders whether the "beyond being," "source of the Forms" passages are to be taken seriously: "Are they merely *daimonias hyperbolēs* [509c1–2], pious ejaculations thrown out at an object, forms of emotional expansion[?]" Even though Shorey indeed took Plato seriously, I can adduce another passage to neutralize Shorey's wonder; Plato states his belief that it is a major fault to mislead others about the good: "I suspect that it's a lesser crime to kill someone involuntarily than to mislead people about fine, good, and just institutions" (*Republic* V 451a5–7). Questions of course remain about whether Plato himself "came out of the cave"—that is, actually possessed the knowledge he discusses and claims exists, or whether he was just being poetic, or describing an ideal concerning knowledge. But, at least in my view, to question Plato's sincerity in his statements on the Good is not a plausible interpretive move.

Out of all the commentators with whom I agree that the Platonic Good is "really" beyond being,[11] Bowe has made an excellent point in its favor that I have not seen rebutted:

> Many attempts have been made to qualify the characterization of the Good as [beyond being] in the *Republic*, for fear that the most rational of philosophers may lapse into mysticism at the summit of his greatest work. But Plato has said that the Good is beyond being. To deny this or attempt to qualify it fails to account for why Glaucon is so incredulous. That is, once Glaucon accepts the principle of Forms in general, it is hard to imagine why he is so surprised at the mention of a superior Form. The characterization of that Form as 'beyond being' is the only thing that explains Glaucon's incredulity.[12]

It would not be stunning either for Glaucon to hear that the Good is more dignified and powerful than being—since Glaucon does not even know what being is, per se—or is "more valuable than" Being or other Forms, or is the equivalent of certain well-organized Forms, to mention just a few of the many options commentators have defended. Furthermore, in the same vein as Bowe, why would Socrates be ashamed of his opinion and unable to give an excellent account of the Good, if all he believed about it was that it is supremely dignified, powerful, valuable, or equivalent to certain Forms? Note that I will refer to this paragraph collectively as the Bowe Defense, hereafter.

A further reason that may hold less weight but should be mentioned is that philosophers before Plato arguably had the view that the One was beyond being,[13] and philosophers between Plato and Plotinus also took Plato to believe that the Good or One was beyond being.[14]

Thus, Plato holds both that the Good is a being and yet is beyond being, and we will find that Plotinus does the same. I am not making a claim about whether the beyond being claim implies that the Good does not exist;[15] I only note that, for Plato, it seems that, on the one hand, if the Good is not being but beyond being, then it is plausible that the Good is not a being and does not exist. However, on the other hand, Plato claims that the Good is the brightest thing that is (*Republic* VII 518c9–d1);[16] so one cannot *only* claim that the Good is beyond or not a being. Some commentators have mentioned only one of these options,[17] on which I need not adjudicate: what is necessary for this project is to show that Plotinus also states that the Good or One is both a being and beyond being, which I will do shortly.

Before continuing with the Good's causational aspect, I will address some alternative problematic views of Plato's claim that the Good is beyond being. Leaving some objections to be dealt with in the notes,[18] I will move on to these three interpretations of "beyond being", that I find unsatisfactory: "beyond being" only means that the Good has more dignity and power than being; "beyond being" means that the Good is more valuable or precious than being; "beyond being" means that the Good is a condition of Intellect or rational order that permits intelligibility.

First, Hitchcock argues that:

> A neoplatonizing interpreter might point to the statement at [*Republic* VI] 509b8–10 that the good is beyond being, *ousia*, in dignity and power. But the qualifying phrase is crucial. Plato does not mean that the good is beyond being in the sense that it is a principle which transcends the realm of what exists, but only that it is a Form more dignified and more powerful than being, which he presumably thinks of here as a Form (as he does at [*Republic* V] 478e1–2). The statement is parallel to the earlier statements at [*Republic* VI] 508e5–6, and 509a4–5 that the good is more beautiful, *kallion*, and still more greatly to be honored, *eti meizonos timeteon*, [than] being and truth.[19]

Reminding ourselves of the all-important line once again: "the Good is not being, but something yet beyond being, superior to it in rank and power" (*Republic* VI 509b8–10), we see that Plato begins the phrase with the claim that the Good is *not being* but beyond it. We cannot know that Plato was not trying to claim that the Good is beyond being—albeit this is admittedly paradoxical—*while also* having superior rank and power. In this case, the Good would have a higher rank because nothing else is beyond being in his philosophy, and, because it is the source of the Forms, more power. Lastly, Hitchcock fails to counter the Bowe Defense; namely, why is Glaucon so amazed if all Plato is saying is that the Good has more power and dignity than other Forms or anything else?

Second, Rawson (and perhaps Shorey)[20] take the view that "beyond being" means that it is not the Form of Being but more valuable than it:

> When Socrates says that the Good 'is not being, but is yet beyond being, surpassing it in dignity and power,' he means to emphasize that although the Good is the *cause* of being in the objects of knowledge, it is not the *form* of being, and is yet more *valuable* than being.[21]

I agree that Plato believes the Good is the cause of being and that it is not the Form of Being, but these cannot be the only things that he intends when he states that the Good is beyond Being. Again, the Bowe Defense asks, what is the big deal with the Good's not being the same as Being? It is not any other Form: for example, Beauty, Justice, or Largeness. Why bother pointing out that the Good is not the same as Being without mentioning other Forms, for instance? Now, specifically on the "more valuable" point, is it not merely tautologous to argue that the Good is more valuable—better than—the other Forms, when in fact it is the best? (Yet again, the Bowe Defense comes to mind—*this* is all Plato has in mind? Where is the oddness,[22] or the need for any hesitation?)

Third, Luban and Reeve have similar but not identical interpretations. Luban[23] states that the Good's "being does not go beyond the being of all the Forms," but instead that the Good is "neither on the Line nor off it; it is nothing more than *the Line itself*, taken as a whole... . The Good is the *logos*, the underlying pattern of the Line." Luban's interpretation is too paradoxical even for Plato. It does not explain why the Good should *be* both the line and the reasoning or logos underlying the Line. I agree that the Good is in some sort the cause of not only Forms but of other things as well; however, this does not imply that the Good is just everything that exists on whatever Platonic level, because then the Good is eternal and not eternal, immortal and mortal, immaterial and material, immutable and mutable.[24] Again, if Plato wanted to say that the Good is just everything that exists on whatever level, then why is this amazing (though it would certainly be paradoxical)?

Finally, Reeve argues that the Good:

> Like other Forms, it is a component of the intelligible realm. But, unlike them, it is a condition of the existence of the realm itself, since if there were no rational order, nothing could be intelligible. That explains why the Good is characterized as 'not substance, but superior to it in rank and power.'[25]

This is certainly the best candidate of all of these interpretive options, but still has its problems: First, how would the rational order of the intelligible realm be able to be the *cause* of that realm? How can graph paper cause the dots and lines on it to exist? Perhaps this is a weak analogy in some hopefully non-fallacious way, but I believe that the point (how can rational order itself cause Beings such as Largeness to exist?) stands. Second, should not the Cave Allegory look a lot different than it does, with Logos being the top object, or, if not, at the very least an explanation that the rational order that underlies the whole process of enlightenment out of the cave just *is* the Good? Third, the Bowe Defense applies here yet again: why would it be amazing to Glaucon that rational order underlies, and is a precondition of, the intelligible realm (as it most certainly is)?[26]

Let us now address the Good's creation, or the aspect of its being the Source of the Forms.[27] Besides *Republic* VI 509b, there is another major passage from Book X that should be reviewed. From 596a–597d, Plato makes several claims concerning God: God is described as "the one who makes all the things that all the other kinds of craftsmen severally make" (596c2). He continues: "this same craftsman is able to make, not only all kinds of furniture, but all plants that grow from the earth, all animals (including himself), the earth itself, the heavens, the gods, all the things in the heavens and in Hades beneath the earth" (596c4–9).[28]

One might immediately object that in the lines thereafter the character Socrates states that anyone can produce these things (as images) by producing a mirror and creating their reflections. However, Plato then proceeds (at 597b–d) to claim that God produces the Forms themselves, including furniture (the Bed Itself at 597b5) and "everything else" (597d8), which strongly implies that the being who truly creates the Forms is the same being who creates the other things mentioned beforehand—the furniture, plants, animals, the earth, heavens, gods and so on. Moreover, nowhere does Plato state that Nous or Intellect creates the Forms; Nous just *is* the intelligible region on my reading of Plato. Thus, these claims are compatible with what Plato states about the Good in *Republic* VI (Sun Simile) and VII (Cave Allegory), namely, that the Good is the source of Being, and the cause of everything right and beautiful and the cause in some way of everything that we see.[29]

In addition, Adam[30] argues: "If God and the Idea of Good are the same (see on VI 505 A ff.), Plato is merely saying in theological language what he formerly said in philosophical, when he derived the [*ousia*] of all other Ideas from the Idea of Good (VI 509 B)." I agree with Adam here, except that there is no identification of God and the Good at *Republic* VI 505a or in the rest of Book VI, as he suggests.

Using the principle of charity, then, I am justified in interpreting God in *Republic* X, the creator of the Forms and cause of all natural things, as being equivalent to the Idea of the Good, which is beyond being and generates the Forms and perceptibles, as asserted in Books VI and VII of the *Republic* (Plato usually intends to refer to Nous or Intellect when he uses the word God in his later works).

I concede that I do not have enough textual evidence to claim that Plato believes that the Good causes itself to exist, as Plotinus states (VI.8.14.41). However, I believe we can make a reasonable inference to that effect given that the Good is the unhypothesized first principle or beginning; for what else—that is beyond being or not a being—could possibly cause the Good?[31]

Before turning to Plotinus' view, let us consider some further objections[32] concerning Plato's view of the Good: the Good is not really a transcendent source; and the Good is improperly conceived as put forth above.

First, Pistorius argues: "Nor can Plato be absolved from the charge that he regarded his highest Idea, the Good, as God, because that particular Idea is as powerless as the others. There is nothing in its nature to make it a creator."[33] I acknowledge that, if one simply asks oneself: "Should the Good be (a) the top of the hierarchy of being, or (b) beyond being?," options (a) or (b) should not immediately come to mind. However, the fact that Plato actually states this forces us to interpret him as believing that it is so, no matter what further complications arise. The Forms *are* causes for Plato, and the Platonic Good causes the Forms to exist, so, in spite of Pistorius's frustration, his claims do not show us that we should not interpret Plato in this way.

Second, commentators have argued that the Good forms "a single, closely knit organic whole" of "several propositions" (Robinson),[34] the Good is a complex of Forms (Reeve),[35] a Form of Forms (Lachterman and Sayre),[36] or the essence of other Forms (Santas).[37] I hold that these views fall short in explaining why the Good is beyond being and a source of the Forms.[38]

Thus, for Plato, the Good is beyond being and the source of the Forms and, plausibly, by implication, the source of itself.

**Plotinus**: Plotinus also believes that the Good is beyond being and is the cause or source of the Forms. First, the following commits him to the view that the Good is beyond being, showing that he agrees with Plato:[39]

> But since *he is the Good and not a good*, he must have nothing in himself, since he does not even have good in himself. For what he will have is either good or not good; but that which is not good cannot be in the Good, the authentically

> and primarily Good, nor does the Good have the good. If then he does not have what is not good or what is good, he has nothing. *If then 'he has nothing' he is 'alone and isolated' from all other things.* If then the other things are either goods, but not the Good, or not goods, and he has neither of these, he has nothing and is the Good by having nothing. But then *if anyone adds anything at all to him, being [ousian] or intellect or beauty, he will deprive him of being the Good by the addition.* If then one takes away everything and says nothing about him and does not say falsely about anything that it is with him, he allows him his 'existence' without attributing to him anything which is not there, as those do who compose inartistic panegyrics, and diminish the reputation of those who are being praised by adding matters inferior to their worth, since they are incapable of making true speeches about their subjects. We also, then, must not add any of the things which are later and lesser, but say that he moves above them and is their cause, but not that he is them. For, again, it is the nature of the Good not to be all things and not to be any of one of them; for [if he were] he would come under one and the same classification as all of them, and if he came under the same classification, he would differ only by his individuality and specific difference and some added attribute. Then he would be two and not one, and one of the two, what was common to him and the others, would be not good, and one would be good; he would, then, not be purely and primarily good, but that would be by participating in which, over and above what was in common, he became good. So the nature of the Good would be good by participation; and what it participated in would not be any one of all things. But if this Good was in the composite thing—for it would be the specific difference by which the composite was good—it would have to derive from something else. But it was simply and solely good; so, much more, that from which it derived was good. That which is primary and *the Good has therefore been revealed to us as above all realities*, and only good, and having nothing in itself, but unmixed with all things and *above all things and cause of all things*. (V.5.13.1–36; adapted from A. H. Armstrong; emphasis added)

Here Plotinus makes many claims about the Good, but, for our purposes, he states that the Good is "not *a* good" and that we deprive the Good's being good if we ascribe being, intellect, or even goodness to it. At the same time (in the quotation's last sentence), Plotinus states that the Good is above all realities (the Forms), above all things and the cause of all things. Thus, Plotinus implicitly confirms the second characteristic listed for Plato above: the Good is the source of the Forms' existence. Note one additional thing: Plotinus argues that, if the Good were in the composite of things, it would have to derive from something else, which responds to the Platonic commentators who think that Plato's Good is the rational order that makes the Forms or intelligible region possible (Reeve), or that it is the whole Line (Luban).

In the next passage, Plotinus affirms that the Good *is not* a Being or "not the *is*":[40]

> But *he is not even the 'is'*; for he has no need whatever even of this; for 'he is good' is not applicable to him either, but to that to which the 'is' applies; but the 'is' [when said of him,] is not said as one thing of another, but as indicating what he is. But we say 'the Good' about him, speaking of him himself nor predicating of him that good belongs to him, but saying it is himself; so then, since we do not think it proper to say 'is good' nor to put the article before it, but are unable to make ourselves clear, if one takes it away altogether, we say 'the good' so as not to still need the 'is,' that we may not make one thing and then another. But who is going to accept a nature which is not in a state of perception and knowledge of itself? What then will he know? 'I am'? But he is not. Why then will he not say 'I am the Good'? Again he will predicate the 'is' of himself. But [perhaps] he will only say 'good,' with some addition; for one could think 'good' without 'is,' if one did not predicate it of something else. But he who thinks that he is good will in every case think 'I am the Good'; if not, he will think good but the thought will not be present to his mind that he is this good. The thought, then, must be 'I am good.' And if the thought itself is the Good, it will not be a thought of himself but of good, and he himself will not be the Good, but the thought will. But if the thought of the Good is different from the Good, the Good is there already before the thought of it. But if the Good is sufficient to itself before the thought, since it is sufficient to itself for good it will have no need of the thought about it; so, as good, it does not think itself. (VI.7.38.1–25)

Besides emphasizing that the Good does not have being and is not being (but yet the "is" indicates what he is), Plotinus states that the Good is associated with sheer negation and is void of self-thought. I will examine the way in which the One of Plato's *Parmenides* First Hypothesis is indicated by many negations, which is compatible with what Plotinus is referring to regarding the Supreme or the Good.

Plotinus argues that the Good is the first, and is prior to substance, which again implies that it is beyond being:

> But why are not the beautiful and the good and the virtues among the primary genera—and knowledge and intellect? As for the good, if it is the first, the nature which we certainly do call that of the good, of which nothing is predicated, but we call it this because we cannot indicate it in any other way, it could not be the genus of anything. For it is not predicated of other things, or each of the other

things of which it was predicated would be spoken of as the good. And that good is before substance, not in substance. (VI.2.17.1–7)

It is important to note that there are many more passages in which Plotinus claims that the Good or One (or the other names Plotinus uses) is beyond being. Since Plotinus scholars do not dispute this claim, though, these passages should suffice.[41]

Let us now show several passages by Plotinus that verify—as with Plato—that Good *is* a being.[42] First, Plotinus explicitly states that he is dealing with difficult concepts, and doing so metaphorically:

> But one must go along with the words, if one in speaking of that Good uses of necessity to indicate it expressions which we do not strictly speaking allow to be used; but one should understand 'as if' with each of them. If then the Good is established in existence, and choice and will join in establishing it—for without these it will not be—but this Good must not be many, its will and substance (*ousian*) must be brought into one; but if its willing comes from itself, it is necessary that it also gets its being from itself, so that our discourse has discovered that he has made himself. For if his will comes from himself and is something like his own work, and this will is the same thing as his existence, then in this way he will have brought himself into existence; so that he is not what he happened to be but what he himself willed. (VI.8.13.47–59)

Thus, while he does state that the Good exists, he also warns that we must be patient with language, and read "as if" with various expressions about the Good. With this warning, Plotinus himself provides the interpretive explanation as to why he states that the Good exists; the Good exists as one on account of its will, but being and will must be taken to be equivalent. And Plotinus is making all of these points to show the necessity of the Good, as opposed to its existing by chance. Here is a similar passage:

> For this is the good to this one nature, belonging to itself and being itself; but this is being one. It is in this sense that the good is rightly said to be our own; therefore one must not seek it outside. For where could it be if it had fallen outside being? Or how could one discover it in non-being? But it is obvious that it is in being, since it is not non-being. But if that good is being and in being, it would clearly be for each individual in himself. We have not, then, departed from being, but are in it, nor has it departed from us: so all things are one. (VI.5.1.18–26)

Plotinus' purpose is to show that Being must have its source from the Good, and that the Good is never a non-Being, which can be taken to imply that the Good is not nothingness, though it is not necessarily a being, given the other passages and justifications that Plotinus asserts for the Good's being "beyond being." He is also trying to show that all beings are in some sense one, which is compatible with Plato's view that knowledge is of being, and being is the realm of the Forms, which is the top level of the upper section of the Divided Line. There are other passages where Plotinus apparently claims that the Good is a being,[43] but in order to be charitable to his view they must be seen as serving some other purpose for the moment, or being metaphorical, as V.5.13.1–36 suggests.

Not every commentator agrees with my view that Plato and Plotinus both argue that the Good or One is a being and beyond being; though there are many different kinds of arguments,[44] I will address criticisms from three authors here: R. E. Allen: Plotinus is merely projecting his view onto Plato; A. H. Armstrong: Plato's Good is an all-inclusive Form containing all the others; Plotinus' One has unique transcendence and otherness; Inge: "Plotinus exalts 'the Good' to a more inaccessible altitude than Plato has done." I begin with Allen, who argues (with my bracketed numbers added for convenience):

> [1] The Good is beyond Being because it surpasses Being in dignity and power. It surpasses Being because both good things and evil things participate in Being, whereas only good things participate in Goodness insofar as they are good. [2] This presupposes, of course, that evil is not merely the privation of goodness, and this presupposition is accurate for Plato, who acknowledged the existence of Ideas of various kinds of evil as the opposites of various kinds of good, just as the theory of Ideas Socrates puts in the *Parmenides* (128e–130a) requires. [3] Plotinus, on the other hand, supposing that evil is purely privative and that whatever is is good, inferred that if the Good is not Being and is beyond Being, surpassing it in dignity and power, it must surpass it in and through not being. That is, the Good does not exist by reason of its excellence. [4] It is a lovely piece of what, in psychological terms, is called projection.[45]

Let us analyze these points in turn: (1) The view that Plato *only* means by "beyond being" in dignity and power is not true for Plato, nor is it for Plotinus. Allen's claim that the Good surpasses Being because both good and bad things participate in Being is not necessarily true of Plato or Plotinus, since ignorance causes bad things, and ignorance is only a lack of knowledge as opposed to a positive quality that exists *per se*. (2) There is certainly a question as to whether there are bad Forms for either Plato or Plotinus; I have not the space to argue against that view here.[46] But for now, Allen's citing of *Parmenides* 128e–130a (where Socrates mentions the Forms Likeness, Unlikeness, Oneness, Multitude,

Rest, and Motion et al.) does not show that some of these Forms are evil; for instance, Rest and Motion are two of the Five Greatest Kinds, neither of which is ever said to be evil in the corpus. (3) Evil is a privation for both philosophers, not just Plotinus, so Allen needs more evidence that evil is only privative for Plotinus but not for Plato. Moreover, they both hold that the Good is the cause of what is right and beautiful, so Plato is not necessarily saying, any more than Plotinus, that the Good causes evil. Furthermore, as we saw, Allen states that "beyond being" in Plato only means "beyond being in dignity and surpassing power," while in Plotinus "beyond being" means "surpassing Being in and through not being."[47] Contra Allen, I point to this Plotinian passage, which confirms Plato's statement about the power of the Good all the more: "for [the One] is the greatest of all things, not in size but in power… . And it must be understood as infinite not because its size and number cannot be measured or counted but because its power cannot be comprehended" (VI.9.6.7–12). (4) Given the preceding considerations, we cannot conclude that Plotinus is merely projecting his view of the Good onto Plato.

A. H. Armstrong argues as follows:

> For Plato the One or Good, the First Principle of the World of Forms was itself a Form and a substance, the all-inclusive Form containing all the others. It had not this unique transcendence and otherness which Plotinus gives the One.[48]

The Good is transcendent for Plato as well; it is the entity that is the source of being of the Forms (besides knowledge and truth),[49] making it unique. So the Good is neither all-inclusive containing all the other Forms, nor is it merely another Form that causes only goodness.

Lastly, Inge quite curiously appears to defend Plotinus against the charge that there is a large difference between his "beyond being" view and Plato's, but then says that there *is* a difference:

> It has been said that Plotinus alters Plato's doctrine of the Good, inasmuch as for Plato the Good is within the circle of the Ideas, while for Plotinus it is above them. But this overstates the difference. For Plato the Good is the supreme source of light, of which everything good, true, and beautiful in the world is the reflexion… .
>
> It is undoubtedly true that Plotinus exalts 'the Good' to a more inaccessible altitude than Plato has done. It is not for us only, but for the highest intelligence, that the Good is 'beyond being.' But if the Good is the Absolute, the question at once arises whether we can rightly use such a name for it as 'the Good.' Plotinus insists that the Absolute cannot be 'the Beautiful,' but

> Beauty, or the source of the Beautiful. Why does he not say that it cannot be the Good, but Goodness, or the source of the Good? In fact, this is his view; but in loyalty to Plato he retains the name, and explains that in reference to *us* the One is the Good, and so may be called by this name, though it is not strictly accurate.[50]

I disagree with the first paragraph's statement that Plato believes that the Good is just an Idea, as anything else, especially in the *Phaedo* and the *Republic*; I agree with the rest of the first paragraph, but believe it to be true of Plotinus as well. As for the second paragraph, I disagree that Plotinus has exalted the Good to a more inaccessible altitude than Plato—it is beyond being, and perhaps beyond knowledge. My disagreement here is also tied to the One's being the Good for Plato. Moreover, neither philosopher states that the Good is identical with Beauty, though they admittedly say similar things about them. Thus, his loyalty is more than in name only, unfortunately for Inge.

Plotinus unsurprisingly[51] believes that the Good is the source of the Forms:

> This is why that Good is said to be the cause not only of substance but of its being seen. And just as the sun, which is cause for sense-objects both of their being seen and their coming into being, is also in some way cause of sight—and therefore is neither sight nor the things which have come to be—in this way also the nature of the Good, which is cause of substance and intellect and light, according to our analogy, to the things seen there and the seer, is neither the real beings nor intellect but cause of these, giving by its own light thinking and being thought to the real beings and to intellect. (VI.7.16.22–31)[52]

Since Plotinus states that the Good is the cause of substance and the real beings, we can infer that, for Plotinus, the Good is the cause of the Forms.

Let us now consider objections against the view that both philosophers believe that the Good is the source of the Forms in the same way. There are many different criticisms,[53] but I will examine those of Bechtle, Louth, Lynch, Mohr, and Rist.

First, Bechtle translates the anonymous commentator of Plato's *Parmenides* (hereafter "the commentator") as saying:

> Plotinus is not content with the confirmation of the highest's, i.e., the Good's, [*epekeina*] character only in relation to being and thus acknowledges a higher rank of the Good in relation to mind… . What Plotinus additionally does (against Aristotle), is to emphasize the Good's superiority to mind so consistently and emphatically that eventually no link at all remains between the mind and the Good.[54]

I believe the commentator is mistaken on several fronts: First, if I am correct about Plato's view, if the Good is not a being but the source of being, and Being is the realm of the Forms and Nous, then Plato believes that the Good has a higher rank than mind as well.

Second, Plato and Plotinus still claim that there is a link between the Good or One and Nous; they each have a "light" metaphor, where the light of the sun (Good or One) and the sun's power causes being (which is the realm of Nous), so they agree on the same kind of relation between the Good or One and Nous.

Third, Louth argues that Nous is the ultimate reality for Plato, but not for Plotinus:

> There is the more unified realm of Intelligence, *nous*. This is Plato's realm of the Forms. Here knower and known are one, here knowledge is intuitive: it is not the result of seeking and finding, with the possibility of error, but a possession, marked by infallibility. For Plato this was ultimate reality. For Plotinus, not so; for here, among the Forms, there is still duality, there is still multiplicity; there is the duality of knower and known, even if they are united; there is multiplicity in that there are many Forms, even if they are a harmonious unity. Beyond the realm of Intelligence, for Plotinus, is the One.[55]

I agree that, in Plato's view, Nous is the realm of the Forms and that knowledge there is infallible, but not that knower and known are one, or that one cannot seek knowledge (by recollecting it). I do not know of any Platonic passages that state that knower and known are one at the level of Nous; the converse seems true, given that the *Republic*'s seer or seen metaphor and the Demiurge's looking up to the Forms to create the universe in the *Timaeus* each imply duality. Nonetheless, I would put the issue this way for now, until I discuss the non-dual issue in the conclusion: if the ultimate reality is Being-Forms-Nous (because reality implies being and not "beyond being"), then I would claim they each have the same view of ultimate reality; if, however, the ultimate reality is what causes Being-Forms-Nous (even if that is paradoxically named), then again they have the same view of ultimate reality.

Fourth, in his analysis of the *Parmenides*, Lynch states:

> We have no absolute reason to think that the Good was viewed by Plato in the special Neoplatonic sense that is sometimes ascribed to it. That is to say, we need not view it as an entity that has an existence separate from the Ideas, as the transcendental source, according to a relation of priority and posteriority, of the Ideas.[56]

Indeed, we must read Plato as holding that the Good is a transcendental source of existence, because the texts demand it as the best explanation, while keeping in mind that he also held that the Good is a being, just as Plotinus does. If the Platonic Good is said not to be a being and you cannot have knowledge of it, then it is not just another Idea.

Fifth, Mohr argues that:

> This simple existence of the Forms is bad news for … full-tilt Neoplatonists … because the content of Forms other than the Form of the good is not contained within the Form of the good; the other Forms are not emanations from it.[57]

Assuming that Mohr views Plotinus as a "full-tilt" Neo-Platonist, I fail to see how Plotinus is committed to the view that the contents of the Forms are contained in his One any more or less than they would be in Plato's Good.[58] They both state that the Good causes the Forms' existence and essence, but they also both agree that the Forms are eternal. Again, they both use the metaphor that the sun's (Good's) light flows out from itself to everything else and that the Good has causal power for goodness and the existence of the Forms.

Lastly, Rist argues that:

> The system of Plato is ultimately a dualism, composed of the motionless, unchanging World of Forms on the one hand and the world of movement, potential or actual, typified at its highest by the souls of the Gods and of the [godlike men] on the other. This 'separation' which is the mark of a truly platonizing system is absent in the world-view of Plotinus where all, ultimately, is in a sense contained in the One.[59]

As for Rist's comment that everything is, ultimately, in a sense contained in the One, see my replies to Mohr. When claiming that Plato has the two-worlds view that is absent in Plotinus' view, Rist is ignoring Plato's statements about the Good's transcendence to make his case, as well as Plotinus' similar statements about "here" (the realm of becoming) and "there" (the realm of being). Plato and Plotinus share the same levels and kinds of being (and becoming).

I have one final claim to confirm about the One's creation for Plotinus; namely, that the One causes itself:[60] "His being then comes by and from himself" (VI.8.16.37).[61] That I know of, no commentator in English has argued either in favor of, or against, the view that Plato and Plotinus aver that the Good or One causes itself.

There are two more remaining sets of objections against my view to consider: that Plato and Plotinus have differing views of the Good or One; and that the

Platonic Good of the *Republic* and the *Philebus* is not the same as the Plotinian One.

First, let us consider one objection to the effect that they might have distinct conceptions of the Good or One, leaving others aside.[62] A. H. Armstrong argues:

> This phrase of Plotinus [that the Good's radiance is a grace playing upon the Forms' beauty] brings home very strikingly the difference between him and Plato. For Plato the One or Good, the First Principle of the World of Forms was itself a Form and a substance, the all-inclusive Form containing all the others. It had not this unique transcendence and otherness which Plotinus gives the One.[63]

I have tried to show that the Platonic Good does indeed have a transcendence and otherness, and does not contain the Forms any more or less than Plotinus' One is said to cause the Forms. Plotinus also referred to the Good as a Form; ignoring these similarities and others can really help our opponents' case.

Let us now consider an objection concerning the Good of Plato versus the One or Good of Plotinus. Hampton's interpretation of the *Philebus* leads her to reject the Neo-Platonic notion of seeking union with the One as a Platonic goal:

> If my general interpretation of the *Philebus* is essentially correct, then Plato has come a significant way towards tying up some loose threads left hanging in the *Republic*'s account of the relations between pleasure, knowledge, and being. In the *Philebus*, the Good which unites all of reality is depicted as an organic whole. The highest form of knowledge is the realization of this truth—by both *nous* and *phronesis*—in our lives. The ideal of the good life is one in which the various types of knowledge and pleasure are properly arranged in imitation of the universal order provided by the Forms. Thus, our goal is not the Neoplatonic life of contemplation which seeks mystical union with the One. Neither is it the Aristotelian ideal of the life of practical virtue, since Plato insists that we can realize our human good only by shaping our lives so that they are true to the universal Good which unites all things. While the exact nature of the good life in the *Republic* may have remained unclear, in the *Philebus* the Good is shown to be neither Neoplatonic nor Aristotelian. Plato remains to the end a Platonist.[64]

I have two replies to Hampton's view. First, Plato's account of the Good in the *Republic* was not rejected in the *Philebus* on my reading of the latter: the *Philebus* mainly concerns the good for humans and other living things, especially when the discussion is centering around pleasure and intelligence, and not the Good that causes the Forms; Plotinus clearly makes this argument himself at VI.7.24–5. Second, Plato has rejected neither contemplation nor the ultimate experience in the *Philebus*; the ultimate experience can still be the necessary and sufficient condition for human happiness, which in turn will be the reason why one is just, temperate (that is, having a well-proportioned life), and experiences true pleasure. Thus, Hampton's dismissal is perhaps premature.

Before concluding, it is fitting to underscore the way in which both Plato and Plotinus are being inconsistent, but in the same ways. They both seem to hold that you can and cannot have knowledge of the Good.[65] I have shown that the Good or One is beyond being and a being. Note Rist's apropos comment:

> If, however, the Platonic dialogues themselves contain unresolved contradictions, either explicit or implicit, then clearly by enlarging upon certain portions of the corpus and neglecting the rest, one could produce a system which, though more consistent than that of Plato, would by this very consistency be open to the charge of being unplatonic.[66]

Granting Rist his argument, I maintain that Plotinus and Plato are inconsistent in the same ways, which only confirms my thesis.

Thus, I have confirmed that Plato and Plotinus have the view that the Good is beyond being and is the source of the existence of the Forms. Both posit that the Good also causes other things than just the Forms.

## 1.2 The Good is "in some sort" the cause of all things, seasons, years, the sun, earth, and so on

**Plato**: In Chapter 1, we saw the way in which Plato in the Cave Allegory describes the pain of ascending from the cave, but Plato positively states something about the Good in that passage. In the allegory, the sun outside the cave represents the Good (as Plato explicitly avers), and Plato makes an analogy from the eyes' seeing the sun and the soul's knowing or seeing the Good:

> Finally, I suppose, he'd be able to see the sun, not images of it in water or some alien place, but the sun itself, in its own place, and be able to study it.
>
> Necessarily so.
>
> And at this point he would infer and conclude that the sun provides the seasons and the years, governs everything in the visible world, and is in some way the cause of all the things that he used to see. (*Republic* VII 516b4–c2)[67]

So, for instance, (assuming for the moment that the sun in the allegory is the Good), the Good-seer can finally see what goodness itself is, and not the reflections and imitations of goodness in our everyday lives and actions; also, once we see the Good, we can infer that everything else is in some sense caused by it. We can be quite certain about this interpretation, for Plato verifies it shortly thereafter in the text, as we shall see in the following section.[68]

Not every commentator agrees with me[69] here. For instance, Gerson claims that "a connection in Plato's dialogues is nowhere made between the first principle and everything else besides the divine mind and Forms."[70] Plato is explicit enough that the Good causes the Forms and being, which are part of the intelligible region, of which God and the Demiurge are a part, the Demiurge or Nous creates the World-Soul, and soul is prior to body. Moreover, for Plato, Forms cause their likenesses,[71] so if the Good causes, though perhaps in a different way, the Forms, and the Forms cause every thing of that kind to have the share of character that it does, then I have another way of showing that the Good causes many things.[72] Lastly, in the Cave Allegory, the sun—the Good—causes reflections in water and shadows to occur (*Republic* VII 516a6–7; which I take to be analogous to the second highest section of the Divided Line); and, at 514a2–5, Plato states that the cave wall, where the shadows in the cave are cast, is open to the light of the sun, which implies that the sun (Good) aids somehow even in the production of cave shadows, the lowest objects that exist.

**Plotinus**: Plotinus believes that the Good is in some way the cause of All Things, the earth, and so forth, with this passage and others (VI.7.16.22–31 and those cited on p. 160n. 74), which discusses his view that the Good causes the Intellect and the Forms:[73]

> How then do the parts in heaven last, but down here the elements and living things do not last? Because, Plato says, the heavenly things derive their being from God, but the living things down here from the gods derived from him; and it is not lawful for the things which derive their being from him to perish. (II.1.5.1–8)

Assuming that "God" here is *either* the Good *or* Intellect (Nous) for Plotinus, which is no interpretive stretch, Plotinus explicitly agrees with Plato that God causes gods to exist, which cause living things to exist. Supposing "God" to refer to the Good, this passage states that the Good causes the gods which cause the living things; supposing "God" to refer to Intellect, then the Good causes Intellect, which in turn causes the gods, which cause living things.

Plotinus states that matter needs a light, Being, in order to be visible at all, metaphorically implying that Being—which in turn needs a higher light, the Good—is in some sense the cause of the visible realm:

> Just as with bodies, though light is mixed into them, all the same there is need of another light for the light, the color, in them to appear, so with the things there in the intelligible, though they possess much light, there is need of another greater light that they may be seen both by themselves and by another. (VI.7.21.13–17)

We have confirmation from Plotinus, therefore, that the Good causes Being,[74] and Being (via the Receptacle, among other things) causes material forms to be visible, which is compatible with Plato's view. Moreover, Plotinus believes that the Good emanates (metaphorically) the Intellect and the World-Soul, which in turn is the cause of the visible universe.

Only one commentator, possibly, agrees with me on this issue;[75] two of my opponents on this issue—Gerson[76] and Rist[77]—have the view that, for Plotinus, everything is contained in the One, but, for Plato, it is not. See my reply to Mohr (p. 16) for my defense against this kind of objection, and allow me to add that creation seems to occur in the same way for Plato and Plotinus, so, if everything is contained in the One in some sense (even though it is beyond being and unqualified, for instance), then Plato makes the same claims about the Good or One.

Anton[78] says that the Plotinian One outshines Plato's Good, in part because it "sustains the cosmic hierarchies, being the sole demiurgic power and progenitor of all with the exception of evil," but we can see the way in which the Platonic Good indeed sustains cosmic hierarchies and generates everything but evil; moreover, they both believe that a Demiurge created the All-Soul, despite Anton's implication to the contrary.

Lastly, Zeller[79] claims: "Neo-Platonism concentrates its whole efforts on deriving the sensual from the super-sensual world," but this charge does not apply to Plotinus, given his discussions about everything from the One to unformed matter, and the relation of everything between, not to mention Plato's effort to derive the sensual from the super-sensual world.

Therefore, besides the Forms, the Good is "in some sort" the cause of all things, seasons, years, the sun, and the earth, according to both thinkers.

## 1.3 The Good is the cause of all that is right and beautiful, the authentic source of reason

**Plato:**

> This whole image, Glaucon, must be fitted together with what we said before. The visible realm should be likened to the prison dwelling, and the light of the

fire inside it to the power of the sun. And if you interpret the upward journey and the study of things above as the upward journey of the soul to the intelligible ream, you'll grasp what I hope to convey, since that is what you wanted to hear about. Whether it's true or not, only God knows. But this is how I see it: In the knowable realm, the Form of the Good is the last thing seen, and it is reached only with difficulty. Once one has seen it, however, one must conclude that it is the cause of all that is correct [*orthōn*] and beautiful in anything, that it produces both light and its source in the visible realm, and that in the intelligible realm it controls and provides truth and understanding [*noun*], so that anyone who is to act sensibly in private or public must see it.

> I have the same thought, at least as far as I'm able. (*Republic* VII 517a8–c6; adapted from Grube and Reeve)[80]

Here we have the best summation of the experience of the Good: it is the cause of everything that is right (*orthōn*) and beautiful, causing the sun to exist, and the authentic source of truth and understanding (*noun*).[81] Moreover, I highlight Plato's statement that the Good is the source of reason, perhaps implying that the Good causes Nous as well, as is additionally implied by the claim that the Good causes being and the Forms.

On the Platonic side, I disagree with Majumdar,[82] who claims that her interpretation places "the Good in the monistic position of being the only source behind both the good and evil." For Plato does not state that the Good is the source of evil, and instead asserts that ignorant human souls cause evil, and not God (*Republic* II and III) or the Good. Majumdar continues:

> [Plato] understands that the Good is the cause of even the ignorance in the cave. He cannot conclude that so long as the Good continues to permit shadows on the cave wall, a revolutionary overthrow of the immediate human causes of the prisoners' bondage (the puppeteer-performers) must fail in the ignorance of the prisoners symbolized by their fetters cannot be removed.[83]

Majumdar incorrectly assumes that allowing something to occur is the same thing as causing it to occur. Furthermore, it is not evil per se that shadows are produced on the wall; it is the soul's reaction to the shadows and its decision to ascend or not, or whether the soul accepts the shadows as real, that determines whether or not the soul is evil. Also, Plato and Plotinus argue that the ignorance is caused by actions and thoughts in past lives and an evil condition of the soul where one is mastered by pleasure, love, and/or fear.

Thus, Plato holds that the Good causes all that is right and beautiful, and is the source of reason.

**Plotinus**: One might think it difficult to confirm the Good is in some way the cause of beauty, since Plotinus identifies the Good with Beauty in some places (see especially I.6.6 and I.6.7). However, since he believes that Beauty Itself is the source of beautiful things—even if we assume, *per impossibile*, that Beauty Itself is identical with the Good for Plotinus—Plotinus believes that the Good or Beauty Itself is indeed the source of beauty in other things. Nonetheless, later in his writings, Plotinus seems to deny that Beauty and the Good are identical:

> Both [the Good and Beauty] participate in the same and the One is before both, and that in the higher world also the Good itself does not need beauty, though beauty needs it… . But the Good is older, not in time but in truth, and has the prior power: for it has all power; that which comes after it has not all power, but as much as can come after it and derive from it. (V.5.12.31–34, 37–40)

This passage implies that the Good and Beauty are closely related, and this, too, is compatible with Plato's view, because, in the *Symposium* (210e–212b), Plato makes claims that are similar to those made about the Good in the *Republic*; namely, that one can have a final vision of Beauty is a life-transforming experience. For instance, Plato says that having a vision of Beauty Itself appears to radically reduce—if not remove—one's sex drive (*Symposium* 211d). Plato does not make such claims about any of the other Forms, such as Justice, Temperance, or Courage.

The relevant issue on commentators' minds is whether the Plotinian One is the progenitor of evil: Anton[84] believes it is not; but O'Brien[85] believes that it is (and that Plato's Receptacle can be made evil so he can account for evil's not being produced by the Good), so that Plotinus has a problem accounting for what is intrinsically evil. I will analyze this issue further when I discuss the Receptacle below.

Therefore, Plato and Plotinus each have the view that the Good is the cause of all that is right and beautiful, the authentic source of truth and reason.

## 1.4 The Good is the source of ethical truth

The Good, for both philosophers, is not merely a metaphysical cause of truth, knowledge, seasons, years, just and beautiful things; it is also the source of ethical goodness. If one knows the Good, one knows how to live well and be happy. Here I differ with Platonic commentators who claim that the Good is *chiefly* or *solely* a metaphysical entity, or *chiefly* or *solely* an ethical entity, because I believe that Plato holds that the Good is equally the chief epistemological, metaphysical, and ethical entity. Others claim, for instance, that Plato has a problem in the *Republic* when he tries to link the Good both to metaphysics and to ethics, that we distort Plato's meaning if we base his ethics on the Good, and that the fundamental insight of Plato's ethics is that nothing can be said about the content of the Good.

On the Plotinian side of the issue, we only find one argument, from Ciapolo, that Plotinus and Plato do not have the same view.

**Plato**:[86] Plato actually adds to the Cave Allegory summary that, along with one's discovering the source of truth and reason:

> Anyone who is to act wisely [*emphronōs*] in private or public must see it [the Good].
>
> I have the same thought, at least as far as I'm able. (*Republic* VII 517c4–6; adapted from Grube and Reeve)

Thus the Good is the entity that one must know in order to be a good person. In fact, putting together what we've seen so far about the Good, it appears to be the answer to the three most significant philosophical questions (or *at least* to play a key role in answering them): what can we know, what exists, and how should we live?

Let us now consider objections[87] from Benitez, Shorey, and Voegelin on Plato's view. First, Benitez explains:

> If we adopt the view that Plato first came to see the problem of unity of ethical and metaphysical good when he wrote the *Republic*, we are better placed to understand his reticence to speak there about the Good itself... .
>
> Whether or not Plato saw a problem about the unity of good in the *Republic*, he certainly came to see such a problem by the time he wrote the *Philebus*.[88]

A few replies are in order. First, and most importantly, one of the reasons that the Good is arguably the source of ethical truth is that it is the universal object of living things' desire, and Plato never veers, even in the *Philebus*, from this view. Second, one wonders why Benitez did not mention that the Good is also Plato's view of the unity of epistemological—as well as of ethical and metaphysical—good, given that Plato also says that the Good is the greatest object of knowledge. Lastly, on my reading of the *Philebus*, Plato is discussing the human good (*qua* beauty, proportion, and truth) as opposed to the Good

Itself. So perhaps there is not a problem with the Good's being the supreme object of knowledge as well as the supreme metaphysical good.

Shorey argues:

> The [unhypothesized first principle] is the Idea of Good so far as we assume that idea to be attainable either in ethics or in physics. But it is the Idea of Good, not as a transcendental ontological mystery, but in the ethical sense already explained.[89]

Of course I agree that the Good is an attainable ethical good for Plato, but I fail to see why the Good cannot be both transcendent and mysterious (being beyond being) but also the entity that one must ultimately know in order to be an ethically good person.

Shorey also counters: "If we base Plato's ethics on the idea of good, or on any other metaphysical principle or schematism, we shall distort his meanings."[90] I do not think that it is a distortion of Plato's meaning to hold that he is claiming in the Cave summary that one must know or see the Good in order to be a good and wise person (VII 517c), that one will not benefit from any other knowledge unless one has knowledge of the Good (VI 505a–b), and that when one knows the Good, one will be happy and virtuous. My reading of Plato demands that the Good plays a central metaphysical, epistemological, and ethical role.

Lastly, Voegelin perhaps emphasizes the mystery of the Good too much:

> What is the Idea of the Agathon? The briefest answer to the question will best bring out the decisive point: Concerning the content of the Agathon nothing can be said at all. That is the fundamental insight of Platonic ethics. The transcendence of the Agathon makes immanent propositions concerning its content impossible.[91]

One can protest Voegelin's claim by pointing to Plato's claim that the true dialectician can give an account of the Good (*Republic* VII 534b–d), but one can also make the point that, whether or not one can express the content of the Good,[92] Plato nonetheless is urging us (and the guardians) to know the Good in order to be truly good, and I believe that this is the more fundamental insight of Platonic ethics.

Thus, Plato holds that the Good is the source of ethical truth.

**Plotinus**: Plotinus agrees with Plato: the Good is the source of happiness and the Good (via Intellect) generates righteousness and virtue:[93]

> That Good has not given its gifts and then gone away but is always bestowing them as long as it is what it is. But we exist more when we turn to him and our

> well-being [*to eu*] is there, but being far from him is nothing else but existing less. There the soul takes its rest and is outside evils because it has run up into the place which is clear of evils; and it thinks there, and is not passive, and its true life is there; for our present life, the life without God, is a trace of life imitating that life. But life in that realm is the active actuality of Intellect; and the active actuality generates gods in quiet contact with that Good, and generates beauty, and generates righteousness, and generates virtue. It is these the soul conceives when filled with God, and this is its beginning and end; its beginning because it comes from thence, and its end because its good is there. (VI.9.9.9–22)[94]

So Plotinus confirms that the soul's well-being lies in the Good, and that Intellect, via the Good, is the generator of righteousness, virtue, and beauty. I can also affirm this basic point by noting that Plotinus believes along with Plato that the Good is the source of the Forms—including Justice, Temperance—and that every living thing desires the Good.

Ciapolo is the only major dissenter found in my research, arguing:

> Plotinus's position on *eudaimonia*, as well as his view of its relation to seriousness and true life, while profiting from Platonic, Aristotelian, and Stoic insights, is nevertheless an original one. For him, perfect and superabundant life is to be found in *Nous* and in the intelligible nature of man. Both *Nous* and human beings (that is, the inner man in each human being) are life, while all other living things merely have life, precisely because they are less perfect and dimmer versions of Primal Life, the life of *Nous*. Hence, *eudaimonia*, the good state of one's inner reality, is identical with the attainment of identity with the One-Good by any being which has life superabundantly, that is, possesses an intelligible nature.[95]

I counter that these are all Platonic claims, beginning with Ciapolo's last sentence, that one must attain the "One-Good" (leaving aside the non-dual aspect for the conclusion). Plato holds that like resembles like, and analogizes in the Sun Simile that one must be "goodlike" in order to see the Good. Moreover, I will review Plato's claims that Nous has life and, together with the Platonic and Plotinian claims that the philosopher uses her Reason (part of her soul), thereby using her intelligible nature to achieve happiness, we will be able to show that Plotinus and Plato agree on these claims as well. Lastly, I will still argue for Plotinus' originality in the conclusion, so I agree with Ciapolo about Plotinus' originality, but not about its nature.

Therefore, each thinker holds that the Good is the source of ethical truth.

## 1.5 The One is interpretively equivalent to the Good [that is, especially in Plato, the One of Parmenides' First Hypothesis (*Parmenides* 137c–142b) is the Form of the Good]

Plotinus refers to the Good as the One frequently, and states that the One is not a being, but even more paradoxically that it is unlimited, is not even one, cannot have a name and that one cannot have knowledge or perception of it. Admittedly, Plato does not make these latter claims—except perhaps the knowledge claim—of the Good in *Republic* VI or VII, or elsewhere for that matter. However, in the *Parmenides*, Plato makes just these claims about one version of a "One." Thus, if, as I claim, Plato and Plotinus have the same view about the highest principle of their philosophies, an argument is needed that attempts to prove that, when Plato refers to a One in the relevant section of the *Parmenides*, he is somehow referring to the Form of the Good, or an entity that could be reasonably interpreted as having characteristics of the Form of the Good is said to have. When I get to specific claims that are made by Plato in the *Parmenides* about the One, I will also confirm that these features are found of the One in Plotinus.

This is one of the most controversial sections of the book. Few commentators agree with my interpretation of Plato, and thus few also believe that Plotinus interprets Plato correctly on this point.

**Plato**: I have largely refrained from mentioning Aristotle to make our case thus far, and will in general continue to do so. It is, however, worth noting that Aristotle, and his contemporaries thereafter, seemed to take Plato as believing that the One is the Good.[96]

In what is known as the second section[97] of the *Parmenides* (137c–166b), Plato lays out either eight or nine hypotheses, depending on your interpretation of those pages, concerned with whether a One is, or a One is not. Plato, through the character Parmenides, lists, and in some cases appears to argue for, characteristics that a One would have and not have, were it to exist—as well as characteristics that a One that is *not* would have and not have, were that the case. The standard Neo-Platonic reading of this second section is that in the First Hypothesis (*Parmenides* 137c–142b; regardless of whether there are eight or nine hypotheses), where Plato runs through the characteristics of a One if a One is, he is describing perfectly the One of Plotinus (or Iamblichus, or Proclus, for instance). The thesis of this book does not require that the Neo-Platonic interpretation of the entire second section (or any of the other sections) be correct, so that detailed argument will not be attempted here. However, it can be shown that the first set of characteristics attributed to—or, more accurately, *not* attributed to—the One from *Parmenides* 137c–142b in the First Hypothesis are consistent with what Plato says elsewhere of the Good.[98]

Before I attempt such an argument, one might object that it is prima facie implausible to suggest that anything said in the second section of *Parmenides* refers to anything other than the character Parmenides' hypothesis, since he himself states that he will begin with his hypothesis (*Parmenides* 137b).[99] My responses are, first, if we normally take characters who speak for Plato to contain Plato's view, then we can take Parmenides here—usually taken to speak for Plato—to at least *possibly* contain some of Plato's views elsewhere; and second, I take this to be Plato's style, loosely alluding to the philosopher Parmenides' view that a one exists, but, if it can be shown that characteristics of the One of the First Hypothesis are consistent with what Plato says elsewhere about the Good, then we are justified in so taking the second section.

In order to demonstrate this, I provide twenty conclusions that Plato gives in the First Hypothesis about what characteristics the One would lack, if a One is.

To make this task more manageable, I sort these 20 conclusions into two groups: the first contains a list of characteristics that all Forms presumably have; the second contains a list of characteristics that not all Forms have,[100] and in the second list characteristics will be shown to uniquely refer to the Good Itself.

I begin with the first list of eleven conclusions that can be plausibly and consistently interpreted as referring to characteristics of all Forms. Through the character Parmenides, Plato posits the following attributes with respect to the One:

1. "If the one is to be one [and not many], it will neither be a whole nor have parts" (137d1–2);
2. "It could have neither a beginning nor an end nor a middle" (137d4–5);
3. "It is also without shape" (137d8);
4. "It would be nowhere, because it could be neither in another nor in itself" (138a2–3);
5. "[It is] even more impossible for it to *come* to be" (138d4–5);
6. "It doesn't change places by going somewhere and coming to be in something, nor does it move by spinning in the same location or by being altered. . . . The one, therefore, is unmoved by every sort of motion" (138e7–139a3);

7. "The one is never in the same thing" (139a8);
8. "The one … is neither at rest nor in motion" (139b2–3);
9. "It won't be different by being one" (139c6);
10. "The one could not be younger or older than, or the same age as, itself or another" (141a2–4);
11. "[The one] has no share of time, nor is it *in* any time" (141d4–5).

(1) Every Form is said by both philosophers to be one, and the Good is no exception.[101] If the Good is truly one, then it cannot have parts. If something is a whole, it is implied that it has parts. From this perspective, the Good would not be a whole either. Now, an objection should be immediately present: if *every* Platonic Form is one and not many (and if these first ten characteristics in general apply to all Forms as well), then the One mentioned in the First Hypothesis could be equivalent to every Form, and not, as required by the current thesis, only the Form of the Good. This is an excellent point, but I withhold that judgment for now; as I continue, further conclusions will narrow down the number of possible Forms to the Good, given Plato's statements about the One in the *Parmenides* and about the Good in the *Republic* and elsewhere. Notice that all of the remaining ten conclusions can be true of at least one other Form other than the Form of the Good—Oneness or the One Itself.[102]

(2) The claim, "no beginning, end, or middle" does apply to Forms in general, again, since, for one reason, they are held to be eternal by both philosophers. The number of Forms may be infinite—and if numbers are Forms, as I believe, the infinity of Forms is likely—but also since one of the characteristics of a One in the first hypothesis is "it will neither be a whole nor have parts" (137d1–2), this option of the infinite set of Forms' being the One will not satisfy all of the criteria.

(3) All Forms are said to be immaterial, therefore implying that they have no shape. Thus this conclusion can be said to be true of every Form, not just the Form of the Good.

(4) Again, if all Forms are immaterial, they cannot be anywhere, either in another or in themselves.

(5) All Forms are said to be beings and not changing or coming to be, as is attributed repeatedly to perceptible, physical things.

(6) Besides the "changing" and "coming to be" points which are consistent with every Form, immaterial Forms would not revolve in the same place either, so it is reasonable to conclude that they would also not partake of any kind of motion.

(7) Forms cannot be in any place, and it would not be reasonable to think that Forms are in a certain condition, given that they are immutable natures.

(8) Even though Plato holds that there is a Form of Rest and a Form of Motion, he does not claim that Motion moves and Rest rests (see *Sophist* 250a–d). Thus, this conclusion could also apply to all Forms and not merely the Form of the Good.

(9) All Forms are one, so, viewed as being one, they are not other. Alternatively, the Form, One Itself, would presumably not be other in virtue of its being one. However, this characteristic of not being other might also be alluding to some other "One" that is beyond being, so that it is not *other* to anything, given that it is not anything besides one, or given that it *is* not anything at all. Hence, this conclusion does not clearly indicate that Plato is referring to any Form, the Form One Itself, or some entity that is beyond being. I need to look elsewhere.

(10), (11) Since Forms are eternal, it is reasonable that all Forms would lack these qualities of being younger or older than itself, the same age as itself, or being in time. At *Timaeus* 37d, Plato states that time is a moving image of eternity, implying that, just as matter imitates Matter Itself, the latter of which is eternal, time imitates eternity, the latter of which is associated with the realm of the eternal Forms.[103] However, if all Forms are eternal, this conclusion does not uniquely identify the Form of the Good.

Thus far, these conclusions are not necessarily helping to narrow down my interpretation of the Good, but there are still nine conclusions or characteristics that the One is said to lack, and the only entity in Plato's philosophy that fits these characteristics is the Form of the Good. Namely:

1. The One is without limits;
2. The One cannot be the same as itself or as another, nor other than itself or other than another;
3. The One cannot be like or unlike itself or another;
4. The One cannot have any other character distinct from being one;
5. The One will not be equal or unequal to itself or to another;
6. The One in no way has being, and in no sense is;
7. The One neither is one or is at all;
8. The One cannot have a name or be spoken of;
9. There cannot be knowledge, perception, or opinion of the One.

### 1.5.1 The One is unlimited (*Parmenides* 137d7–8)

**Plato**: The One is unlimited (*apeiron*—also rendered "boundless" or "infinite"). As far as Plato's view goes, the number of Forms, for instance, may be infinite, and if numbers are Forms, as I believe, the infinity of Forms is certain; but, since one of the characteristics of a One in the first hypothesis is also that the One "will neither be a whole nor have parts" (137d1–2), this option of the infinite set of Forms' being the One will not satisfy all of the criteria. Thus, "unlimited" is not a characteristic that Plato attributes to each and every Form, and, therefore, we are warranted in searching Plato's dialogues for something that is unlimited. Indeed, if the Good is beyond being and the source of truth and knowledge, it stands to reason that the Good would be an entity that is not limited. For instance, it is not limited to being a being, or to having to be the thing that it is—because it is not a thing if it is beyond being, and "it" is not an "is." This argument by itself may not be convincing for Plato's view, but it is certainly plausible, and there are other traits that must point us uniquely to the Form of the Good.

**Plotinus**: Plotinus believes that the One is unlimited, without limits, or infinite (all of which are legitimate translations of *apeiron*):[104]

> He is the Good—for he is the productive power of thoughtful, intelligent life, from whom come life and intelligence and whatever there is of substance and being—that he is One, for he is simple and first—that he is the Principle—for all things come from him: from him comes the first movement (for it is not in him); from him comes rest, because he had no need of rest: for 'he does not move, nor does he stand still';[105] for he has no place to stand still in and no place to move in: for round what or to what or in what [should he move]? For he is the First. But he is not limited (*apeiron*): for by what? But he is not unlimited: for by what? But he is not unlimited like a magnitude either: for where should he proceed to, or what should he intend to gain when he lacks nothing? But he has infinity in the sense of power: for he will never be otherwise, or fail, since the things which do not fail exist through him. (V.5.10.11–23)

Plotinus apparently equates the Good and One, and states that its Being is not limited, because at that level what *could* limit it? But it is not infinite in magnitude because that implies spatial location, which the One does not have. Speaking of infinity, the Plotinian One is also infinite[106] in this way:

> And this has infinity (*apeiron*) by not being more than one, and because there is nothing in which anything belonging to it will find its limit: for by being one it is not measured and does not come within range of number. It is therefore not limited in relation to itself or to anything else: since if it was it would be two. It has no shape, then, because it has no parts, and no form. (V.5.11.1–5)[107]

Besides confirming that the One is "under no limit," externally or internally, Plotinus states that it accepts no pattern and forms no shape, the latter of which was also a conclusion of the One of Parmenides' First Hypothesis.[108]

A. H. Armstrong[109] argues that Plotinus uses *apeiros* differently than Plato:

> Plotinus ... appears to shrink from applying [*apeiros* and *apeiria*], terms traditionally used to express the negative indefiniteness of matter, to the primary and absolute infinity of the One. When he does use the term 'unbounded' of the One it is in one of the restricted senses in which he applies it to the other Hypostases [Intellect and the All-Soul] which are not absolutely without limit but in some senses limited. Thus the Divine Intellect, which is very often called 'unbounded' in the restricted senses, is also limited because the Forms or Ideas which are its content are definite realities and their number is finite. This was the normal Platonist doctrine.[110]

First, it is far from clear that Plotinus shrinks from applying *apeiros* to the One, just because he uses this term (not absolutely) of Intellect and the All-Soul; Plotinus also uses *apeiros* of matter, body, evil, and other entities,[111] so this argument is not well founded. Second, Armstrong admits that the One is absolutely unlimited, but why is the First Hypothesis One not absolutely unlimited as well? Third, it is unclear that the number of Platonic Forms is finite; if numbers are Forms, it seems that their number would be infinite.

Therefore, they each believe that the One is unlimited (or without limit), and, in Plato's case, this lack is compatible with what he states about the Good.

### 1.5.2 The One will not be the same as another thing or itself, nor could it be different from itself or another thing (*Parmenides* 139b4–5)

**Plato**: Let us analyze these claims, that the One cannot be the same (*tauton* or self-identical at 139b4) as itself or as another, nor other than itself or other than another.[112] At *Sophist* 254d, Plato claims that each of Being, Motion, and Rest are different from the other two and the same (*tauton* at 254d15) as itself. But here, in the *Parmenides*, he states that the one cannot be the same as itself, or even different from another, so he cannot be alluding to either Forms of Sameness[113] or Difference. More importantly, in the *Sophist*, Plato states that every Form is different from the others (255e3–6) and every Form is the same as itself (256a7–8).[114]

Thus, if this One refers to anything in Plato's philosophy, it is not any of the standard Forms, including the Form Oneness, since it—like other Forms—would presumably be different than the other Forms.[115] Moreover, since the Good is not a being, then one could argue that it is not the same as itself, because there is no "it" for it to be like; it is not the same as another, because it is beyond being, and everything else that *is* is a being, a Form. From this perspective, it cannot be other than itself because it is not a being; and it cannot be other than another because somehow it is the source of everything else—at least of good. There is no question but that these claims are paradoxical, but we have already seen that Plato is paradoxical on the subject of the Good—it is but may not be a Form, is a being but is not a being, and knowledge thereof is possible but may not be so. We will need to look at additional characteristics of the One to ensure that we should best interpret it as being the Good.

**Plotinus**: For these characteristics let us examine the propositions that the One cannot be the same or like another.[116] Plotinus writes that the One "is the most sufficient and independent of all things" (VI.9.6.17–18); if the One is independent of all things, then it presumably cannot be like another.

Moreover, Plotinus states: "[The] One ... has no otherness" (VI.9.8.33–4), which is more evidence for the claim that the One is not other than itself or another.

However, Plotinus does state that the One has an identical nature to the Good (II.9.1). On the other hand, if the One is beyond being, then it is not a being, but it is also not becoming, and therefore it is not the same as nor like any Being, nor the same as nor like anything that is becoming. Thus, these characteristics—same as, equal to, like itself or another—are not obviously confirmed nor denied in Plotinus' thought. As for the One's not being the same as itself or equal to itself, in order for the One to be the same or equal to itself it would have to be a being, or indeed an "it;" again, Plotinus strictly denies being of the One—even though he uses the terminology of being with the One, on occasion, just as we saw that Plato used being of the Good as well.

Therefore, both philosophers affirm that the One cannot be the same as itself or as another, nor other than itself or other than another, and, since the Good is not a being according to Plato, the Good is the most likely candidate to lack these qualities.

### 1.5.3 The One cannot be like or unlike itself or another (*Parmenides* 139e7–8)

**Plato**: Here, Plato is denying likeness (*homoion* at 139e7) of the One to itself and others, and unlikeness (*anomoion* at 139e7) to itself and others. This *homoion* relation implies that the One cannot be the same as another One (namely, itself), or unlike another One, or unlike some other thing. Thus, this is not the same denial made at *Parmenides* 139b4–5, about the One's not being self-identical (represented by *tauton* there).

This denial is plausible, since in this First Hypothesis there is only one One and it is not many, so it cannot be the same as another One. For the same reason, it cannot be unlike another One because there is no such other One. Moreover, not being a being, it cannot be like any other being—which also disqualifies all the Forms from being this One. Lastly, it cannot be unlike itself, because there is only one One.

Suppose for the moment, though, that this passage refers instead to the Form Oneness, then it is difficult to fathom why the One Itself also would not be *like* another—that is, the other Forms—eternal, immutable, immaterial and so on, while at the same time being *unlike* all the other Forms, in order to be unique; both of these claims are denied by the claim that "the First Principle is king and unique." Lastly, the Form Oneness would presumably be the same as itself (per the *Sophist*), but here it is stated that it cannot be so.

As in the last section, if the Good is beyond being it cannot be like itself because it is not an "it" at all; it cannot be unlike itself, because there is nothing for it to "be;" it cannot be like another, because nothing else is the source of the Forms and beyond being; it cannot be unlike another, because it is the source of everything, and everything that exists is ultimately one—keeping in mind that matter for Plato is technically between being and not being, so, even if it is many, it is becoming, so it is not stably many. We have puzzling statements made about this One; but let me examine the other claims in order to see what Plato might be referring to by these statements.

**Plotinus**: I have already confirmed this claim for Plotinus; however, he denies these claims of the One just as they are written in the Plato section immediately above.

Therefore, Plato and Plotinus both hold that the One cannot be like itself or another, and these attributes also fit what Plato says about the Good.

### 1.5.4 The One cannot have any other character distinct from being one (*Parmenides* 140a1–3)

**Plato**: First, note that Plato paradoxically denies even this characteristic at 142a. From one perspective, if the One were in any way many, that would guarantee that it is not One, which is impossible, so it can only have the character of being one. From another perspective, however, if the One cannot be the same as itself (*Parmenides* 139b4–5) or like itself (*Parmenides* 139e7–8), then, if it were one, it would presumably be the same as itself and like itself. This is certainly paradoxical, but let us look at the claim a bit closer:

> If the one has any property apart from being one, it would be more than one; and that is impossible. (*Parmenides* 140a1–3)

First, I have already shown that this One cannot refer to the Form of Oneness.

Second, I can connect oneness with the Good of the *Republic*, as follows: Plato claims that our soul needs to be "goodlike" in order to see the Good (VI 508b).[117] At X 611a–e, Plato claims that the purified soul of a presumably good person is unified,[118] and not teeming with diversity and contradictions. Together, these passages imply that goodness is oneness and that the good person, if she is like the good or unified, would be good and unified to the extent possible given that she is still incarnated while contemplating the Good. If the Good is the One (as Plotinus uses this word), it makes more sense for Plato to claim that we must be one or unified, in order to see the One.

It is thus plausible that the One referred to here refers to the Good.

**Plotinus**:

> The One—that which is before this Intellect, this marvel of the One, which is not existent, so that 'one' may not here also have to be predicated of something else, which in truth has no fitting name, but if we must give it a name, 'one' would be an appropriate ordinary way of speaking of it, not in the sense of something else and then one. (VI.9.5.29–33)

This implies that the One is only one or a unity,[119] but note that Plotinus nonetheless denies being of the One.[120]

Therefore, though this is a paradoxical issue, the One cannot have any other character other than being one, and Plato's statements about the Good uniquely point it out as having this characteristic.

### 1.5.5 The One will be neither equal nor unequal to itself or another (*Parmenides* 140b6–7)

**Plato**: Since the equality relation implies two objects, and since there is only one One and it is not many, the One cannot equal another One. From this perspective, it is not a being, so it cannot be unequal (or equal) to others because there is technically nothing it "is." For the same reason, it cannot be unequal to itself, because there is no it for it to be unequal to.

This is yet another indication that Plato cannot be referring to the Form Oneness here. For One Itself would be equal to itself, and the One Itself would be equal in *some* ways to other Forms as well—eternality, immateriality and immutability.

Admittedly, from the viewpoint that the One only has the characteristic of being one, the characteristic of its not being equal to itself is puzzling, because, if the One can only be one, then the One would presumably be equal to itself. However, Plato ultimately denies oneness of the One (as does Plotinus).

Since the Good is said uniquely by Plato to be not a being but beyond being, with these lacks of characteristics, it is the best candidate for a One.

Thus it is plausible that the One here refers to the Good.

**Plotinus**: Assuming that, if something is not the same as itself, it is not equal to itself, and that something is not unlike itself or another also implies that that thing will not be unequal to itself or another, I have already confirmed this claim for Plotinus.

Therefore, they each hold that the One will not be equal or unequal to itself or to another, and these lacks of properties can only be referring to the Good.

### 1.5.6 The One in no way partakes of being, and in no sense is (*Parmenides* 141e9–10)

**Plato**: Plato argues for this conclusion as follows: (1) The One has nothing to do with time; (2) The One never has become, was becoming, was, has become now, is becoming, is, will be becoming, will become, or will be in the future; (3) a thing can only have being in one of these ways; therefore (4) the One in no way has being and in no sense is.[121]

Now, since all the Forms are eternal (not in time), the claims in premises (1) and (2) (except for the claim that the One never "is") are certainly applicable to generic Forms. But premise (3) and the conclusion—that these are the only ways in which something can have being, so the One in no way has being and in no sense is—are unique. At this point, we have certainly—and again, in another way—been informed that the One Itself is not being referred to here, because the One Itself is a being if it is a Form.

However, the *only* entity that Plato negates being of is the Form of the Good, when he claims that the Form of the Good is not being, but beyond being in dignity and surpassing power (*Republic* VI 509b8–10). Plato also claims that the Good is a being, but remember that Plotinus states the same thing of the Good, so this does not imply that they cannot be discussing the same Good. Thus, it is plausible that the First Hypothesis One is the Platonic Good.

**Plotinus**: Plotinus believes that the One is beyond being and not a being.[122] However, he also holds that the One—here rendered "the first nature"—is outside of time:

> Since it is the first nature and is not measured or bounded to the size it ought to be—for in this way it would be again measured by another nature—it is all power, nowhere of this particular size. For this reason it is not in time either, but outside all time, for time is continually dispersed into distancing. (VI.5.11.11–15)[123]

Therefore, Plato and Plotinus each believe that the One in no way has being, and in no sense is, and this is compatible with what Plato says about the Good.

## 1.5.7 The One neither is one nor is (*Parmenides* 141e12)

**Plato**: This claim is admittedly paradoxical if not contradictory, given Plato's statement that the one must have the character of being one. It shows that Plato is not referring here to the One Itself—or any generic Form, because they all are one and are beings—but to something else entirely, that is not one or a being. The only entity in the Platonic corpus to which this statement could possibly refer is the Good Itself, since Plato claims that it is beyond being. And, if the entity is beyond being, it is not technically one. Recall that both Plato and Plotinus have said that the One or Good is a being, not a being and beyond being. Thus, this One is plausibly thought to be the Good.

**Plotinus**: Plotinus believes that the One "is not at all," the One is beyond being. However, the first part of the claim, that the One is not one, just as in Plato, contradicts what Plotinus had said about its being a unity:

> The One—that which is before this Intellect, this marvel of the One, which is not existent, so that 'one' may not here also have to be predicated of something else, which in truth has no fitting name, but if we must give it a name, 'one' would be an appropriate ordinary way of speaking of it, not in the sense of something else and then one (VI.9.5.29–33).

Here we can see his reluctance to name it at all, and for it to be a being, because " 'one' may not here also have to be predicated of something else"—I can only point out that this paradoxical feature of the One is said by both of the philosophers to belong to it (or not).

Therefore, each thinker holds that the One neither is one nor is at all, and the most likely entity of Plato's philosophy that fits this description is the Good.

### 1.5.8 The One is not named or spoken of (*Parmenides* 142a4–5)

**Plato**: Admittedly, the statement that we cannot name or speak of the One actually contradicts what Plato says about the Good in several places. For instance, he claims that we are in the habit of *naming* a Good Itself for all the many perceptible good things (*Republic* VI 507b, and cf. X 596a–b).

There are several responses that can be made here: if the One is in no way a being,[124] we cannot stably refer to it, just as Plato states of "becomers" that are constantly changing from one kind of thing to another, and never "are" anything, other than constantly changing (*Timaeus* 37c–8b);[125] if the Good is beyond being, then technically it cannot have a name either, and this may explain why Plato gets noticeably hesitant to discuss it in *Republic* VI as the topic is being introduced, and says that he can only discuss its offspring, the sun; since Plotinus and Plato both seem to refer to the Good as a Form and not as a Form, they can in places seem to emphasize one or the other feature, without always acknowledging the alternative feature. Thus, it is consistent for Plato to claim that, qua the Good (the source of the Forms), the Good cannot be spoken of; and since Plotinus himself constantly refers to the Good and the One, and in fact names the One even after stating that no name is truly fitting (VI.9.5.31–2), it is possible that Plato may be doing that very thing more stealthily in the *Parmenides*. In other words, Plotinus attempts to provide an explanation as to why naming the One is difficult, and the *Parmenides* (141e–2a) gives the same kind of reason as to why it is difficult—that it is not one nor is, so nothing can belong to it or be of it.

As far as the ineffability claim is concerned—that the One cannot be spoken of—it is relatively easy to show that Plato says that the ultimate experience as well as the First Principle is ineffable.[126]

So, in the rest of Plato's philosophy, I represent that "the One cannot have a name or be spoken of" is the Form of the Good.[127]

**Plotinus**: Plotinus claims that the experience of the One is ineffable,[128] so, in focusing on the inability of it to have a name, a passage we have just examined helps: "The One—that which is before this Intellect, this marvel of the One, which is not existent, so that 'one' may not here also have to be predicated of something else, which in truth has no fitting name, but if we must give it a name, 'one' would be an appropriate ordinary way of speaking of it, not in the sense of something else and then one" (VI.9.5.29–33).

Another passage confirms that the Plotinian One cannot be named or spoken of:

> It is, therefore, truly ineffable: for whatever you say about it, you will always be speaking of a 'something.' But 'beyond all things and beyond the supreme majesty of Intellect'[129] is the only one of all the ways of speaking of it which is true; it is not its name, but says that it is not one of all things and 'has no name,' because we can say nothing of it: we only try, as far as possible, to make signs to ourselves about it. But when we raise the difficulty 'Then it has no perception of itself and is not even conscious of itself and does not even know itself,' we should consider that by saying this we are turning ourselves round and going in the opposite direction. (V.3.13.1–9)[130]

Not everyone agrees that Plotinus has properly interpreted the First Hypothesis of the *Parmenides*.[131]

Therefore, Plato and Plotinus each hold that the One cannot have a name or be spoken of, and given what Plato says about the ineffability of the ultimate experience (and the Good), this One is interpretively equivalent to the Good.

### 1.5.9 There cannot be knowledge, perception, or opinion of the One (*Parmenides* 142a3–4)

**Plato**: Noting the Platonic claim that knowledge is of Forms, Plato's statement that there cannot be knowledge of the One implies that he is not referring to the Form Oneness; this statement might also refer to the Good.

Admittedly, however, if we suppose that the One here is the Good, in several places this actually contradicts what Plato says about the Good. For instance, he states that *knowledge* of the Good is necessary to benefit from other knowledge (*Republic* VI 504e–505b); and *knowledge* of the Good is necessary for one to be a true dialectician (VII 534c). In order to salvage my interpretation, however, recall the hints in Plato that the Good is not just another Form in at least three ways (besides that it is the source of the Forms):

First, Plato says the Good in *Republic* VI is not a being but beyond being (509b9), and the source of knowledge, but other than, and superior to, knowledge[132] (508d–509a); he also states that we *are* able to have knowledge of Forms, so these statements themselves are incompatible. No other "Form" or entity is said to be beyond being and knowledge by Plato—except, according to my argument, the One of the first hypothesis in the *Parmenides*.

Second, we may not be able to know the Good; in the wrap-up of the Cave Allegory, for instance, Plato says, "in the knowable, the Idea of Good is the last thing to be seen, but hardly" (*Republic* VII 517b8–c1; my translation),[133] which implies that the Good technically may not be known, but that a glimpse of the Good will give its seer enough understanding to see the layout of the universe, as it were, and understand the source of goodness.

Third, Plato claims that we can have a *vision* of the Good, as well as of the Beautiful, in many places,[134] which implies that, in those passages, he is trying to get away from the idea that we can *know* the Form of the Good, to articulate that it is more of an experience.[135] In addition, an analogous precedent has been made at *Symposium* 211a–b, where Plato states that the vision of Beauty will not be any kind of knowledge.

On one's lack of being able to perceive or opine the One, leaving aside Plato's statements of seeing or having a vision of the Good—as they allude instead to the soul or mind—if the Good is not a being but beyond being, it arguably cannot be perceived, certainly not with one's senses.[136] Moreover, one cannot opine the One (or any Form, for that matter), because opinion is a faculty whose objects are between being and not being.

Thus, it is plausible that the One referred to here is the Good.

**Plotinus**: Plotinus confirms these claims, that there cannot be knowledge, perception, or opinion of the One:[137]

> If the Good is anything, it is so in a greater way than by knowledge and thought and self-perception; since it is not anything for itself; for it does not bring anything into itself, but itself suffices. It is not, then, even good for itself, but for the others; for they need it, but it could not need itself; that would be ridiculous; for if it did it would be in need of itself. Nor, certainly, does it look at itself; for it must have and get something from the looking. For it has left all these things to the beings which come after it, and, so it seems, none of the additions to the others are with it, just as even substance is not; so not thinking either, since that is where substance is and the primary and authentic thinking and being are both together. Therefore "there is neither discourse nor perception nor knowledge" because it is impossible to predicate anything of it as present with it. (VI.7.41.25–38)[138]

So Plotinus holds with Plato that there cannot be knowledge, perception, or opinion of the One, and I have confirmed these claims for each philosopher at this point.

Note a major objection to my position[139] from those who claim that Plato's Good is knowable (but the Plotinian One is unknowable). Hitchcock's argument will represent this group:[140]

> The interpretation has links with the neoplatonist reading, but Plato clearly differs from the neoplatonists in holding (at least in the *Republic*) that the good is a Form … exists, … and can be known.[141]

Both Plato and Plotinus refer to the Good as a Form, but they also use "Good" in other ways, as the source of knowledge, truth, and being. Both philosophers refer to the Good or One as a being and not being, but beyond being. Additionally, the Plotinian Good can be known, and there is reason to believe that the Platonic Good may be unknowable (unlike any other Form), but an object of intellectual vision or some other experience. Thus, I am far from being able to dismiss the unknowable One of the First Hypothesis as possibly being interpretively equivalent to the Platonic Good, not to mention this entity's being equivalent to the Plotinian One or Good.

Plotinus holds that all of the conclusions in Parmenides' First Hypothesis uniquely pick out the Form of the Good in Plato's writings, and Plato's assertions of the One—or, rather, mostly characteristics that the One could *not* have, if a One "is"—are in fact equally attributed to the One which Plotinus discusses in his writings.[142]

For Plotinus, the Good is the One:

> Since, then, the simple nature of the Good appeared to us as also primal (for all that is not primal is not simple), and as something which has nothing in itself, but is some one thing; and since the nature of what is called the One is the same (for this is not some other thing first and then one, nor is the Good something else first, and then good), whenever we say 'the One' and whenever we say 'the Good,' we must think that the nature we are speaking of is the same nature, and call it 'one' not as predicating anything of it but as making it clear to ourselves as far as we can. And we call it the First in the sense that it is simplest, and the Self-Sufficient, because it is not composed of a number of parts. (II.9.1.1–9)

So the Good is identical to the One[143] and can also be referred to as "The First"[144]; they have identical natures.

I will examine this telling passage of Plotinus', which I believe is precisely what we find in Plato—a statement of the paradox of the One's relationship to the Forms: "It is none of these things and all of them: none of them because the real beings are later, but all of them because they come from it"

(VI.7.32.12–14). Since Plotinus' idea is that the One is all the Forms, because it is their source, and similarly none of them because the Forms are later than their source, we again see just how parallel Plato's statements of the Good are to Plotinus' One.

Consider Plato's corpus and ask this question: Does Plato explicitly claim that the One is identical to the Good? Admittedly, he does not. I argued that the conclusions of the *Parmenides*' First Hypothesis are best interpreted in the Platonic corpus as referring to the Form of the Good, given that several of the conclusions are that a One has no being and is nothing at all, and the only other entity that Plato describes as being beyond being is the Good.

Given how indeterminate Plato is about the relation between the One and the Good, we cannot conclude that Plato and Plotinus disagree on the issue of whether the One is the Good. Therefore, invoking the Compatibility Principle, their views are at least in principle compatible with each other. It is unfortunate that Plato is not as clear as Plotinus on the relation between the Good and the One, though Plotinus' view itself is certainly in need of explanation. The most likely interpretation of the *Parmenides*' First Hypothesis remains, even if it cannot be proven for certain: the Plotinian One or at least something close (if not identical) to Plato's Form of the Good.

**Commentators**: Let us now consider what commentators have said in general about Plotinus' view of the One or Good and its connection, or lack thereof, to the *Parmenides*. First, I should mention A. H. Armstrong's discussion concerning the negative theology of the First Hypothesis:

> The early history of this 'negative theology' – the description of God by saying what he is not rather than what he is – is bound up with a particular interpretation of Plato's most difficult dialogue, the 'Parmenides' which was accepted by all later Platonists and finds defenders even now. This indirect knowledge of God by negation is very far from the direct contemplation or full and clear intuition which is what Platonists mean by knowledge.[145]

It should be noted that both Plotinus and Plato do not consistently use the word God for the Good or One as opposed to Intellect, Nous, or the Demiurge. Nonetheless, even discounting the *Parmenides* that we have carefully examined, there is negative theology even in the description of the Good in the *Republic*, where Plato claims it is unhypothesized and not truth, knowledge, or being and hardly seen. On the other hand, both philosophers obviously attribute positive qualities to the Good or One, as Bussanich lists in Plotinus' case.[146] In addition, few commentators[147] hold, as I do, that Plotinus and Plato have the same view of the One and Good, and that the *Parmenides*' First Hypothesis should be interpreted similarly to mine.

There are many representative arguments against my position, because this is such a crucial point of interpretation.[148]

**First**, Allen retracts his concession that the Good of the *Republic* is connected to the One of the *Parmenides*:

> For the sake of argument, I have supposed that the Good of the *Republic* and the Unity of the *Parmenides* are connected. Plotinus, indeed, thought they were identical, and identical with God. But of course they are not; for what it is to be good is not identical with what it is to be one; otherwise it would be the same to be good and be one.[149] Plotinus' One and Good is not an exemplary cause. Nor does Plotinus's scheme, despite stout asseveration to the contrary, and reasoning by modern commentators of such tortuousness as to defy analysis, fit the *Parmenides*.
>
> This is clear for reasons we have already seen. Even in respect of the 'first hypothesis,' there are clear disparities… . The nonexistence of Unity in Deduction I.1 is derived from the premise that to be is to be in time, a premise which both Plato and Plotinus thought false.[150]

We have already seen that both Plato and Plotinus refer to the Good and/or the One as God, so Allen dismisses this connection too quickly. In addition, I do not claim that Plato and Plotinus believe that oneness and goodness are identical but that their philosophical entities the Good and the One are identical—in part because the Good, for example, is said to be being and not being but beyond being, and the One is said not to be as well. Moreover, it has been demonstrated that the One of the First Hypothesis is not the Form Oneness, which *would* be what it is to be one; this is one more reason for not taking Plato to be discussing oneness in general in *Parmenides*' First Hypothesis. Finally, we have no reason to believe that when Plotinus discusses the One he is referring to oneness in general. Though it is generally true that Plato and Plotinus deny that "becomers" have being, when Plato says at *Parmenides* 141e7–8 that something can partake of being only in one of three ways: "was," "is," and "will be" (and their variants; see 141e3–7), it is perfectly plausible to posit that he is suggesting but not endorsing these options. That is, he is suggesting "was," "is," and "will be" as the only possible options for something's being in time, while at the same time denying elsewhere that "is" can be said of beings, since "is" is only properly said of eternal, non-temporal, Forms (see, for example, *Timaeus* 37d1–8b5—we improperly apply "was" and "will be" to everlasting being, at 37e). Thus we cannot infer that this false premise nullifies the fact that the One is said to be beyond time, and "was," "is," and "will be" do not apply to it.

**Second**, A. H. Armstrong gives an alternative view of what Plato is arguing for the First Hypothesis:

> Very closely related to this Pythagorean way of approach is the quite illegitimate interpretation of Plato's dialectical exercise on the subject of the One in his dialogue 'Parmenides' which had been current among Platonists and Pythagoreans ... and which Plotinus, the later Neo-Platonists and some modern writers accept. According to this interpretation the first hypothesis about 'the One,' which Plato probably intended to show that if you posit an absolute unity in the strict sense all sorts of impossible consequences follow, is a description of a transcendent Unity, the First Principle of all things, which can only be described by negations.[151]

I have shown that the First Hypothesis One is best interpreted as being the Good in Plato's philosophy. Moreover, if Plato only intended to show that impossible consequences follow, if you posit an absolute unity in the strict sense, then we would have to keep in mind that, since Plato begins the analysis either four or five times (depending on your count) after positing whether a One exists, then we must also conclude by this reasoning that no "One" can exist, including knowable ones that are beings, which, quite counter to the remainder of the Platonic corpus, would also disqualify the Forms themselves from existing.[152]

**Third**, Chen argues that Neo-Platonists (such as Plotinus, explicitly named immediately before this quotation):

> ... failed to perceive that the premisses from which the inferences follow are not categorical but hypothetical. Such inferences can never be held to be objectively valid without a categorical assertion of their premisses; but no such assertion, covering all the hypotheses alike, is to be found anywhere in the dialogue. In its absence how is it possible to ascribe to our philosopher a metaphysical system having no other foundation than these inferences? It is not possible; and this is fatal not only to the Neoplatonist interpretation but to all others which, without regard to the hypothetical form of the demonstration, introduce a metaphysical system into the second part of the dialogue.[153]

However, my interpretation can and does grant the hypothetical structure, but finds that the conclusions made about the First Hypothesis One in the *Parmenides* are compatible with, and point to, the Good as described in *Republic* VI and VII. And, I have rejected the logical reading (with A. E. Taylor) in favor of the metaphysical reading, and I have not introduced any new Platonic principles or entities as part of a new metaphysical system (see the Appendix). Thus, Chen's charges that there is no other foundation for the metaphysical reading, and that interpreters such as myself fail to regard the hypothetical form of the demonstration, are not persuasive.

**Fourth**, Cornford makes several points absent from the objections I have considered thus far:

> This revelation of mystical doctrine could never have been discovered by anyone who had nothing more to go upon than the text of the dialogue itself. What Parmenides offered to Socrates was a gymnastic exercise, not the disclosure of a supreme divinity. He also said that he would begin 'with himself and his own supposition that there is a One,' and Parmenides' One Being was not a god, nor was it 'beyond being.' The language throughout is as dry and prosaic as a textbook of algebra; there is as little here to suggest that the One has any religious significance as there is in the other case to suggest that x, y, and z are a trinity of unknown gods.
>
> The Neoplatonic interpretation rests in the first place on the assumption that, when Plato says that this One has no positive attributes and cannot even 'be' in any sense, he means that it is somehow 'beyond' or 'above' being and all other attributes. There is not the slightest hint anywhere in the text to warrant this assumption.[154]

I contest the claims of the first two sentences by countering that the First Hypothesis One is an entity that is not a being and is unknowable, so we are warranted in asking ourselves about the nature (or lack thereof) of such an entity. If it is possible to have an experience, vision, or knowledge of a Good that is not a being but beyond being, as Plato urges in *Republic* VI and VII, then I am warranted in noting the parallel. So it does not matter if one can find a supreme divinity in the First Hypothesis just by reading the dialogue. Also regarding Cornford's first two sentences, I read the second section as being an exercise to help Socrates work out some of the answers to the criticisms of the Forms; Parmenides called it a laborious game, because every option had to be examined; but if it is the case, as Cornford admits (and I agree), that Parmenides (Plato) is serious here, then why are we not warranted in thinking about the relation between the ultimate entity, about which Plato is serious in *another* major dialogue, and the First Hypothesis, and *their* nature(s)? Moreover, the alleged dry nature of the second section does not tell us that the subjects of the hypotheses cannot be the Good, or Forms, the soul, or particular things. We must look at each conclusion (or set of conclusions) and see if they might be referring to other Platonic entities, based on the rest of his corpus (see the Appendix). Lastly, acknowledging that Cornford did, in fact, mention the possibility of a "mystical construction" of the "beyond being" passage[155] in the sentence that follows his quotation, the quibble between beyond being versus not being is reduced when we remember that Plato *said* that the Good is "*not being*, but beyond being" at *Republic* VI 509b8–9 (emphasis added).[156] My interpretation is not, therefore, a stretch, but, at a bare minimum, quite plausible.

**Fifth**, Gerson makes four arguments against the view that the Plotinian One is the Good of the *Republic*:

1. "Plato does not explicitly claim that the Form of the Good is the cause in any sense of the demiurge or divine mind. It is explicitly said only to be the cause of the being and knowability of the Forms."
2. "Plato does not even analogously attribute 'personal' attributes to the Form of the Good as does Plotinus."
3. "Plato evinces no reticence or qualification in calling his first principle an Idea even though it is 'beyond [*ousia*].' This is quite unlike the case with the One, as we have seen."
4. "Plato is silent about any causal relation between the Form of the Good and anything else besides Forms. On the contrary, his sketchy remarks suggest that this Form is only indirectly related to what participates in the other, subordinate Forms. I shall argue, however, that the proper effect of the One's activity is the existence of everything else."[157]

My reply to (1) is that, though I admit that Plato does not explicitly state that the Good is the cause of the divine mind (Nous) or the Demiurge (so Gerson is technically correct), Nous is being and is good; the Good causes being as well as everything that is good; thus I can infer that Plato believes that the Good causes Nous. I will argue that Nous or God is best interpreted as referring to the Demiurge (of the *Timaeus* and the *Statesman*).

Re: (2): Assume that the One's willing something is a personal attribute, as opposed to eternality, infinity, omnipresence and like attributes,[158] then, from *Republic* X, I have evidence that Plato attributes willing and wishing to God, the creator of the Forms. As I argued, however, Plato's use of God must almost certainly refer to the Good, since he claims that the Good is the source of the Forms in VI and VII. The passages are: "Now, God, either because he didn't want to [*ebouleto*] or because it was necessary for him not to do so, didn't make more than one bed in nature, but only one, the very one that is the being of a Bed" (X 597c1–3; adapted from Grube and Reeve); "God knew this, I think, and wishing [*boulomenos*] to be the real maker of the truly real Bed and not just *a* maker of *a* bed, he made it to be one in nature" (X 597d1–3; adapted from Grube and Reeve); "Do you want us to call him [the Bed's] natural maker?" (X 597d5–6). Thus, it at least appears that—by implication of the best reading of X 597c–d—the Platonic Good wills or wishes, and so has at least this personal attribute in common with the Plotinian One.[159]

Re: (3): Even if Plato shows no reticence in calling the Good a Form as well as not a being and beyond being, Plotinus *does* call the Good a Form as well, so this point does not, or should not, decide the issue.

Re: (4): I have already shown this claim to be mistaken; the Platonic (as well as Plotinian) Good of the Cave Analogy is in some sort the cause of everything outside the cave, as well as the visible sun and ultimately—via the Demiurge in the *Timaeus*—the visible world (*Republic* VII 516b–c).

**Sixth,** Robin argues his claim about the Plotinian One:

> In itself it is 'formless,' like Plato's 'receptacle' or Aristotle's potential intellect, in order to be all forms. It is, therefore, not a unity and not a being; it is the One and 'What is.' Or rather, it is 'beyond and above Being,' but not in the same way as Plato's Good, for it is also 'above the Good.'[160]

Plotinus does not say that the One *is* all the Forms, but that it contains them, is their cause and source, which is parallel to what Plato says of the Good. Moreover, Plotinus believes in the existence of Plato's Receptacle (see Chapter 6.1), but the reader should not surmise from Robin that the Plotinian One is Plato's Receptacle. Next, Robin's paradoxical statements, about the One's being a being and yet being beyond being, are something I have already shown also to be Platonic. Lastly, if my interpretation is correct, the statement that the One is beyond the Good is arguably Platonic, because, as we have seen and argued, based on the Sun Simile and Cave Allegory, the *Republic* VI and VII Good is not always goodness per se in Plato's view but not a being and the source of being. In addition, the First Hypothesis One is not the One Itself, so Plato is simply not discussing Forms there.

**Seventh**, Rochel concludes his analysis of the First Hypothesis One and the Neo-Platonic interpretation:

> Hence the One that is non-existent, therefore not capable of being One, not knowable, and not thinkable, cannot be anything positive, let alone more than positive, beyond positive. Rather it is what it is, i.e. a mere negation. And thus the neo-Platonic interpretation, which for the rest of the dialogue is a treasury of good ideas, can only be indicative of the nature of the non-existent

> One—indeed, indicative of contradiction, namely that the non-existent One is nothing but a simple nothing.[161]

All of these negations have been made or implied by Plato about the Good, which commentators have failed to see, for one reason or another.[162] Further, the One of Plotinus is also said to be not One, unknowable, and beyond being, but also to be the source and container of everything; Plato declares the same about the Good, so it is not true that each philosopher claims only negative attributes of their highest principle. In fact, they both give the same kinds of positive statements about the One or Good.[163] Lastly, if the First Hypothesis One is a nothing but a simple nothing, then it would appear that Plotinus' One and perhaps (if I am correct) Plato's Good are simple nothings as well. However, this is not the message that Plato and Plotinus are trying to make about the Platonic Good or the Plotinian One, even though these are claimed to not be truth, knowledge, being, and so on. For both philosophers say other similar paradoxical things about both entities, which is precisely why I am arguing that it appears that they share the same nature.

**Eighth,** and finally, Stace argues that:

> Plato had shown that the idea of the One, an exclusive of all multiplicity, was an impossible abstraction. Even to say 'the One is,' involves the duality of the One. The Absolute Being can be no abstract unity, but only a unity in multiplicity. Plotinus begins by ignoring this extremely important philosophical principle. He falls back upon the lower level of oriental monism. God, he thinks, is absolutely One. He is the unity which lies beyond all multiplicity. There is in him no plurality, no movement, no distinction.[164]

Even if Plato has shown that the First Hypothesis One is a paradoxical entity, it nonetheless shares qualities with the *Republic* VI and VII Good—in part because the Good is paradoxically described as well. Moreover, the Absolute Being is the intelligible region, the realm of the Forms, but the Good is the source or cause of being, and so cannot be Absolute Being. In addition, Plotinus does not ignore what Plato says in the relevant section of *Parmenides*, but seems to be describing precisely that kind of entity, and Plato seems to be describing the same entity in *Republic* VI and VII. Lastly, Plotinus is not the only philosopher who calls God that which lies beyond all multiplicity; Plato's "beyond being" Good is referred to as God in *Republic* X.

Therefore, from a careful reading of the relevant passages and from addressing the objections of commentators, it is plausible to read the First Hypothesis One as being interpretively consistent with the Form of the Good, as Plato writes of it in *Republic* VI, VII, and X; I have also shown that the attributes of Plato's One or Good are consistent with those of the Plotinian One.

In conclusion, my goal in this chapter was to show that Plato believed that the One of the First Hypothesis of the *Parmenides* is equivalent to the Good, to show that Plato held that there are many characteristics of the Good or the One (mostly that it lacks, as opposed to possesses), and that Plotinus does not essentially differ on any of these characteristics. Without a doubt, all of these major claims are the most controversial claims of this book.

# 2

# Beauty

Both philosophers hold the following claims to be true: beauty is a Form; beauty is similar to but not identical with the Good; one can have a transformative vision of Beauty; the imitator (artist, poet) of Beauty does not know if the imitations are in fact beautiful or how bad his imitations are.[1]

## 2.1 Beauty is a Form

The main interpretive issues here are whether Plotinus continues to hold that Beauty is a Form in his middle and later writings, and whether Plotinus agrees with Plato that Beauty is symmetry.

**Plato:** As with the Good, Plato claims that Beauty is a Form in many passages across the dialogues,[2] just as if it is a Form as all the other Forms; in the *Symposium* and *Phaedrus*, however, Plato passionately describes a transformative vision of the Form of Beauty similarly to the vision of the Good in the Cave Allegory.

In the *Phaedo*, Plato certainly holds that beauty is a Form, which is the real nature of beauty or what beauty really is:

> Do we say that there is such a thing as the Just Itself, or not?
>
> We do say so, by Zeus.
>
> And the Beautiful, and the Good?
>
> Of course.
>
> And have you ever seen any of these things with your eyes?
>
> In no way, he said.
>
> Or have you ever grasped them with any of your bodily senses? I am speaking of all things such as Size, Health, Strength and, in a word, the reality of all other things, that which each of them essentially is. (*Phaedo* 65d4–e1; adapted from Grube)[3]

Thus, for Plato, Beauty is a Form that we do not access with our senses, and Beauty is the real nature of beauty, or what beauty essentially is.

**Plotinus:**

> Therefore, even when it is called beauty, one must even more avoid shape of this kind; but it must not be set before the eyes, that you may not fall out of beauty into what is called beauty by obscure participation. But the shapeless form is beautiful, since it is form [*eidos*], and is so in proportion to the length you go in stripping all shape from it, the shape in reasoning, for instance, by which we say that one form differs from another, as we say that righteousness and temperance are different from each other. (VI.7.33.1–7; adapted from A. H. Armstrong)[4]

Plotinus confirms that the Form of Beauty is not physical, and that physical beauty participates but is not identical with the Form, just as Plato states. He adds that Beauty is beautiful, though not physical, which is obviously Platonic.

Anton and Rist[5] object that Plato holds that Beauty is symmetry, but Plotinus does not. First, Anton argues:

> In a later tractate we read: 'Beauty is that which irradiates symmetry rather than symmetry itself and is that which truly calls out our love [VI.7.22].' It is not necessary to pause here to give a detailed account of Plotinus' answer, but it is significant to note that he views symmetry as an outcome, in fact, one of the outcomes of beauty. Part of his theory is, then, to demonstrate why and how symmetry is an effect and not the cause of beauty, and why it is philosophically false to define beauty as symmetry.[6]

Note that VI.7.33.1–7, which states that Beauty is a Form, is written by Plotinus later in the same treatise (VI.7) as the passage quoted by Anton. Plotinus has an odd way of veering from Plato's view if he is disputing or refuting that view in VI.7.22, but returns to embrace it in tractate 33. Moreover, consider A. H. Armstrong's translation: "So here below also beauty is what illuminates good proportions rather than the good proportions themselves, and this is what is lovable" (VI.7.22.24–6). Anton misses the "So here below" [*dio kai entautha*], which definitely signals that Plotinus is referring to perceptible beauties, and not Beauty Itself. Lastly, on Anton's general point of beauty's not being best defined as symmetry, just as Equality Itself is a Form for Plato (and Plotinus), it would stand to reason that Symmetry would be its own Form as well, such that Symmetry is not identical with Beauty—though they may be closely related as are, say, Equality and Sameness and Likeness.

Second, Rist has a similar argument:

> For Plato, symmetry, as we read repeatedly, and especially in the *Republic* and *Phaedo*, is of the very essence of Goodness and Beauty; for Plotinus, on

> the other hand, the essence of Beauty is Life. Why is there more beauty on a living than a dead face? Why are portraits which are more alive considered more beautiful than those which are more symmetrical? Because it is wrong to suppose that symmetry is the bringer of beauty. The truth is that beauty is the cause of symmetry.[7]

In the *Phaedo*, however, Plato claims that Beauty Itself is the real nature of beauty or what beauty actually is—and *mutatis mutandis* for the Good Itself; thus, even if symmetry is involved in beauty and goodness, it is not the essence of Beauty or Goodness. Further, the context of Plotinus' comments on beauty in the relevant part of VI.7.22 concerns perceptible beauty and not Beauty Itself—and his claim that Beauty is a Form comes in VI.7.33, so Plotinus is not equating Beauty with Life. In addition, I will show that Nous for Plotinus (and Plato) is a region that has life, and is a living creature, so it is plausibly Platonic that something living is more beautiful than something that is not.[8] Lastly, it is also Platonic for Plotinus to argue that, in beautiful perceptibles, symmetry does not cause beauty by itself, it is beauty that causes beauty.

Therefore, since I have shown that both philosophers have similar views about symmetry and beauty, and that the passages confirm that Beauty is a Form, I can conclude that they both hold that view.

## 2.2 Beauty is similar to but not identical with the Good

The Form of Beauty is similar for both philosophers, as they seem to hint that the entities might be equivalent, and describe a vision of each Form in the *Symposium* and *Republic* VI and VII that seems to be equally important and even life-transforming. It is not identical, in the sense that, in their works taken as whole, they do not ultimately claim that Beauty just *is* the Good.

**Plato:** Plotinus asserts in some places that the Good and Beauty are identical—but not in all places, and he denies it elsewhere; so let us confirm Plato as raising the possibility that the Good and the Beautiful are identical. In the *Greater Hippias*, via Socrates, where "fine" throughout translates καλόν or its derivatives:

> He'll say, 'Then this is what you say is the fine [καλόν]—beneficial pleasure?' 'Apparently so,' I'll say. And you?
>
> [Hippias:] Me too.
>
> He'll say: 'The maker of good is beneficial, but we just saw that the maker and what is made are different. Your account comes down to the earlier account.

> The good would not be fine, or the fine good, if each of these were different.' 'Absolutely,' we'll say, if we have any sense. It's not proper to disagree with a man when he's right. (*Greater Hippias* 303e8–4a3)

On one hand, we should not take Plato's considered view to be that the Good and Beautiful are identical, because Socrates does not conclude that the Good is the Beautiful thereafter. On the other hand, I should note that Plato at least raised the possibility of the good being identical with beauty.

The connection between beauty and good—but still not necessarily the *identity* of Beauty and the Good—is also hinted at in the *Republic* in several places:

> It's foolish to think that anything besides the bad is ridiculous or to try to raise a laugh at the sight of anything besides what's stupid or bad or (putting it the other way around) it's foolish to take seriously any standard of what is fine and beautiful other than the good.
>
> That's absolutely certain. (*Republic* V 452d6–e3)[9]

Plato seems to imply that the standard of the beautiful is nothing other than the good. In the second place where Plato connects beauty and goodness, Socrates states, and Glaucon repeats, that the Idea of Good is beautiful, and more beautiful than even knowledge or truth:

> So that what gives truth to the things known and the power to know to the knower is the Form of the Good. And though it is the cause of knowledge and truth, it is also an object of knowledge. Both knowledge and truth are beautiful things, but the Good is other and more beautiful than they. In the visible realm, light and sight are rightly considered sunlike, but it is wrong to think that they are the sun, so here it is right to think of knowledge and truth as goodlike but wrong to think that either of them is the Good—for the Good is yet more prized.
>
> This is an inconceivably beautiful thing you're talking about, if it provides both knowledge and truth and is superior to them in beauty. (*Republic* VI 508d4–509a7; adapted from Grube and Reeve)

Again, however, we should not interpret either of these passages as stating that the Good just *is* the Beautiful, since there are at least two passages in the *Republic* that state that Beauty and Good are separate Forms:

> I think that you will agree to this.
>
> To what?
>
> Since the Beautiful is the opposite of the ugly, they are two.

Of course.

And since they are two, each is one?

I grant that also.

And the same account is true of the Just and the unjust, the Good and the bad, and all the Forms. Each of them is itself one, but because they manifest themselves everywhere in association with actions, bodies, and one another, each of them appears to be many. (*Republic* V 475e6–76a7; adapted from Grube and Reeve)[10]

Socrates first states that Beauty is one (and ugly is one as well), and then states that the Good is also one. The next passage is even more explicit about the difference between Beauty and the Good:

> And Beauty Itself and Good Itself and all the things that we thereby set down as many, reversing ourselves, we set down according to a single Form of each, believing that there is but one, and call it 'the being' of each.
>
> That's true. (*Republic* VI 507b5–8; adapted from Grube and Reeve)

Beauty is the Form differentiated from the many beautifuls, as is the Good from the many goods.[11]

Thus, Plato hints in several places of an identity between Beauty and the Good (admitting that the Good is certainly beautiful), but ultimately he is best read as thinking that the two are distinct entities.

**Plotinus**: Plotinus actually does identify Beauty and the Good; in another passage he equates Beauty and Being, and in yet another he denies that Beauty and the Good are identical:

> And first we must posit Beauty which is also the Good; from this immediately comes Intellect, which is Beauty; and soul is given Beauty by Intellect. (I.6.6.25–7; adapted from A. H. Armstrong)[12]

Plotinus identifies Beauty and Goodness, additionally identifying Intellect with Beauty. Plotinus believes, as Plato does, that Beauty is a Form; also, at *Republic* VI 509a, Plato refers to the Good as an inconceivably beautiful thing; and Plato and Plotinus agree that Intellect is good and beautiful; so neither of these claims is necessarily un-Platonic. But I need to review the other passages, as this is not Plotinus' final word on this issue.

The next passage identifies Being and Beauty, and discusses what Plato refers to as the "many beautifuls:"

> The power in the intelligible world has nothing but its being and its being beautiful. For where would its beauty be if it was deprived of its being? And

> where would its reality be if it was stripped of its being beautiful? For in deficiency of beauty it would be defective also in reality. For this reason being is longed for because it is the same as beauty, and beauty is lovable because it is being. But why should we enquire which is the cause of the other when both are one nature? This reality here below, which is not genuine, does indeed require a phantasm of beauty brought in from outside in order to appear and in any way to be beautiful, and it is beautiful in proportion as it has a share in the beauty which is according to Form, and when it has it it is more perfect the more of it it has: for it is more reality insofar as it is beautiful. (V.8.9.36–47)

In what follows, Plotinus identifies Beauty and Being—he has already claimed that Intellect is beautiful. A charitable reading of this passage, and the other passages, where Beauty is a Form that is not identical to Being, is that there is still a Form of Beauty for Plotinus, but All that exists (Nous, Intellect, all of the Forms, for instance) is beautiful as well. And:

> The grasp of the beautiful and the wonder and the waking of love for it come to those who, in a way, already know it and are awake to it. But the Good, since it was there long before to arouse an innate desire, is present even to those asleep and does not astonish those who at any time see it, because it is always there and there is never recollection of it; but people do not see it, because it is present to them in their sleep. But the passionate love of beauty, when it comes, causes pain, because one must have seen it to desire it. Beauty is shown to be secondary because this passionate love for it is secondary and is felt by those who are already conscious. But the more ancient, unperceived desire of the Good proclaims that the Good itself is more ancient and prior to beauty.
>
> All men think that when they have attained the Good it is sufficient for them: for they have reached their end. But not all see beauty, and when it has come into existence they think it is beautiful for itself and not for them; this applies also to beauty here; it belongs to the one who has it. And it is enough for people to seem to be beautiful, even if they are not really; but they do not want to have the Good in seeming only.
>
> Then they dispute the first place with beauty and wrangle contentiously with it, considering that it has come into being like themselves. It is as if someone who holds the lowest rank at court were to want to attain equal honor with the man who stands next to the king, on the ground that they both derive from one and the same source; he does not realize that though he too depends on the king the other ranks before him.
>
> The cause of the error is that both participate in the same and the One is before both, and that in the higher world also the Good itself does not need beauty, though beauty needs it. The Good is gentle and kindly and gracious,

> and present to anyone when he wishes. Beauty brings wonder and shock and pleasure mingled with pain. It even draws those who do not know what is happening away from the Good, as the beloved draws a child away from its father; for Beauty is younger. (V.5.12.9–37; my paragraphs)[13]

In the first paragraph, Plotinus states that the Good is prior to Beauty, and desiring it is inherently present to everyone, whereas Beauty is for those already awakened to it in some way. In the second paragraph, Plotinus claims that more people have possessed the Good and felt it sufficient, whereas fewer possess Beauty[14] and think it exists for itself. The third paragraph is similar to Plato's claim at *Republic* VI 505d–e, that no one wants the semblance of Good, whereas they do not mind the semblance of justice and beauty. In the final paragraph, Plotinus mentions an error that one might make, thinking that beauty is just the First Principle, and there he sets the reader straight: The One precedes both the Good and Beauty—both of which participate in the One—and the Beautiful needs the Good, whereas the Good does not need the Beautiful.[15] These claims are not consistent with the view that Beauty is numerically identical with the Good or that Beauty is identical with Being. Therefore, we must look elsewhere for a charitable reading of these passages.

Taken together, the most promising reading of these passages is to interpret Plotinus as claiming that there is a Form Beauty, which is what the nature of Beauty is; the Good is beautiful, but the Good Itself is not the nature of what beauty is (in part because Beauty needs the Good); the Intellectual, or Living, Principle is beautiful as well, but, again, is not Beauty Itself; and Beauty is not the One or the First, but is one of the first offspring thereof.[16] Whether this interpretation entirely succeeds or not, note that Plato makes similar comments about how the Good is the most beautiful, and that the vision of either is supreme, so the thesis that Plotinus and Plato are saying the same thing here about Beauty is not only disproved but implies that the two had similar, if not identical, views on Beauty.

Let us now consider some objections[17] from Rist.[18] First, Rist[19] finds it striking that Plotinus does not refer to the One as the Beautiful, but he does say that Beauty is also the Good. I need not review Rist's hypotheses as to why Plotinus does not make that statement, but notice that Plotinus does not hold Beauty and the One or Good as identical. Second, Rist argues:

> This insight [in Plato's *Statesman*] that although both courage and moderation are 'parts of virtue' they can be in opposition to one another is nowhere paralleled in Plato by the recognition that there might be any divergence in the claims

> on man of Goodness and Beauty. Indeed the search for Beauty in the *Symposium* and the journey to the Good in the *Republic* are always rightly supposed to be different ways of looking at the same philosophic procedure. And in Plotinus too this is often the case, for example in *Ennead* 1.6, which perhaps best fulfils Porphyry's description of Plotinus as living in accordance with the methods prescribed by the *Symposium*. Yet in 5.5.12 Plotinus is able to see that at times the love of Beauty and the love of the Good may not be compatible. The Good is superior to Beauty and its effects are different; it is gentle and friendly, where Beauty brings violence and astonishment. Love of Beauty may even prevent the aspirant to philosophy from attaining the Good. There is no need to go further here in the exegesis of this difficult chapter. Suffice it to say that Plotinus' respect for Plato does not prevent him from saying some very un-Platonic things if he feels they are necessary.[20]

Contra Rist's first sentence, Plato does not make strong claims that Goodness and Beauty are identical, and indeed does argue that they are not the same concepts, even though a vision may be had of both of them. Moreover, the fact that the philosophical procedures to attain to the vision of the Good and Beauty are similar in the *Republic* and *Symposium* respectively does not imply that they are the same entity. Further, Rist notes that Plotinus has the same view, at least in I.6—that Beauty and Goodness seem closely related in his view, as they are in Plato's—but claims that the major difference is that the love of Beauty and the love of the Good may not be compatible for Plotinus. Plato does not state in the *Symposium* that the vision of Beauty tells one that Beauty is beyond being, the source of being, all knowledge and truth, for instance, as he states of the Good. Plato is describing the awesome experience—just as Plotinus does—of coming to know, or having a vision of, Beauty. Both agree that the Good is the cause of Beauty, even though we have also seen that they both seem to hint that Good and Beauty are similar. Lastly, it is not inconceivable that a person can fail to attain the Good by focusing only on Beauty, especially if they do not understand the nature of the latter. Plato would agree with this statement, because he does not claim that, if one knows Beauty, one thereby knows the Good; in fact, he implies the opposite in the Sun, Line, and Cave Analogies and especially at *Republic* VI 505a, where he states that even if we know other things this will not benefit us without knowledge of the Good.

Plato and Plotinus are thus best read as holding that, though Beauty and the Good are said to share some identical properties, ultimately Beauty is not identical with the Good.

## 2.3 One can have a transformative vision of Beauty

Plato makes a major claim in the *Symposium* concerning beauty (which he repeats in the *Republic* and the *Phaedrus*), when through Diotima he poetically states that one can have a transformative vision of beauty, which changes its experiencer from thence onwards. It is important to review these passages so that I will be able to demonstrate the similarity between the claims made by Plato and those made by Plotinus concerning beauty.

**Plato:**

> 'Try to pay attention to me,' she said, 'as best you can. You see, the man who has been thus far guided in matters of Love, who has beheld beautiful things in the right order and correctly, is coming now to the goal of Loving: all of a sudden he will catch sight of something wonderfully beautiful in its nature; that, Socrates, is the reason for all his earlier labors:
>
> First, it always *is* and neither comes to be nor passes away, neither waxes nor wanes. Second, it is not beautiful this way and ugly that way, nor beautiful at one time and ugly at another, nor beautiful in relation to one thing and ugly in relation to another; nor is it beautiful here but ugly there, as it would be if it were beautiful for some people and ugly for others. Nor will the beautiful appear to him in the guise of a face or hands or anything else that belongs to the body. It will not appear to him as one idea [*logos*] or one kind of knowledge [tis *epistēmē*]. It is not anywhere in another thing, as in an animal, or in earth, or in heaven, or in anything else, but itself by itself with itself, it is always one in form; and all the other beautiful things share in that, in such a way that when those others come to be or pass away, this does not become the least bit smaller or greater nor suffer any change. So when someone rises by these stages, through loving boys correctly, and begins to see this beauty, he has almost grasped his goal. This is what it is to go aright, or be led by another, into the mystery of Love: one goes always upwards for the sake of this Beauty, starting out from beautiful things and using them like rising stairs: from one body to two and from two to all beautiful bodies, then from beautiful bodies to beautiful customs, and from customs to learning beautiful things, and from these lessons he arrives in the end at this lesson, which is learning of this very Beauty, so that in the end he comes to know just what it is to be beautiful.' (*Symposium* 210e1–11d1)[21]

First, note that Diotima states that one can liken the journey to the vision of Beauty as the goal of Loving and the mystery of Love. Second, Diotima mostly emphasizes the experience of Beauty's being a vision—"sight," "appear to" and "see"—as opposed to knowledge; but then, in the last sentence of this quotation, she describes the vision of Beauty as ultimately being knowledge of Beauty. The vision is everlasting, does not increase or decrease, is the same to every perceiver, is not physical, is not propositional, is not inherent in any physical object and subsists always one in form, even though the physical partakers of Beauty wax and wane in reference to beauty. Lastly, we are to use the method of understanding the beauty of individual bodies on all bodies, customs, and education until we can understand Beauty Itself.

Diotima then introduces the transformative feature of one's vision of Beauty:

> 'And there in life, Socrates, my friend,' said the woman from Mantinea, 'there if anywhere should a person live his life, beholding that Beauty. If you once see that, it won't occur to you to measure beauty by gold or clothing or beautiful boys and youths—who, if you see them now, strike you out of your senses, and make you, you and many others, eager to be with the boys you love and look at them forever, if there were any way to do that, forgetting food and drink, everything but looking at them and being with them.' (*Symposium* 211d1–8)

If one has this vision of Beauty, one will no longer be significantly attracted to any perceptible instance of beauty that used to attract one. It may be possible to realize and acknowledge the varying degrees to which perceptible objects partake in Beauty; however, this realization is not equivalent to being attracted to these perceptible objects.

> 'But how would it be, in our view,' she said, 'if someone got to see the Beautiful itself, absolute, pure, unmixed, not polluted by human flesh or colors or any other great nonsense or mortality, but if he could see the divine Beauty itself in its one form? Do you think it would be a poor life for the human being to look there and to behold it by that which he ought, and to be with it?' (*Symposium* 211d8–12a2)

Socrates does not answer the questions posed by Diotima in this sentence, but presumably the answer to the second question is, No; the person who beholds beauty does not have a poor life.

In the *Republic*, Plato also alludes to the experience of knowing more about Beauty and its relation to perceptibly beautiful things after one exits the cave and re-enters it:

> When you are used to it, you'll see vastly better than the people there. And because you've seen the truth about beautiful [*kalōn*], just, and good things, you'll know each image for what it is and also that of which it is the image. (*Republic* VII 520c3–6; adapted from Grube and Reeve)

Note that Plato refers to the experience of beauty (justice and goodness) as being seen, even though elsewhere he describes the Forms as knowable.

Plotinus makes a lot of the *Phaedrus*, and Plato there again links love and beauty, and mentions the pre-incarnation vision of beauty, so it is important to review the relevant passages. In the first passage, Plato likens the desire or love of beauty to a divine madness, wherein one can recollect Beauty:

> Now this takes me to the whole point of my discussion of the fourth kind of madness—that which someone shows when he sees the beauty we have down here and is reminded of true beauty; then he takes wing and flutters in his eagerness to rise up, but is unable to do so; and he gazes aloft, like a bird, paying no attention to what is down below—and that is what brings on him the charge that he has gone mad. This is the best and noblest of all the forms that possession by god can take for anyone who has it or is connected to it, and when someone who loves beautiful boys is touched by this madness he is called a lover. (*Phaedrus* 249d4–e4)

As in the *Symposium*, Plato claims that the lover cares nothing for the worlds beneath, though in this passage, the person who is called demented by the many does not, as of yet, have knowledge of beauty. Here Plato initially raises the notion of growing one's wings as one ascends toward the knowledge or vision of Beauty. In the next passage, Plato mentions the vision of beauty that we have had before being incarnated:

> Justice and self-control do not shine out through their images down here, and neither do the other objects of the soul's admiration; the senses are so murky that only a few people are able to make out, with difficulty, the original of the likenesses they encounter here. But beauty was radiant to see at that time when the souls, along with the glorious chorus (we were with Zeus, while others followed other gods), saw that blessed and spectacular vision and were ushered into the mystery that we may rightly call the most blessed of all. And we who celebrated it were wholly perfect and free of all the troubles that awaited us in time to come, and we gazed in rapture at sacred revealed objects that were perfect, and simple, and unshakeable and blissful. That was the ultimate vision, and we saw it in pure light because we were pure ourselves, not buried in this thing we are carrying around now, which we call a body, locked in it like an oyster in its shell. (*Phaedrus* 250b1–c6)

As in the *Symposium*, Plato relates the hindrance of the body to knowing beauty, and the privation and evils inherent in perceptible beauty.[22] In the last relevant passage from the *Phaedrus*, once again Plato describes the awesome, life-transforming nature of the experience of Beauty:

> A recent initiate, however, one who has seen much in heaven—when he sees a godlike face of bodily form that has captured Beauty well, first he shudders and a fear comes over him like those he felt at the earlier time; then he gazes at him with the reverence due a god, and if he weren't afraid people would think him completely mad, he'd even sacrifice to his boy as if he were the image of a god. Once he has looked at him, his chill gives way to sweating and a high fever, because the stream of beauty that pours into him through his eyes warms him up and waters the growth of his wings. Meanwhile, the heat warms him and melts the places where the wings once grew, places that were long ago closed off with hard scabs to keep the sprouts from coming back; but as nourishment flows in, the feather shafts swell and rush to grow from the roots beneath every part of the soul (long ago, you see, the entire soul had wings). Now the whole soul seethes and throbs in this condition. Like a child whose teeth are just starting to grow in, and its gums are all aching and itching—that is exactly how the soul feels when it begins to grow wings. It swells up and aches and tingles as it grows them. But when it looks upon the beauty of the boy and takes in the stream of particles flowing into it from his beauty (that is why this is called 'desire'), when it is watered and warmed by this, then all its pain subsides and is replaced by joy. When, however, it is separated from the boy and runs dry, then the openings of the passages in which the feathers grow are dried shut and keep the wings from sprouting. Then the stump of each feather is blocked in its desire and it throbs like a pulsing artery while the feather pricks at its passageway, with the result that the whole soul is stung all around, and the pain simply drives it wild—but then, when it remembers the boy in his beauty, it recovers its joy. From the outlandish mix of these two feelings—pain and joy—comes anguish and helpless raving: in its madness the lover's soul cannot sleep at night or stay put by day; it rushes, yearning, wherever it expects to see the person who has that beauty. When it does see him, it opens the sluice-gates of desire and sets free the parts that were blocked up before. And now that the pain and the goading have stopped, it can catch its breath and once more suck in, for the moment, this sweetest of all pleasures. This it is not at all willing to give up, and no one is more important to it than the beautiful boy. It forgets mother and brothers and friends entirely and doesn't care at all if it loses its wealth through neglect. And as for proper and decorous behavior, in which it used to take pride, the soul despises the whole business. Why, it is even willing to sleep like a slave, anywhere, as near to the object of its longing as it is allowed to get! That is because in addition to its reverence for one who has such beauty, the soul has discovered that the boy is the only doctor for all that terrible pain. (*Phaedrus* 251a1–2b1)

There are many words related to the pain of coming to know, or receding from the knowledge of Beauty, filling in the brief description in the Cave Allegory of the rough and steep ascent out of the cave. The more we remember Beauty, the more our wings grow; the less we remember beauty, the more shriveled our wings and encrusted our wings' outlets become. Once we allow the flood of Beauty to pour in on us, we experience "the sweetest of all pleasures," which is entirely consistent with the account of the final revelation of Beauty in the *Symposium*: that is, this vision will make us forget our relatives, neglect wealth, and despise "proper and decorous behavior"—this vision will cease our soul's suffering.

Though Plato refers to Beauty in *Letter* VII (342d–3a), it is not exactly clear what he is saying there about beauty or Forms, besides a view that language is inadequate to describe Forms, implying that it is the experience of seeing or knowing the Forms that is all-important.

**Plotinus**: It is easily demonstrated that Plotinus believes what Plato says about the vision of Beauty in the *Symposium* and the *Phaedrus*.[23] Plotinus believes that Diotima is correct about the vision of Beauty in the *Symposium*:

> So he must be taught not to cling round one body and be excited by that, but must be led by the course of reasoning to consider all bodies and shown the beauty that is the same in all of them, and that it is something other than the bodies and must be said to come from elsewhere, and that it is better manifested in other things, by showing him, for instance, the beauty of ways of life and laws—this will accustom him to loveliness in things which are not bodies—and that there is beauty in arts and sciences and virtues. Then all these beauties must be reduced to unity, and he must be shown their origin. But from virtues he can at once ascend to intellect, to being; and There he must go the higher way. (I.3.2.5–13)[24]

This passage reflects the idea behind Plato's Ladder of Love passage (*Symposium* 210a4–e1 and 211b5–d1), where the seeker of the vision must not pursue physical beauty but use his mind to discern what all beautiful things have in common, recognizing beauty in the arts, sciences, virtues and so on. This passage also alludes to the top two sections of the Divided Line, where Plato argues that one must ascend from the assumptions made by the mathematicians and kindred sciences to the unhypothetical first principle. Noting that he begins the discussion by referring to it as an ascent to the Good, Plotinus also ecstatically confirms the awesome nature of the vision of Beauty that Plato passionately describes in the *Symposium*:

> So we must ascend again to the Good, which every soul desires. Anyone who has seen it, knows what I mean when I say that it is beautiful. It is desired as good,

> and the desire for it is directed to Good, and the attainment of it is for those who go up to the higher world… . If anyone sees it, what passion will he feel, what longing in his desire to be united with it, what a shock of delight! The man who has not seen it may desire it as good, but he who has seen it glories in its beauty and is full of wonder and delight, enduring a shock which causes no hurt, loving with true passion, and piercing longing; he laughs at all other loves and despises what he thought beautiful before; it is like the experience of those who have met appearances of gods or spirits and do not any more appreciate as they did the beauty of other bodies. (I.6.7.1–4, 12–21; adapted from A. H. Armstrong)[25]

Plotinus, along with Plato, argues that having a vision of Beauty puts an end to one's travail of love toward beauty:

> The man could reach ['the true region' which contains 'the glory above' from V.9.1] who is by nature a lover and truly disposed to philosophy from the beginning, in travail over beauty, since he is a lover, not enduring the 'beauty of body' but escaping from it up to the 'beauties of soul, virtues and kinds of knowledge and ways of life and laws'; and again he ascends to the cause of the beauties in soul, and again to anything there may be beyond this, till he comes to the ultimate which is the first, which is beautiful of itself. When he has arrived there he ceases from his travail (*ōdinos*), but not before. (V.9.2.2–10)[26]

Plotinus again alludes to the Ladder of Love, as well as making the point that the vision of Beauty assuaged one's pain. The Greek, *ōdinos*, translated here as "travail," can also be translated as labor pains, anguish, or agony. Plotinus also gives advice on appropriate and inappropriate physical love.[27]

In addition to the important claims about the vision of Beauty in the *Symposium*, Plotinus also has passages that parallel the passages in Plato's *Phaedrus*. He mentions the soul's wing being broken in IV.3.7. Plotinus discusses how the soul is stirred to love by beauty, and grows strength by seeing all that is beautiful and true:

> The soul … loves that Good, moved by it to love from the beginning. And the soul which has its love ready to hand does not wait for a reminder from the beauties here, but because it has its love, even if it does not know that it has it, it is always searching and in its wish to be borne away to that Good has a contempt for the things here, and when it sees the beauties of this world it distrusts them, because it sees that they are in bodies of flesh and polluted by their present dwelling and disintegrated by magnitudes and are not the true beautiful things themselves; for those, being as they are, would never bring themselves to enter the mud of bodies and dirty themselves and disappear. But

> when it sees the beauties here flowing past it, it already knows completely that they have the light which plays on them from elsewhere. And then it is borne away there, skilled in finding what it loves, and not leaving off till it catches it, unless someone were to take even its love away. There certainly it sees that all things are beautiful and true and gains greater strength, since it is filled with the life of real being, and has become truly real itself also, and has true awareness, and it perceives that it is near to what it has long been seeking. (VI.7.31.17–34)

In the next passage, Plotinus asks if the Beauty Itself maintains its purity, being uncontaminated by flesh or body when one contemplates it, and answers that in contemplating Beauty, one needs no other beauty, and all other additions to beauty are external, so Beauty does maintain its purity even when contemplated:

> What then are we to think, if anyone contemplates the absolute beauty which exists pure by itself, uncontaminated by flesh or body, not in earth or heaven, that it may keep its purity? All these other things are external additions and mixtures and not primary, but derived from it. If then one sees That which provides for all and remains by itself and gives to all but receives nothing into itself, if he abides in the contemplation of this kind of beauty and rejoices in being made like it, how can he need any other beauty? For this, since it is beauty most of all, and primary beauty, makes its lovers beautiful and lovable. (I.6.7.21–30)

Since Plotinus agrees with Plato about recollection, I can confirm their agreement that we already have the vision of Beauty before we incarnate on earth.

Thus, Plotinus agrees with Plato about the transformative nature of the experience of having a vision or gaining knowledge of Beauty.

Hadot argues:[28]

> Platonic love rises, through a series of intellectual operations, up to the contemplation of Beauty; Plotinian love, by contrast, waits for ecstasy, ceasing all activity, establishing the soul's faculties in complete repose, and forgetting everything, so as to be completely ready for the divine invasion. The soul's highest state is complete passivity, and she tries to maintain herself in this state. Platonic love, once it has reached Beauty, displays its fertility in multiple thoughts and actions, producing science, education, and the organization of the state. Plotinian love, by contrast, refuses to return to day-to-day activity. It redescends to the world only when forced to do so by the needs of the human condition.[29]

My replies: In I.6.7.21–30, we see Plotinus agree with Plato that we should contemplate "absolute beauty which exists pure by itself," which obviously denotes Beauty Itself. Moreover, for Plato as well as Plotinus, dialectic plays a crucial role in one's coming to know the Forms. In addition, as we have seen, Plato and Plotinus have the same view about the Ladder of Love. Further, nowhere does Plotinus state that the goal of love is *only* or *exclusively* a readying for ecstasy; in fact, Plotinus (VI.7.31.17–34) says that the soul loves the Good and is moved by It to love in the beginning. Thus Hadot seems to overstate the case. Also, Plato does not say that science, per se, or education is produced from the vision of Beauty. If Hadot is mistaken about this, then it damages his claim that Plotinian love refuses to return to day-to-day activity. Instead, I would put Plato's view this way: the Good produces the Forms; this makes both knowledge and science (no matter the translation) possible, as well as education. Love is either an irrational desire for bodily beauty, or a rational manifestation of the desire of the Good. Lastly, admittedly, it is true that at *Symposium* 212a, Plato says that the vision of Beauty produces true virtue, but it is plausible to suggest that Plotinus holds that the vision of Beauty makes one happy because such a vision implies knowledge of Beauty; if one does not have a vision of the Good at that point, one can be encouraged to continue the ascent. Moreover, they both hold that in order for one to be happy, one must be virtuous; and they both agree that one must see the Good in order to be truly virtuous. Thus, I submit that Plotinus effectively agrees with Plato that a vision of Beauty produces true virtue.

In sum, both Plato and Plotinus claim that you may have a vision of Beauty where Beauty is nonphysical, and similar to, but not identical to, the Good. Moreover, we humans have already seen Beauty before being incarnated, but we can work back towards that vision by contemplating and ascending the Ladder of Love, through understanding what all beautiful things have in common.

## 2.4 The imitator (artist, poet) of Beauty does not know how beautiful or ugly his imitations are

**Plato:** In the *Republic*, Plato argues that the imitator of Beauty—the artist or poet who imitates perceptible things in his paintings, sculptures, or poems, for instance—does not know if the imitations are in fact beautiful or how bad his imitations are:

> Does an imitator have knowledge of whether the things he makes are fine or right through having made use of them, or does he have right opinion about

them through having to consort with the one who knows and being told how he is to paint them?

Neither.

Therefore an imitator has neither knowledge nor right opinion about whether the things he makes are fine or bad.

Apparently not.

Then a poetic imitator is an accomplished fellow when it comes to wisdom about the subjects of his poetry!

Hardly.

Nonetheless, he'll go on imitating, even though he doesn't know the good or bad qualities of anything, but what he'll imitate, it seems, is what appears fine or beautiful to the majority of people who know nothing.

Of course. (*Republic* X 602a3–b5)[30]

Plato also makes several claims about beauty in the *Philebus*, but I will not review those in detail now.[31]

**Plotinus**:

> If art makes its work like what it is and has—and it makes it beautiful according to the forming principle of what it is making—it is itself more, and more truly, beautiful since it has the beauty of art which is greater and more beautiful than anything in the external object. For a thing is weaker than that which abides in unity in proportion as it expands in its advance towards matter. Everything which is extended departs from itself: if it is bodily strength, it grows less strong, if heat, less hot, if power in general, less powerful, if beauty, less beautiful. Every original maker must be in itself stronger than that which it makes; it is not lack of music which makes a man musical, but music, and music in the world of sense is made by the music prior to this world. But if anyone despises the arts because they produce their works by imitating nature, we must tell him, first, that natural things are imitations too. Then he must know that the arts do not simply imitate what they see, but they run back up to the forming principles from which nature derives; then also that they do a great deal by themselves, and, since they possess beauty, they make up what is defective in things. (V.8.1.22–38)[32]

Plotinus warns in I.6.8 to remember that material beauty is only a vestige and copy of Beauty, which is precisely one of Plato's main points about artists and poets in Book X of the *Republic*.

Admittedly, I cannot explicitly confirm that Plotinus states that artists per se do not understand true Beauty, or the extent to which their beautiful creations fail to match Beauty's beauty; however, it is clear that Plotinus would argue that an artist who is not a philosopher, and who has not had the vision of Beauty, would not know Beauty, and therefore not realize the (extent of the) difference between her artwork and Beauty. Further, from the Platonic side, we must keep in mind that Plato did not state that every kind of art was worthless and evil; in fact he states: "We can admit no poetry into our city *save only* hymns to the gods and the praises of good men" (*Republic* X 607a3–5; emphasis added). In other words, there is such a thing as good poetry, and, in Plato's view, by writing poetry about the gods we are writing about entities higher than the perceptible universe, imitating the Form of Beauty as we do so.

I will consider objections from Gerson and Fuller on the difference between the philosophers' views on artists, beauty, and Beauty. First, Gerson argues: "Plotinus also claims that artistic beauty is superior to natural beauty, counter to what Plato says in book 10 of the *Republic* [V.8.1]."[33] In response, let us review the passage I believe Gerson has in mind:

> Let us suppose, if you like, a couple of great lumps of stone lying side by side, one shapeless and untouched by art, the other which has been already mastered by art and turned into a statue of a god or of a man… . The stone which has been brought to beauty of form by art will appear beautiful not because it is a stone—for then the other would be just as beautiful—but as a result of the form which art has put into it. Now the material did not have this form, but it was in the man who had it in his mind even before it came into the stone; but it was in the craftsman, not insofar as he had hands and eyes, but because he had some share of art. So *this beauty was in the art, and it was far better there; for the beauty in the art did not come into the stone, but that beauty stays in the art and another comes from it into the stone which is derived from it and less than it.* And even this does not stay pure and as it wants to be in the stone, but is only there as far as the stone has submitted to the art. If art makes its work like what it is and has—and it makes it beautiful according to the forming principle of what it is making—it is itself more, and more truly, beautiful since it has the beauty of art which is greater and more beautiful than anything in the external object. (V.8.1.6–26; emphasis added)

In the italicized portion of the text, Plotinus seems to claim that the beauty in the arts is far better than the beauty of the natural stone, but then claims that the beauty in the statue is derived from it and less than it—and in the next sentence states that it does not remain in the stone but only to the extent that it submits to the arts. Hence we have qualifications from Plotinus. Moreover, Plotinus also argues that living beauty is more glorious than dead beauty, and even that living ugly humans are more attractive than sculptured handsome ones:

> For why is there more light of beauty on a living face, but only a trace of it on a dead one, even if its flesh and its proportions are not yet wasted away? And are not the more lifelike statues the more beautiful ones, even if the others are better proportioned? And is not the uglier living man more beautiful than the beautiful man in a statue? Yes, because the living is more desirable; and this is because it has soul; and this is because it has more the form of good; and this means that it is somehow colored by the light of the Good, and being so colored wakes and rises up and lifts up that which belongs to it, and as far as it can makes it good and wakes it. (VI.7.22.24–36)[34]

Since Plotinus also claims that uglier living men are more beautiful than a beautiful human statue, we cannot simply take Plotinus in V.8.1 as saying that artificial beauty is, or can be, more beautiful than natural beauty. We must also keep in mind that Plato states that beautiful perceptibles are made beautiful by Beauty Itself; if this is the case, then artists must also look to Beauty if their products are to be beautiful, even though Plato and Plotinus both agree that the perceptible product will be a (better or worse) imitation of Beauty. Lastly, note that Plotinus says that the person who despises the arts because they produce their works by imitating nature "must know that the arts do not simply imitate what they see, but they run back up to the forming principles from which nature derives" (V.8.1.34–6). By using the words "simply imitate," Plotinus implies that the arts do in fact imitate nature, but that they can do more than simply imitate, because they can look to the Forms to put the nature of the form into the work, just as Plato argues that the craftsperson (carpenter, shuttle-maker) makes shuttles according to nature by putting the form of the shuttle into the shuttle, not looking to broken shuttles to do his or her work (*Cratylus* 389a–d). Thus, at the very least, when we look at Plotinus' view on the issue of whether artistic creations are more beautiful than natural things, we are faced with inconclusive passages in both Plato and Plotinus' works.

Fuller[35] observes that: "Plotinus, however, does not, like Plato, scorn the artist as a mere imitator, and the work of art as the copy of a copy and therefore further removed from reality than the sensible object it portrays." Admittedly, Plotinus does not scorn the artist per se as a mere imitator, but we must keep in mind that Plotinus would not sit for a sculptor or a painter, replying to Amelius' urging for his portrait to be made: "Why really, is it not enough to have to carry the image in which nature has encased us, without your requesting me to agree to leave behind me a longer-lasting image of the image, as if it was something genuinely worth looking at?" (*Life*, Ch. 1).

To conclude, Plato and Plotinus do not essentially differ on the claims that: Beauty is a Form; Beauty is similar to but not identical with the Good; One can have a transformative vision of Beauty; the imitator (artist, poet) of Beauty does not know if the imitations are in fact beautiful or how bad his imitations are.

# 3

# Intellect: The Intelligible Region

I will discuss Nous or Intellect, the intelligible region, affirming four related entities and qualities thereof that both philosophers posit: (1) God and gods; (2) the Demiurge; (3) Forms or Ideas; (4) the Five Greatest Kinds: Being, Sameness, Difference, Motion, and Rest.

## 3.1 Nous: The intellectual principle

Nous is alternatively referred to as Intellect, the Intelligible Region, Divine Mind, the realm of Being, the intelligible realm, the realm of the Forms, or what others sometimes call the Platonic Heaven.[1] I will discuss the relation between the One, Intellect and the World-Soul after I have examined what the philosophers say about the World-Soul. Plato and Plotinus both claim that: (1) Nous is Being, the Realm of the Forms, and that Nous has knowledge; (2) Nous has intelligence, wisdom, life, soul and is immutable.[2]

### 3.1.1 Nous is Being, the realm of the Forms, and has knowledge

**Plato:**[3] Plato believes that Nous is being,[4] Nous is the realm of the Forms[5] and Nous has knowledge:[6]

> The place beyond heaven—none of our earthly poets has ever sung or ever will sing its praises enough! Still, this is the way it is—risky as it may be, you see, I must attempt to speak the truth, especially since the truth is my subject. What is in this place is without color and without shape and without solidity, a being that really is what it is, the subject of all true knowledge, visible only to intelligence, the soul's steersman. Now a god's mind is nourished by intelligence and pure knowledge, as is the mind of any soul that is concerned to take in what is appropriate to it, and so it is delighted at last to be seeing what is real and watching what is true, feeding on all this and feeling wonderful, until the

> circular motion brings it around to where it started. On the way around [the soul] has a view of Justice as it is; it has a view of Self-control; it has a view of Knowledge—not the knowledge that is close to change, that becomes different as it knows the different things which we consider real down here. No, it is the knowledge of what really is what it is. And when the soul has seen all the things that are as they are and feasted on them, it sinks back inside heaven and goes home. On its arrival, the charioteer stables the horses by the manger, throws in ambrosia, and gives them nectar to drink besides.
>
> Now that is the life of the gods. (*Phaedrus* 247c3–8a1)[7]

Plato claims that there is a realm of true being ("a being that really is what it is"), that is immaterial—no color, shape, or solidity,[8] and that is the object of reason's true knowledge; this knowledge nourishes the mind of gods as they discern Justice, Temperance and so on, which in turn shows that this is the realm of Forms for Plato. It is true that Plato does not refer to Nous or the Intellect in this passage from the *Phaedrus*; however, the notions mentioned—"a god's mind" and an immaterial realm that is only beheld by reason—are quite compatible with what we see Plato say in the *Timaeus* about Nous or Mind, or what we see about the Intelligible region in the *Republic*.[9]

**Plotinus:**[10] First, Plotinus argues for the existence of Intellectual or Nous; there must be something beyond the corporeal and material :[11]

> There must be something before soul… . For if what is in the universe is what is in body and matter, nothing will remain the same: so that man and the other rational forming principles will not be eternal or the same. One can see then from these and many other arguments that there must be an intellect before soul. (V.9.4.15–19)

Plotinus also argues that Intellect cannot be the First or the One, but must be a distinct entity:

> The One is primary and the Forms and being are not primary. For each Form is of many parts and composite and posterior; for those elements from which an individual thing is composed are prior to it. (VI.9.2.29–32)[12]

Plato agrees with Plotinus' argument as follows: Mind cannot be the First in Plato's view; if we examine the Sun Simile and Cave Allegory passages, where Plato states in both metaphors that the Form of the Good makes knowledge possible and is the source of the Forms, and that when the cave escapee sees the Good, she must infer that the Form of the Good is the source of reason in the intelligible world (in the Cave Allegory).

Plotinus holds both that Intellect has knowledge,[13] and that *our* knowledge is of Intellect's objects:

> The life and activity of Intellect is the first light shining primarily for itself and an outshining upon itself, at once illuminating and illuminated, the truly intelligible, both thinker and thought, seen by itself and needing no other that it may see, supplying itself with the power of seeing—for it is itself what it sees—known to us by that very power, so that the knowledge of it comes to us through itself; otherwise from where should we have the ability to speak about it? It is such a kind that it apprehends itself more clearly, but we apprehend it by means of it. (V.3.8.36–45)[14]

For now, I can confirm that Plotinus holds that Intellect knows itself and that, when we have knowledge, it is of and through Intellect that we have it.

Plotinus confirms that Nous—here rendered "Intellect"—is Being:[15]

> Intellect, therefore, really thinks the real beings, not as if they were somewhere else… . So the statements are correct that 'thinking and being are the same thing' and 'knowledge of immaterial things is the same as its object' and 'I searched myself' (as one of the real beings); so also are 'recollections.' (V.9.5.26–7, 29–32)[16]

Plotinus also implies here that there are many beings in Nous, besides confirming that Nous is Being, Nous (or Intellect) contains all beings:[17]

> Intellect is the real beings, possessing them all not as if [they were in it] as in a place, but as possessing itself and being one with them. 'All things are together' there, and none the less they are separate. (V.9.6.1–3)[18]

Assuming that the real beings are the Forms, I have confirmed that Plato and Plotinus agree that Nous is the intelligible region that contains the Forms. Here is a passage on Plotinus' view concerning Nous' relation to the Good:

> We say that Intellect is an image of that Good; for we must speak more plainly; first of all we must say that what has come into being must be in a way that Good, and retain much of it and be a likeness of it, as light is of the sun. But Intellect is not that Good. How then does it[19] generate Intellect? Because by its return to it it sees: and this seeing is Intellect. For that which apprehends something else is either sense-perception or intellect; (sense-perception is a line, etc.) but the circle is of a kind which can be divided; but this [intellectual apprehension] is not so. (V.1.7.1–9)[20]

That the Intellect is an image of the Good is also seen in the Allegory of the Cave, when Plato states that the released prisoner outside the cave, once his eyes have adjusted to the blinding light, sees "the things themselves" (*Republic* VII 516a8), stars ("the things in the sky" at 516a8 and "stars" at 516a8–b1), "the sky itself" (which may be an indirect metaphor for Nous, actually; 516a8–9) and the moon (516b1), before finally seeing the sun, which is the Good (517b1–2). Of course, Plato also states that he will conclude after seeing the sun that it "is in some way the cause of all the things that he used to see" (516c1–2).

Further, Plato states that the metaphor is to symbolize the "the upward journey of the soul to the intelligible realm" (517b4–5), and he refers to the Good as the "last thing to be seen" (517b8–c1) in the "knowable [realm or region]" (517b8), both of which in my view refer to Nous, or the intelligible region. Plato implies again that the Good generates Intellect in the Cave Allegory by concluding that "in the intelligible realm [the Good] controls and provides truth and understanding" (517c3–4). We cannot conclusively confirm—though there are hints[21]—that Plato believes that by Intellect's return to the Good it sees and *is* Intellect.[22] However, since there is no statement in Plato's philosophy that disagrees with this claim, we do not have a contradiction between Plato and Plotinus that Nous or Intellect is Being, the realm of the Forms, and Nous has knowledge.

Rist[23] was the first, to my knowledge, to raise this objection:[24]

> The real issue was whether the Forms are inside or outside the world of life. If they are outside of it, quite apart in their essence from souls, even from the souls of the Gods, as Plato held, they can only be contemplated; if, however, they are 'inside,' then an ascent beyond mere contemplation, a mystical union with the One, is possible, and indeed not only possible but the only worth-while [*telos*] of the philosophic life.[25]

Leaving the issue of whether Nous has life aside for the moment, contra Rist, I think *Phaedrus* 247c3–8a1 shows that, for Plato, the Forms are in Nous, the intelligible region. Moreover, given that ascent to knowledge of the Good or One is possible in both philosophers' views, do we not have to find an interpretation that philosophically allows the soul to so ascend?

Rist continues:

> It is no service to our case to go into matters where Plotinus produces an un-Platonic doctrine by unwittingly *misinterpreting* Plato himself. Mistakes of exegesis are unimportant to a philosopher. The fact that Plotinus should not have found his doctrine that the Forms are 'not outside the Intellect' in the dialogues does not affect the question of his attitude to the Platonic text. For that purpose all that matters is that he thought he could find it in that text.[26]

It is far from clear that the Platonic Forms are outside the Intellect. Certainly, Plato's view is that our intellects do not and cannot create the Forms with our thoughts (*Parmenides* 132b–c), but this is irrelevant to the point of whether the Forms exist in Nous or the intelligible region.[27] If the Forms are eternal beings, Nous is an eternal being and God is an eternal being, then we have some evidence that these entities are, at the very least, at the same metaphysical level in Plato's view. The All-Soul (and all individual souls), for instance, is in time, so it is not on the same level. If we then consider that God can contemplate something, then why would an immaterial God not be able to access the immaterial Forms? Admittedly, Plato's—and Plotinus' for that matter—precise position on exactly what the relation is between these entities is not crystal clear, but it is certainly plausible for the Forms to be inside, or a part of, Nous. Thus, I deny that Plotinus is "unwittingly *misinterpreting* Plato himself."

Therefore, Plato and Plotinus have the view that Nous is Being, the realm of the Forms, and Nous has knowledge. From these claims, it is plausible that Plato believes with Plotinus that Forms are not outside Intellect.

### 3.1.2 Nous has intelligence, wisdom, life, soul and is (somehow) mutable

**Plato:** In the *Sophist*, Plato implies and argues for the view that change, life, soul, and wisdom[28] or intelligence are part of the intelligible region[29] (here rendered "that which is perfectly real"):[30]

> Are we really to be so easily convinced that change, life, soul, wisdom [*phronēsin*] have no place in *that which is perfectly real* [*tōi pantelōs onti*]—that it has neither life nor wisdom [*phronein*], but stands immutable in solemn aloofness, devoid of intelligence [*noun*]?
>
> That, sir, would be a strange doctrine to accept.
>
> But can we say it has intelligence [*noun*] without having life?
>
> Surely not.
>
> But if we say it contains both, can we deny that it has soul in which they reside?
>
> How else could it possess them?
>
> But then, if it has intelligence [*noun*], life, and soul, can we say that a living thing remains at rest in complete changelessness?
>
> All that seems to me unreasonable.
>
> In that case we must admit that what changes and change itself are real things.
>
> Certainly. (*Sophist* 248e7–9b4; adapted from Cornford; emphasis added)[31]

I read this passage as generally saying: *That which is perfectly real*, because it has intelligence (and wisdom—assumed at the passage's beginning), must have life; and if it has life, then it must have a soul of some sort in which intelligence, wisdom and life reside; and if it has intelligence, wisdom, life and soul, then it must change in some sense.

There are obviously interpretive issues here, however. First, for Plato, that which is perfectly real is the realm of the Forms, or the Intelligible Region. I am labeling that region Nous in this section, as this is Plotinus' name for it (besides Intellect and others). Confusion may occur here, though, because Plato says that what I am referring to as Nous has nous, among the other characteristics. It is clear, however, that Plato is attributing intelligence (nous) to the Intelligible Region. Moreover, I can adduce another passage from the *Philebus*, wherein Plato confirms that Nous has intelligence and wisdom:[32]

> Whether we hold the view that the universe and this whole world order are ruled by unreason and irregularity, as chance would have it, or whether they are not rather, as our forebears taught us, governed by reason and by the order of a wonderful intelligence.
>
> How can you even think of a comparison here, Socrates? What you suggest now is downright impious, I would say. The only account that can do justice to the wonderful spectacle presented by the cosmic order of sun, moon, and stars and the revolution of the whole heaven, is that reason arranges it all, and I for my part would never waver in saying or believing it.
>
> Is this what you want us to do, that we should not only conform to the view of earlier thinkers who professed this as the truth, repeating without any risk what others have said, but that we should share their risk and blame if some formidable opponent denies it and argues that disorder rules?
>
> How could I fail to want it? (*Philebus* 28d5–29a5)[33]

The other interpretive issues are the ways in which we should read the life, soul and change characteristics of Nous.

In the *Timaeus*, the Intelligible Region is a living thing (or has life):

> Now when the Father who had begotten the universe observed it set in motion and alive, a thing that had come to be as a shrine for the everlasting gods, he was well pleased, and in his delight he thought of making it more like its model still. So, as the model was itself an everlasting Living Thing, he set himself to bringing this universe to completion in such a way that it, too, would have that character to the extent that was possible. (*Timaeus* 37c6–d2)

Along with de Vogel,[34] I believe that Plato is being consistent between the *Sophist* and the *Timaeus* on the point of the Intelligible Region's living.[35]

On the issue of Nous' having a soul in some sense, I believe that this is compatible with the claims that either Nous works with and through the All-Soul—the soul of the universe—or perhaps that Nous contains the Form, Soul Itself.[36]

Lastly, the claim that change is present in Nous or that Nous is not changeless[37] is certainly puzzling, but fortunately I just need to confirm that we find the same view in Plotinus. The only related comment is that—noting that the Greek for "change" is *kinēsin* in the *Sophist* 248e7–9b4 passage, as well as for "motion" in the Five Greatest Kinds—I can safely state that Plato believes that motion[38] or change is real.

On this point, Carone[39] argues that the Demiurge is a Nous that moves, and I would like to note that prima facie this is compatible with what Plato says in the *Sophist* (as well as with what Plotinus says at II.2.3.20–2, that Nous circles the Good). However, Carone goes on to argue that motion presupposes space, and space implies body, so Nous cannot exist without a body. I disagree that motion necessarily implies space, because souls exist between lives for Plato without bodies, and their intellects can be moved—especially in the case of the gods' souls that move around Nous, in the *Phaedrus*. In addition, the Form of Motion itself does not move, but we can still say that Nous has Motion without implying that Nous requires a body.

**Plotinus:** Let us confirm that Plotinus holds that Nous has life,[40] intelligence,[41] wisdom, soul and in some sense moves or changes (*kinēsin*).[42] First, Plotinus claims that Nous has life:

> Since this universe is certainly a living being containing all living beings and deriving its being and its being as it is from another, and the origin of that from which it derives is traced back to Intellect, its whole archetype must necessarily be in Intellect, and this Intellect must be an intelligible universe, which Plato says exists in 'the absolute living being.'[43] (V.9.9.3–8)[44]

Plotinus implies that if living things on earth have life, there must be a source of their life, and that is in Nous, the living being, as Plato says at *Timaeus* 37c6–d2.

Lastly, on the claim that Nous or Intellect is living, Plotinus claims that Intellect is the Absolute Living Being and substance:

> Since, then, it is the primary living being, and for this reason the Absolute Living Being, and is Intellect and substance [*ousia*], real substance, and we claim that it contains all living things and the whole of number, and the Absolutely Just and

> Beautiful and all other such things—we speak in a different way of Absolute Man and Absolute Number and Absolute Justice—we must enquire how each of these exists as an individual and what it is. (VI.6.8.1–6; adapted from A. H. Armstrong)[45]

Plotinus has confirmed that Nous is living, the Absolute Living Being and it contains the Forms, which we have already seen claimed by Plato in the *Timaeus* and the *Sophist*.

Obviously, since we've already seen that Plotinus believes that Nous has knowledge, it follows that Nous is intelligent as well; nonetheless, this brief passage can explicitly commit Plotinus on this score:

> See how in this great, this overwhelming Intellect, not full of talk but full of intelligence. (VI.2.21.3–4)[46]

Lastly, Plotinus also says that Intellect *thinks* the real beings (Forms), thereby creating them, and hence also *is* the real beings:

> It is clear that, being Intellect, it really thinks the real beings and establishes them in existence. It is, then, the real beings. (V.9.5.12–13)[47]

As with Nous and intelligence, imputing wisdom to Nous is not a long interpretive stretch, given that Nous is the realm of real beings that have knowledge, and is the object of knowledge. Plotinus declares that Nous is the very essence of, and has the greatest, wisdom:

> This life is wisdom, wisdom not acquired by reasonings, because it was always all present, without any failing which would make it need to be searched for; but it is the first, not derived from any other wisdom; the very being of Intellect is wisdom: it does not exist first and then become wise. For this reason there is no greater wisdom: Absolute Knowledge has its throne beside Intellect in their common revelation, as they say symbolically Justice is throned beside Zeus. (V.8.4.36–42; adapted from A. H. Armstrong)

Plotinus ties wisdom together with the notion of Nous' embracing of, and creation of, the real beings:

> The greatness and power of this wisdom [*sophia*] can be imagined if we consider that it has with it and has made all things, and all things follow it, and it is the real beings, and they came to be along with it, and both are one, and being is wisdom [*sophia*] there. But we have not arrived at understanding this, because we consider that the branches of knowledge are made up of theorems and a collection of proportions; but this is not true even of the sciences here below. (V.8.4.44–51; adapted from A. H. Armstrong)

Plotinus not only discusses wisdom, but also explicitly declares that true knowledge—even of sciences in the sense realm—is not of theorems and proportions; in fact, believing the opposite will produce in one a lack of wisdom.

With Plato, Plotinus believes that Nous has a soul through which it works. Recall that the Athenian Stranger in the *Sophist* argues that, if Nous has intelligence, and therefore must have life, then it must also have a soul in which the real beings reside (*Sophist* 248e7–9b4). Assuming for now that All-Soul is the offspring of Intellect, Plotinus claims that the All-Soul has an upper and lower phase, where the upper phase circles Nous:

> And the offspring of Intellect is a rational form and an existing being, that which thinks discursively; it is this which moves round Intellect and is light and trace of Intellect and dependent on it, united to it on one side and so filled with it and enjoying it and sharing in it and thinking, but, on the other side, in touch with the things which came after it, or rather itself generating what must necessarily be worse than soul. (V.1.7.42–8)[48]

So Plotinus believes that Nous has a soul, the All-Soul. Let us move on to the notion of change in Nous.

A quick reminder: Plato stated at *Sophist* 249a–b that if the realm of real beings has intelligence, life, and soul, then it would be unreasonable to deny any change of it at all. A simple way of confirming that Plato believes that Nous *in some sense* allows change is that Motion is one of the five greatest kinds. Plotinus generally denies any change at all, but he does allow for change in Nous. Plotinus argues that Intellect cannot and does not change:

> Intellect is as it is, always the same, resting in a static activity. (II.9.1.29–30)[49]

So, paradoxically, Plotinus is claiming, on the one hand, that Intellect is always the same, resting, and, on the other, performing an activity; but the activity is static. Allow me to hypothesize: according to Plotinus, Intellect already knows everything, but still contemplates, just as the philosopher-king of the ideal state would wish to do if he weren't required to return to the cave to rule. One can ask then, what will Intellect discover, when it has nothing but Beings before it? It stands to reason that it will gain nothing by contemplating, but the thinking can be seen as form of motion. (In at least two places, Plotinus also denies memory of Nous, since the Forms are not in time and do not change; they are in a state of unbroken identity [IV.3.25 and IV.4.1]). The bottom line on this issue, though, is that, even though Plotinus has a paradoxical position here, Plato still claims that Forms never change (which qualifies them as objects of knowledge), but "that which is completely real" must have life, change and the rest; in short, they both have this paradoxical view, which is consistent with my thesis.

Lastly, there is another passage where Plotinus discusses the stationary act of movement of Intellect:

> This is how Intellect is moved; it is both at rest and in motion; for it moves around Him [the Good]. So, then, the universe, too, both moves in its circle and is at rest. (II.2.3.20–2; adapted from A. H. Armstrong)[50]

Thus, Plotinus believes, as Plato does, that Nous is in some sense a living thing, has intelligence and wisdom, works through a soul and in some sense changes.

Plato and Plotinus have compatible views of the nature of Nous. They each believe that Nous is Being, the realm of the Forms, and has knowledge, intelligence, wisdom and understanding, life, works through soul, and in some sense changes.

## 3.2 God and Gods

Plato and Plotinus both discuss many characteristics of a singular God, and plural gods.[51] Both philosophers posit the following claims concerning God: God is the creator at the level of Nous (with one exception) and is wise; it is possible to know God via philosophy; God is good and is blameless for your life because each soul chooses its life beforehand; God creates humans as a toy so we should play our role well, not taking our lives and mortal concerns too seriously.

In addition, they do not essentially differ on the following claims concerning gods: the gods exist, are mindful of humans and cannot be swayed from justice through prayer or sacrifice; the stars are gods (though not all gods are stars); the universe is a perceptible god; the gods follow Zeus; the gods are good, beautiful, just, and wise; humans are a possession or a toy for the gods.

Unfortunately, here I will only be able to cover the claims that (1) God is the creator at the level of Nous (with one exception) and is wise; (2) the gods exist, are mindful of humans, and cannot be swayed from justice through prayer or sacrifice.

### 3.2.1 God is the creator (usually Nous) and is wise

One might ask for a definition of "creator" for Plato and Plotinus. If or when "God" refers to the Good or One, I suppose the creator would be that which creates *ex nihilo*, since the Good or One is said to be beyond being. However, if and when "God" refers to either Nous or a being at that level, then I believe that creation is performed via beings (Forms, gods, and the rest) and entities (the Receptacle) that exist. For example, Nous has soul and life, so those entities already exist in order to be prior to Soul and life. Moreover, attempting to define God in Plato and Plotinus' view is best done—and this is admittedly and unavoidably unhelpful—by seeing the major claims they make about God in the Dialogues and the *Enneads*, especially because they both seem to shift from using God for the Good or One and Nous or the Demiurge.[52]

I must admit that I do not fully understand the precise nature of God in Plato's view; for example, is God a being that is at the level of Nous but not identical to Nous? In this way, one might think, God would create the Forms in the sense of sustaining them in existence by being cognitively identical with them. Whether or not I take this view with Plato, it does not preclude me from doing the same for Plotinus (because on my reading he is equally vague on this issue), so I will make no such judgment here.[53]

**Plato:** In one major (exceptional) passage concerning God in the middle dialogue,[54] *Republic* X 596b–7e, Plato is best interpreted as saying that God is the Good, since he says there that God creates the Forms, which is consistent with his claims that the Good causes the Forms to exist.[55]

Moving on to passages where I take God to be Nous, in the *Timaeus*,[56] Plato claims that God is good, free from jealousy, ordered the universe, and installed intelligence in the soul and soul in body:[57]

> Now why did he who framed this whole universe of becoming frame it? Let us state the reason why: He was good, and one who is good can never become jealous of anything. And so, being free of jealousy, he wanted everything to become as much like himself as was possible. In fact, men of wisdom will tell you (and you couldn't do better than to accept their claim) that this, more than anything else, was the most preeminent reason for the origin of the world's coming to be. God wanted everything to be good and nothing to be bad so far as that was possible, and so he took over all that was visible—not at rest but in discordant and disorderly motion—and brought it from a state of disorder to one of order, because he believed that order was in every way better than disorder. Now it wasn't permitted (nor is it now) that one who is supremely good should do anything but what is best. Accordingly, the god reasoned and concluded that in the realm of things naturally visible no unintelligent thing could as a whole be better than anything which does possess intelligence as a whole, and he further concluded that it is impossible for anything to come to

> possess intelligence apart from soul. Guided by this reasoning, he put intelligence in soul, and soul in body, and so he constructed the universe. He wanted to produce a piece of work that would be as excellent and supreme as its nature would allow. This, then, in keeping with our likely account, is how we must say divine providence brought our world into being as a truly living thing, endowed with soul and intelligence. (*Timaeus* 29d7–30c1; adapted from Zeyl)[58]

Nous was also claimed by Plato to be the cause and orderer of the universe, so it is a good bet that God is Nous, at least here in the *Timaeus*:

> Now when the Father who had begotten the universe observed it set in motion and alive, a thing that had come to be as a shrine for the everlasting gods, he was well pleased, and in his delight he thought of making it more like its model still. So, as the model was itself an everlasting Living Thing, he set himself to bringing this universe to completion in such a way that it, too, would have that character to the extent that was possible. (*Timaeus* 37c6–d2)[59]

Further, while explaining the creation of time, Plato relates:

> For before the heavens came to be, there were no days or nights, no months or years. But now, at the same time as he framed the heavens, he devised their coming to be. (*Timaeus* 37e1–3)

Now, because Plato states that the father and creator "saw" the moving universe, one might think that the father and creator is best interpreted as the World-Soul; however, immediately after this passage Plato claims that this father and creator constructed the heaven, which is said of God in the *Republic*, where God was best interpreted as the Good. However, since the Good is said to be "in some sort" the cause of all things, Nous might be more directly responsible for the heavens' creation, perhaps partially explaining the "in some sort" qualifier. Thus, it is compatible that Nous is the direct creator of the heavens, as is stated in the *Timaeus*, while still maintaining that at the relevant spot in *Republic* X, "God" refers to the Good.

Lastly, I can confirm that "God" refers to Nous in another dialogue—the *Philebus*: "For all the wise are agreed, in true self-exaltation, that reason [*noun*] is our king, both over heaven and earth. And perhaps they are justified" (28c6–8).[60]

**Plotinus:**[61] This passage occurs immediately after Plotinus' discussion of Forms and Being:

> This God, then, which is over the soul, is multiple; and soul exists among the intelligible realities in close unity with them, unless it wills to desert them. (V.1.5.1–2; adapted from A. H. Armstrong)[62]

According to Plotinus, Nous is "over" the Hypostasis Soul and/or the All-Soul, so "God" here refers to Nous.

However, as we noted in Plato, it must be said that Plotinus also employs "God" to refer to the One:[63]

> [The One] appears everywhere to him as if before the eyes of his soul and, wherever he fixes his gaze, he is looking at him, unless he leaves the God and fixes his gaze elsewhere and thinks no more about him. And one ought perhaps to understand that it was in this sense that the ancients spoke of 'beyond being' with a hidden meaning, not only that he generates substance but that he is not a slave to substance or to himself, nor is his substance his principle, but he, being principle of substance, did not make substance for himself but when he had made it left it outside himself, because he has no need of being, he who made it. He does not then even make being in accordance with his being. (VI.8.19.9–20)[64]

Admittedly, the quotation begins by assuming that the One is being referred to by Plotinus, but, as the passage continues, it is clear—from his comments about God, beyond being, and multiple references to a "he" that does not need being because he made it—that in this passage God is taken to refer to the One or Good.

Thus, for Plotinus, as we saw in Plato, "God" usually refers to Nous, but also sometimes refers to the One or Good, so the context must be analyzed carefully to determine which is intended.

Similar to what Plato says at *Timaeus* 37c6–d2, Plotinus believes that God was pleased with his creation:

> But when he sees … what does he report? He reports that he has seen a god in labor with a beautiful offspring all of which he has brought to birth within him, and keeping the children of his painless birth-pangs within himself; for he is pleased with what he has borne and delighted with his offspring and so keeps all with him in his enjoyment of his and their glory. (V.8.12.2–7)

**Plato:** Late in the *Laws*, Plato places prohibitions on our thoughts on God as creator and provider, while also claiming that God is supremely wise:

> Let's not treat God as less skilled than a mortal craftsman, who applies the same expertise to all the jobs in his own line whether they're big or small, and gets more finished and perfect results the better he is at his work. We must not suppose that God, who is supremely wise, and willing and able to superintend the world, looks to major matters but—like a faint-hearted lazybones who throws up his hands at hard work—neglects the minor, which we established were in fact *easier* to look after.

> No sir, we should never entertain such notions about gods. It's a point of view that would be absolutely impious and untrue. (*Laws* X 902e4–3a6)[65]

Here we have the unsurprising Platonic claims that God is not inferior to human craftspersons, but supremely wise, and that God does not neglect even small issues, so—because it's false and impious—we should never think these things of the gods.

The last issue that needs to be examined dealing with God as creator provides us with more detail about the creation of earthly mortal beings: God assigned to "the gods"[66]—the stars, planets and "more retiring gods"—the task of actually creating humans, animals, and plants:

> When all the gods had come to be, both the ones who make their rounds conspicuously and the ones who present themselves only to the extent that they are willing, the begetter of this universe spoke to them. This is what he said:
>
> 'O gods, works divine whose maker and father I am, whatever has come to be by my hands cannot be undone but by my consent. Now while it is true that anything that is bound is liable to being undone, still, only one who is evil would consent to the undoing of what has been well fitted together and is in fine condition. This is the reason why you, as creatures that have come to be, are neither completely immortal nor exempt from being undone. Still, you will not be undone nor will death be your portion, since you have received the guarantee of my will—a greater, more sovereign bond than those with which you were bound when you came to be. Learn now, therefore, what I declare to you. There remain still three kinds of mortal beings that have not yet been begotten; and as long as they have not come to be, the universe will be incomplete, for it will still lack within it all the kinds of living things it must have if it is to be sufficiently complete. But if these creatures came to be and came to share in life by my hand, they would rival the gods. It is you, then, who must turn yourselves to the task of fashioning these living things, as your nature allows. This will assure their mortality, and this whole universe will really be a completed whole. Imitate the power I used in causing you to be. And to the extent that it is fitting for them to possess something that shares our name of "immortal," something described as divine and ruling within those of them who always consent to follow after justice and after you, I shall begin by sowing that seed, and then hand it over to you. The rest of the task is yours. Weave what is mortal to what is immortal, fashion and beget living things. Give them food, cause them to grow, and when they perish, receive them back again.' (*Timaeus* 41a3–d3)[67]

If God created humans, animals, and plants, they would be gods, God reasons, so the gods must create them after God installs the divine part of humans, animals, and plants, which is presumably the souls of these living beings.

**Plotinus:** Plotinus agrees that God or a god created living things:[68]

> When God or one of the gods was sending the souls to birth he put 'light-bearing eyes' in the face and gave them the other organs for each of the senses, foreseeing that safety would be ensured in this way, if one saw and heard beforehand and by touching could avoid one thing and pursue another. (VI.7.1.1–5)[69]

Admittedly, Plotinus only says "souls to birth," which does not show per se that he believes that god created humans, animals, and plants, as Plato said. One need only read a few more lines below to confirm this, however: "He afterwards gave what human beings and other living things were going to avoid suffering by having" (VI.7.1.7–8).

I need to confirm that Plotinus thinks with Plato that God qua Nous is wise. I can do that here, keeping in mind that for Plotinus, as for Plato, Kronos is a reference to Intellect or Nous:

> Kronos, the wisest God, before the birth of Zeus [All-Soul] took back and kept within himself all that he begat, and in this way is full and is Intellect in satiety. (V.1.7.33–5; adapted from A. H. Armstrong)[70]

We can also infer that the Plotinian God is wise as follows: since Intellect is Kronos, the wisest God, and given that we have shown that Plotinus believes that "God" usually refers to Nous or Intellect, we can infer that for Plotinus, God—qua Nous—is wise.[71]

Therefore, both philosophers believe that God (usually) refers to Nous and is wise.

### 3.2.2 The gods exist, are mindful of humans, and cannot be swayed from justice with prayer or sacrifice

**Plato:** Plato via the Athenian summarizes three conclusions in the *Laws*, which will serve as a springboard for his further views on the gods:[72]

> Our three theses—that the gods exist, that they are concerned for us, and that they are absolutely above being corrupted into flouting justice—have been adequately proved … (*Laws* X 907b5–7)[73]

Plato sets up the discussion about whether gods exist, care for humans, and can be bribed, with this claim: "No one who believes in gods as the law directs ever voluntarily commits an unholy act or lets any lawless word pass his lips" (*Laws*

X 885b4–6). The Athenian continues to say that, if anyone does commit such a deed, he either does not believe in the gods, believes that gods exist but take no thought for the human race, or that they are influenced by sacrifices and supplications and can easily be won over (*Laws* X 885b6–9).

**Plotinus:** First, it is obvious that Plotinus believes that gods exist, since he discusses them and their nature.

Second, on the issue of gods' care for humans, Plotinus says, "God in his providence cares for you" (II.9.9.64)—and, given other statements Plotinus makes, such as that gods will answer prayers of good persons (implied at IV.4.40 and III.2.8) and that there are guardian spirits who care for us, Plotinus agrees with Plato.

However, Plotinus also says that the gods—familiar with all that Intellect sees—"know all things and are acquainted, not with mortal matters, but with their own divine ones" (V.8.3.26–7),[74] which certainly implies that gods do not care for humans. My response is twofold. First, if we read on, Plotinus discusses *other* gods,[75] the ones in heaven (presumably stars) contemplate things in the "higher heaven" (including earth, sea, plants, animals, and humans), all of which are "heavenly" (V.8.3.27–33), and he concludes: "The gods in it do not reject as unworthy men or anything else that is there; it is worthy because it is there, and they travel, always at rest, through all that higher country and region" (V.8.3.34–6). Second, given that Plotinus states that good persons have their prayers answered by gods (IV.4.40.27–32, IV.4.41; cf. IV.4.42), it is pretty clear that he agrees with Plato on this issue in general.[76]

Lastly, on the issue of the gods' not being unduly influenced by humans away from justice, Plotinus agrees with Plato once again:

> The law says that those who fight bravely, not those who pray, are to come safe out of wars; for, in just the same way, it is not those who pray but those who look after their land who are to get in a harvest, and those who do not look after their health are not to be healthy... . It is ridiculous for people to do everything else in life according to their own ideas, even if they are not doing it in the way which the gods like, and then be merely saved by the gods without even doing the things by means of which the gods command them to save themselves... . The wicked rule by the cowardice of the ruled; for this is just, and the opposite is not. (III.2.8.37–52)[77]

Plotinus states that it would be unjust for the gods to intervene even on behalf of good people who pray (let alone on the behalf of bad people), if one does not help oneself, and that this is a law.

Thus, our philosophers do not essentially differ on the claim that God (usually) refers to Nous and is wise; and Plotinus believes that gods exist, gods care for humans, though he is admittedly less enthusiastic about this claim than is Plato, and the gods' decisions are not to be swayed from justice through prayer or sacrifice.

## 3.3 The Demiurge

Both Plato and Plotinus posit a Demiurge (*ho dēmiourgos*) or craftsman who created the visible universe. Aside from Plotinus' infrequent use of "Zeus" to refer to the Demiurge—which is best interpreted as God, Nous, the Creator—they each agree that there is a non-jealous, good, Demiurge, and that the Demiurge created the universe and rejoiced thereafter in his creation.

**Plato:** To my knowledge,[78] Plato first refers to the Demiurge in the *Republic*: "He'll believe that the craftsman of the heavens arranged them and all that's in them in the finest way possible for such things" (*Republic* VII 530a4–7).[79]

I should state that I take the Demiurge to be the same being as Nous and God, being thoroughly convinced by the text and the arguments of many commentators, especially Menn and Mohr.[80]

We will now focus on the references to the Demiurge in the *Timaeus*,[81] where Timaeus (here the voice of Plato) repeats that the Demiurge created the best universe, and adds that he used the Forms, or eternal patterns to do so:

> Which of the two models did the maker use when he fashioned it? Was it the one that does not change and stays the same, or the one that has come to be? Well, if this world of ours is beautiful and its craftsman good, then clearly he looked at the eternal model. But if what it's blasphemous to even say is the case, then he looked at one that has come to be. Now surely it's clear to all that it was the eternal model he looked at, for, of all the things that have come to be, our universe is the most beautiful, and of causes the craftsman is the most excellent. (*Timaeus* 28c5–9a6)[82]

Timaeus goes on to state that the Demiurge created the universe as one whole, in the form of a globe (32d1–3b8), without senses, organs, hands, or feet, and put it into circular motion (33c1–4a7). Plotinus indeed agrees with Plato that the universe was created without hands or feet: "Planning of this sort is quite impossible—for where could the ideas of all these things come from to one who has never seen them? And if he received them from someone else he could not carry them out as craftsmen do now, using their hands and tools; for hands and feet come later" (V.8.7.8–12).

Remember Plato's passage about the Demiurge's enjoyment of his creation and his desire to make the copy as close to the original as possible:

> Now when the Father who had begotten the universe observed it set in motion and alive, a thing that had come to be as a shrine for the everlasting gods, he was well pleased, and in his delight he thought of making it more like its model still. So, as the model was itself an everlasting Living Thing, he set himself to bringing this universe to completion in such a way that it, too, would have that character to the extent that was possible. (*Timaeus* 37c6–d2)[83]

The Demiurge rejoiced in the creation and strove to make the universe as close to the original—Nous, Intellect, God, that is, Himself—as possible.

In addition, the Demiurge qua God created the All-Soul, World-Soul, or soul of the universe (*Timaeus* 34b–c, 36d–7c)[84] and time.[85] Further, since Plato states that the Demiurge is eternal (*aei te ontōn* at *Timaeus* 37a1), and the World-Soul is in time (*Timaeus* 36d8–e5),[86] we can infer that the World-Soul is not identical to the Demiurge. Contra my view, Carone and Cornford believe that the Demiurge is the World-Soul, so let us address Carone's more recent defense of this view:

> Those who would like the Demiurge to be a soulless *nous* might argue that *genesis* is not to be predicated of him (as it seems to be predicated of ensouled *nous* e.g. at 30b3, 37c3–5). However, it is less than clear that the Demiurge, *qua nous*, should not belong to the realm of becoming or change (*genesis*), or even be a self-generating kind of entity, as we shall see soul is in the *Laws*. After all, in a summary of account of the *Timaeus* ontology, at 52d, we are told that three things existed before the generation of the universe: being, space, and *genesis*; no mention is made of the Demiurge as a separate entity (despite his being alluded to e.g. at 53b4). Even though it might be tempting to include him in the realm of being (which preeminently belongs to the Forms), this possibility is precluded by the fact that such a realm is immutable (38a3), while *nous* is in motion.[87]

However, Nous—the "perfectly real"—changes or is in motion[88] and has a soul (in some sense), according to *Sophist* 248e7–9b4; thus, for Carone to argue that the Demiurge cannot be understood to be at the level of Being or Nous is implausible. I can also arrive at this conclusion by remembering that the Form of Motion itself does not necessarily move, and thus motion per se does not presuppose space—as Carone[89] says—but is an immutable, immaterial

Form at the level of being as well. Additionally, it seems incoherent for Plato to require that an eternal, immutable, living God-Demiurge-Nous (as described in the *Timaeus*) needs an always-becoming body that is in time. Finally, contra Carone, who argues that the Demiurge *is* the World-Soul, we should say that the Demiurge *has* a soul[90] with which it works, to create, order, and govern the universe—namely, the World-Soul.[91] Thus, the Demiurge is best interpreted as its own entity, and not as the World-Soul itself.

Lastly, Plato states that the "begetter ... maker and father" (*Timaeus* 41a5, 7) addressed the gods and children of gods and instructed them to create humans, animals, and plants, with which Plotinus agrees.

Thus, Plato believes in a Demiurge who is equivalent to God or Nous, who created the heavens, the World-Soul and, in some way[92] the body of the universe.

**Plotinus:** First, Plotinus[93] assents to Plato's attribution of joy to the Demiurge upon completing his creation as well as his striving to make the copy resemble the original[94] as much as possible:

> For this reason Plato, wishing to indicate this by reference to something which is clearer relatively to ourselves, represents the Demiurge approving his completed work, wishing to show by this how delightful is the beauty of the model, which is the Idea. For whenever someone admires a thing modeled on something else, he directs his admiration to that on which the thing is modeled. But if he does not know what is happening to him, that is no wonder: since lovers also, and in general all the admirers of beauty here below, do not know that this is because of the intelligible Beauty: for it is because of the intelligible Beauty. Plato deliberately makes it clear that he refers the 'was delighted' to the model by the words which follow: for he says, 'he was delighted, and wanted to make it still more like its model,' showing what the beauty of the model is like by saying that what originates from it is itself, too, beautiful because it is an image of the intelligible Beauty. (V.8.8.7–20; adapted from A. H. Armstrong)[95]

As with Plato, Plotinus also emphasizes that the Demiurge is not in time—which implies that the Demiurge is Nous,[96] which is said by both philosophers to be eternal:

> But Plato's 'He was good' takes us back to the thought of the All [the physical universe]; he indicates that by virtue of the transcendent All it has no beginning in time; so that the universe, too, did not have a temporal beginning because the cause of its being provides what is prior to it. But all the same, after saying this for the sake of explanation, he objects to this expression, too, afterwards, as not

> being entirely correctly used about things which have a part in what we speak and think of as eternity. (III.7.6.50–7)

"He was good" comes from Plato's *Timaeus* 29e2.[97] Plotinus and Plato agree that there was nothing before the universe, since Plato states that God "took over all that was visible—not at rest in discordant and disorderly motion—and brought it from a state of disorder to one of order" (*Timaeus* 30a3–5).[98] Plotinus also agrees with Plato's claim that the Demiurge cast the soul around the universe from outside (*Timaeus* 36e), because Plotinus explains why it must be that way at V.1.10.

The only interpretive issue I saw initially—that is, not as a result of reading commentators—with respect to the Demiurge, came from Plotinus' first use of the term, when he explains the ordering principle:

> But since the ordering principle is twofold, we speak of one form of it as the Demiurge and the other as the Soul of the All; and when we speak of Zeus we sometimes apply the name to the Demiurge and sometimes to the ruling principle of the All. (IV.4.10.1–4; adapted from A. H. Armstrong)

This is an interpretive issue, since everything else that Plotinus claims about the Demiurge agrees with Plato's account of what the Demiurge is and what he does or did. But if Plotinus uses "Zeus"—which normally denotes the Plotinian All-Soul—for the Demiurge, then the Demiurge is not Nous.

Plato himself uses "Zeus" to refer to "the soul of a king" with "king's reason" in it, at *Philebus* 30d1–2, and both Plato and Plotinus claim that the All-Soul orders and governs the perceptible universe, so this is entirely compatible with Plato. Moreover, this issue seems to be analogous to Plato's treatment of "God;" namely, Plato used "God" to refer to the Good in the *Republic* but as Nous in the *Timaeus*, and similarly "King" is best interpreted as Nous in the *Philebus* but the Good in *Letter* II. Since Plotinus agrees with every major statement Plato makes about the creation of the universe and the Demiurge's role in that creation, I can only conclude from this passage that Plotinus and Plato did not use the term "Zeus" consistently; we cannot therefore infer, however, that they have incompatible views concerning the Demiurge.

Let us now consider an objection[99] from Corrigan (Bréhier and Majumdar), who argues:

> Plotinus gives a powerful analysis of what this means in practice in VI.7.2 in an extended discussion of the meaning of divine causality in relation to the *Timaeus*'s description of the Demiurge's making of the world. Plato represents the Demiurge planning and acting like a human craftsman, but divine

> forethought cannot be like this, Plotinus argues, for to represent God as having to work things out by reasoning would be to impute an anthropomorphic deficiency to the intelligible world (VI.7.1). We see a part and work out laboriously its relation to the whole, but in each divine act everything is complete without reasoning and already included in the totality of intelligible being so that we can reason out the purpose in things later.[100]

Since the Demiurge is Nous or God in Plato's view (in general), and God has immediate access to all the Forms, it stands to reason that God already has everything worked out when creating the universe. There is no notion in Plato's *Timaeus* of the Demiurge's having to deliberate and figure out what would be best for the universe—He just said to create it. In addition, in spite of Corrigan's passages, Plotinus does refer to the Demiurge's planning at V.9.3 and V.8.7. Thus, the lack of Plotinus' mentioning of the anthropomorphic features of the Demiurge in VI.7.1–2 does not constitute a major difference between Plato and Plotinus on the Demiurge.

Therefore, we can see that both philosophers agree on the nature and works of the Demiurge; the Demiurge is alternatively Nous, God, or the Creator.

## 3.4 Forms or ideas

Plato and Plotinus certainly agree that Forms exist, so I will only add here that they uncontroversially agree at least to the following major characteristics of the Forms: the Forms: (1) are eternal; (2) are immutable; (3) are immaterial; (4) are accessible by Reason or intelligence; (5) are unities and each is one; (6) are the cause of everything of that kind and Forms are what each thing really is; (7) "blend;" (8) are referred to by words; (9) are originals, perceptibles are images; (10) exist of things done according to nature.

## 3.5 The five greatest kinds

Both philosophers agree that the five most important (*megista*) Kinds (*genē*) or Forms,[101] or "Five Greatest Kinds," are Being, Sameness, Difference, Motion, and Rest.

**Plato:** Plato examines the Five Greatest Kinds in the *Sophist*, starting with Being, Motion, and Rest, differentiating them from one another (250a–4d),[102] calling them "most important"[103] kinds (254d4). He then adds and differentiates Sameness and Difference, making five Kinds (254d–7b).[104]

**Plotinus:**[105]

> So all things are being, rest and motion; these are all-pervading genera, and each subsequent thing is a particular being, a particular rest, and a particular motion. Now when anyone sees these three, having come into intuitive contact with the nature of being, he sees being by the being in himself and the others, motion and rest, by the motion and rest in himself, and fits his own being, motion and rest to those in Intellect: they come to him together in a sort of confusion and he mingles them without distinguishing them; then as it were separating them a little and holding them away from him and distinguishing them he perceives being, motion and rest, three and each of them one. Does he not then say that they are different from each other and distinguish them in otherness, and see the otherness in being when he posits three, each of them one? And again, when he brings them back to unity and sees them in a unity, all one, does he not collect them into sameness and, as he looks at them, see that sameness has come to be and is? So we must add these two, the same and the different, to those first three, so that there will be in all five genera for all things, and the last two also will give to subsequent things the characters of being different and same; for each individual thing is a particular 'same' and a particular 'different'; for 'same' and 'different' without the 'particular' would apply to genera. These are the primary kinds because you cannot apply any predicate to them which forms part of the definition of their essence. You will certainly predicate being of them, for they exist, but not as their genus, for they are not particular beings. Nor can you predicate being as the genus of motion and rest, for they are not specific forms of being; for some things exist as species of being, others as participating in being. Nor again does being participate in these others as if they were its genera: for they do not transcend being and are not prior to it. (VI.2.8.25–49; adapted from A. H. Armstrong)[106]

Plotinus even starts off with Being, Rest, and Motion, and then adds Sameness and Difference, just as Plato does in the *Sophist*. He also avers that they are "primary kinds" and why they are the primary—we cannot predicate anything of them to denote their essential nature except Being.

Therefore, I argue that Plato and Plotinus do not essentially differ on many significant claims concerning Nous, God and gods, the Demiurge, Forms, and the Five Greatest Kinds.

# 4

# The All-Soul or World-Soul

Plato and Plotinus agree that there is one soul of the universe, variously referred to as the All-Soul, World-Soul, Soul of the All, Soul of the Universe, Zeus, or the Divine Soul.[1] "All-Soul" or "World-Soul" will be used here, although Plato, Plotinus, commentators, and some translations may use these alternatives. I will define and address Soul, or what Plotinus refers to as the Third Hypostasis; behind the First Hypostasis (the One or Good) and the Second Hypostasis (Nous or Intellect).

In this chapter, I will show that Plato and Plotinus do not essentially differ in their claims that the All-Soul: (1) must exist; (2) has Nous as its source; (3) circles, contemplates, and knows Nous; (4) has an upper part or phase that circles Nous, and lower parts or phases that are individual souls; (5) is in time.[2]

## 4.1 The All-Soul must exist

**Plato:**[3] Socrates asks the first question, and Protarchus answers:

> Of the body that belongs to us, will we not say that it has a soul?
>
> Quite obviously that is what we will say.
>
> But where does it come from, unless the body of the universe [*to ge tou pantos sōma*],[4] which has the same properties as ours, but more beautiful in all respects, happens to possess a soul [*empsychon*]?
>
> Clearly from nowhere else… .
>
> We had better pursue the alternative account and affirm, as we have said often, that … there is, above them, a certain cause, of no small significance, that orders and coordinates the years, seasons, and months, and which has every right to the title of wisdom and reason.
>
> The greatest right.
>
> But there could be no wisdom and reason without a soul.
>
> Certainly not. (*Philebus* 30a3–8, c2–11)[5]

**Plotinus:**[6]

> 'So he [Love] must exist only there above, where the soul which is pure abides. But since the universe, too, had to have a soul' (III.5.3.26–8).[7]

## 4.2 The All-Soul's source is Nous

Plato and Plotinus both refer to the All-Soul as Zeus, and Nous as Kronos (where Zeus is the son of Kronos), so there is already one way of showing that Plato and Plotinus hold that Nous is the source of the All-Soul.

**Plato:** In the *Timaeus*, Plato states that an eternal God created the All-Soul,[8] the soul of the universe:[9]

> Applying the entire train of reasoning to God that was yet to be, the eternal God made it smooth and even all over, equal from the center, a whole and complete body itself, but also made up of complete bodies. In its center he set a soul, which he extended throughout the whole body, and with which he then covered the body outside. And he set it to turn in a circle, a single solitary universe, whose very excellence enables it to keep its own company without requiring anything else. For its knowledge of and friendship with itself is enough. All this, then, explains why this world which he begat for himself is a blessed god. (*Timaeus* 34a8–b9; adapted from Zeyl)[10]

For the precise claim that God *created* the All-Soul—as opposed to its already somehow existing, and God merely needed to "set" the soul into the universe's center—see *Timaeus* 34c1: "It isn't the case that God devised [the soul] to be younger than the body."

**Plotinus:**[11]

> In the *Timaeus* when speaking about this All he praises the universe and calls it a blessed god, and says that the soul was given by the goodness of the Demiurge, so that this All might be intelligent, because it had to be intelligent, and this could not be without soul. The Soul of the All, then, was sent into it for this reason by the god, and the soul of each one of us was sent that the All might be perfect: since it was necessary that all the very same kinds of living things which were in the intelligible world should also exist in the world perceived by the senses. (IV.8.1.41–50; adapted from A. H Armstrong)[12]

Plato believes the universe would not have been complete without, for instance, individual souls and animals: "This world of ours has received and teems with living things, mortal and immortal. A visible living thing containing visible ones, perceptible god, image of the intelligible Living Thing, its grandness, goodness, beauty and perfection are unexcelled" (*Timaeus* 92c5–8).

Even though Plato states that Nous created soul, he also claims that it is impossible for soul to come into being:

> This self-mover is also the source and spring of motion in everything else that moves; and a source has no beginning. That is because anything that has a beginning comes from some source, but there is no source for this, since a source that got its start from something else would no longer be the source. And since it cannot have a beginning, then necessarily it cannot be destroyed. (*Phaedrus* 245c9–d4)[13]

Thus, Plato holds that soul can be neither destroyed nor come into being, and Plotinus agrees: "Universal Soul did not come to be anywhere or come to any place, for there was no place; but the body came near to it and participated in it" (III.9.3.1–2).

## 4.3 The All-Soul circles, contemplates, and knows Nous

**Plato:**[14]

> Now Zeus, the great commander in heaven, drives his winged chariot first in the procession, looking after everything and putting all things in order. Following him is an army of gods and spirits arranged in eleven sections. Hestia is the only one who remains at the home of the gods; all the rest of the twelve are lined up in formation, each god in command of the unit to which he is assigned. Inside heaven are many wonderful places from which to look and many aisles which the blessed gods take up and back, each seeing to his own work… . When they go to feast at the banquet they have a steep climb to the high tier at the rim of heaven; on this slope the gods' chariots move easily, since they are balanced and well under control. (*Phaedrus* 246e4–7b2)

Zeus, Plato's reference to the All-Soul, is the first of the gods and leads the others around, sometimes climbing to the summit of the arch that supports the heavens, which may allude to Nous:

> Now a god's mind is nourished by intelligence and pure knowledge, as is the mind of any soul that is concerned to take in what is appropriate to it, and so it

> is delighted at last to be seeing what is real and watching what is true, feeding on all this and feeling wonderful, until the circular motion brings it around to where it started. On the way around [the soul] has a view of Justice as it is; it has a view of Self-control; it has a view of Knowledge—not the knowledge that is close to change, that becomes different as it knows the different things which we consider real down here. No, it is the knowledge of what really is what it is. And when the soul has seen all the things that are as they are and feasted on them, it sinks back inside heaven and goes home. On its arrival, the charioteer stables the horses by the manger, throws in ambrosia, and gives them nectar to drink besides.
>
> Now that is the life of the gods. (*Phaedrus* 247d1–8a1)[15]

Zeus is leading the gods around in a circle; the gods—including Zeus, the first god—contemplate truth, Justice Itself, Temperance (Self-control) Itself, Knowledge Itself; and thus, as the Forms are in Nous, we can reasonably say that Zeus circles Nous and contemplates and knows Nous.

**Plotinus:**[16] First, the All-Soul circles around Nous, or God:

> If it is the center of soul that is in question, soul runs round God and embraces him lovingly and keeps round him as far as it can; for all things depend on him: since it cannot go to him, it goes round him. (II.2.2.12–15)[17]

Plotinus also believes that the All-Soul contemplates Nous:

> The Soul of the All contemplates the best, always aspiring to the intelligible nature and to God, and that when it is full, filled right up to the brim, its trace, its last and lowest expression, is this productive principle that we are discussing. (II.3.18.9–13)[18]

Lastly, Plotinus states that Zeus truly knows an unlimited eternal one thing existing as one life—Nous—forever:

> Now [Zeus] will know that his work is one and a single life for ever—this is how the number is unlimited—and will know the unity not externally, but in his work; the unlimited in this sense will always be with him, or rather follows upon him and is contemplated by a knowledge which has not come to him from something other than himself. For as he knows the unlimitedness of his own life, so he knows his activity exercised upon the All as being one single activity, but not that it is exercised upon the All. (IV.4.9.13–18)

## 4.4 The All-Soul has upper and lower parts or phases; the upper circles Nous, and the lower are individual souls

Interestingly, both Plato and Plotinus believe that there are two parts to the All-Soul; they each refer to soul in the singular, and then differentiate between the upper All-Soul and the lower. The upper, All-Soul, circles Nous, as we've already seen. The lower is what Plato calls "divided soul" or individual souls, and Plotinus confirms this view.

**Plato:** Plato claims in the *Phaedrus* that there is a perfect part of soul which traverses and cares for the whole universe; but there is another part, when it sheds its wings and fastens onto something solid taking on a body, which is presumably an individual star, human, animal, or plant soul:[19]

> And now I should try to tell you why living things are said to include both mortal and immortal beings. All soul [*psychē pasa*] looks after all that lacks a soul, and patrols all of heaven, taking different shapes at different times. So long as its wings are in perfect condition it flies high, and the entire universe is its dominion; but a soul that sheds its wings wanders until it lights on something solid, where it settles and takes on an earthly body, which then, owing to the power of this soul, seems to move itself. (*Phaedrus* 246b5–c4)

If our soul can somehow—presumably when it is good and not incarnate—have dominion over the whole universe, then Plato must think that somehow individual souls are a part of the All-Soul, or at least definitely *can be* a part of the All-Soul.

Plato also discusses an indivisible and divisible soul in the *Timaeus*:

> The components from which he made the soul and the way in which he made it were as follows: In between the *Being* that is indivisible and always changeless, and the one that is divisible and comes to be in the corporeal realm, he mixed a third, intermediate form of being, derived from the other two. Similarly, he made a mixture of the *Same*, and then one of the *Different*, in between their indivisible and their corporeal, divisible counterparts. And he took the three mixtures and mixed them together to make a uniform mixture, forcing the Different, which was hard to mix, into conformity with the Same. (*Timaeus* 35a1–8)[20]

So there is an indivisible and immutable soul, and the kind that comes to be in the corporeal realm (by mixing the indivisible with the divisible kind) and arduously blending them together, which again implies that somehow the individual souls are connected and similar to the All-Soul.[21]

**Plotinus:**[22] First let us see some of his discussion concerning the two phases of soul:

> And the offspring of Intellect is a rational form and an existing being, that which thinks discursively; it is this which moves round Intellect and is light and trace of Intellect and dependent on it, united to it on one side and so filled with it and enjoying it and sharing in it and thinking, but, on the other side, in touch with the things which came after it, or rather itself generating what must necessarily be worse than soul. (V.1.7.42–8)[23]

Technically, Plotinus is referring in most of this passage to the Third Hypostasis, Soul—that is, the Soul that is a purer version of what the All-Soul and individual souls have in common. However, he then alludes to this Soul's being in touch with the things which come after soul, which would be perceptible things, or matter, which in turn implies that All-Soul and individual souls are, or can be, in touch with Intellect on one side and with perceptibles on the other. Thus, Plotinus states that the higher phase circles Nous and the lower contacts the realm beneath, which is obviously body or matter.[24]

Now let us see Plotinus' interpretation of the indivisible and divisible soul of the *Timaeus*:

> There is, then, this primarily indivisible being which dominates in the intelligible and among real beings, and there is also that other in the perceptible world which is altogether divisible; and, bordering on the perceptible, and rather near it, and in it, there is another nature which is not primarily divisible, like bodies, but all the same does become divisible in bodies; so that when bodies are divided, the form in them is divided too, but is a whole in each of the divided parts, becoming many and remaining the same, when each of the parts is completely separated from another part, since it is completely divisible. (IV.1.1.29–38)[25]

There is no question but that this is a plausible interpretation of the *Timaeus*, given what we see in the *Phaedrus* and the *Timaeus*: all soul is governing the universe, providing motion, caring, governing, and either using their intellect or intelligence toward the Forms or dealing with matter in individual bodies; the former is indivisible, and the latter is divisible soul. The soul divisible in bodies refers to individual souls.

An implication of there being upper and lower phases of the All-Soul is that all soul is one. We have already seen passages to this effect in Plato, and Plotinus states it many times,[26] in part by arguing that there are many similarities between individual soul and the All-Soul, as we see in this representative passage:

> For each of them is a principle of movement, and each of them lives of itself, and each of them apprehends the same things by the same means, thinking the things in heaven and the things beyond heaven and searching out everything which has substantial existence, and ascending to the first principle. (IV.7.12.4–8)

Therefore, both Plato and Plotinus believe that there are two phases of soul: the All-Soul, which circles Nous and governs the universe, and the individual souls which also govern the universe, but usually only part of it at a time. I have also confirmed that all soul is one, in some sense.

## 4.5 The All-Soul is in time

**Plato:**[27]

> Once the whole soul had acquired a form that pleased him, he who formed it went on to fashion inside it all that is corporeal, and, joining center to center, he fitted the two together. The soul was woven together with the body from the center on out in every direction to the outermost limit of the universe, and covered it all around on the outside. And, revolving within itself, it initiated a divine beginning of unceasing, intelligent life for all time. (*Timaeus* 36d8–e5)[28]

**Plotinus:**[29]

> The same is true also of the Soul of the All. Is time, then, also in us? It is in every soul of this kind, and in the same form in every one of them, and all are one. (III.7.13.65–7)[30]

In conclusion, Plato and Plotinus do not essentially differ in their claims that the All-Soul: (1) must exist; (2) has Nous as its source; (3) circles, contemplates, and knows Nous; (4) the All-Soul has upper and lower parts or phases, the upper circles Nous, and the lower are individual souls; (5) is in time.

5

# The Three Hypostases and Emanation

Now that I have covered the One, Intellect, and All-Soul in detail, we are in a better position to discuss the relation between these three principal entities (which Plotinus refers to as Hypostases)[1] in Plato and Plotinus' works.

The second and last issue is emanation; namely, it is often written that Plotinus believes that, from the One, Nous emanates (or "outflows therefrom"), and from Nous, Soul emanates. Because Plotinus mentions emanation and Plato apparently does not, it is commonly held on this score that Plato and Plotinus have different views; I contest that interpretation.

## 5.1 The Three Hypostases

**Plotinus:** Plotinus relates his view to the first three Hypotheses of Plato's *Parmenides*:[2]

> Parmenides in Plato speaks more accurately, and distinguishes from each other the first One, which is more properly called One, and the second which he calls 'One-Many' and the third, 'One and Many.' In this way he too agrees with the doctrine of the three natures. (V.1.8.23–7)

According to Plotinus, the First Hypothesis in the *Parmenides* (namely, what follows "if a one is") concerns the One or the Good, a Primal One, or a pure Unity; the Second Hypothesis is Nous, a secondary one, or a One-Many; the Third is the Soul (which I designate in this chapter as "$\text{Soul}_{3H}$," the Plotinian Third Hypostasis), or One-and-many;[3] therefore, Plato and Plotinus have the same view. I believe that Plotinus is correct about the First Hypothesis' referring to the One or Good.

It is possible, but not entirely conclusive, that Plotinus is correct about the *Parmenides*' Second Hypothesis' referring to Nous (see the Appendix). Note, however, that, even if Plotinus is not correct in interpreting the Second Hypothesis as referring to Nous, that does not imply that Plato and Plotinus have different philosophies, because Plato and Plotinus hold in common all the essential claims about Nous. This "misinterpretation" would be just that, a misinterpretation, which in itself obviously entails no incompatibility between Plato and Plotinus' views. Moreover, there is nothing in the *Parmenides*' Third Hypothesis (157b9–9a8) that I am aware of that prima facie disqualifies the One from referring to the Soul$_{3H}$.

Plato makes the following claims or conclusions about the one in the Third Hypothesis:

1. "Since in fact they are other than the one, the others are not the one" (157b9);
2. "The others are not absolutely deprived of the one, but somehow partake of it" (157c1–2);
3. "Things other than the one must be one complete whole with parts" (157e4–5);
4. "Things that partake of the one partake of it, while being different from it" (158b1–2);
5. "Things different from the one would surely be many" (158b2–3);
6. "Those things themselves that get a share of the one [must] in fact be unlimited in multitude" (158b6–7);
7. "For things other than the one that from the one and themselves gaining communion with each other, as it seems, something different comes to be in them, which affords a limit for them in relation to each other; but their own nature, by themselves, affords unlimitedness" (158d3–6);
8. "Things other than the one, taken both as wholes and part by part, both are unlimited and partake of a limit" (158d7–8);
9. "They [are] both like and unlike each other and themselves" (158e1);
10. "In respect of either property they would be like themselves and each other, but in respect of both properties they would be utterly opposite and unlike both themselves and each other" (159a2–4);
11. "Things other than the one are both the same as and different from each other, both in motion and at rest, and have all the opposite properties" (159a6–8).

(1) The "they" here can plausibly refer to individual souls, because we saw both authors refer to the similarity between the All-Soul and individual souls (such as immateriality and rationality); but it was also stated by both philosophers that All-Soul never ceases circling Nous and remains above, whereas individual souls can "fall" to earth by losing their wings and being attracted to the body.

As individual souls are in a sense other than the All-Soul—even though they are also in a way part of the All-Soul—we can say that the first conclusion is compatible with the one's being the All-Soul.

(2) The "others" can be interpreted as individual souls again, and, if they are so taken, it would be true that they are not deprived of the All-Soul, and partake of it in a way. Individual souls can circle Nous as well, if they are worthy of so doing. Again, this is compatible with the one's being the All-Soul.

(3) Again, taking the "things other than the one" as individual souls, one can argue that it is interpretively plausible to think that Plato and Plotinus believe that individual souls are wholes with parts (for example, the three parts of the soul). For both philosophers, individual souls are wholes, because they each get judged at the end of their lives, and thereafter can be incarnated in animals, separately, for their behavior, be sent singly to Tartarus for eternal punishment, or they may be sent to the "Isles of the Blessed."

(4) Individual souls will share in the one All-Soul, because Plato and Plotinus agree: "All soul looks after all that lacks a soul" (*Phaedrus* 246b6; cf. Plotinus' IV.8.2.19–32), and these individual souls are different from the All-Soul that they share in.

(5) There are many individual souls, so this is compatible with the one's being All-Soul in this hypothesis.

(6) As Plato says in *Republic* X 611b–612a, if an individual soul is unmarred and good, it is a unity, so the phrase "come to acquire unity" can be viewed as jibing with what we see Plato say elsewhere concerning individual souls. The claim that the one in the Third Hypothesis must be without limit of multitude is explained (158b–c) as those things that acquire unity are not one when they become so (as with the First Hypothesis, these things cannot be Forms), and that they are multitudes, but there is no limit to how many ways in which they can be a multitude. All of this is compatible with the Third Hypothesis' being the All-Soul (and the other souls which are in some sense part of it).

(7) The individual souls are unlimited in what they can do, in the sense that they are mostly reason, and therefore can be in many states and have many thoughts: one soul can focus on the material realm, for example, and there are many, if not infinite, material experiences a soul can have; another soul can focus on contemplating the Forms, for example, which are infinite, so this activity by itself makes what the soul can do infinite. Moreover, there is a limit to where one soul starts and the other ends; and, given past actions or habits of each soul, there are limits as to what each soul can achieve when compared to another.

(8) Both the Appetite and Spirit parts of the individual soul can be limited, in the sense that, if the Reason part primarily follows either of these, one cannot experience the ultimate knowledge or vision. On the other hand, one soul can spend multiple (and in principle unlimited) lives pursuing appetites, or honor, or emotional experiences, being repeatedly reincarnated to experience these goals over and over again.

(9) Individual souls are similar in having the same parts and capacities, but they are also different because of their diverse past experiences and present circumstances, levels of virtue and other characteristics. They are like themselves for obvious reasons, and unlike themselves because they can change their level of virtue over time. Lastly, one might argue that an incarnated soul is not the same as a soul that has been separated from a body.

(10) Since each soul has limit, and unlimit, in it, they are both like themselves and others; but they are also unlike themselves, because they have contrary characters in themselves, and it seems pretty obvious that different individual souls are different from one another.

(11) Most of these conclusions have already been shown to be true of individual souls, except the "motion and rest" and "contrary characters" statements. For motion and rest, souls are self-movers that move bodies, but bodies can be kept at rest, and souls can cease thinking as well, while unconscious or in certain comas. Souls have contrary characters, because they can be good in some aspects and bad in others, neither good nor bad in some aspects, and so on. They can change from being partly just and partly unjust to essentially unjust or totally just. And the same goes for all the other moral Forms such as Temperance, Piety, Courage, and Magnanimity. Therefore, an argument can be made that the Third Hypothesis refers to the All-Soul and the individual souls that are part of the All-Soul, or all of soul (see also the Appendix for more on my overall view of the second section of the *Parmenides*).

In any case, I will not argue that the Third Hypothesis of Plato's *Parmenides* must be taken to be Soul. The issue is whether we are warranted in believing that Plato believes in Three Hypostases, since we know that Plotinus does. Thus, we may grant to those who deny the presence of the Plotinian Three Hypostases in the *Parmenides* that they may be right;[4] nonetheless, it can still be true that both philosophers believe in Three Hypostases.[5]

But, assuming that it is pretty clear what the First Hypostasis (the Good or the One) and Second Hypostasis (Intellect or Nous) are, and that Plato and Plotinus believe in their existence, we should clarify the nature of the Third Hypostasis, which is Soul (hereafter I will refer to this soul in this section as $\text{Soul}_{3H}$ for ease of reference). Here I will accept Gerson's definition of the Plotinian Soul$_{3H}$ as "an [*eidos*] of soul in virtue of which [the soul of the universe and the soul of individuals] are the same" and as an *archē* that is the Form of Soul.[6]

**Plato:** Since no one doubts the existence of Soul$_{3H}$ in Plotinus,[7] I need only examine whether we find Soul$_{3H}$ in Plato's dialogues. There are at least six reasons to believe that we do.

First, we are justified in believing that Plato believes that there is an eternal Form of Living Thing, based on the *Timaeus* (37c6–d3, 39e7–9, 92c5–9), and the *Phaedo* (106d5–6). Moreover, there is (eternal) life in Nous. This Form would be the essence or nature of what it is to be living, which for Plato is soul, since soul is the one thing that all life or living things have in common, keeping in mind that Plato also holds that Nous has soul and life. For one cannot suppose that Living Thing is essentially the nature of soul *and* body (even though the World-Soul has a body and other living things do as well), since every thing that is living in Plato's view is not an entity with a body and a soul, given his view on reincarnation and that Nous has life and soul. Furthermore, the Demiurge created the World-Soul and individual souls (and indeed the whole universe) after this eternal Living Thing (*Timaeus* 37c6–d7, 39e7–9, 92c5–9). Thus, given that Soul$_{3H}$ is the Form of Soul that all souls (World and individual) have in common, and Plato believes in an eternal Living Thing, Plato believes in Soul$_{3H}$.[8]

Second, the *Timaeus* also attests to the idea that the universe (that which has an All-Soul and individual souls, among other things) resembles the eternal intelligible Living Thing, which *contains* within it all the living things that exist (30c5–41a1, with 31a2–b3 and 39e7–9), even to the point of referring to living things in the universe as "parts" (*moria* at 30c6) (both individually and by kinds) of the Living Thing (30c6). This feature of the Living Thing Itself mirrors the idea that Soul$_{3H}$ is what all souls have in common.

Third, I have shown that Plato (and Plotinus, for that matter) holds that there is some kind of soul in the "perfectly real" so Nous must have soul; this Soul is the plausible equivalent of the Plotinian Soul$_{3H}$.[9]

Fourth, at V.1.8.5–6, Plotinus refers to Soul$_{3H}$ as being alluded to when Plato refers to his mixing bowl, at *Timaeus* 41d4–5. This is a fair comparison, because Plato says that the Demiurge went once more into the former bowl, where he had blended the All-Soul, in order to form the stars' souls and human souls.

Fifth, Plotinus (in V.1.8.1–14) interprets Plato's reference to three kinds in *Letter* II 312e–3a (the "king of all," the "second," and the "third") as claiming that there is the One or Good, Intellect or Nous, and Soul. I defend that interpretation in the Plotinus section immediately following.

Lastly, Plato plausibly believes that all souls are one, which implies that he also believes in $Soul_{3H}$, which is what all these souls have in common.[10] This implies, again, a Platonic Form of Soul, which—at least according to Gerson's and my conception—is equivalent to $Soul_{3H}$.

Thus, I can confirm that Plato believes in the Plotinian Third Hypostasis, $Soul_{3H}$.

**Plotinus:**

> That, then, to which perfection belongs will exist before thinking; it will therefore have no need of thinking; for he is sufficient to himself before this; so he will not think. This, then, does not think, and the other is the primary thinking principle, and another again will think in a secondary way. (V.6.2.14–17)[11]

The One or Good has no intellection, Nous (here "the other") has intellection or is intellection primarily, and $Soul_{3H}$ (here "another again") has thinking in a secondary way, because it is mainly a principle of motion and life and governing the universe, though it does possess intellect. I need not review Plotinus' metaphor that the Good is in the center of a circle, that Nous is an unmoving circle around the Good, and that the $Soul_{3H}$ circles Nous, moving to aspire to Nous (I.7.1–2),[12] or his claims about the Three Hypostases in his diatribe against the Gnostics (II.9).[13]

Plotinus alludes to Plato's *Letter* II 312e–13a:

> This is the reason why Plato says that all things are threefold 'about the king of all'—he means the primary realities—and 'the second about the second and the third about the third.' But he also says that there is a 'father of the cause,' meaning Intellect by 'the cause': for Intellect is his craftsman; and he says that it makes Soul in that 'mixing-bowl' he speaks of. And the father of Intellect which is the cause he calls the Good and that which is beyond Intellect and 'beyond being.' And he also often calls Being and Intellect Idea: so Plato knew that Intellect comes from the Good and Soul from Intellect. And [it follows] that these statements of ours are not new; they do not belong to the present time, but were made long ago, not explicitly, and what we have said in this discussion has been an interpretation of them, relying on Plato's own writings for evidence that these views are ancient. (V.1.8.1–14)

Here Plotinus sums up the Three Hypostases and plainly declares that he is not devising some new philosophy (as he states Platonic views that we have now confirmed) but a philosophy that directly follows Plato, and we have now seen the passages that state that both philosophers believe that there is a One or Good that transcends being (and Nous) and causes Nous; that being is Nous, and Being Itself is contained in Nous and one of the five greatest kinds of Forms; Nous or God begets the All-Soul or soul of the universe, which is based on $Soul_{3H}$.

We must examine one further passage on Plotinus' interpretation of *Letter* II, because A. E. Taylor heavily criticizes Plotinus' reading, claiming that it is not clear what Plato is claiming there and that Plotinus misquotes Plato's letter. So, keeping in mind that in Plotinus' view the First is the One or Good, the second is Nous, Intellect, or the Forms (for "seconds") and the third is $Soul_{3H}$ or $Souls_{3H}$ (for "thirds," which presumably is the World-Soul with individual souls), let us look at Plotinus' interpretation of Plato's *Letter* II:

> But when in this kind of enquiry you adopt a rational approach to these things and get into difficulties and enquire where you should put them, put away these things which you regard as majestic on the second level, and do not add the seconds to the first or the thirds to the seconds, but set the seconds around the first and the thirds around the second. For thus you will leave each of them as they are and will make the things which come after depend upon those higher realities which exist in independence as the later things circle around them. This is why it is rightly said in this regard also "all things are around the King of all and all are for the sake of that King"; Plato is speaking of all the real beings and says "for the sake of that King," since he is the cause of their being and they, we may say, strive after him, who is other than all of them and has nothing which belongs to them; otherwise they would not still be "all things" if any of the other things which come after him belonged to him. If then Intellect is one of "all things" it does not belong to him. But when Plato calls him "Cause of all beauties" he is clearly putting beauty in the world of Forms, but the Good itself above all this beauty. Now when he puts these second, he says that the thirds depend on them, that is the things which come to be after them, and what he posits around the thirds, clearly the things that came to be from the thirds, this universe here, he makes depend on Soul. But since Soul depends on Intellect and Intellect on the Good, so all things depend on him through intermediaries, some close to him, some neighbors of those close to him, and the things of sense dependent on Soul at the ultimate distance from him. (VI.7.42.1–24)[14]

Plotinus demonstrates that he believes that the King in Plato's second letter refers to his "First" or Good, the seconds, or secondaries, are Forms in the Intellect, and the thirds, or tertiaries, are souls—All-Soul and individual souls—which depend on $Soul_{3H}$. I have already shown Plato's view of the Good and its causation of the Forms (and Beauty, which implies that Plotinus rightly infers that Plato's "Cause of all beauties" refers to the Good there), which are in the intelligible region. In addition, I have demonstrated that Plato holds that (1) Nous is Being and the realm of the Forms; (2) All-Soul comes from, circles, contemplates, and knows Nous; (3) individual souls are in some sense part of the All-Soul. Thus, when Plotinus states that he finds the Three Hypostases in Plato, Plotinus indeed has a quite plausible interpretation of Plato.

Though there are many objections to Plotinus' finding of the Three Hypostases in Plato,[15] I will consider one of A. E. Taylor's criticisms of Plotinus' reading of Plato's *Letter* II:

> The sentence from the second *Epistle* (the only one in which any reference is made to a "triad" of any kind), occurs in a reply to a difficulty raised by Dionysius II. He had complained, we are told, that Plato had not sufficiently explained his views on "the nature of the first principle." … Plato replies that he will convey his meaning in a "hint" or "riddle" … in order that no mischief may be done if the latter comes into the wrong hands. Then follow (312e) the words which Plotinus has quoted inaccurately. "The facts are these. All things center in the King of All and are for His sake, and He is the cause of all that is fair; the second things center on a second, and the third in a third." Nothing is said to explain either what is meant by the "second" and "third" things, or the nature of the principles in which they "centre," or the relation between these principles and the "King of All." Nor is it even made very clear who or what this "King" is. It ought not to be hard to see that, as Harward, the last English translator of the *Epistles* says, Plato is using the "riddle" as a humorous way of "parrying" a question prematurely put by a mind too immature to understand the answer to it. As he tells us partly in this very letter (313a) and more fully in one written a few years later (VII.341a–e, 345a–c), he was unfavorably impressed by the fact that Dionysius, after a single lesson, professed to understand the whole "secret" of philosophy, to the bottom.[16]

Beginning with the reference to Dionysius' complaint that Plato has not sufficiently explained the nature of the first principle: this is surely an allusion to the Good and sets up what follows as having to deal with that entity.

Next, A. E. Taylor accuses Plotinus of misquoting Plato. Here is Morrow's translation of the relevant Plato passage: "Upon the king of all do all things turn; he is the end of all things and the cause of all good. Things of the second order turn upon the second principle, and those of the third order upon the third" (*Letter* II 312e1–4). From this translation, we can see that Taylor's misquotation charge is not accurate, though he is correct that Plato does not explain what the second or third principles are in *Letter* II. However, since Platonic Nous is said to exist due to the Good, and since Nous thinks and contemplates the Forms, it is plausible that Nous can contemplate the Good as well. Moreover, it is said that Nous circles, and it stands to reason that it would "circle" (or "be around," as Plotinus says) the Good; and Taylor ignores that the Good is said to cause all that is right and beautiful in *Republic* VII. Lastly, it is true in Plato's view that, since the Good is the first, the second is Nous-God-Demiurge, the second things (Forms) center on a second (Nous-God-Demiurge, as Plotinus says); since Nous is eternal and the All-Soul is in time, the third is $Soul_{3H}$ or All-Soul, and the third things (individual souls) center in a third thing (All-Soul) *or* individual souls and the All-Soul together center in $Soul_{3H}$, as Plotinus says. Hence, this misquotation is not a vicious one, so to speak.

Next, A. E. Taylor claims that, since Plato does not state clearly what the seconds and thirds are, or what principles they center on, we cannot tell what they are, or what the King is. However, since the King clearly denotes the Good (due to Plato's reference to the King's causing everything to exist, *and* all beautifuls—just as is claimed in *Republic* VI and VII), then the only real seconds and thirds can be as described in the previous paragraph, and as Plotinus interprets the passage.

Lastly, A. E. Taylor states, per Harward, that Plato is merely using a riddle, and parrying, because Dionysius has an immature mind and is unimpressive.[17] However, this is a red herring—even granting that Plato believes that Dionysius is not sharp—because this fails to show that Plato is deceiving him, or not actually discussing his philosophy, especially because he states that he is going to put the doctrine into code. In short, just because (or assuming) Dionysius cannot figure out Plato's ontology, this does not imply that Plato is not discussing his ontology.

Thus, A. E. Taylor is much too hasty when he says: "The attempt to find neo-Platonic doctrine in the *Epistles* seems then to be a complete failure",[18] or: "Wherever in later philosophy or theology we come upon the 'scale of being' or 'ladder of perfection' we may be sure that we are dealing with the influence of Plato transmitted through Plotinus."[19]

Therefore, the Plotinian doctrine of Three Hypostases is quite definitely, and with much justification, to be found within Plato's dialogues.

## 5.2 Emanation

It is false to say that Plotinus has the view that lower entities or Hypostases ($Soul_{3H}$ and Intellect) emanate from, or are outflows of, higher principles or Hypostases ($Soul_{3H}$ emanates from Intellect, Intellect emanates from One), but

Plato does not.[20] Plotinus himself states that emanation is only a metaphor, implying that his emanation references should not be taken literally. It can also plausibly be argued that Plato is also committed at least to the spirit, metaphor, or idea, if not the letter or doctrine, of emanation.

**Plotinus:** Plotinus refers to overflowing and immediately says "as it were," which implies that emanation is a metaphor,[21] while he claims that the One generates Intellect:

> It is because there is nothing in it that all things come from it: in order that being may exist, the One is not being, but the generator of being. This, we may say, is the first act of generation: the One, perfect because it seeks nothing, has nothing, and needs nothing, overflows [*hypererruē*], *as it were*, and its superabundance makes something other than itself. This, when it has come into being, turns back upon the One and is filled, and becomes Intellect by looking towards it. (V.2.1.5–9; emphasis added) [22]

We have already seen that Nous contains soul, that Living Thing Itself is eternal and intelligible (VI.2.21–2), and that Nous is the source of $\text{Soul}_{3H}$,[23] so $\text{Soul}_{3H}$ metaphorically emanates from Nous. Plotinus also mentions the emanation of the universe from $\text{Soul}_{3H}$,[24] the emanation of $\text{Soul}_{3H}$ from Nous from the One,[25] and other combinations.[26] If asked to define Plotinian emanation (leaving other possibilities open), I would describe it as a metaphor for the outflowing from a higher principle to a lower principle, an outflowing which does not diminish the power or capacity of the higher principle in any way, and implies some kind of causation of the lower entity's existence. But it must immediately be added that the One does not cause Intellect in the same way that Intellect causes $\text{Soul}_{3H,}$ or in the way that $\text{Soul}_{3H}$ causes the universe to come to be, so defining emanation even just for Plotinus is problematic.

For the moment, however, I have shown that, though Plotinus definitely discusses emanation of the Hypostases from one another, and of the universe from the $\text{Soul}_{3H}$, he also states that emanation is a metaphor, which implies that emanation should not be taken literally to describe his view.

**Plato:** Even if one doubts the claim that Plotinus is not really committed to emanation in a strong sense, but only metaphorical emanation,[27] there is a second way to show that Plato and Plotinus have similar views on the issue of emanation. Namely, if it can be shown that Plato is implicitly (if not explicitly), committed to the view of metaphorical emanation as well, then Plotinus' mentioning of emanation does not prove that the views of Plato and Plotinus are irreconcilably incompatible. In fact, we will see that it is not an interpretive blunder to suggest that Plato thought that the $Soul_{3H}$ emanated from Nous, which emanated from the Good or One.[28]

First, then, let us review what we have shown concerning the Good, Nous, and the All-Soul (the latter, which is part of the Third Hypostasis, $Soul_{3H}$). Plato believes that the Good or One is beyond being and caused Nous or Intellect to exist; Nous or God caused the All-Soul to exist; and it is uncontroversial that he believes that soul is prior to body, all of which imply that Plato believes that the All-Soul (and individual souls) emanates from Nous, and Nous from the One.[29] Nous via the All-Soul causes the universe to come into being (Nous put the body of the universe in soul), which shows interpretive compatibility between Plato and Plotinus on the universe's emanating from Nous and the All-Soul. In addition, All-Soul would not exist without there being a Form, Soul Itself, so we can infer that All-Soul and individual souls are caused by Soul Itself or $Soul_{3H}$, in part because Forms cause everything of that kind to have that nature.

Second, in the Cave Allegory, three points can be made that are relevant to Platonic emanation. (i) Plato states that the sun's light enters the cave and aids in causing the puppets' shadows to be cast on the cave wall: "Imagine human beings living in an underground, cavelike dwelling, with an entrance a long way up, which is both open to the light and as wide as the cave itself" (*Republic* VII 514a2–5). (ii) If the sun in the allegory is analogous to the Good, and the light from the sun reaches the inside of the cave, then, analogously, the Good reaches all the way down the metaphysical scale.[30] (iii) When the released prisoner finally sees the sun (which is analogous to knowing or seeing the Form of the Good): "At this point he would infer and conclude that the sun provides the seasons and the years, governs everything in the visible world, and is *in some way* the cause of all the things that he used to see" (*Republic* VII 516b4–c2; emphasis added). This is metaphorical for the Good's being connected in some way to even the last vestige of becoming, which implies that the Good emanates from the highest to the lowest. Also, note that Plato's phrase "in some way" is compatible with even a robust sense of emanation that is commonly attributed to Plotinus—even though Plotinus himself refers to emanation as a metaphor. Interestingly, Plotinus actually uses the "light as outflow" metaphor alongside his emanation metaphor, which can further confirm the similarity between Plato and Plotinus' views:

> If we are to make a rational statement, we shall state that the first activity, which, so to speak, flows from it like a light from the sun, is Intellect and the whole intelligible nature, but that he himself, staying still at the summit

> of the intelligible, rules over it; he does not thrust the outshining away from himself—or we shall make another light before light—but he irradiates for ever, abiding unchanged over the intelligible. For what comes from him has not been cut off from him, nor is it the same as him, nor is it the sort of thing not to be substance, or to be blind, but it sees and knows itself and is the primary knower. (V.3.12.39–47)

Plotinus uses Plato's metaphor of the sun's light (and "so to speak, flows") to explain how the Good's power emanates to lower Hypostases and entities.

Let us now consider objections[31] from Dodds and Sinnige (and Majumdar, who agrees with the latter), who claim that there are differences between emanation in Plato and Plotinus; that is, they both—implicitly or explicitly—concede that Plato has some level of emanation, but that Plotinus' is different in kind. First, then, Dodds argues—where "Outgoing" is equivalent to emanation—that:

> There are three distinctive marks which differentiate this Plotinian Outgoing from other ancient theories of substance.
> (i) It is a dynamic conception… .
> (ii) The Plotinian theory is not a historical or mythological account of the *origin* of the universe… . This differentiates Plotinism from … the kind of Platonism which took the *Timaeus* literally.
> (iii) The relationship between cause and effect is for Plotinus *non-reciprocating*: that is to say, the higher determines the lower without itself being determined or modified by its own causative activity.[32]

I will only defend Plato's ancient theory of substance here, as opposed to anyone else's, using Dodds' numerals for convenience: (i) Plato has a conception of his Good or One that is just as dynamic as Plotinus', given that they both claim that the Good or One is and is not a being, and agree on most if not all of the major properties and qualifications it has and lacks. They also agree that it is indeed the cause of Being, Forms, and Nous, that Nous is (usually) God or the Demiurge, that the Demiurge causes the All-Soul, and that soul is prior to body; (ii) This is a puzzling statement: I fail to understand how Dodds can know whether Plotinus is indeed giving an historical account of the universe's origin; if Plotinus is not giving such an historical account, what other account is available for Plotinus to make if not "mythological?" Dodds *also* seems to imply that Plotinism cannot even be said to take the *Timaeus* literally, which I suppose undermines the "mythological" account denial, since Timaeus says that it is only a likely myth (29c–d; cf. 30b); (iii) Plato's view of causation from the Good to the material universe seems to be entirely consistent with what is said here: the Forms do not determine or modify the Good, the All-Soul does not determine or modify Nous, the Forms, or Being and so forth.

Second, Sinnige gives four features of emanation and says that Plato's version thereof only satisfies the first of these features:

> (1) All existence has its origin in a first principle which is perfectly One;
> (2) A stream of creative energy flows out from the One, creating and penetrating the universe to its utmost limits. The first duality is found in Intellect, which surrounds as it were the One. Then follows the All-Soul, and from these onwards the life-giving force manifests itself in the infinite multitude of living beings;
> (3) The mechanism of emanation has a double phase: there is an indefinite flow of energy issuing from the first One. This outflowing energy becomes aware that it is leaving its origin, and turning around contemplates its origin. In the act of contemplation it receives light from the One and First, and by that light is given its Form; [and]
> (4) The creative mechanism repeats itself throughout the universe down to the lowest level of existence… . Plotinus stresses everywhere that it is not the One itself that descends to the created being, but the light emanating from it: 'the origin itself stays above.'
>
> Only the first of these points can be explained by reference to Plato. The other points contain the specific features of Plotinus' theory of emanation.[33]

Given Sinnige's concession concerning (1), I will continue with the remaining points: (2) Nous circles in some sense, and what it circles would most likely be the Good, its source. The Good's light in Plato's Cave Allegory reaches to the cave wall, so it, too, reaches the utmost limits, except that in each philosopher's view the Good does not cause evil. Plato's Nous has a dual nature as well: it contains the Forms but also thinks, so there are objects of knowledge and a knower there, and, for both philosophers, the All-Soul circles Nous. Their view of the creation of the physical universe is similar if not identical. So Plato's view satisfies Sinnige's second feature; (3) I have shown that life is both in Nous, and imitated by the perceptible universe, via the All-Soul; Plato argues that we need to convert our soul to the Good, which is our origin, and that every soul pursues the Good and for its sake does what it does (*Republic* VII with VI). Moreover, if Nous thinks, then it stands to reason that it would contemplate the Forms and even the Good. So Plato's view satisfies the third feature; (4) The Platonic "mechanism" is creative in the same way as in Plotinus: the Platonic Good does not descend to the created being, but is in some sense the cause of "everything" except evil, just as Plotinus states. The fact that Plotinus mentions emanation as a metaphor does not make it another entity (like a creative mechanism); it is said by both philosophers that the Good creates everything, but then more specifically that the Good causes Nous-Forms-Demiurge-God; God causes the World-Soul, gods cause mortal souls, and soul is prior to body. So Plato's view satisfies the fourth feature as well. Therefore, I can explain all four of these points in reference to Plato—and note that Sinnige does not address Plotinus' statement that emanation is a metaphor.

It is not important to insist on Plato's committal to the emanation from the Good; all that is minimally necessary for my thesis is to show that, when Plotinus speaks of emanation (as a metaphor, as he states at V.2.1), this is not, in principle, incompatible with Plato. In fact, Plato and Plotinus seem to have the same view; but again, even if that is contestable, the views are arguably best seen as being compatible—either they are both committed to real emanation, or they are both only committed to metaphorical emanation.

Therefore, both philosophers are committed to Three Hypostases or major metaphysical entities: the One or Good, Nous, and the $\text{Soul}_{3H}$. Additionally, the commonly held notion that Plotinus is an emanationist is in principle compatible with Plato's view, given that Plotinus states that emanation is a metaphor, and Plato also is arguably committed to the same idea.

# 6

# Matter and Evil

Plato and Plotinus both think that matter (or place or space) is a Receptacle, wherein perceptible objects are generated through receiving Form-copies in and out of it; that is, they both refer to a third nature that is apprehended by a spurious kind of reasoning: the Receptacle (*hupodoxēn*), which can be interpreted as matter, place, or space.

They also do not essentially differ on the views that evil is a privation of the Good, it must always exist and must "haunt" our mortal nature.

## 6.1 Matter: The Receptacle?

**Plato:** Plato introduces and discusses this entity only in the *Timaeus*, after referring to the Forms (those which always are) and perceptible things (those which are always becoming) as the first two kinds of being. Plato at times seems to imply that the Receptacle is both a kind of stuff, or matter,[1] and an ever-existing place:

> We distinguished two kinds, but now we specify a third, one of a different sort. The earlier two sufficed for our previous account: one was proposed as a model, intelligible and always changeless, a second as an imitation of the model, something that possesses becoming and is visible. We did not distinguish a third kind at the time, because we thought that we could make do with the two of them. Now, however, it appears that our account compels us to attempt to illuminate in words a kind that is difficult and vague. What must we suppose it to do and to be? This above all: it is a *receptacle* of all—becoming its wetnurse, as it were. (*Timaeus* 48e3–9b6; emphasis in the original)

The Receptacle is the "wetnurse" of all becoming, difficult to illuminate and vague. The Receptacle receives all bodies, never departs from its own character, assumes a form like those imitations of Forms which enter it without taking on their characteristics; namely it is an intelligible, most incomprehensible, invisible, characterless being:

> The same account, in fact, holds also for that nature which receives all the bodies. We must always refer to it by the same term, for it does not depart from its own character in any way. Not only does it always receive all things, it has never in any way whatever taken on any characteristic similar to any of the things that enter it. Its nature is to be available for anything to make its impression upon, and it is modified, shaped and reshaped by the things that enter it. These are the things that make it appear different at different times. The things that enter and leave it are imitations of those things that always are, imprinted after their likeness in a marvelous way that is hard to describe. This is something we shall pursue at another time. For the moment, we need to keep in mind three types of things: that which comes to be, that in which it comes to be, and that after which the thing coming to be is modeled, and which is the source of its coming to be. It is in fact appropriate to compare the receiving thing to a mother, the source to a father, and the nature between them to their offspring. We also must understand that *if the imprints are to be varied, with all the varieties there to see, this thing upon which the imprints are to be formed could not be well prepared for that role if it were not itself* [*tout' auto en hōi*][2] *devoid of any of those characters that it is to receive from elsewhere. For if it resembled any of the things that enter it, it could not successfully copy their opposites or things of a totally different nature whenever it were to receive them. It would be showing its own face as well. This is why the thing that is to receive in itself all the elemental kinds must be totally devoid of any characteristics.* Think of people who make fragrant ointments. They expend skill and ingenuity to come up with something just like this [i.e., a neutral base], to have on hand to start with. The liquids that are to receive the fragrances they make as odorless as possible. Or think of people who work at impressing shapes upon soft materials. They emphatically refuse to allow any such material to already have some definite shape. Instead, they'll even it out and make it as smooth as it can be. In the same way, then, if the thing that is to receive repeatedly throughout its whole self the likenesses of the intelligible objects, the things which always are—if it is to do so successfully, then it ought to be devoid of any inherent characteristics of its own. This, of course, is the reason why we shouldn't call *the mother or receptacle of what has come to be, of what is visible or perceivable in every other way,* either earth or air, fire or water, or any of their compounds or their constituents. But if we speak *of it as an invisible and characterless sort of thing,* one that receives all things and share in a most perplexing way in what is *intelligible, a thing extremely difficult to comprehend,* we shall not be misled. (*Timaeus* 50b5–1b2; emphasis added)

Before this passage, Plato makes an analogy about gold being continuously shaped into every shape there is, claiming that the Receptacle has an analogous nature (*Timaeus* 50a4–b5). This might imply that the Receptacle has a nature that is best described as matter. From the passage above, the Receptacle is characterless so as to receive all manners of impressions, thereby implying that the Receptacle is formless matter (as well as invisible, as he states in the second and third italicized passages).

As plausible an interpretation as this *may* sound, Plato also states that the third "thing" (besides being and becomers) is ever-existing space:

> The third type [of thing] is space, which exists always [*tēs chōras aei*] and cannot be destroyed. It provides a fixed state for all things that come to be. It is itself apprehended by a kind of bastard reasoning that does not involve sense perception, and it is hardly even an object of conviction. We look at it as in a dream when we say that everything that exists must of necessity be somewhere, in some place and occupying some space, and that that which doesn't exist somewhere, whether on earth or in heaven, doesn't exist at all. . . . Let this, then, be a summary of the account I would offer, as computed by my 'vote.' There are being, space, and becoming, three distinct things which existed even before the universe came to be.
>
> Now as *the wetnurse of becoming turns watery and fiery and receives the character of earth and air, and as it acquires all the properties that come with these characters*, it takes on a variety of visible aspects, but because it is filled with powers that are neither similar nor evenly balanced, no part of it is in balance. It sways irregularly in every direction as it is shaken by those things, and being set in motion it in turn shakes them. (*Timaeus* 52a8–b5, d2–e5; emphasis added)

Plato clearly states in the beginning of this quotation that this third thing is ever-existing space (sometimes translated as place). However, he also states shortly thereafter that the nurse of becoming—the Receptacle—gets liquefied and fiery (receiving the forms of water and fire), and receives the characters of earth and air; but how can an indestructible space that occupies some place get liquefied or fiery, and be formless space? Instead, it is more plausible to suggest that formless matter somehow—though mysteriously, and comprehensible only through spurious reasoning, as Plato says in these passages—allows these processes to occur by receiving Form-copies without itself being changed.

Though I have argued that interpreting the Receptacle as matter is plausibly Platonic, I need not look at D. Miller's[3] or Mohr's[4] arguments that the Receptacle must be interpreted as space, or Zeyl's[5] argument that it is best interpreted as "room" (and is consistent with the idea that the Receptacle is matter as well),[6] because I am only concerned with whether Plotinus agrees with Plato on this issue. Plotinus, as with Plato, mentions both matter and space or place while discussing the Receptacle, and does not argue against the latter (though Plotinus certainly leans towards matter).

**Plotinus:** Though Plotinus usually thinks of the Receptacle as being matter, he also unflinchingly acknowledges the "space, place, or seat" interpretation as a possibility, thus accepting Plato's view of the Receptacle (or as a plausible interpretation thereof):[7]

> For if [matter] is receptacle and nurse, becoming is other than it, but that which is altered is in becoming, so matter would be existent before becoming, and before alteration; and *the words 'receptacle' and also 'nurse' imply its maintenance in the state in which it is free from affections; and so does 'that in which each thing appears on its entrance, and again goes out from it' and the statements that it is 'space' [chōras] and 'seat' [hedran].*[8] And the statement which has been criticized as speaking of a 'place of the Forms' does not mean an affection of the substrate, but is trying to find another way [of participation]. What is this way, then? Since this nature of which we are speaking must not be any real thing, but must have escaped altogether from the reality of real beings, and be altogether different—for those real beings are rational principles and really real—it is necessary for it by this difference to guard its own proper self-preservation; it is necessary for it not only to be irreceptive of real beings but as well, if there is [in it] some imitation of them, to have no share in it which will really make it its own. In this way it would be altogether different; otherwise, if it took any form to itself it would in conjunction with it become something else and would cease to be different and space for all things, and the receptacle of absolutely everything. But it must remain the same when the Forms come into it and stay unaffected when they leave it, so that something may always be coming into it and leaving it. So certainly *what comes into it comes as a phantasm, untrue into the untrue.* (III.6.13.13–32; adapted from A. H. Armstrong; emphasis added)[9]

Besides all of the familiar Platonic terminology and qualities of the Receptacle that are mentioned here, Plotinus implicitly confirms that Form-copies enter the Receptacle ("what comes into it comes as a phantasm, untrue into the untrue"). Second, what is fortuitous for my thesis is that Plotinus, in the first italicized phrase, actually acknowledges that Plato has stated that the Receptacle is a place (*chōras*) or base (*hedran*), and seems to see no interpretive problem with equating matter and place (*topos*). Thus, Plotinus seems to assume that Plato is referring to both matter and place with his use of "Receptacle."

However, Plotinus argues that matter must come before place or space:

> So here in the material world the many forms must be in something which is one; and this is what has been given size; but this is different from size. We can see that this is so because in our present experience things that are mixed together come to identity by having matter, and there is no need for any other medium, because each constituent of the mixture comes bringing its own matter. All the same, there is need of some one kind of vessel or place to receive bodies; but place is posterior to matter and bodies, so that bodies would need matter before they need place. (II.4.12.6–13)

Since Plotinus argues that space and place are preceded by both matter and body, he implies that matter is the Receptacle, even though he seems comfortable claiming that we might be able to refer to the Receptacle as a seat, place, or space as well.

As Plotinus believes that the Receptacle is ultimately matter, can we confirm that he believes, as Plato states, that matter is invisible, formless, imperceptible and apprehended by a spurious reason?[10] In fact we can:

> So, then, matter is necessary both to quality and to size, and therefore to bodies; and it is not an empty name but it is something underlying, even if it is invisible and sizeless. If we do deny the existence of matter we shall by the same argument be prevented from asserting the existence of qualities and size; for everything of this kind could be said to be nothing taken alone by itself. But if these have an existence, though in each case an obscure one, still more would matter exist, though it is not obvious since it is not by the senses that it is apprehended: not by the eyes, for it is without color; not by the hearing, since it makes no noise; nor has it taste or smell, so it is not nostrils or tongue that perceive it. Is it touch, then? No, because it is not a body, for touch apprehends body, because it apprehends density and rarity, hardness and softness, wetness and dryness; and none of these apply to matter. It is apprehended by a process of reasoning, which does not come from mind but works emptily; so it is spurious reasoning, as has been said. (II.4.12.20–34)[11]

There are many other passages that show Plotinus' commitments to matter's being formless,[12] quality-less,[13] invisible (III.6.7), immutable (namely, unaffected by Form-copy entrances and departures),[14] acceptance of Form-copies,[15] being seen by spurious reasoning (II.4.10), and matter's being unextended and unembodied.[16]

Let us now consider two objections concerning matter made by commentators: (1) Plato and Plotinus differ on matter, since the One contains and creates everything in Plotinus' view, and so Plotinus also has a problem of evil issue (given that matter is evil);[17] and (2) Plato holds that pre-cosmic matter exists and therefore is somehow not created by the Demiurge, whereas Plotinus says that the One contains and creates everything; thus they have different views.[18]

Re: (1), Plato states that the sun—the Good—is the cause in some sort of everything that the prisoner has seen, and that the sun's light extends to the cave wall; thus in some sense, they agree. However, they both also argue that the One or Good only cause or create good things, so they both have paradoxical views on this issue, and it is not accurate to portray only Plotinus as saying that the One causes "everything" without acknowledging Plato's similar passages. Moreover, they both argue that soul is prior to body, implying that matter exists somehow after soul and the Forms exist.[19] Further, if—as they both believe—matter is in time and time is created as an image of eternity, how can pre-cosmic matter already exist before time does? Lastly, they both believe that matter is the furthest entity away from the Good, and that matter is a privation, so it is not clear that Plotinus has a theodicy issue that Plato does not have.

Re: (2), there are Plotinian passages which imply that matter is indestructible as well, and always in existence (even granting the spots where he—like Plato—claims that the One or Good causes everything): "That which is altered is in becoming, so matter would be existent before becoming, and before alteration" (III.6.13.14–15); "Things that are said to have come into being did not just come into being [at a particular moment] but always were and always will be in process of becoming: nor will anything be dissolved except those things which have something to be dissolved into; that which has nothing into which it can be dissolved will not perish" (II.9.3.15). Even if Plotinus is only referring to "becomers," these in turn cannot exist without the Receptacle or matter,[20] so if "becomers" always exist—and there was no moment at which they came into being—the Receptacle always exists, according to this argument. "What comes into [the universe] from God is good; the evil comes from the 'ancient nature' (Plato means the underlying matter, not yet set in order)" (I.8.7.5–7).[21] Since Plotinus quotes Plato's "ancient nature," directly alluding to the idea that there is pre-cosmic matter, he is implicated on the same charges that affect Plato, contra this objection. These commentators need to account for these passages in order to have a convincing view on this issue.

## 6.2 Evil

Plato and Plotinus believe that evil is a privation of the Good, it must always exist, and haunts our mortal nature.

A word should be said about the connotation of the word evil (*kakos*), versus badness. In this section, I will take evil roughly as Leibniz defines metaphysical evil in his *Theodicy*, namely mere imperfection, or the lack of goodness. "Evil" should not, however, be taken to imply that someone can willingly do something wrong.

### 6.2.1 Evil as privation

**Plato:** Plato states: "The bad is more opposed to the good than is the merely not good" (*Republic* VI 491d4–5).[22] Also, while Plato is arguing for the immortal soul, he claims that evil is that which destroys and corrupts:

> Do you talk about good and bad?
>
> I do.
>
> And do you think about them the same way I do?
>
> What way is that?
>
> The bad is what destroys and corrupts, and the good is what preserves and benefits.
>
> I do.
>
> And do you say that there is a good and a bad for everything? For example, ophthalmia for the eyes, sickness for the whole body, blight for grain, rot for wood, rust for iron or bronze. In other words, is there, as I say, a natural badness and sickness for pretty well everything?
>
> There is… .
>
> Therefore, the evil that is natural to each thing and the bad that is peculiar to it destroy it. However, if they don't destroy it, nothing else will, for the good would never destroy anything, nor would anything neither good nor bad. (*Republic* X 608d13–609b2)

In Plato's examples, every evil is a privation of a good: ophthalmia is a privation of good sight; disease is a privation of health; blight is a privation of healthy grain.

Moreover, if we look at the ontology examined in Chapter 1, the Good or One is the highest principle and source of all being, truth, knowledge, and goodness. Of the entities thereafter, only the individual soul is capable of evil, and even then this is only possible when the soul is incarnated. Thus, evil is related to matter, which is the furthest thing away from the Good, and, as such, is a privation.

**Plotinus:**[23]

> In general, we must define evil as a falling short of good; and there must be a falling short of good here below, because the good is in something else. This

> something else, then, in which the good is, since it is other than good, produces the falling short; for it is not good. Therefore 'evils will not be done away with,' because some things are less than others in comparison with the nature of good, and the other things which have the cause of their existence from the Good are different from the Good and have certainly become the sort of things they are because of their distance from it. (III.2.5.25–32)[24]

Therefore, Plotinus believes that evil is a privation, just as Plato does. Is evil necessary, though? Both philosophers respond in the affirmative.

### 6.2.2 Evil must always exist

**Plato:**[25]

> But it is not possible, Theodorus, that evil should be destroyed—for there must always be something opposed to the good. (*Theaetetus* 176a5–7)

So evils are indestructible because there must always be something to oppose the good. Leibniz in his *Theodicy*[26] used a similar line of argument, when he argued that metaphysical evil (mere imperfection, or any imperfect thing that exists, other than the perfect God) must exist.

**Plotinus:**[27]

> Therefore 'evils will not be done away with,' because some things are less than others in comparison with the nature of good, and the other things which have the cause of their existence from the Good are different from the Good and have certainly become the sort of things they are because of their distance from it. (III.2.5.29–32)[28]

Plotinus even goes so far as to say: "But if anyone says that there is no evil at all in the nature of things, he must also abolish the good and have no object to aim at" (I.8.15.3–5), and: "Those who make the demand to abolish evil in the All are abolishing providence itself" (III.3.7.5–6). Let us take the example of reincarnation and undergoing the same punishments that one has caused others to suffer: Plato and Plotinus both believe that this principle is true; thus evil must exist, in order to provide a mechanism for retribution.

As both philosophers acknowledge that evil must always exist, this *may* also imply that matter has always existed (as Plato says of the unordered matter in the *Timaeus*), which counters some commentators' charges that Plotinus' view has no inchoate matter, as there is in Plato's.

Thus, Plotinus and Plato believe that evil necessarily exists.

### 6.2.3 Evil haunts our mortal nature

**Plato:**[29]

> Nor is it possible that it should have its seat in heaven. But it must inevitably haunt human life, and prowl about this earth. (*Theaetetus* 176a7–8)[30]

Plato also states: "There is one form of virtue, and an unlimited number of forms of vice" (*Republic* IV 445c5–6), which, together with each thing having its own evil (X 608d13–9b2), implies that, as there are so many ways in which to come into contact with evil, evils must be earthly.

**Plotinus:** Plotinus thoroughly agrees with Plato's *Theaetetus* passage: "For the evils are here below, because there is [only] a trace of life and a trace of Intellect" (VI.7.15.9–10).[31] Thus, they both agree that evil is a necessary feature of mortal life.

To summarize this chapter, Plotinus does not essentially differ with Plato that the Receptacle exists, receives impressions of Form-copies, is invisible and formless and remains what it is in spite of the constant entrances and departures of Form-copies. I raised the issue of whether the Receptacle is matter, space, or perhaps somehow both, and tried to show that Plato and Plotinus both think that the Receptacle is either only matter, or both matter and place, given what they said about the Receptacle. Lastly, they also do not essentially differ on the view that evil is a privation of goodness, evil must always exist, and evil necessarily exists as part of our mortal lives.

# Conclusion

I have tried to show as conclusively as possible, while addressing my opponents' objections and given space constraints, that Plotinus' metaphysics did not essentially differ from Plato's on 38 separate major (and some minor) philosophical claims. I hope that I have lent much credence to the following kinds of comments:[1]

> It might be Plotinus' merit to have, generally speaking, fully understood the details and implications of Plato's philosophy together with their background. In any case, he presents us with a consistent and 'universal' interpretation of Plato's philosophy. It might be in this sense that he marks a climax and *peripeteia* in the development of Platonism, rather than the starting point of Neoplatonism.[2]

> In general Plotinus' views must be seen in the light of the views of his predecessors. Plotinus was a Platonist. In fact he was so much of a Platonist that he thought that his most important doctrines contained nothing new, that he himself was merely an exegete who unfolds what lies implicit in the doctrines of Plato.[3]

Moreover, I hope I have provided much to doubt about these comments concerning the dissimilarity between Plato and Plotinus' views—where the claims concerning Neo-Platonists at least do not apply to Plotinus:[4]

> We can at least try to keep matters straight by insisting that regardless of family resemblances, Plotinus was not a Platonist.[5]

> We still have not entirely dropped the habit of seeing Plato through the eyes of Plotinus,– a habit which once made it possible for that Renaissance philosopher Ficino to declare that Plato was speaking through the mouth of Plotinus.[6]

> Plotinus-the-Mystic, like Heraclitus-the-Obscure, was unable to express his thoughts clearly and convincingly. Heraclitus composed riddles. Plotinus wrote the *Enneads*… . Plotinianism is the death spasm of Greek philosophy. J. B. Bury said in trying to characterize the change from Plato to the Neoplatonists, 'It is not a rise; it is a fall or failure of something, a sort of failure of nerve.' But it is a noble failure.[7]

> That Plotinus professed to follow the Platonic teachings is certain: certain too that he believed that his own written words were true Platonism. But perhaps he was deceiving himself, for the history of philosophy teems with examples of those who, while professing to follow their master's doctrines, have in fact changed those doctrines radically and set them forth in an unrecognizable form.[8]

> The word Neo-Platonism is a misnomer. It does not stand for a genuine revival of Platonism. The Neo-Platonists were no doubt the offspring of Plato, but they were the illegitimate offspring. The true greatness of Plato lay in his rationalistic idealism; his defects were mostly connected with his tendency to myth and mysticism.[9]

> From the Early Academy onwards all of whom have been traitors to Plato, especially the Neoplatonists.[10]

Be that as it may, before I conclude that Plotinus is indeed *the* Platonist (at least metaphysically), I still need to address six major objections of a general sort that have been made against the idea that Plato and Plotinus have the same philosophies:

(1) **Aristotelian and Stoic Elements**: Plotinus has Aristotelian and Stoic elements in his thought, so he is not a Platonist; he may even be better characterized as an Aristotelian;[11]
(2) **Forms of Individuals**: Plotinus endorses the existence of Forms of Individuals such as the Form of Socrates, but Plato does not, so he fails to be a Platonist in this respect;[12]
(3) **Non-Originality**: Plotinus will not be an original philosopher if he merely follows what Plato says;[13]
(4) **Non-Dual Experience**: Plotinus claims that the ultimate experience is a non-dual union, where one's soul somehow literally becomes one with the One, to the point where there are not two things but only One; Plato never declares this, so Plotinus has a different view of the ultimate experience and fails to be a Platonist in this respect;[14]
(5) **Plotinus is Monist; Plato is Dualist**: Due to Plotinus' description of a Non-Dual Experience (see (4) above), Plato's lack of such a description, and other expressions, Plato is best described as a dualist; Plotinus is a monist;[15]
(6) **Plotinus is Selective of Plato's Thought**: Since Plotinus only mentions a handful of dialogues, he cannot be a full-fledged Platonist.[16]

**Replies to (1) Aristotelian and Stoic Elements**: One might concede that this book demonstrates that Plotinus definitely held views similar to those of Plato, but still want to emphasize that Plotinus had Aristotelian and Stoic views as well, and certain commentators actually claim that Plotinus is more Aristotelian than Platonist. It is certainly open to any Platonist to believe—as Plotinus did—that Aristotle's categories hold true for the sensible realm but not entirely for the Intelligible Realm. A Platonist may also rightfully hold that certain Stoic elements, such as cosmic sympathy or downplaying death by comparing life to a play, are true as well, especially given Plato's view that individual souls are a part of the All-Soul, and that life is like a play.[17] And it is true that Porphyry tells us that Plotinus' philosophy has much of Aristotle's *Metaphysics* in it (*Life*, Ch. 14.4–7).

So, first, it must be granted that there are Aristotelian and Stoic[18] elements in the thought of Plotinus[19] and that Plotinus was fully versed in Aristotle's philosophy and arguments. However, the real question is whether those elements disqualify Plotinus as a Platonist, and the answer is obviously No, due to the preponderance of evidence. Thus, a first response is that the objection—especially in its weaker form, that Plotinus' works contain Aristotelian elements but that Plotinus is not more aptly described as an Aristotelian—does not take anything away from my argument that there are such elements present in Plotinus, even granting Gerson's thesis[20] that Aristotle is a Platonist.

Second, one might argue that we already see the notion of cosmic sympathy in Plato, so that this concept is not only Stoic in origin. For instance, after stating that Plotinus has the Stoic notion of cosmic sympathy, Wilberding[21] says that cosmic sympathy "begins with a vitalistic conception of the universe—the cosmos is a single and continuous living thing," which is, of course, straight out of the *Timaeus*, especially when one adds that in Plato's view, "All soul [*psychē pasa*] looks after all that lacks a soul" (*Phaedrus* 246b6).[22] Thus, we can question whether certain Stoic elements are uniquely Stoic or whether they have Platonic origins.

Lastly, Plotinus is not more aptly thought of as being an Aristotelian[23] for several reasons: Aristotle did not believe in Forms, a Good beyond being, an All-Soul, reincarnation, recollection, guardian spirits, or the nature of matter (among many other things), as Plato did. Moreover, if Plotinus were more of an Aristotelian, there should be much more discussion than there is of Aristotle's theory of knowledge [that is, that intuition (seeing a universal in a particular), plus induction, plus experience (multiple memories of multiple sense perceptions), leads us to understand the starting points of a syllogism, form and matter, rhetoric and animals]; and Plotinus explicitly criticizes both Aristotle and the Stoics,[24] while the most criticism Plato, famously, receives is being inconsistent about the nature of the soul's relation to body (both sides of which ironically Plotinus himself endorses). If Plotinus criticizes Aristotle[25] and the Stoics' positions and not those of Plato (even disregarding the 38 claims reviewed in the present work), my opponents must adequately account for this evidence.

Therefore, Plotinus is essentially a Platonist, and not essentially an Aristotelian or a Stoic.

**Replies to (2) Forms of Individuals**: First, admittedly, Plotinus mentions that there are Forms of individuals, such as Socrates Itself (V.7), while Plato does not. While there is some question as to whether Plotinus actually does commit himself to this view,[26] I can grant that Plotinus believes in Forms of individuals, and still not concede my thesis that this is not necessarily an incompatibility (per the Incompatibility Principle), because we do not have a statement from Plato that denies the existence of Forms of individuals. One might think that Plato's *Parmenides* and *Republic* X definitively show that a Form is a one over many and not a one over one, thereby implicitly denying the possibility of Forms of individuals for Plato. However, as Gerson[27] states, Plotinus' reason for postulating Forms of individuals does not conflict with Plato's one-over-many argument for the Forms,[28] with some qualifications.[29] Further, we also find the same one-over-many statements concerning the Forms in Plotinus,[30] so, if the one-over-many statement disqualifies Plato from having Forms of individuals, then it should also disqualify Plotinus.

Second, it should be noted that Plato does, in my view at least, admit the Form of Man at *Philebus* 15a (despite young Socrates' puzzlement about such a Form at *Parmenides* 130c).[31] With Gerson's reading of Plotinus' view of Forms of individuals—the Form of Socrates is in reality a Form of an individual that is now Socrates, then Aristotle, then an animal of some sort—and his defense of Plotinus' view of reincarnation,[32] it is even more clear that this kind of view is Platonic, given that Plato believes in reincarnation as well. However, I do not need to argue, and should not be taken as arguing, that Plato definitely believed in Forms of individuals; I simply reiterate that this is not a *bona fide* incompatibility.

Plotinus' view that there are Forms of individuals does not itself differentiate his view from that of Plato, because it fails to rise to the level of a contradiction between their views.

**Replies to (3) Non-Originality**: First, Plotinus is still original in that he is the first person to have claimed to "ascend from Plato's Cave" and to have actually experienced the Good.[33]

Second, it is incredibly rare for any philosopher to agree on 38 major and minor claims and to *state* in his or her writings that he or she has the same view as a previous philosopher. I believe that they had the same experience which conveyed to them the same epistemology, metaphysics, and ethics. Moreover, if this suggestion is correct, it makes originality impossible to an extent, since they would have seen the same reality and will inevitably describe it in much the same ways or defer to earlier descriptions thereof. Nonetheless, even if I am wrong about my main thesis, and Plato and Plotinus do not agree on every one of these claims, it remains infrequent that a philosopher states that they have the same philosophy as anyone else, so *in this sense* Plotinus is an original. Lastly on this point, if my thesis is correct, I believe that it helps us understand Plotinus better, since the received view is that there are at least a few, if not many, essential differences between Plato and Plotinus' views; and upon deeper inspection, some views (e.g. that individual souls are part of the World Soul) that do not appear immediately obvious in Plato can indeed be found in Plato's work as well.

Third, Plotinus (as Gerson states) deserves to be studied as a critic of Aristotle just as much as Aristotle deserves to be studied as a critic of Plato. Plotinus' originality, then, comes in part from his perspective as a Platonist responding to Aristotelianism.

Fourth, Plotinus made arguments against materialists that definitely merit further study, as well as his analysis of Aristotle's categories, to name only two promising subjects of future Plotinian research; it is a *non sequitur* to argue that if Plotinus either does not essentially differ from Plato or has essentially the same view as Plato, therefore there is no reason to study his view.

Lastly, from my perspective, Plotinus filled in the details and had insight into Plato's view, showing details that others missed both before and after Plotinus.[34] So I argue that he is original in the sense of being one of the best (if not the best) interpreter of Plato, at least of *his* (if not *any*) time.

Therefore, we should not worry about Plotinus' originality if we refer to him as a Platonist.[35]

**Replies to (4) Non-Dual Experience**: First, we do not have a statement in Plato that denies that this happens, so, according to the Compatibility Principle, we do not have a *bona fide* incompatibility on our hands.

Second, Plato implies in the Sun Simile that one must be like the Good in order to know or see the Good (*Republic* VI 508a–b); and, if the Good is the One, then we can infer that Plato implies in the Sun Simile that a person must be as unified as possible in order to know—or see—the Good or the One.

Third, in *Republic* X 611a–e, Plato claims that the purified soul of a presumably good person is unified, and not teeming with diversity and contradictions, which again implies that the good person, if she is like the Good or One, would be good and one to the extent possible given that she is still incarnated while contemplating the Good.

Fourth, in the *Symposium*, Plato mentions that people love the good and want the good to be theirs (206a) so that they can be happy (205a);[36] these passages echo the view of the dialogues (especially *Republic* VI and VII) that every soul desires the Good and is happy by knowing the Good. Moreover, Plato mentions that we will not benefit from any other possession or knowledge "without the possession of the good" (*Republic* VI 505b2). In short, these passages may imply that the Good-experiencer makes the Good part of her in some sense (all paradoxes to the contrary, just as these same paradoxes occur in Plotinus' thought).[37]

Fifth, both thinkers use vision and touch metaphors to describe the experience of the Good,[38] the latter of which implies that two entities may become one. Moreover, knowledge of the Good is non-discursive, and this is at least compatible with a non-dual experience; further, I have tried to show that Plato seems to hint that knowledge of the Good may actually not be possible, which is also consistent with a non-dual experience.[39]

Lastly, if I am correct that the One of the *Parmenides*' First Hypothesis is interpretively equivalent to the Good, given that Plato says that we should have a vision of the Good, then some of the First Hypothesis' conclusions actually hint at a non-dual experience. For instance, suppose that knowledge, perception and opinion require a dualistic experience—the knower and the object known, the perceiver and the perceived, and the opiner and the opined. As "there [cannot] be any knowledge or perception or opinion of it," if one's soul can have a "vision" of the Good, then the vision must be a non-dual one.

Therefore, it is possible to find even this feature in Plato's thought, or, at least, we cannot state that we can be certain that Plato does not have this view.[40]

**Replies to (5) Plotinus is Monist; Plato is Dualist**: First, I have just addressed the Non-Dual Experience objection, so that feature by itself should not warrant our believing that Plotinus is a monist or that Plato is necessarily not a monist (to the extent that my replies above succeed).

Second, Majumdar (2007: 157) posits that Plato has a dualistic "blessed encounter" (knowing the Good) because of this deeper reason: "the larger explicit forces propelling the ascent are merely political and not theological." This thesis does not account for Plato's view that all souls desire the Good,[41] Love's role in our desiring that beauty and the good become our own,[42] and

Plato's urging us to become godlike by the use of the divine Reason part of our soul to gain knowledge.[43] Admittedly, the immediate context of the Cave Allegory is to state what the metaphysical and epistemological stages are, in order for a guardian to become an excellent ruler; but the larger theological, psychological, and erotic contexts cannot be ignored either.

Third, I have shown above that Plato and Plotinus agree that there are two sets of three major metaphysical kinds: Set One: (1) The Good or One; (2) Intellect or Nous; (3) the All-Soul; and Set Two: (A) Forms; (B) particulars (Form-copies); (C) the Receptacle. Thus, one can argue that each of them is a dualist or a tri-generist, depending on how one classifies these entities; that is, for "Set One," eternal [(1) and (2)] versus in time [(3)], or beyond being [(1)] versus being [(2)] versus becoming [(3)]; for "Set Two," immaterial and eternal [(A) and (C)] versus material and in time [(B)], or being [(A)] versus becoming [(B)] versus seat or place that allows for becoming [(C)]. Regardless of the non-dual experience mentioned by Plotinus, he appears to be committed to these other entities in the same way and to the same extent as Plato. Arguably, as one goes, so goes the other.

Lastly, and related to the previous point, one can indeed argue that both philosophers are monist, in this sense. Based on what I have just referred to as "Set One," each of these real existents (the Good, Nous, and All-Soul) are immaterial, and I have shown that Plato believes they each exist, so he would be best construed as a monist in that case. Moreover, based on "Set Two," they each claim that the only things that truly exist are the Forms, which are immaterial (and eternal), as is the Receptacle; and that particulars (a) are not knowable but only appear to be and not be, (b) do not change the Receptacle, and (c) are essentially privations of existents. Thus, Plato (and Plotinus) could be best read as monists in that sense as well.

**Replies to (6) Plotinus is Selective of Plato's Thought**: First, had Plotinus used more of the early dialogues, scholars would, or could, have accused him of failing to understand the difference between Socrates and Plato. So, for anyone who believes that there is a major difference between Socrates in the early aporetic dialogues and Socrates in the middle and late dialogues, Plotinus' comparative lack of mentioning them is to be expected. For those, such as myself, however, who believe that we find basically the same view throughout the dialogues between Socrates and Plato (the Unitarian view), I have noted passages from early dialogues (*Apology*,[44] *Alcibiades* I,[45] *Greater Hippias*,[46] *Cratylus*, *Euthydemus*, *Gorgias*, *Meno*, *Phaedo*, and *Symposium*)[47] that are similar to what Plotinus says, despite the Oxford Classical Text's [OCT] lack of listing some of these dialogues in Henry et al.'s *index fontium* of the *Enneads*.[48] As I have shown, it is not necessary for Plotinus to refer to an exact passage in order to show that he has the same view as that passage.

Second, I cite parallels in Plotinus' thought with views in the rest of the dialogues as well: *Republic, Parmenides, Theaetetus, Phaedrus, Timaeus, Sophist, Statesman, Philebus, Laws, Epinomis*, and *Letters*.[49] Moreover, the idea that Plotinus should have to declare somewhere that the three rejected views of knowledge in the *Theaetetus* are rightfully rejected in order for him to be thought to be a Platonist misses the point; he picks out the most major things that Plato definitively says there concerning evil, justice, and becoming like god.

Third, of the 18 "early" dialogues Brandwood attributes to Plato (including *Alcibiades* I, which Plotinus takes—and I took it so here—as being authentic), Henry et al.'s *Enneads*' OCT *index fontium* finds citations or allusions to nine of these, including one in the *Apology*. As far as the middle and later dialogues are concerned, all are referred to other than the *Critias* (where Brandwood includes the *Epinomis*). The main point is that, just because Henry et al. found only these citations or allusions, does not entail their being in fact the only allusions to Plato's dialogues in the *Enneads*—though that index is certainly a fine starting point.

Lastly, the fact that Plotinus does not write out that he agrees with every pronouncement concerning the ideal state or the bad constitutions, say, in the *Republic* is not important, because it can arguably be shown that he does not essentially differ from Plato in his view of the Good, justice, reincarnation and eschatology, knowledge of Forms, opinion, three parts of the soul, and pleasure. Plotinus also tried to establish an ideal state based on Plato's laws, which implies that he agreed with the *Republic*'s contents, as well as those of the *Laws*.

Therefore, it is false that Plotinus is unfairly selective in his use of texts, given that his doctrine is consistent with what Plato says throughout most of his dialogues; and Plotinus can still be a Platonist.

Given the foregoing passages, my analysis, and the hopefully successful responses to all major and most minor objections (those that I am aware of) against the view that Plotinus is not a Platonist metaphysically, I feel warranted in declaring that Plotinus is entirely deserving of the title "Platonist," more so than the popular designation of "Neo-Platonist." Plotinus is the best example of a Platonist, even though there has been neither the time nor the space to show that no other Platonist—of whatever stripe: Aristotle, the spin-off schools of the Academy such as Skepticism, Cynicism, Stoicism, other Neo-Platonists such as Cambridge Platonists, Christian Platonists, or contemporary Platonists—shares *more* beliefs (assuming I cannot say "knowledge") in common with Plato than does Plotinus. From my scholarly and personal experience, most self-declared Platonists throughout history—including the present moment, where Thomas Taylor is an obvious notable exception—do not think that Plato is correct about reincarnation, guardian spirits, stars having souls, or even perhaps that the Good is beyond being, which makes each of them less of a Platonist than Plotinus.

Assuming that I have successfully argued for the conclusion that Plotinus and Plato do not have essentially different metaphysical views, there are two implications: first, Platonic commentators not familiar with Plotinus' work should now examine his work more carefully to explore its connections and details; second, that, at most, Plotinus is confirming, in non-dialogic prose form, that he has had an experience that proved that Plato (or at least many of the claims that are made by characters in his dialogues) is correct, and, at the very least, that Plotinus effectively claims to have ascended from the cave and came to know the Good.

I hope this work has changed some minds about the importance of studying Plotinus' work more closely, since it will give us a good, though not necessarily infallible, sense of the view that Plato was most probably intending to convey throughout his dialogues. Of course, I do not think that everyone will agree with me. As Tigerstedt[50] warns: "What some scholars regard as a faithful picture of Plato the man and his philosophy, is to other scholars an outrageous caricature or a pure invention." I sincerely hope that my interpretation is neither of these things, nor a mere wind-egg, as Socrates mentions in the *Theaetetus*, but on the contrary: a plausible—if not the most plausible—overall reading of Plato's metaphysics.

To conclude, since I have shown that there are numerous compatible passages, effectively saying the same thing on many major and minor metaphysical claims, and since I have defended this against most attacks in English on alleged essential differences between the two philosophers, perhaps I am warranted in suggesting that their views are essentially the same, and that Plotinus is *the* Platonist with respect to metaphysics.

# Appendix

## A Plotinian Interpretation of Plato's Eight Hypotheses in the *Parmenides*

*Subject in the* Parmenides = *Equivalent in Plotinian Ontology*

**First Hypothesis** (If a One is—137c4–42a8) = The Good or the One (see Chapter 1.5 and its subsections)

**Second Hypothesis** (If a One is—142b1–55e3) = Nous or the Forms (namely, the "parts"—142d–e—of Nous), the One-Many (see Chapter 5.1 and *Parmenides* 145a)

[Space does not permit my reviewing every conclusion of this One to attempt to demonstrate that the Second Hypothesis is best interpreted as Nous or Intellect; however, I should address two obvious problems with this strategy: (1) One of the Second Hypothesis' conclusions is that the one is in time [*Parmenides* 151e–2a and 155c-d, and the related conclusion that it both is and is not becoming older and younger than itself (among others), at *Parmenides* 152b–155d], whereas Plato (*Timaeus* 37c–8c) and Plotinus (III.7.5) state that both Nous and the Forms are eternal; and (2) The one is said there to "touch" itself and the others (*Parmenides* 149d). Re: (1), in *Sophist* 249a–b (quoted in Chapter 3.1.2), Plato claims that "that which is perfectly real" must have life, soul, and change, among other characteristics. In short, if change, life and soul *do* have a place in the perfectly real, or Intellect, given that each of these, *especially soul*, implies *time*, then *in some sense* it might be said that (*part of?*) Nous is in time. Re: (2), Plato can be asserting nothing other than immaterial contact between immaterial objects; namely, that the intelligibles are related to one another, just as he claims that our immaterial souls can "touch" the immaterial Forms (see my replies to the Non-Dual Experience objection in the conclusion); and, further, the Forms blend (see citations in note 101 in Chapter 3).]

**Third Hypothesis** (IIIA: If a One is—155e4–7b5) = Soul or the World-Soul (see Chapter 5.1)

[This Hypothesis is traditionally numbered IIA, but the text clearly states that they are starting over for the third time; hence my numbering of IIIA.]

(IIIB: If a One is—157b6–9b1) = The One = Soul or the World-Soul; the others = individual souls; the One-And-Many is soul collectively [see Chapter 4.4 and Inge (1929a: 214)]

**Fourth Hypothesis** (If a One is—159b2–60b4) = The One = Forms; the others = perceptibles

[Forms are separable from perceptibles—159b; when we have named the Forms and perceptibles, we have named all things—159b–c; what is really and truly one (the Form) does not have parts—159c; Forms are not *in* perceptibles as a whole or as parts—159c–d; perceptibles do not possess unity—159d; perceptibles are not many in the sense of consisting of many ones—159d; Likeness Itself and Unlikeness Itself are not in perceptibles, or they would *be* Likeness or Unlikeness Itself—159b; perceptibles are not truly the same, different, in motion, at rest (or they would be Forms), or coming to be or ceasing to be (because then they would have to acquire or be a being or change from not-being to being or lose being, which Forms cannot do)—160a–b.]

**Fifth Hypothesis** (If a One is not—160b5–3b6) = What follows if Forms do not exist; shows that the Forms must exist

[Largeness and smallness mentioned at 160c; Forms are something knowable and different from the other things (perceptibles)—160c–d; Forms are different in character—160d–e; if Forms do not exist, then the other things can have as many characters at the same time—160e–1a; only Equal Itself is truly equal—161c; the ones that in some sense possess being and the things that are, are Forms—161e–2a; the non-existent one must *be* non-existent and also *not be* existent—162a-b; the nonexistent one that becomes and does not become unlike is perceptibles—163a.]

**Sixth Hypothesis** (If a One is not—163b7–4b4) = Absolute Non-Being

[Many of these claims are true of the One of the First Hypothesis; but in this hypothesis he does not assert even the character of oneness of the One—164a–b.]

**Seventh Hypothesis** (If a One is not—164b5–5e1) = What follows if no Forms exist and, *per impossibile*, **only** perceptibles exist (in some sense)

[The perceptibles must differ from each other as multitudes from multitudes, but not in the sense of being many ones, because there are no ones (that is, Forms)—164c–d; perceptibles might appear to be one, but are not really one—164d–e and 165b; they might appear to be even or odd (per the *Phaedo*, for instance), but they are not either—164e; will appear to be equal but will not be so—165a; these multitudes are truly many and cannot be conceived to be a one because there are no ones on this Hypothesis—165a–b; the perceptibles will appear both like and unlike, same and different from one another—165c–d; they are both in motion and at rest in every respect, both coming to be and ceasing to be and doing neither (reminiscent of *Republic* V 479d's rolling around between being and not-being claim)—165d–e.]

**Eighth Hypothesis** (If a One is not—165e1–6c2) = Others or perceptibles are technically not many; what follows if Forms do not exist; the necessity of the One's existing

[The others (perceptibles) will not be one—165e; and they will not be many because that necessitates their being made of ones, and there are no ones—165e; so they will be neither one nor many—165e–6a; since the perceptibles would have no being of any kind, there cannot be opinion of them either—166a–b; they cannot be imagined to be one because one does not exist, and they cannot be many because many is made up of ones—166a–b; and if there is no one, the others cannot be or appear like or unlike, the same or different, in contact or apart, and the same for the other characters—166b; if there is no Form(s) or Good or One, there is nothing at all.]

# Notes

## Preface

1 Apparently my initial reaction was similar to Anton (2010, p. 7): "… does [the term Neo-Platonism] suggest that we are dealing with a special type of Platonism? I ask the question because like many others had once thought that Plotinus was a true Platonist …" Unlike Anton, however, my initial reaction has not changed.

2 Findlay (1978, p. 216). I should point out that I disagree with Findlay's assessment here: "it is in Hegelianism that Platonism finds its highest fulfillment" (1970, p. 263; see also 1975, pp. 679–80). Also, Findlay is a "hylozoist and an animist," and believes that "all these beings have their own life and consciousness" (1970, p. 265).

3 While I agree with Findlay that Plato and Plotinus have very similar eschatological views, space constraints unfortunately do not permit me to cover those here.

4 Rist (1967a, p. 187) and I are in agreement on the basic point: "There is no polemic against Plato in the *Enneads*. The honor due to the Master who had seen so much would render that impossible."

5 Another option, of course, is that we do not have enough material on which to base an accurate judgment, which includes the Old Academicians and Middle Platonists, for instance.

6 One such example is Jordan (1983, p. 1), who states: "No philosophical theory fools all the people all of the time … the theory of Forms—criticized and modified by Plato himself in his later works, and further modified or abandoned by his immediate successors—has perhaps found less adherents than most philosophical theories. And yet it retains its interest today, and will doubtless continue to do so." Jordan believes that Forms were conjured up in order to fool people and that it has few adherents, without stating his objections to the theory. In contrast, Plotinus not only enthusiastically argued for the Forms but for every other major Platonic ontological entity, as we will see.

7 O'Meara, 2003, pp. 154–8.

8 See Tigerstedt (1974, p. 18); Gatti notes Ficino's remark as well (1996, p. 22).

9 See Tigerstedt (1974, p. 19): "Ficino composed a vast *Corpus* of writings which in his eyes were only a little less holy and revealed than the Scriptures." See also the entry for Ficino in *Britannica* (1991, v. 4, p. 761): "He saw Plato's thought as one of the most noble expressions of the spirit, exceeded only by the truth of

Christianity." This high opinion of Christianity's correctness is where I disagree with Ficino, though I will not argue that point here.

10 In *Life*, Porphyry relates that Plotinus wanted to use the former city of Campania to found Platonopolis, and indeed tried to found it, prevented only by courtiers unfriendly to the idea (Ch. 12). Nonetheless, Plotinus was a living counter to Bernard Knox's claim that "Plato is a great artist and philosopher, but there is surely no one reading this who would abandon even the most corrupt and inefficient democracy to live in his republic" (1993, p. 98).

11 This should not be taken to mean that no one else can rightly be referred to as a Platonist, but rather as suggesting that Plotinus saw himself as merely filling in details of Plato's thought, and not as fitting Platonic views into his own. Of course, there are many different followers of Plato, including, but not limited to, Aristotle, the Skeptics, Middle Platonists, other Neo-Platonists (Porphyry, Iamblichus, Syrianus, and Proclus), early Christian Platonists (Augustine, Ficino), Renaissance Platonists, Cambridge Platonists (Cudworth, More, Smith and others), and Thomas Taylor. And we should note that Plotinus believed Platonism was (1) a view that preceded Plato, since other philosophers had his view as well (see, for example, III.7.1, V.1.8–9); and (2) that it included what we find in Plato's dialogues, as well as in Aristotle's testimony concerning Plato, and that we could reconcile much of Aristotle and Plato (so the former was not necessarily an enemy of the latter), and that it even possibly included oral traditions concerning Plato's view. Though I will focus this study upon what Plato states in the dialogues, I consider myself justified in stating that Plotinus is a Platonist, where Platonism per se may not, or does not, limit itself to what Plato writes in the dialogues.

12 Having written this sentence, I found A. H. Armstrong's (1947, p. 222) similar wish: "If I have managed to persuade anybody that Plato and Aristotle, Plotinus and Augustine are something more than musty historical curiosities who can be left to the attention of specialists with nothing better to do, then I shall have done something well worth doing. After all, we may reject the conclusions of the ancients if we like, but their thought is of sufficiently high quality and has affected that of later ages sufficiently deeply to make it very unwise for us to ignore them completely in making our own decisions about what we believe to be true."

## Introduction

1 Dillon et al. (2004, p. xiv) state: "*Alcibiades* I is the one that was most important for Neoplatonists because that dialogue was apparently read first among the works of Plato in the Neoplatonic curriculum. Among the *Epistles* of doubted authenticity, the second and the philosophical portion of the seventh are

unquestionably the most significant for the Neoplatonists, who used them regularly to bolster their interpretations of the dialogues." See also Gerson (2005, p. 258) for a repeat of *Letters* II and VII being important to the Neo-Platonists. I merely want to note that we have no evidence that the students of Plotinus were part of the "Neoplatonic curriculum;" that is, that they started off their Platonic studies by reading *Alcibiades* I, or indeed that they had a specified syllabus or reading schedule of Plato (or Aristotle, or anyone else). Sheppard notes that this schedule may have been developed by Iamblichus, but nonetheless was used by Proclus in his training as well as by his students (2005, p. 838).

2 See Wilberding (2006, p. 15n. 94) for passages where Plotinus takes the *Epinomis* to be genuine.

3 See Brandwood (1976, p. 1992) and Ledger (1989, p. 150).

4 See, for example, Findlay (1978, p. 15), keeping in mind that he takes the *Epinomis* to be genuine: "The *Epinomis*, a sort of addendum to the *Laws*, and classified in the past as its thirteenth Book, is either Plato's last piece of writing or the writing of Philip of Opus, his pupil. As the *Laws* is undoubtedly the work of Plato, and as the *Epinomis* is, on the whole, a worthier philosophical effort than the *Laws*, and also continues the themes of the latter, we may with uninterested hesitation attribute it to Plato: despite the glassy structure of its re-entrant sentences, it is what Plato, in some happier moment in his last phase, may have written" (Findlay 1974, p. 343). But see Ledger's (1989, pp. 199–200) rebuttal of the Philip of Opus hypothesis. Many others, such as Wilberding, argue that it is inauthentic (2006, p. 14n. 93).

5 Denyer, 2001, pp. 14–26; see also Ledger (1989, pp. 75, 144: "Of the group of early dialogues in Plato this must surely be one of the prime candidates for inclusion in the genuine corpus"); cf. Annas (1999, p. 58) on *Alcibiades* I's authenticity. For the opposite view, see N. Smith, 2004.

6 Brandwood (1976); Duncan (1940, p. 362), implied; Edelstein (1962, p. 1): "usually considered genuine" by others, but Edelstein argues against *Letter* VII's authenticity in Edelstein (1966).

7 Irwin (1992, p. 78n. 4: "I am inclined to agree with those who reject all of them"); Ledger (1989, p. 75, but see pp. 224–5); Shorey (1933, p. 50); de Vogel (1986, p. 76), implied – we should be skeptical about them all.

8 Cooper, 1997, pp. 1634–5, and Robin (according to Friedländer, 1969, p. 236).

9 Most *Letters* (except I and XII) are authentic: A. E. Taylor (1934, pp. 150–1) states there that he agrees with "Raeder, Burnet, Novotny … and historians like Grote and E. Meyer" on this issue (though they may have been proponents of all the letters' authenticity; it is not clear from the context). *Letter* II is authentic: Atkinson (1983, p. 188) and Findlay (1975, p. 660: "it fits in with and categorizes all that is taught in the most profound and representative of the Dialogues"). *Letter* VI is authentic: Friedländer (1969, p. 236). *Letter* VII is authentic: Brandwood

(1992, p. 112); Desjardins (2004, pp. 203–4); Doherty (1956, p. 460: "now proven beyond reasonable doubt to belong to the Platonic Corpus"); Frank (1940, p. 36: "now generally supposed to be authentic"); Friedländer (1969, p. 236); Harward (1928, p. 143); Inge (1948b, p. 152: "the genuineness of which almost all scholars are now convinced"); Morrow (1929, pp. 326, 348–9); Penner (1992, p. 130; due to its "sheer power and brooding, pessimistic tone" which is compatible with the same in the *Republic* and *Laws*); White (1976, p. 200–1). *Letters* II, III, VII, VIII and XII are authentic: Ledger (1989, pp. 151–3, 168–9, 197, 215, 220–1, 199, 224–5). *Letter* VII is inauthentic: Cherniss (1945, p. 13); Irwin (1992, p. 51: "probably spurious"); Press (2007, pp. 21, 146: "is not authentic").

*Letter* VIII is authentic: Friedländer (1969, p. 236) and Harward (1928, p. 143). Post (1927, p. 121) claims that *Letters* IX and XII may not be authentic, but that there is no case against the authenticity of *Letter* V.

A. E. Taylor (1934, pp. 150–1) said there was a general consensus against the authenticity of *Letters* III and VI, but he took them to be genuine.

Finally, Richards (1900, p. 344) is not clear on the issue: "It is true then that if we judged by the Greek alone we should have no reason for doubting. But, if we take into account the tone and spirit of the letters, we hesitate. When we weigh the extraordinary things they contain, we give judgment against them. The spuriousness of some does not of course necessarily entail the spuriousness of all. But, if the important letters are false, the trifles are probably false too, and in any case it matters little whether they are or are not."

10 Findlay, 1975, p. 660.

11 Desjardins. 2004, p. 227.

12 Tigerstedt, 1977, p. 19; see also p. 22.

13 Ibid., p. 13.

14 See, for instance, Pond's question-begging commentary: "In the writings of Plato, we behold a great mind placed (to use one of his own comparisons) in a dark cavern, searching after a reality of things, but perceiving little more than empty shadows. He is 'feeling after God, if haply he might find him;' and yet, though the true God is near, he finds him not" (1856, pp. 154–5). Pond assumes that, since Plato did not discover Pond's idea of the true God, he fails to hold any real view (due to his constant search), but only perceives shadows thereof.

15 Anderson, 2004, p. 71. See also Press (2007, pp. 89, 145, 159–71, for example), who claims that Platonism is not a system of doctrines but an intellectual vision; I do not see these approaches as mutually exclusive; cf. Schleiermacher (1973, pp. 7–8). I also do not go as far as Findlay (1974, p. 205) when he says: "Plato, it is clear, was capable of infinite mental reservation: he wrote all the Dialogues with his tongue in his cheek." I believe that Plato is serious, given statements to that effect, such as at *Republic* V 451a5–7: "I suspect that it's a lesser crime to kill someone

involuntarily than to mislead people about fine, good, and just institutions", and many other statements that should encourage us to be philosophers concerned with the truth.

16 The *Parmenides* is an exception to this rule regarding the character of Socrates.

17 See also Press, 2007.

18 While I am "laying my interpretive cards on the table" to inform the reader of my Unitarian view, I do not think that I am *assuming* Unitarianism in my method for these reasons: First, I give passages *across* Plato's dialogues in the notes whenever possible, to avoid the criticism that I only give one passage that matches up with Plotinus to perhaps deceptively convince the reader. Second, the most important argument for Platonic developmentalism is that Plato changed his mind on moral psychological views (which I address elsewhere in my unpublished ethics analysis, but that is not relevant here). Third, I am not adducing passages at liberty; I have chosen passages that give a good, or the best, impression of what Plato believes on a given metaphysical topic, and have then done the same for Plotinus. I leave it to the reader to assess whether I have misrepresented Plato in some way.

19 Gerson, 1989, p. 85. On the Platonic side of the issue, I agree with Benitez's characterization of the Unitarian view, not only with respect to the Forms but also with basically every Platonic view (1989, p. 2). To my knowledge, on the Plotinian side, at least in contemporary scholarship, developmentalism in Plotinus is a non-issue; see, for example, O'Meara (1993, p. 11). I will not be investigating whether Plotinus developed or modified his views in general here.

20 See Prior (1985, pp. 51–167) and Silverman (2002, pp. 155ff.).

21 Shorey, 1903a, p. 88. He also raises the issue of development even within the *Republic* itself, where he lists the commentators of his day who argued for the unity of the *Republic* (Hirmer, Campbell, and Grimmelt), as opposed to those "extreme partisans of 'development'" who "break it up into distinct sections which they assign to different periods." Shorey retorted that the partisans held their view "in the total absence of evidence" (p. 79).

22 Here I am thinking of Owen's (1953) infamous article, in which he argues that the *Timaeus* and *Critias* are not in the later period (p. 79), and the *Timaeus* is in the *Republic* group (p. 81), preceding the *Parmenides, Theaetetus* (p. 87) and *Statesman* (p. 91), and the *Timaeus* and *Critias* are middle dialogues (p. 94). Sayre (1983) argues that the *Parmenides* comes after the *Timaeus*, around the *Philebus* (pp. 15–16). Instead, I agree with Mohr (2005, p. xxv) who said, "Plato's ontology did not shift from middle dialogues to late."

23 Tigerstedt, 1977, p. 54.

24 See Shorey (1903a) and Cherniss (1957; denies the developmentalism of Owen; and cf. 1945, p. 85).

25 See, for example, Szlezak (1999) for a recent defense of this view; see Gonzalez

(1998, p. 278n. 16) for references to other members of the Tübingen school (Krämer, Gaiser, and Reale) and their works.

26 By "Plotinian Unitarianism," I intend to point out the way in which Plotinus views Plato's thought, as opposed to raising the issue of Unitarianism in the thought of Plotinus. With regard to the latter, in contemporary Plotinian scholarship, developmentalism is a non-issue.

27 My hesitation is based on the idea that, while Plotinus may certainly endorse the Unwritten Teachings (because what they purportedly claim is consistent with what we see in Plotinus and he does not explicitly deny the Unwritten Teachings), and while he makes many direct references to Aristotle's *Metaphysics* and *Eudemian Ethics* equating the Platonic Good with One or Oneness, three concerns arise: (1) Plotinus never refers to the Unwritten Teachings in his written work (he does refer to "unwritten" once at the end of V.1.9, but this passage does not clearly refer to Plato – that is, the context has nothing to do with first principles – and A. H. Armstrong believes Plotinus might instead be referring to Ammonius there); (2) Plotinus makes no (clear) allusion or reference to Aristotle's *Physics* 209b, where the latter refers to Plato's Unwritten Teachings, or to Aristoxenus' account of Plato's lecture "On the Good;" (3) contra Gerson (1997, p. 295), Plotinus is a proponent of unwritten doctrines in part because "Plotinus reads the second part of the *Parmenides* as a positive statement about the One" and "does so partly on the basis of Aristotle's testimony that Plato in his unwritten doctrines equated the Form of the Good and the One." Plotinus might have believed that the One as described in Plato's *Parmenides* is just the One he describes in the *Enneads*, and in turn with the way in which he and Plato describe the Good. We cannot be sure, though it could certainly be true, that Plotinus bases his view of Plato concerning goodness and oneness on reading Aristotle; but other possibilities include reading Plato's work or indeed himself experiencing the Good.

28 Tigerstedt: "Grote's work will always remain a healthy and necessary antidote against the never-ending attempts at systematization and harmonizing which overlook or explain away obvious contradictions, ambiguities, or gaps in Plato. But it cannot convince us that the interpretation of Plato constitutes no problem, for that thesis is disproved by the very attempts to prove it, of which the most radical and, in a sense, most successful is the elimination of the obnoxious texts" (1977, p. 18). I mention this here only to assure the reader that the present work does not intend to eliminate obnoxious texts, but to mention and attempt to account for them whenever possible. Cf. Gerson (2005, p. 264). Here is M. Miller's approach toward interpreting Plato's dialogues: "By my concern for structure, in turn, I require myself to approach each part of the dialogue with an eye to its relationship to the others, hence with an eye to its place in the whole; this serves as a check against the danger – always present when one is examining small stretches

of text at a time – of reading out of context and under the spell of inappropriate concerns" (1986, pp. 11–12). I completely agree with M. Miller's approach here, but add that I am using as many of Plato's dialogues as possible as a check against any one claim made therein.

29 Katz, 1950a, p. xi.

30 On this point, I agree with Gerson (2005, p. 264) and Press (2007).

31 For example, I concur with Rist (1967a, p. 247), who warns: "When one is reading the *Enneads*, it becomes clear that it would almost not be too much to say that the whole philosophy of Plotinus can be deduced from every individual sentence, or that a prerequisite for understanding any of the *Enneads* is to have read all of them."

32 See Nails 2002, an excellent resource.

33 I am convinced by Edwards (2000, pp. 117–19), who argues that Plotinus was born in the year 204, and not the almost universal birth year of 205. Incidentally, I am also convinced by Nails (2002, pp. 245–6), who argues for Plato's dates as born 424 or 423 BCE, died 348 or 347 BCE.

34 I have written an account of Plotinus' life in O'Grady (2005, Ch. 48); for much more on Plotinus' life, and an alternative translation to A. H. Armstrong's translation of *The Life of Plotinus*, see Edwards (2000). O'Meara (1993, pp. 111–16) gives a great account of the history of the *Enneads* and Plotinus since his death. For instance, in 1580 CE, the first printed edition of the Greek text of the *Enneads* was printed (p. 116). Sells (1994, pp. 220–1, n. 14) relates the claim that Arabic and Judaeo-Arabic people read Plotinus under the title *Theology of Aristotle*, but that work did not contain the whole of the *Enneads*.

35 From the Plotinian side of the scholarship, see Inge (1929a, p. 12); Pond (1856, pp. 139–40); Turnbull (1948, pp. xvi, 249). Hopefully the reader will not agree with one of my reviewers that I have hastily dismissed Plotinus' historic place and role in distinctively organizing and articulating Plato's themes as principles that allows us to trace a strong and substantive tradition of philosophers over the centuries after Plotinus. I simply and regrettably do not have enough time to review all of the schools of thought and trace the history, tradition and distinctions here.

36 One of the heaviest sources of criticism is Plotinus' writing style: for example, Gerson's humorous comment regarding Porphyry's statement that Plotinus made no revisions: "To my knowledge no one who has read Plotinus' Greek has ever questioned this astonishing statement" (Gerson 1996b, p. 8). Harris (1976, p. 2), a deeply devoted scholar of Neo-Platonism, says this of the *Enneads*: "Although extremely profound and provocative, the *Enneads* probably deserves to be called the world's worst written book since Plotinus seems to presume that the reader already has a complete knowledge of his system when he discusses any topic." As will be shown, Plotinus is praised in spite of his writing style.

37 A. H. Armstrong, 1947, p. 197. He also states: "the philosophy of Plotinus, who is with Plato and Aristotle one of the three supremely great masters of pagan Hellenic thought, and whose influence on later thinkers of many different schools has been very considerable" (ibid., p. 175). And: "Plotinus is not only the most vital connecting link in the history of European philosophy, as being the philosopher in whom the Hellenic tradition in full development and maturity was brought into touch with the beginnings of Christian philosophy. He is also one of the few ancient philosophers whom we can still honor, though not uncritically, as a master, and not simply study as a historical curiosity" (1940, p. 120).

38 Dodds, 1928, p. 142.

39 Fuller, 1938, p. 282.

40 K. S. Guthrie, 1896, p. 56. Several commentators' word for Plotinus is "great": Hardie (1936, p. 8); Strong (1895, pp. 107–8); Underhill (1974, p. 455); de Vogel (1986, p. 85) has "a high opinion of Plotinus as a philosopher."

41 Turnbull (1948, pp. xv–xvi). She also explains her colleagues and her admiration: "we chiefly delight in him ... because he has risen higher than any other into the clear stratosphere of the spirit" (ibid., p. xvii).

42 Hadot, 1993, p. 1.

43 Inge (1929a, p. 120). See also K. S. Guthrie (1896, p. 57); Harris (1976, p. 2) gives a possible explanation as to why Plotinus was not well known: "it was not widely circulated." Lastly, Wallis (1972, p. ix) states that his work's last chapter was meant to show his view as to why the neglect of Neo-Platonism was unjustified.

44 See, for example, Clark (1949, p. 137) and Inge (1935, p. 145: "Plotinus was profoundly loyal to the Greek philosophical tradition, and never willingly deserts his master Plato"). Cf. Miles (1999, p. ix: "[Plotinus] studied Plato intensively and passionately until he was able to see the world as Plato saw it").

45 For instance, Emilsson (1988, p. 3); Gatti (1996, p. 18); Gerson (1996b, p. 3); Harris (1976, pp. 2–3); Henry (1917–30, pp. xxxix–xl); Inge (1929a, pp. 81, 109–12); Katz (1950b, p. 2); O'Meara (1993, p. 6); Rist (1967a, p. 187); Wallis (1972, p. 3). Cf. Dillon et al. (2004, pp. xiii–xiv), who restate that Plotinus and other Neo-Platonists see themselves as Platonists, but add that we "need not of course accept such protestations of absence of originality at face value. There is admittedly a fine line between saying what one thinks the master meant and saying something, in fact, new." Rist (1999, p. 271) said the question of whether Plato would think Plotinus had his view "interests and puzzles" him.

46 Emilsson, 1988, p. 3. Tigerstedt (1977, p. 63) notes that Merlan and de Vogel had strongly stressed the connection between Platonism and Neo-Platonism, and on the next page facetiously claims (in his opponents' mouths) that "Plotinus was in fact what he claimed to be: Plato's true heir and successor" (1977, p. 64).

47 Gatti, 1996, p. 18.

48 Findlay, 1976, p. 25.

49 Findlay, 1970, p. 248.

50 Annas, 2000, p. xiv.

51 Ibid., p. 107.

52 See Anton (2000, pp. 52, 138; 2010, p. 15): "regardless of family resemblances, Plotinus was not a Platonist;" and cf. where he states that he initially thought Plotinus was a Platonist (2010, p. 2).

53 Gerson, 1997, p. 295. Gerson goes on to explain some of the reasons why Plotinus' view is different from Plato's: he is a proponent of the Unwritten Doctrines view and he formulates his arguments in Aristotelian terms (1997, pp. 295–6).

54 For instance, Plotinus mentions the non-duality of what I refer to as the ultimate experience (I address this issue in the conclusion); the One or Good causes itself (addressed in 1.1); the Good is self-love or simply love; Nous lacks memory, is a number, thinks itself and knows the future; there are Forms of individuals (e.g. a Form of Socrates; addressed in the conclusion); there is a logos that administers to the material world and leaves the All-Soul to contemplate; Gnostics and Gnosticism; the relevance of Aristotle's categories to the sensible realm; the superiority of stars' recollection over that of humans; the ability for humans to remember their past lives, guardian spirits having senses, memories and emotions; astrology and the effect of magic on good and bad souls; optics, potentiality and actuality; complete transfusion of material substances.

55 Stace, 1967, p. 372. See also Friedländer (1969, p. 64) and Majercik (1995, p. 43) for the "Plotinus is not a Neo-Platonist" view; for an argument as to how Plotinus could believe that he is a Platonist even though he was not really true to the letter of Plato, see Natorp (2004, p. 10). For a comment that leans toward Plotinus as a Neo-Platonist, see O'Meara (1993, p. 7), who reminds us that Porphyry states that Plotinus' view of Plato was "hardly orthodox." This is not surprising, however, given what I understand of the Middle Platonists and even the early Platonists, such as Speusippus' alleged non-belief in Forms.

56 Miles (1999, p. 9, see also pp. 8, xi): "Plotinus constructed his answer to the ancient question, How should we live?, in direct response to other proposals existing in his own intellectual and social situation. There is little that is abstract, timeless, or perennial about Plotinus's philosophy. If it is useful – as a whole, or in part – for the present, that will only be seen when we carefully replace it in its own society, critically examine its function in that setting, and then identify features of our own very different situation to which it may offer usable suggestions."

I take issue with Miles's assessment that Plotinus' view is not abstract, timeless or perennial and her questioning of its utility. It is abstract because it deals (as Plato's philosophy does) with Forms and the Good, which are transcendent entities; it is timeless for the same reason, because these are eternal entities; it is perennial, if my argument in this project succeeds, because Plotinus is in fact confirming the truth of Plato's philosophy, and not merely agreeing in the abstract with Plato's writing. To the utility point, if Plotinus (and Plato for that matter, as I will show) is correct that the most important thing that one can do with one's life is to experience the Good, and therein lies one's happiness, then it is difficult for me to understand what experience or knowledge could be more useful. Contrast Turnbull (1948, p. xvi) on Inge: "Dean Inge himself says of him: 'No other guide even approaches Plotinus in power and insight and profound spiritual penetration… . I have tried … to take him as a guide to right living and right thinking'"; thus, at least Inge takes Plotinus as giving useful advice on the way in which we should think and live.

57 See also Tripolis (1978, p. 140): "['The thinkers of the period'] believed that Plato's teachings represented a philosophy which satisfied the religious needs of the time"; Anton (2010, p. 7); Fuller (1938, p. 284); Robin (1928, p. 374).

58 A. H. Armstrong, 1945, p. 142; emphasis added.

59 Gerson's warning in his introduction to *The Cambridge Companion to Plotinus* could not be more fitting than here: "Do not be put off by ignorant detractors or uncritical enthusiasts or by the essentially empty label 'Neoplatonist,' which in some circles has become nothing more than a term of abuse" (1996b, p. 1).

60 Tigerstedt, 1974, p. 6. Tigerstedt's (1977, pp. 65–6) view puzzles me, because he states that, if the Neo-Platonist interpretation of Plato is correct, then "the interpretation of Plato ceases to be a problem. There is one and only one way of understanding him, and that is to study the Dialogues as interpreted by the Neoplatonists. Neoplatonism being a metaphysical system, founded by Plotinus and brought to its perfection by Proclus, the difficulty of combining Plato's various often divergent statements into a unity disappears. Only when the Neoplatonic interpretation becomes questionable or is openly rejected, the problem of Platonic interpretation emerges again" (1977, p. 66). I call his view "puzzling" because Tigerstedt does not seem to think that it would be a good thing if we could understand what Plato was saying, but instead seems to take it as axiomatic that no one has understood, can understand, or ever will understand what Plato believes. Contra Tigerstedt, I try to show why Plotinus' interpretation of Plato's metaphysics seems to be the best one, based on many divergent texts, even while acknowledging that the same (infrequent) paradoxes exist in both Plato's and Plotinus' texts, which they themselves admit.

61 For one example here, see Katz (1950a, p. xii).

62 See also I.4.5, and I.4.7–9; for more on the Sage's control of fear, see I.4.15.

63 See also VI.9.7.23–8 for Plotinus' reference to King Minos, a possible philosopher-king whom Plotinus posits may have legislated on the basis of his experience of the One. Notably, this passage is parallel to Plato's *Minos* 319b–20b, *Laws* I 624a, and *Republic* VI 505d–e.

64 Lewy, 1978, p. 315.
65 Rist, 1964, p. 7.
66 Ibid.
67 Robinson, 1953a, p. 4.
68 Ibid. Cf. Penner, who may or may not be justly placed here; he states, in his dialogue in the mouth of Plato: "My works have inspired many different thinkers – and especially neo-Platonists and Christian theologians. But you can't hold me to everything everyone has ever thought about me" (1987, p. 98). Charitably, due to the use of Penner's blanket term "neo-Platonists," I will only claim that Penner's claim does not hold true specifically of Plotinus.
69 Katz (1950a, p. ix) uses the fact that Plato wrote dialogues, and that Plotinus did not, to argue that there is no doctrine in Plato, so comparing Plato's view with Plotinus is wrong from the start.
70 Besides Porphyry's account in *Life* (Ch. 23), see *Ennead* I.6.7.
71 *Life*, Ch. 23.
72 Ibid.
73 I realize that this is a contentious view, but I consider this as an objection in the conclusion.
74 I will consider an objection concerning Aristotle and the Stoics in the conclusion.
75 Here I agree with Emilsson (1988, p. 4), that Plotinus is "not merely borrowing ideas from them [Parmenides, Anaxagoras, Plato, Aristotle, Pythagoreans, and Stoics] when it suits him."
76 See Mohr, 2005, p. 31.
77 The fact that I am stating in my introduction that I believe these philosophers do not have essentially different views, and then go on to amass quotations and argue for it, may appear to the reader to be a non-inductive, question-begging, procedure. However, the reverse is the case: after having read each corpus, I have induced that they do not have essentially different views, so here I can at most demonstrate that it is highly likely that they do not have essentially different views. I concede from this project's outset that I cannot prove my thesis with a deductive argument.

## Chapter 1

1 I do not have space to show that they also do not essentially differ on the claims that the Good or One: (1) is sufficient for, complete, desirable and satisfying to all souls, and is an absolute good; (2) is self-sufficient and perfect; (3) is alternately referred to as the Father.
2 Here is a reasonably complete list of where Plato refers to the Good as a Form (including those passages where he claims that it is the Source of All Things):

*Cratylus* 439c–d, *Greater Hippias* 287b–d, *Phaedo* 65d, 75d, 76d–7a, 100b, *Republic* V 476a, VI–VII 505a–b, 506d–7c, VII 517b–18a, 532a–4c, *Parmenides* 130b, 134c, 135c–d, *Theaetetus* 186a, *Philebus* 15a.

3 See Inge, 1929a, p. 85.

4 The following commentators say that the Good is not just another Idea or Form, in so many words: Findlay (1978, p. 28); Gadamer (1986, pp. 20, 27); de Vogel (1970, p. 184); cf. White (1979, p. 180) who bristles at the view that somehow the Good might be "beyond or outside the class of Forms."

5 Bréhier (1958, p. 134) and de Vogel (1986, p. 15) seem comfortable declaring the transcendence of the Good; cf. Hampton (1990, p. 89). McCabe (1994) simply states that this passage is "pretty mysterious" (p. 72) and then explains "beyond being" in terms of the Sun Simile and Divided Line Analogy (pp. 72–3).

6 In other translations of this key passage, *ousias*, here translated as "being" (in "beyond being"), is translated as "essence" (by Shorey [and see Grote (1875, p. 90), who argues that the Good is beyond essence, but not being]). However, several points can be made here: First, it can be argued that the Greek *ousias,* that some translate as "essence", really alludes to "being," so that, even if we should translate *ousias* as "essence," they are fundamentally equivalent, so it comes to the same claim. Second, at least one commentator, Rawson (1996, p. 111; cf. p. 112n. 4), has argued for the "being" translation over the "essence" translation, supporting Reeve's rendering here. In either of these cases, we are warranted in believing that Plato is claiming that the Good is not being but beyond being.

7 See *Parmenides* 130b, 134c, and 135c–d.

8 See *Theaetetus* 186a.

9 See also *Philebus* 15a1–7. Also, note that, according to Brandwood's stylometric analysis, the *Philebus* was written after the *Sophist.*

10 Shorey, 1895, p. 65.

11 See Bowe (2003, pp. 16–19); Findlay (1978, p. 28); Friedländer (1969, pp. 62–3); Gadamer (1986, pp. 27, 89); Jessop (1930, p. 47); Joseph (1948, pp. 23–40); Rawson (1996, pp. 103–4, 110), though he argues that Plotinus misinterprets Plato; Voegelin (2000, p. 167); de Vogel (1969, p. 229; 1970, p. 187; 1986, p. 15) and White (1979, p. 180).

12 Bowe, 2003, p. 19.

13 Ferguson (1963, p. 193) believes that Parmenides' poem gave Plato the notion that the Good was beyond being. Sextus Empiricus stated: "The sons of Pythagoras then placed the One in a position of transcendence over the class of Things Conceived by Themselves. For it is through this One that this class has self-existence, so that each distinct entity is a single thing and can be contemplated on its own" (*Against the Mathematicians* X, as quoted in Findlay, 1974, p. 428).

14 See Bechtle (1999, pp. 86–7, 87n. 216) for the anonymous commentator of Plato's *Parmenides* who provides Aristotelian evidence (via Simplicius *in Cael.*); cf. *Eudemian Ethics* 1248a27–9. Bechtle's anonymous commentator also lists all of the pre-Plotinian philosophers and interpreters who describe Plato's beyond being or substance formulation as transcendent, besides Aristotle and Speusippus: Brontinos, Alcinous, Celsus at Origen, Corpus Hermeticum, various Gnostic versions and Calcidius (p. 87n. 219).

15 For commentary on both sides of this issue, see Allen (1983, p. 193); Gerson (1993, pp. 568–9) (commenting on Plotinus); Murphy, 1951, p. 183; White, 1979, p. 180. One might also question why a "beyond being" Good is not nothing at all. I would respond that we need to make our interpretation of the Good also compatible with passages that claim that the Good is the brightest of beings (see the next note), and that claim that the Good is the source of the Forms. It would be nonsense to claim that Plato thinks that nothing causes the Forms and all else that exists.

16 Here is the "brightest thing that is" passage: "This instrument ['present in everyone's soul' at 518c5] cannot be turned around from that which is coming into being without turning the whole soul until it is able to study that which is and the brightest thing that is, namely, the one we call the good" (*Republic* VII 518c8–d1). See also 505a2, 508e2, 517b8, 534b9 for other references to where Good is a being.

17 Desjardins (2004, pp. 119, 229) and Reeve (2003, p. 43) note the passage with little additional comment; de Vogel (1970, pp. 185–6) argues that, for translation reasons, *Republic* VII 518d should be read that the Good does not belong to being; Brisson (2005, pp. 7–9) argues that Good is still a being, as does Carter (1975, p. 260). Rist (1964, pp. 53, 91) seems to be one of the few who note the "duality" of the Good's being and not being a Form.

18 I will address four additional interpretations of "beyond being": (1) Bréhier (1958, pp. 134–5) argues that the "necessarily transcendent" Good is a unit of measure beyond the things we measure. If the Good were some kind of unit of measure, first (à la Bowe), I fail to see why this should be as amazing as Glaucon states the Good to be; second, it is tough to see why Plato would not simply state here that the Form, One Itself, would not be the measure as opposed to the Good. It seems that the Good is the One, but the properties the One is said to have are as paradoxical as those said of the Good. (2) Inge (1929a, p. 85) puzzlingly says: "Plato, in his writings at least, had not clearly envisaged any principle prior to the Ideas, and supreme over them" and then adds: "It is difficult to say how much importance we should give to the isolated passage of the *Republic*, in which he speaks of the Good as 'beyond Being'" (p. 85n. 2). (Inge also states that the doctrine that the Good is beyond being goes back to,

and even precedes, Plato, at 1929b, p. 110.) In short, if the Good is the source of the Forms, the unhypothesized beginning, the last thing experienced once one exits the cave, I think it is safe to argue that it is in some sense "prior" to the Ideas, and "supreme over them." (3) Irwin (1992, pp. 272–3) posits that "beyond being" implies that the Good is constituted by an appropriate arrangement and combination of virtues, making the Good superior to any and all of them because "it cannot be understood, defined, or achieved without reference to them." However, how can any combination of virtues be the *source* of all of them? Also, on this model, would not Plato just say that, upon exiting the cave and after much habituation (and initially seeing reflections only at night), the prisoner would simply see the trees, stars and "things themselves" in a certain arrangement and thereby would know the Good? Instead, Plato says that until we see the Good—as if it were a separate "object"—we will not know or benefit from the other things. If Irwin is correct, in other words, Plato is misleading us about the Good, while in the same dialogue he avers that such a thing is deplorable. Lastly, (4) Reale (1997, p. 203) argues that "beyond being" is explained by the Unwritten Doctrines; there may be some truth in this view, given Aristotle's testimony that Plato discussed the Good in his unwritten doctrine; however, my project is not to assess Aristotle's understanding of Plato, but merely to examine, and argue for the consistency of, Plato and Plotinus' views, which I think can easily be done in the case of "beyond being."

19 Hitchcock, 1985, p. 90n. 56. Murphy (1951, p. 183) and Penner (2003, p. 221) make a similar argument. Penner also states that the beyond being claim is another way of expressing Plato's view that "the Form of the Good is the cause both of the knowledge and of the being of all the other Forms," which Penner interprets in pp. 218–20. Without going into Penner's views on the latter, I cite the Bowe Defense as an objection against his overall view. Cf. Doherty (1956, p. 448; he sums up Jaeger's view as being that the Good is "beyond essence … in its dignity and power" and is the "highest Being"); and Denyer (2007, p. 284) mentions that "the Good has the privileged position of being what accounts for the existence and intelligibility of Forms, much as the Sun has the privileged position of being what accounts for the growth and visibility of plants." However, he does not mention that the Good is beyond being or not a being, there, or anywhere else, in his otherwise excellent analysis of the Sun Simile and Divided Line Analogy.

20 Shorey (1895, pp. 36–7) says: "The Idea of Good, though the wellspring of knowledge and Being, is not Being, but something beyond and above it in dignity and power. The practical ethical outcome of all this, as Plato hints in the words [at 509a], is merely that goodness is more precious than any knowledge of intellectual faculty." Unlike Rawson though, Shorey limits his view of preciousness to the practical ethical outcome.

21 Rawson, 1996, p. 105. He continues: "The Good is more valuable than being for at least three reasons. First, it is more valuable than being because it is the cause of being (509ab). Second, all knowledge is of 'what is,' but is useless without knowledge of the Good (505ab). Third, the Good is 'beyond being' in its extremely valuable epistemic function: the Good, even more than being, is a cause of knowledge" (p. 105). Of course I agree that the Good is valuable, and even for these reasons, though I would add further ones, such as that the Good is what every soul desires, for instance. The interpretive problem is that Rawson does not do justice to the amazed tone of Glaucon in the context: namely, at *Republic* VI 509a (just before the key passage), where Glaucon says that Socrates is probably not referring to pleasure as being the Good (because it is the source of, and surpasses, knowledge and truth), Socrates says *euphēmei*, usually translated "Hush," but other alternatives are "Avoid all unlucky words" or "Keep a religious silence!" Clearly, the context shows that Plato is trying to convey that he is discussing something special, and not merely something that causes being, is not a being, and is more valuable than it.

22 I cannot resist one more reason why the Good's being beyond being and the source of Forms is odd: why would Goodness per se be *the* entity that should be the source of the Forms or the source of knowledge? The Plotinian, mysticism interpretation handles this kind of issue quite well in my view.

23 Luban, 1978, p. 162.

24 I assume that attributing a contradictory position to Plato such as this is not warranted, though, as I have shown, Plato certainly makes a small number of paradoxical claims. The difference between my extrapolation of Luban's interpretation and my claim that Plato's view is paradoxical is that it is my intent to show that, in certain cases, we must interpret Plato's view as paradoxical when the texts warrant it, such as that the Good is a being and is beyond being. Another problem I see with Luban's view would be that the Good causes evil, or just is evil, because matter is both evil and the source of evil, via humans' ignorance, but the Good only causes all that is right and beautiful in the Cave summary.

25 Reeve, 2003, p. 44. Lachterman (1989–90, pp. 156–7, 169n. 22) makes a similar argument, that the Good is what enables each and every one of the Forms to do the work for which it is suited by its own nature. I believe my replies to Reeve effectively deal with this objection as well.

26 Given the considerations against the interpretation of the Good as a rational order that makes Forms possible, as well as those against the interpretations that the Good may just be the Forms, I can be reasonably assured that Plato does not hold this view. Consequently, it must be the case that, either I can know some of the Forms before I know the Good or I know the Forms in

general once I know the Good. We should confirm this view in Plotinus, however, given the nature of this project, and this confirmation is relatively easy. For instance, Plotinus says that the One gives us substance, Intellect and everything at the level of Intellect, but is not these himself, at V.3.14.19; he also states that Intellect is not the Good at V.1.7.4–5 – if the Good just were the Forms, as Intellect just is the Forms, for Plotinus, we would not expect him to deny the identification of the Good and Intellect. See also VI.9.3.39–40 (since the One generates all things, it is not any one of them); III.8.10, VI.9.2, VI.7.18; cf. V.3.13.4. Thus, we can infer that Plotinus also does not subscribe to the view that knowledge of the Good or One just is knowledge of the Forms (due to their identity), but that perhaps one knows the Forms before or after knowing the Good or One.

27 The following commentators explicitly hold that the Good causes the Forms: Benitez (1995, p. 118); Findlay (1974, pp. 40, 281); Gerson (1994, p. 67); Kolb (1974, p. 138; the "One" causes the Forms); Lachterman (1989–90, p. 156); Mohr (2005, p. 256); Murphy (1951, p. 183); de Vogel (1970, p. 187; 1986, p. 74); cf. Hitchcock (1985, pp. 74–5; The Good qua Form of Oneness must be able to cause mathematics). Bussanich (1996, p. 50) points out that Plotinus claims that the other things that the One creates are like and are not like that One at V.2.2.24–9; it is interesting that in the Second Hypothesis of *Parmenides*, at 146a–b, Parmenides concludes that "it must be (a) the same with itself and (b) different from itself, and similarly both (c) different from and (d) the same with the others." For my interpretive sketch of the second section of the *Parmenides*, see the Appendix.

28 See also *Republic* X 597c1–5 and d1–3.

29 Compare *Letter* II 312d–13a, where Plato states that the First Principle (which I take to be equivalent to the Good as well) is the source of all that exists.

30 Adam, 1902, p. 391.

31 And cf. *Republic* X 596c, where Plato mentions a craftsman who could make all kinds of furniture including himself, among other things, keeping in mind the considerations above for taking 596a–e as referring ultimately to God, which I have posited is the Good.

32 Desjardins (2004, pp. 11, 106, 119, 229) argues that we need to use what Plato says about the Good in the *Philebus* and *Republic* in order to really understand what he had meant about its role in reason and knowledge (cf. Sayre 1987, p. 70). But he claims that it is "wholeness as such, of Unity-in-multiplicity" (p. 106), and that "The source of such 'measure,' the principle itself of Unity as Wholeness which thus maximizes being, Plato calls the Good (cf. *Phil* 66a6–8). As the source and condition of all being (being now recognized as power) this Good must itself be 'beyond being … and of surpassing power' (*Rep* VI, 509b8–10)"

(p. 229). It is my contention that the good mentioned at *Philebus* 65a—beauty, proportion, and truth, by which we can take hold of goodness if we cannot capture it in one form—is the human good, as opposed to the Form of the Good, although I do believe that the Form makes its appearance at *Philebus* 15a and perhaps also when he refers to the "absolute Good" that everyone desires at 67a. This is consistent with the *Republic* and other dialogues because, for example, in the *Republic*, as we have seen, the Good causes truth but is not truth. I make a distinction between the human good (which is the end for humans, and can be associated with, among other things, knowledge of the Good and the Forms, happiness, true pleasure, being just) and the Good (which is the metaphysical, epistemological, and ethical first principle).

33 Pistorius, 1952, pp. 23–4. Shorey (1895, p. 38) argues that we must assume that evil is a privation and that things exist only insofar as they are good, in order to hold that the Idea of Good is the cause of all existence. I agree with these claims as stated; however, I disagree with Shorey when he adds that these claims (evil as privation and things exist insofar as good) must be "read into Plato", since they will be shown in the sections of this book, "evil as privation", and it can be shown that matter is the source of badness and the furthest thing from the Good for Plato. Generally, I will also be showing that Plato and Plotinus do not essentially differ in their view of existence.

34 Robinson, 1953b, p. 111.

35 Reeve, 1988, p. 96.

36 Lachterman, 1989–90, p. 169n. 22; Sayre, 1987, p. 70.

37 Santas, 1985, p. 238–239.

38 For a hint, look back at all the replies that involved Bowe (2003, p. 19) and what I have called the Bowe Defense. On another note, I have two further quibbles. First, with Gadamer (1986, p. 27), who claims: "That Plato uses only the word *idea*, and never *eidos*, for the *agathon*, surely has something to do with that transcendence"; this is not true, as Plato uses *eidōn* with *agathou* (and bad, just, unjust and all the others) at *Republic* V 476a. Second, with Rawson (1996, p. 103), where he says: "*Republic* does not contain an explicit account of the Good. Though it is what Socrates most ardently *desires*, the good is beyond his *understanding* - and even his own beliefs about it are too difficult for the occasion." While admitting that Socrates is reluctant to discuss the Good—I argue that it is because of the ineffability of the mystical experience or vision that Socrates begs off his explanations of the Good—it is certainly *not* the case, as Rawson presumably realizes, given his use of these claims in his interpretations, that Plato did not say *anything* about the Good.

39 The following commentators seem to believe that Plato and Plotinus agree that the Good is beyond being: Blumenthal (1993, p. 3); Findlay (1974, p. 184); Fuller

(1938, p. 286); O'Meara (1993, p. 52; but Plotinus "underplays the fact that Plato refers to 'the Good' as a Form"); Reale (1997, p. 207); Rist (1964, pp. 53–4); Sells (1994, p. 6); de Vogel (1986, pp. 47, 86); Whitby (1909, p. 121). Gerson (1993, pp. 568–9) denies that "beyond being" implies that the One for Plotinus is not a being, but only that the One is neither limited nor complex, which may be parallel to Plato—if, as I argue below, the One of the *Parmenides*' First Hypothesis can be interpreted as being the Good of *Republic* VI and VII.

40 I will review passages where Plotinus says that the One or Good *is not* being and beyond being, which shows that both he and Plato made each of these paradoxical claims.

41 For more passages on how (or that) the Good or One is beyond being, see I.7.1.19–20, III.8.9, III.9.9, IV.4.16, V.1.10, V.2.1, V.3.17, V.4.1–2, V.5.5–6, V.5.11, V.8.1, VI.2.3, VI.2.17, VI.6.9, VI.8.12, VI.8.17, VI.8.19, VI.9.2–6, VI.9.11.

42 Mayhall (2004, pp. 1–2) states that Neo-Platonists believe that ultimate reality is the One, which is God and the highest being, with the Good as its character and nature. But Plotinus is much more careful about his phrasing—usually the Good or One is not a being, and usually "God" refers to Nous or Intellect and not the One or Good (as in Plato). Cf. Rist (1996, pp. 389–90). Rist (1964, pp. 54–5, 91–2, 110) argues that for Plato, the Good is a being and beyond being, but, for Plotinus, it is only beyond being; thus, unfortunately Rist fails to account for this.

43 For other passages that claim that the Good or One is a being, see V.3.11, V.4.1 and V.5.13.

44 I will briefly reply to other commentators on this crucial issue: (1) Annas (1981, p. 246) argues that Plotinus (qua one of the Neo-Platonists) has a complex metaphysical interpretation of "beyond being"; while it is true that Plotinus gives more details about why and how the Good is beyond being, this is not necessarily incompatible with Plato's view. (2) Anton (2000, p. 21) said Plotinus went beyond the reaches of classical ontology when he stated that the One is beyond being, transcending activity, mind and thought. However, we have seen Plato claim that the Good is beyond being (as well as a being, just as Plotinus says), and if the Forms are in the realm of Intellect or the intelligible region or Nous for Plato, as they are for Plotinus, then the Good, since it is the source of the Forms, would be beyond mind and thought as well. (3) Brisson (2005, p. 9) claims: "It must be admitted that nothing can be found in the *Dialogues* that explicitly takes up this idea, and that only a reading of the *Enneads* provides us a true metaphysics of the One-Good as situated absolutely beyond being." I find Brisson mistaken—Plotinus says both that the One is a being and beyond being, so I cannot state that Plotinus' One was simply absolutely beyond being (as Bussanich also does in 1988, p. 42) and ignore that Plato made similar statements about it, especially if

I am correct that the One is the Good for Plato too. (4) Cornford (1939, p. 132) objects: "beyond being" just means the reason that something exists is due to its goodness and the good is an end in itself with no final cause beyond it. However, this is not what Plato says, and nowhere else does Plato state that the reason Largeness exists, for example, is due to its goodness. Moreover, it does not make sense to think that goodness, as opposed to Being, would be the highest principle; after all, if something does not exist, then it cannot be either good or bad. Cornford continues on the same page to argue that, in the *Phaedo,* Socrates says that the good of the whole is the ultimate reason beyond the existence it explains; but this cannot be identified with that which has no existence of any kind. I agree that, because both Plato and Plotinus say that the Good is a being and is beyond being, we must interpret the "beyond being" in a careful way, but this does not imply that Plotinus misinterpreted Plato's view. (5) Harris (1976, pp. 4–5) argues that Plotinus' One "ignores" the being of Plato's Good and so is greater than Plato's Ultimate. However, we have seen that they both state that the Good is beyond being and a being, so this analysis is not accurate. (6) Murphy (1951, p. 182; cf. Rochel 1971, pp. 500–3) says that the Neo-Platonic reading, "That the good is 'beyond knowledge' and 'beyond being,' whatever such assertions might be thought to mean, have no place in the text." Contra Murphy, we have seen that they have. (7) Rawson (1996, p. 112n. 5) ponders: "On Plotinus' interpretation of "beyond being," this resonance with [*Republic* V] 478–9 becomes even stranger, for Plato would be claiming that the Good is *clearer* than what is, such that it *not be*." But, without satisfactorily accounting for the beyond being of Plato's Good (see my next sentence) or the fact that Plotinus *also* states that the Good is a being, Rawson is not addressing the issue fairly. Moreover, Rawson (1996, p. 104) argues that the Plotinus' "beyond being," "unknowable cause" interpretation of Plato's Good is not plausible because: (a) the terms of the Sun Simile analogy do not *quite* warrant the inference that the Good has no share in being; (b) Plato says that the Good has being elsewhere in the *Republic*; (c) Plato says that what is, is completely knowable, which must include the Good. Re: (a): Rawson is not accounting for the phrase that Plato uses of the Good immediately before he states that it is beyond being, namely that the Good is not being. Re: (b): My interpretation is that both Plato and Plotinus claim that the Good and One are somehow beings and not beings, so pointing out that Plato says the Good is a being does not damage my interpretation or show that Plotinus necessarily has a different view of the Good than Plato. Re: (c): Similarly to (b), my interpretation is that both philosophers state or imply that the Good is both somehow knowable and unknowable, so Rawson's charge does not affect my interpretation. (8) Rist (1964, p. 74) "For Plato, the Forms are the exemplars of limit and symmetry, and symmetry is almost equivalent to Beauty. Not so for Plotinus. His One is [a non-Idea]; symmetry is irrelevant to it and thus, in a sense, irrelevant to Beauty as well." I assent to Rist's statement about Plato, but not as it might concern the Good; Plato states that the Good, unlike the other Forms, is not a being but beyond being (and the source of the Forms, knowledge and other things), so we must account for this and not ignore it. Lastly, (9) Strong (1895, pp. 107–8) believes that Plotinus is basing his view that the One is beyond being on only one passage and a "bare suggestion" in Plato's thought. Again I point out that Plotinus said the One is a being in places, and hold to the view that Plato did indeed claim that the Good is "*not* a being, but beyond being" so we must account for this passage.

45 Allen, 1983, p. 194.

46 For Plato, see *Sophist* 257d7–8b5 with 260b7–8, where Plato seems to explain at once why the not-beautiful (and the not-just and not-tall) is one thing that exists, while also not committing himself to there being a Form of Ugly Itself or the others. For Plotinus, see V.9.10.18–20, I.8.1.9–12, I.8.10, V.9.14, VI.1.9–10, VI.3.11, 19; VI.7.9. I grant that each philosopher actually gives us some textual evidence for the view that bad Forms do actually exist. But, even if I am wrong that they do not believe in bad Forms, this fact only goes to show that they seem to say the same kinds of things about each option.

47 Ibid, p. 270.

48 A. H. Armstrong, 1947, p. 182. See also his three related charges: In 1967b, p. 236, A. H. Armstrong argues that Plotinus' originality lay in the One or Good's transcending Intellect, which (contra Armstrong) seems to be implied by Plato at *Republic* VI 509b. In 1967b, p. 237, A. H. Armstrong argues that Plotinus based his "beyond being" view on a "curious" Neo-Pythagorean exegesis of the *Parmenides*. Lastly, in 1974, pp. 192–3, A. H. Armstrong argues that Plotinus has a philosophical duty to argue for the One's transcendence because of his having the ultimate experience (as I have phrased the vision of the One). There should be little reason why we cannot attribute the same view to Plato.

49 See *Republic* VI 509b and 508d–9a.

50 Inge, 1929b, pp. 126–7; cf. pp. 110–11.

51 Commentators, without exception, hold that Plotinus believes that the Good causes the Forms to exist, such as Gerson (1994, pp. 31–2); Mayhall (2004, pp. 1–2); O'Meara (1993, p. 52); de Vogel (1986, p. 47; 1953, pp. 52–3). Phillips (1997, pp. 185–7) states that Plotinus' successors have a different view of creation: "In two important respects, however, Plotinus' classification diverges significantly from the Middle Platonic and later Neoplatonic exegeses. First of all, in II.4.5, he – and here he was joined by Porphyry alone among later Platonists – made the eternal intelligibles members of the class of beings that are created… . if only in a qualified sense" (1997, p. 187). Since Plato states that the eternal Forms are

caused (and because Plotinus too believes that the Forms are eternal), I believe Plotinus' reading is correct here. Somehow they both believe that the Forms' creation is not in time. Corrigan (2005, p. 187) reminds us that Plotinus himself states that "you will be amazed" best characterizes the One's production. Lastly, few commentators actually state that Plato and Plotinus seem to agree that the Good causes the Forms: cf. O'Meara (1993, p. 52) and de Vogel (1953, pp. 52–3), though I am sure that there must be others. For example, Hardie (1936, p. 119) states that the Neo-Platonists probably interpret Plato correctly that the Good is the source of Nous or Intellect.

52 For further passages that claim that the Good or One is the cause or source of Being, see I.7.1, III.8.9–10, 13; V.1.5–6, 8, 11; V.2.1, V.3.10, 17; V.5.6, 9–13; VI.8.14, 18–20; VI.9.3, 6; VI.9.3. Cf. III.9.9, V.6.4, V.9.2, VI.7.42, VI.8.15.

53 I will briefly consider several additional criticisms here: (1) Anton (2010, p. 13) states that the place of honor that Plato placed on Beauty in the *Symposium,* or being in the Divided Line Analogy of the *Republic,* Plotinus gave to the One, and outshone Plato's Good by making it beyond being, and the sole demiurgic power and progenitor of everything except evil. But we see that Plato can be interpreted as holding that the Good is not a being but beyond being, as well as that it is the source of good and not of evil. (2) A. H. Armstrong (1945, pp. 139–40; 1967b, p. 236) makes out a difference between Plato and Plotinus, that not only does the One cause Nous and all else "but It sheds upon them an extra grace or glory other than the beauty of their proper natures … a most un-Platonic conception." This shedding of grace or glory is not necessarily un-Platonic because Plato and Plotinus agree that the intelligible world is very beautiful and worthy of reverential admiration; moreover, Plato did not deny that the Good sheds honor on the intelligible region, so we cannot conclude that he would disagree with Plotinus' statement. (3) Bréhier (1958, p. 136) argues that Plotinus got his view that "it is through the One that all beings exist" from the Stoics and not from Plato; however, Plato says that the Good not only causes the Forms, but everything else (other than evil things) in the Cave Allegory, so this can be seen as a Platonic doctrine before becoming a Stoic doctrine. Bréhier (1958, p. 159) also says that Plotinian (but not Platonic) transcendence implies immanence—"absorption of the lower reality in the higher"—so that there can be "real continuity in the spiritual realities;" however, there is continuity in Plato's intelligible realm, as we shall see throughout this chapter. Moreover, the Good's light (in the Cave Allegory) shines into the cave and the Good causes everything either directly or indirectly. It is therefore not a stretch to say that in Plato's view the lower realities have to be connected in some way to the Good, especially human souls, if knowledge or a vision of the Good is possible. (4) Gadamer (1986, pp. 28–9) says Plotinus takes a new step when he calls the One

beyond all thinking, and when he takes all being and thinking as a pointer into transcendence. But Plato refers to knowledge of the Good as a vision, and the way in which he may be implying that knowledge of the Good is not possible, even though he has many passages to the contrary. If something is beyond being in Plato's view, it stands to reason that it would not be thinkable either. So this point relies on one's reading of "beyond being." (5) Lachterman (1989–90, p. 140) says that reading the *Republic* metaphysically—that the Good is the source of being, while the ethical teachings there play a propaedeutic role for the vision of the Good that is beyond being—compromises the integrity of the dialogue. But there is nothing that says that all of this is correct (in the sense that one cannot be evil and still have a chance at knowing or seeing the Good, in Plato's view), *and,* that once one experiences the Good, one then knows what right and wrong are; so Lachterman is creating a false dilemma in my view. (6) Rist (1964, p. 71) claims that Plotinus anthropomorphizes Plato's Good by combining "the functions of the Form of the Good with those of the Platonic Gods, who, as we suggested at the beginning, are little more than perfect Platonic philosophers." Both Plato and Plotinus hold that the Good creates the Forms, that God is in general referred to as Intellect or Nous, which produces in some way the World-Soul, of which individual souls are a part, and that body is prior to soul. One might counter that, since the One produces everything, this makes Nous and Soul instruments of the One. However, in Plato's view the Good produces the Forms (and by implication Nous); Plato also states that the Good is the cause of everything; and the source of Soul is Nous. Thus, assuming Nous and Soul are instruments of the One for Plotinus, we can reasonably say that Nous and Soul are instruments of the Good for Plato. Lastly, they are consistent in their assigning of care of the physical realm to gods, in referring to stars as gods and in claiming that the universe is a perceptible god. For further criticisms, see Bréhier (1958, p. 133); Harris (1976, p. 8); Inge (1929b, pp. 126–7); Pistorius (1952, p. 29); Stace (1967, p. 374); A. E. Taylor (1963, pp. 12–13); Zeller (1931, p. 290).

54 Bechtle, 1999, p. 88.

55 Louth, 1981, p. 38.

56 Lynch, 1959, p. 236.

57 Mohr, 2005, p. 256.

58 Indeed, A. H. Armstrong (194, p. 182) actually argues that it is Plato's Good and not Plotinus' One that is all-inclusive and contains the other Forms, so apparently commentators themselves are not clear on exactly what the Good does or does not contain.

59 Rist, 1964, p. 67.

60 Gerson (1994, p. 32) states that Plotinus only claims that the One (or Good) causes itself, but not its own existence, which stays true to Plotinus' reluctance

to refer to the Good as a being, or substance in general, but as the latter's source. Bussanich (1996, p. 57) and Rist (1973, p. 84) also note this view of Plotinus.

61 See also VI.8.14.41, VI.8.7.53–54, VI.8.16.29. Gerson (1994, p. 32) noted these references.

62 Let us briefly consider four contrary views: (1) Hadot (1993, p. 59) argues that the Good is ultimately Love, for Plotinus; admittedly, Plotinus does claim that the One is love at VI.8.15.1–2, but Plotinus also states that Love is the child of Resource and Need, is midway between ignorance and wisdom, and can either be an irrational desire or a manifestation of the desire for the Good (all of which Plato holds, incidentally), so Hadot's view is in need of more explanation. (2) Merlan (1967, p. 353) charges that Plato only hints at the idea that the One or Good is the highest principle. Since, however, Plato is clear that only the Good fulfills this role, as Merlan must admit, we interpreters are bound to account for what Plato says in these passages. (3) Rist (1967a, pp. 64–5) notes the striking absence in the *Enneads* of the claim that the One is not Beauty and the ultimate experience or vision is of Beauty, since Plato's *Symposium* has Beauty as the end of the mystic's quest. However, one can handle this objection by arguing that Plato's account of the experience of Beauty in the *Symposium* is the coming to know or see Beauty, which is important but not more so than the experience of the Good. Both Plato and Plotinus have the same view that the Good or One resembles, but is not identical to, Beauty. Lastly, (4) Robin (1928, pp. 370–2) argues: "Plato's One was certainly the summit of a hierarchy, but it was so as being measure and limit; the One of Plotinus is the absence of limit, infinity." However, there is a difference in my view of Plato's One Itself, the Form, and Plato's One, the subject of the First Hypothesis of the *Parmenides*; briefly, the One Itself would be a measure and limit, but the One of the *Parmenides* is not limited. Thus Robin's charge is not necessarily well founded.

63 A. H. Armstrong, 1947, pp. 181–2; cf. Inge (1929b, p. 112), who says that the One must be independent of the Forms.

64 Hampton, 1990, p. 93. Gadamer (1986, p. 31) makes a similar argument; Hardie (1936, p. 129) argues that the Plotinian One is not in Plato's *Republic*.

65 See section 1.5.9 below for passages and analysis.

66 Rist, 1964, p. 58.

67 Compare what Socrates says in *Republic* X and the *Philebus*: At *Republic* X 596c5–9, Socrates claims that there is a craftsman who creates "not only all kinds of furniture, but all plants that grow from the earth, all animals (including himself), the earth itself, the heavens, the gods, all the things in the heavens and in Hades beneath the earth," continuing that God creates the Form of Bed—the nature of the truly real bed (597c–d; see also 597b), which is parallel with what he says about the Good's producing the Forms in *Republic* VI (Sun Simile) and

VII (Cave Allegory). At *Philebus* 30c2–7, Socrates relates a "certain cause, of no small significance." Admittedly he claims there that wisdom and reason rule the universe, but this is compatible with the view that the Good causes reason and makes knowledge possible. Cf. *Philebus* 30d.

68 *Republic* VII 517a–c.

69 I agree with Benitez (1995, p. 118), who reminds me that the Sun Simile (508b and 509b) tells us that the Good begets the sun, which begets the visible things; and Hitchcock (1985, p. 74–5) adds that the Good (qua Form of Oneness) must be able to cause mathematics as well.

70 Gerson, 1994, p. 68; see also p. 19.

71 For instance, Beauty causes beautiful things to be beautiful (*Phaedo* 100c4–8, d4–9).

72 Here, I am leaving aside evil or bad things.

73 I agree with Gerson (1994, pp. 28, 31–2).

74 For further passages that state that the Good is a cause, see V.5.13, VI.8.14 and VI.9.3.

75 See Leftow (1990, pp. 585, 590), who holds that both philosophers have the same view, but that they wrongly influenced Christian interpreters thereafter.

76 Gerson, 1994, p. 28.

77 Rist, 1996, p. 391.

78 Anton, 2010, p. 13.

79 Zeller, 1931, p. 290.

80 If every Form causes things of that kind to be that kind—Beauty Itself causes beautiful things to be beautiful—then, since Plato states in many places that the Good is a Form, it causes good things to be good. Cf. *Gorgias* 506c–e.

81 Menn (1995, p. 55) rightly associates the claim that the Good is the source of reason with the Sun Simile as well, as follows: "And as Plato himself pointed out in *Republic* VI, the analogy with vision suggests that something besides the *noêta* may be a cause of intellectual perception: 'The sense of seeing and the power of being seen are yoked together' by light, and by some source of light, or no act of seeing results (*Republic* 507e6–508a2). The sun is the 'cause' of sight (508b9), and sunlight 'makes' (*poiei*, 508a5) sight see and the visibles be seen: if the Good is the analogue of the sun for intellectual perception, then the Good must be a cause of *noêsis*, and it seems that it must be an efficient cause."

82 Majumdar, 2007b, p. 155.

83 Ibid., p. 156.

84 Anton, 2010, p. 13.

85 O'Brien, 1971, pp. 144–5.

86 Here, I agree with Findlay (1975, p. 671; 1978, p. 126). I also agree with Shorey that the Good is the answer to minor dialogues' suggestions needful of the

concept of goodness (1895, p. 48), and that mathematics is part of the best training to enable one to apprehend "higher ethical abstractions" (1895, p. 62); but I disagree with Shorey that these statements somehow negate our thesis that the Good is beyond being and capable of being the object of the ultimate experience a human can have. I also note that Rawson (1996, p. 105) claims: "Generally in Plato's work, and emphatically in *Republic*, metaphysics serves epistemology, and epistemology serves ethics," without taking a stand; it seems that, while ethics is the central concern of the *Republic*, the Good is, equally, the supreme metaphysical, epistemological and ethical entity for Plato. One could argue, for instance, that Platonic ethics serve metaphysics, in the sense that, depending on what exists, one must act accordingly, but I need not resolve this issue here.

87 Other objections include Findlay (1974, p. 191), who argues that ethical concerns are a matter for *pistis* (conviction), the second lowest cognitive faculty of the Divided Line, for Plato. I disagree, because virtues are Forms for Plato, and dialectic works in and through Forms (Ideas) until one arrives at the Good (Divided Line), and one must be a good person in order to see the Good (Sun Simile). Gerson (1989, p. 87) conjectures: "It seems implausible, even assuming the identity of the virtues, that there could be one type of knowledge that would, for example, amount to both temperate and just behavior." I contend that the Good gives one the kind of knowledge that allows one to know what Temperance, Justice and all other virtues are, since being virtuous is good, as well as to act wisely in private and public, as Plato's Cave summary suggests. Luban (1978, p. 162) surmises: "The doctrine of the Good is best understood as an ontological, not a moral or axiological doctrine." However, Luban is ignoring the Cave summary, and that every soul desires and pursues the Good. Santas (1985, pp. 223–4) argues that Plato has two theories of good, but I would briefly argue that *Republic* VI and VII are pretty clear that every good (including Forms of Justice, Temperance, and the rest) come from the Good, and that in order to get any benefit from *any* good (including knowledge of Justice—505a–b), one must know the Good.

88 Benitez, 1995, p. 126; cf. pp. 116–17.

89 Shorey, 1895, p. 70; cf. 1895, pp. 74, 79 and 1903a, p. 17. He seems to think that, if the Good of the *Republic* is the answer to the questions concerning goodness in the "minor ethical dialogues," that this somehow entails that the Good is not a new ontological principle, and that the talk of the Good's being beyond being, knowledge, and truth are mere "mythical and poetical" aspects thereof. I respectfully disagree and hold instead that all of these passages must not be dismissed so easily.

90 Shorey, 1903b, p. 7n. 1.

91 Voegelin, 2000, p. 166.

92 I grant ineffability of the ultimate experience of the Good or One, and address this elsewhere in an unpublished portion of an earlier version of this manuscript.

93 I agree with Gerson (1994, p. 186), who notes that Plotinus does not think that metaphysics is irrelevant to ethics: "As Plotinus puts it, 'everything depends on the One.'" I also agree with Rist (1964, p. 183) when he says: "This is precisely the teaching we find in *Enn.* 6.9.11, where Plotinus comes nearest to describing the nature of mystical experience. In line 16 he writes as follows… . Thus the highest state leaves virtue behind, for if the Divine Mind is virtue, the One is something higher." The One or Good is the source of ethical goodness for both philosophers, I believe, but I hasten to add that, for *both* philosophers, the Good is beyond virtue, just as it is beyond being and time. And yet if one knows the Good, one is thereby virtuous. And so Rist's (1964, p. 184) statement applies equally to Plato: "For Plotinus, both virtue and knowledge are surpassed in the mystic union." It is worthy of note, in general, that, to my knowledge, no English commentator seemed to explicitly put forth that Plotinus and Plato have the same view of the Good's being the source of ethical goodness in the same way.

94 See also I.2.1.46–50; cf. I.2.4.

95 Ciapolo, 1997, p. 489.

96 See the following passages: (1) *Metaphysics* I 988a8–11, where Aristotle says: "Plato, then, declared himself thus on the points in question; it is evident from what has been said that he has used only two causes, that of the essence and the material cause (for the Forms are the cause of the essence of all other things, and *the One is the cause of the essence of the Forms*)" (my emphasis) which is parallel to what Plato claims of the Good; (2) *Eudemian Ethics* 1218a20–1, 25: "unity is the good itself;" (3) Aristoxenus, *Elements of Harmony*, II, 30–1, in Barnes, 1984, p. 2397; (4) *Dialogues*, in Barnes, 1984, p. 2398; (5) Simplicius, *Commentarius in Physica* 151.6–11 (F 28 R3 of the *Dialogues*), in Barnes, 1984, p. 2398; (6) Simplicius, *Commentarius in Physica*, 453.25–30 (F 28 R3 of the *Dialogues*), in Barnes, 1984, p. 2398. Also see Allen (1983, p. 192); Bussanich (1996, p. 52); Gaiser (1980, p. 6); Hardie (1936, pp. 116–7), who mention these arguments.

97 Many commentators take this section seriously and in a positive way: Cornford (1939, pp. vii, ix); Findlay (1978, p. 140); Hermann (2010, pp. vii–x); McEvilley (2002); Ryle (1939a, p. 129); Schofield (1977, p. 140); Scolnicov (2003); Scoon (1942, p. 124); A. E. Taylor (1896, p. 326). Some focus on the character Parmenides saying that it is a gymnastic exercise and a game: Peck (1953, p. 150: "verbal gymnastics" and "game") and A. E. Taylor (1956, p. 360; but see 1896, p. 326). Others have noted that there are many fallacies in the second section: Dodds (1928, p. 134); Findlay (1978, p. 140). McCabe (1994) unfolds her view as follows: "Both conclusions [of the First and Second Hypotheses] are absurd", and the First Hypothesis is "self-refuting" because it states that we cannot even

mention the hypothesis itself (p. 102); the First Hypothesis commits "a clear fallacy of equivocation", and she posits that perhaps Plato does not understand "is" (p. 109) or rather "properties and their possessors" (p. 110); McCabe concludes in part that "This is not a ragbag of philosophical puzzles (as some have supposed), but a connected whole", and she seeks "a single sequence of argument, where one hypothesis is investigated according to two exclusive and exhaustive interpretations, to an aporematic end" (p. 126). I agree with McCabe that we should strive to interpret the hypotheses of the *Parmenides*' second section with a single, unified, view, but not that we must accept an "aporematic (sic) end" of the arguments; More (1916, p. 137: "irrelevant truths"); Robinson (1942b, p. 161: "invalid"; pp. 162, 166–8, 186: "fallacious"); Schofield (1977, p. 151: "set[s] puzzles;" p. 152: "blatantly fallacious" and contains "puzzles"). I am inclined to reject Robinson's (1942b, p. 186) view that Plato "knew there was something wrong; but he could not say what it was with any sureness and abstractness," because I believe that each "One" of the hypotheses has a different subject or subjects—see the Appendix for my sketch thereof, though I yield for now to the criticisms of Brumbaugh (1961, pp. 8–9), Runciman (1959, p. 104) and A. E. Taylor (1934, pp. 156–7) that Neo-Platonists fail to explain recalcitrant details of the whole second section. I can still argue that the First Hypothesis One seems to be best interpreted as the Good until the other subjects are worked out. Yet others claim the second section is absurd: Allen (1983, p. 189); Robinson (1942b, p. 159), "seems bewildering and absurd;" Peck (1954, p. 45), is ludicrous; Robinson (1942b, p. 164), is ambiguous and confusing, is a parody of Parmenides and Zeno; Cherniss (1932, pp. 122, 134, 138), contains no (in) direct statement of doctrine or method; Robinson (1942a, pp. 51, 70), contains confusions the *Sophist* clears up; Ryle (1939b, p. 316), contains Plato's concern for the idea of antinomy itself and conceptual exploration; Schofield (1977, p. 158), is a bewildering metaphysical jest we should not minutely examine; A. E. Taylor (1956, p. 361), is not trying to eradicate the "deeply imbedded" Idea of the Good there; More (1916, p. 138), and is a tool box required for construction of cosmology; Brisson (2002, p. 18). Robinson (1942a, p. 70) fails to prove his case: "Plato is not directly stating a doctrine in the second part of the *Parmenides*. This follows both from his not being a skeptic and from the symmetry of the eight hypotheses and from their indiscriminateness." First, the fact that Plato is not a skeptic seems to imply that he *has* some kind of positive doctrine that he's putting forth. Second, the symmetry of the hypotheses might be due to Plato's aiming the inquiry at different "Ones"—the One or Good, Intellect or Forms, All-Soul and particulars. Moreover, Robinson owes an argument as to why there are eight and not nine hypotheses, which might throw off the supposed symmetry. Third, the indiscriminateness (also noted by Peck [1953, p. 149]) disappears, perhaps along with the fallacies, if each One has a different subject, as I have sketched in the Appendix. Cf. Meinwald (1991, pp. 24–5; cf. p. 78) who argues against different subjects because they reject successive Hypotheses, and Sayre (1983, p. 45), who believes the First and Second Hypotheses have different subjects. It is admittedly difficult to figure out exactly what Plato is saying in the second section, but we should not write off the idea that it contains doctrine, as I hope my argument here will show. One last important interpretive argument about the second section is whether to take it metaphysically or logically, as Cornford (1939, p. v) mentions. A. E. Taylor (1896, p. 300) argued for the metaphysical interpretation and claimed that a majority of interpreters in his day concurred with his view. A good case can be made for Taylor's being right: if we take the second section logically, and we agree with the majority of commentators listed here that it is full of fallacies, then we must interpret Plato as being irrational, deliberately misleading, or ignorant of his writing garbage for his readers. These interpretive options seem highly unlikely, given his first section's criticisms of the Forms, and his argument right before the *Parmenides*' second section that we can answer these kinds of criticisms if we thoroughly examine if something is and if it is not. So our best option is to choose the metaphysical school. See also Morrow et al. (1987, p. xxvii).

98 The following commentators believe that the One is the Good in general throughout Plato's dialogues, but are not committed to my view that the One of the *Parmenides*' First Hypothesis is the Good: Desjardins (2004, pp. 111, 228–9); Findlay (1978, p. 44); Gaiser (1980, p. 12); Hitchcock (1985, p. 90n. 56); Laguna (1934, p. 466); Rist (1962a, p. 13; "in Plato's latest period"). Cf. Reale's (1997, pp. 204, 206–7) view that the Good is not defined as the One in the *Republic,* but it is strongly hinted at, even though Reale does not mention the Good at 233–5 while discussing the second section. Bowe (2003, p. 19) ingeniously argues for "an appreciation of the movement of the text, one which brings us from the Festival of Bendis (Athenian: Artemis, symbol of duality) and *Republic* I to Apollo (symbol of unity) in *Republic* VI," which is precisely where Plato introduces the Good as a supreme entity. Also see Findlay (1976, p. 30), who believes that Beauty of *Symposium* 211a–b is Unity Itself.

Findlay (1974, p. 370), McEvilley (2002, p. 161; I am not clear on his take on the Second Hypothesis, however, on pp. 159 and 568) and Organ (1991, pp. 9–22) believe both that the One is the Good and that my current thesis is correct. Findlay brings in Plotinus as well: "It will be plain that almost everything that Plotinus says of the First Hypostasis simply dots the *i*'s and crosses the *t*'s of what Plato said of the Good or One in *Republic,* VI and in the First Hypothesis of the *Parmenides*" (1974, p. 370). Rist (1962a, pp. 13–14; 1964, p. 52) and de Vogel (1970, p. 187) overtly state that the subject of the First Hypothesis is not the Good. A good number believe that the subject of the First Hypothesis is an abstract or absolute One that is only one: Chen (1944, p. 105); Lynch (1959, p. 248); Walker (1938, p. 498). These commentators do not satisfactorily account for the fact that Plato also says in the First Hypothesis that the one is not even one. Cherniss (1932, p. 126) and Rochel (1971, p. 503) hold that this One is nothing (cf. Peck 1953, p. 150). Lastly, Runciman (1959, p. 103) takes Plato's statement at *Republic* VII 524d as saying that "the study of [*to hev*] will guide the soul to the contemplation of true being," as part of his argument that the One in the second section does not refer to Plato's Good due to the lack of this kind of guidance.

99 See Silverman (2002, pp. 116–17), who claims that the First Hypothesis is of the Parmenidean One, but the Second Hypothesis is of the Platonic One. I question this interpretation, since the character Parmenides remains speaking, and does not indicate, as he moves from "one" to "one" and from whether or how they exist, that he is referring to someone else's "one." As I have said, I do not have the space (and it is not necessary) to defend my interpretation of the second section of the *Parmenides*, but I do believe (with the Neo-Platonists) that the Second Hypothesis does refer to Nous and/or the Forms.

100 My argument will be implicitly arguing against the following commentators, since they believe that the subject(s) of (at least) the First Hypothesis is or are the Forms: Curd (1989, pp. 347–8); Meinwald (1991, p. 176n. 26: referring to another of her works, "I suggest that the One stands in for all the Forms"); Mohr (2005, p. 72); Ryle (1939a, p. 142; cf. pp. 311–12); J. Whittaker (1968, pp. 136–7). Tigerstedt (1977, p. 58) criticizes Hoffman for misinterpreting Plato by equating the Good of the *Republic* with the One in the *Parmenides* and the Demiurge; my view is that the first two are interpretively linked, but the Demiurge is best interpreted as Nous or God. Also, Brumbaugh (1961, p. 211) points out that Plato rejects the First Hypothesis and considers alternative axioms; I want to note that this point is not limited to the First Hypothesis – the rejections continue until the conclusion, and are equally a problem for my interpretation as well as the aforementioned, who believe that one or more of the Hypotheses refer to Forms. My tentative solution is to take the different Ones as applying to different subjects, which explains why Plato would start over, to consider another kind of One.

101 Just considering the *Republic*, see *Republic* V 476a and VI 507b.

102 Certainly Plato is committed to there being a Form of Unity, Oneness, or One Itself: See, for instance, *Phaedo* 101b–c, *Republic* VII 524d–5a, 525d–6b and *Parmenides* 129c–e and 130b.

103 See *Cratylus* 440b–c, *Republic* VI 484b, 485a–b, 500b–c, X 611e–12a, *Timaeus* 27d–8b, 29a–b, 37c–8e, and 50c.

104 De Vogel (1959, p. 39) claims that Plotinus has the best interpretation of unlimited in Plato's philosophy.

105 A. H. Armstrong (1984b, p. 187) reminds us that this quotation comes from Plato's *Parmenides* 139b3.

106 See Bussanich (1996, p. 57; the Plotinian Good is infinite) and Gerson (1994, p. 18; the One is infinite).

107 Note the Platonic parallels to the First Hypothesis especially in VI.7.32.15–16 and VI.9.6.7–12; see also II.4.15, V.5.6 and VI.4.11.

108 The characteristic of no shape was argued in point 3 on p. 28 to be true about Forms in general as well as the Form of the Good, implying that this characteristic did not uniquely pick out the Form of the Good as the entity to which Plato must have been referring.

109 A. H. Armstrong argues that there is no clear evidence that Plato thought the Good was unlimited, so the Plotinian One is not the same as the Platonic One (1954 and 1955, pp. 47–8); my reply is that the First Hypothesis One is said to be unlimited. Armstrong also claims: "A being for Plotinus is always limited by form or essence. An absolutely formless being is impossible, and perfect or absolute being is the unified whole of all forms which is the divine Intellect: therefore that which is beyond the limitation of form is beyond being" (1967b, p. 237), implying that this is not Plato's view, but it is so in my view. And Robin (1928, p. 371) argues: "Plato's One was certainly the summit of a hierarchy, but it was so as being measure and limit; the One of Plotinus is the absence of limit, infinity"; however, Robin is not acknowledging the First Hypothesis One, and I have pointed out that this One cannot be the Form of Oneness, which may be a limit, just as any being is a limit.

110 A. H. Armstrong, 1954 and 1955, pp. 50–1; cf. p. 53.

111 See Sleeman et al. (1980, p. 118).

112 Rist (1962a, p. 13) appears to agree with these (and the other attributes that were denied of the One) that to this One "no predicates can be given;" cf. Rist (1962a), where he takes issue with Runcimann for supposing that the One in the second section is the "Platonic Form of Unity" (p. 1).

113 For references where Plato posits the existence of Sameness or Likeness, see, for example, *Euthydemus* 301b–c, *Parmenides* 129a–e, 130b, 131a, *Theaetetus* 186a, *Timaeus* 35a–b, *Sophist* 254d–5e, 256b–c, 258e–9b.

114 See also *Phaedo* 78d, *Symposium* 211b, *Cratylus* 439e, *Republic* V 479a, 479e and VI 484b; cf. *Phaedo* 79a, 79d–e and 80b.

115 The following commentators believe that the First Hypothesis One is One (that is, like itself) and/or that the Good is Unity Itself, which I take to be denied here in the First Hypothesis: Chen (1944, p. 105); Desjardins (2004, pp. 111, 228–9); Findlay (1975, p. 674); Hitchcock (1985, pp. 74–5, 80); cf. Lynch (1959, p. 248). If

I understand Meinwald's (1991, p. 176n. 26) position, she incorrectly believes that the subject of the First Hypothesis is the Forms.

116 I agree with Bowe (2003, p. 15) that Plotinus' One and Plato's Good are not the Form of Unity, with Inge (1929b, p. 112), that Plotinus' One is independent of the Forms, and with Katz (1950b, p. 21) and Rochel (1971, pp. 500–1, 503), that the One is not one, though they do not agree with my interpretation overall. Cf. A. H. Armstrong (1940, p. 15).

117 As the eye must be sunlike to see the sun, the soul must be goodlike to see the Good.

118 That Plato believes that a good person is unified is also generally implied by what he says throughout the *Republic* concerning justice and the just person, as well as that the analogous just city's being unified makes it great, while divisions incline it toward evil (see *Republic* V 462a9–b2 and IV 423c–d; cf. VIII 551d).

119 Cf. Gerson (1993, p. 571), who states that the Plotinian One is simply and solely the cause of Oneness, which seems to ignore both this passage and the claim that the One is also the cause of being. In addition, I disagree with Hampton (1990, p. 87), who argues that the Good at *Philebus* 20d is the ultimate One, but is unlike the Neo-Platonic One, which "is an absolute simple, the Platonic One is a unity of interrelated parts"; for the First Hypothesis One is not the Form Oneness, so Plato's philosophy does mention an absolutely simple One.

120 Allen (1983, pp. 192–213) draws attention to the Plotinian paradox of being able to say of the One that it is and is not one (is and is not good, God, and being), though he is not sympathetic to my view of Plato.

121 Pater (1893, p. 24) says that others after Plato have quixotically gone after the One, the Absolute, which is, after all, "zero, and a mere algebraic symbol for nothingness." It is not clear that the First Hypothesis One is nothing, though Pater is not alone in his assessment.

122 For relevant favorable commentator passages, see A. H. Armstrong (1940, p. 15); Hardie (1936, p. 119); Inge (1929b, p. 112); cf. Dodds (1928, p. 134). For commentators with whom I disagree on this issue, and have not mentioned elsewhere on this issue, see: Allen (1983, p. 192), Speusippus and not Plato is the first to have the "beyond being" interpretation of the One; cf. Bechtle (1999, pp. 75–6) and More (1923, pp. 218–19).

123 For some other passages that the One is eternal, or beyond time, see II.4.15, III.7.12 and VI.9.9.

124 Note that, yet again, this shows that the Form Oneness cannot be referred to here, because Forms in general are said to be what we are really referring to when we deal with participations of Forms; for example, when we say we have one dollar, the "one" refers to the Idea One, but the one dollar I hold in my hand qua one merely imitates what oneness really is.

125 In fact, I take this to be one of Plato's arguments that the Forms must exist—if we cannot stably refer to anything, then language is meaningless; but since language is not meaningless, we must be able to refer to things that really are; Forms are things that really are; therefore, Forms exist. This kind of argument appears at *Parmenides* 134e7–5c6 and is alluded to in *Theaetetus* 152d–e, 157a–c.

126 A brief review of some of the general ineffable claims may be in order. First, Plato has Socrates say that he cannot quite tell Glaucon what the Good is (*Republic* VI 506b–507a· 509c; VII 517b, 533a) and that it is only his opinion that the Good is the Source of all things right and beautiful in his Cave summary (*Republic* VII 517c). Second, Plato says: "Now to find the maker and father of this universe [*to pan*] is hard enough, and even if I succeeded, to declare him to everyone is impossible" (*Timaeus* 28c3–5). If the universe's father or maker—that is, the Demiurge according to Timaeus—cannot be declared, then one can only imagine what can be said (or rather *not* said) about a "beyond being." Third, Plato via Timaeus says: "So let me now proceed with my treatment in the following way: for the present I cannot state 'the principle' or 'principles' of all things, or however else I think about them, for the simple reason that it is difficult to show clearly what my view is if I follow my present manner of exposition. Please do not expect me to do so then. I couldn't convince even myself that I could be right to commit myself to undertaking a task of such a magnitude. I shall keep to what I stated at the beginning, the virtue of likely accounts, and so shall try right from the start to say about things, both individually and collectively, what is no less likely than any – more likely, in fact, than what I have said before" (*Timaeus* 48c2–d4). Lastly, Plato avers that the cause of all the trouble [that needs to be expelled from the seeker of the first principle(s) or she will never find the truth] is to ask: "What … is the nature of these [first, second, and third] principles?" in *Letter* II, at 312e–13a. See also *Statesman* 285e–6b and *Letter* VII 341b–e, 342e–3a.

127 Only Findlay (1974, pp. 240, 252; 1978:, pp. 214–15) has noted and essentially endorsed the ineffability of the First Hypothesis One in Plato. Brisson (1995, p. 127) argues: "The Good is said to be beyond being in the *Republic*, not in an absolute sense, because if this were the case it would be both unthinkable and unspeakable, but in dignity and power." This may be true, but Brisson needs to account for the fact that Plato says the Good is not being, for the many ineffable statements concerning the Good and First Principle and for the First Hypothesis One.

128 Many commentators are happy to point out this feature of the Plotinian One: Bussanich (1996, p. 38), Organ (1991, p. 42), Sells (1994, p. 15), who say that naming the One limits it, and we have already seen that the One is unlimited. Whitby (1909, p. 121) agrees with me that Plato and Plotinus hold that "God" cannot be named (assuming God is the One or Good for both philosophers).

129 Here Plotinus alludes to *Republic* VI 509b; we will study Nous or Being to show that Plotinus is warranted in reading the "beyond being" passage to refer to the Good's being beyond Nous and Intellect as well.

130 Note the expression of philosophical agony from Plotinus with regard to naming or defining the One, in V.5.6.22–37; see also VI.2.17.

131 The following commentators disagree with my interpretation in this section: (1) Friedländer (1969, p. 63) argues that for Plato, not Plotinus, the highest goal is not a mystery that is profaned by contact with words (because the Good is the greatest thing learned); but we have already seen that Plotinus also affirms that the Good is the greatest thing to be learned and the ineffability of the Good and the ultimate experience thereof. (2) D. Jackson (1967, p. 322) claims that Plotinus goes beyond Plato in that we cannot really name the One; we can point in the direction of the One, however. But Plato can be interpreted as saying this in the First Hypothesis as well as in the *Republic*'s key passages. (3) More (1923, pp. 218–19) says that the Plotinian One is undefinable, and may be called the Good, but it is not Plato's Good; if my argument is correct, then Plato is hinting in the First Hypothesis that the Good is truly unnamable, which again helps to explain his reluctance to discuss the Good Itself in *Republic* VI and VII. (4) Shorey (1938, pp. 45, 49) mentions that the Neo-Platonists took the second section to denote an ineffable One, but he does not believe they are correct in so interpreting it. Lastly, (5) Wolfson (1952, p. 115) argues that Plotinus got his "One cannot be spoken of" statement from Philo, not Plato; if we see the claim made in Plato, I am warranted in claiming that it comes instead from Plato (even if Plotinus is incorrect that his One is the same as the Platonic One or Good).

132 Cf. Brisson (1995, p. 127), who disagrees.

133 Desjardins (2004, p. 231) notes this point as well. See also the next text paragraph and associated notes.

134 For visions of Beauty, see *Symposium* 210c–12a, *Phaedrus* 247b–48b, 249c–d, 249e–51a, *Republic* V 476b; and cf. *Republic* VI 500d.

135 Note, too, the precedent case in what Plato says at *Symposium* 211a5–b2 of the vision of Beauty, which he also paradoxically claims is knowledge of Beauty, at 210c–d—see also *Republic* V 476c–d; cf. *Republic* (V 479e): "*Nor will the beautiful appear to him* in the guise of a face or hands or anything else that belongs to the body. *It will not appear to him as* one idea [*logos*] or *one kind of knowledge* [*tis epistēmē*]. It is not anywhere in another thing, as in an animal, or in earth, or in heaven, or in anything else, but *itself by itself with itself, it is always one in form*" (*Symposium* 211a5–b2; emphasis added); this passage is parallel to the *Parmenides*' conclusions, because he denies words or names [*logos*] of the vision of Beauty as well as knowledge, and predicates eternal oneness of it. These points merely lead to another interpretive problem—if Beauty is not the Good, then

why would Plato predicate (or not) these attributes of Beauty and not of the Good, or even better of the One, outside the *Parmenides*? My response is that we need to look for the best reading of Plato overall, given everything he says; and the best reading of the First Hypothesis of the *Parmenides* and the Good in the *Republic*, and Beauty in the *Symposium*, and the ineffability passages is to take Plato as arguing that one can have a vision or experience of a beyond being which will be remembered afterwards as being good and beautiful, and will lead to knowledge. But, while one experiences it, one will not be thinking that it is good or beautiful. Louth (1981, pp. 11–13) is the only other commentator to my knowledge who really theoretically connects the "no knowledge" point from the *Symposium* to the Good's transcending knowledge point of *Republic* VI and VII. From my perspective, Rawson (1996, p. 108) misses this point by claiming only that the ladder of love "climbs to knowledge" and neglects to mention that Plato also states that the vision of Beauty will not be knowledge.

136 There is evidence that we cannot perceive Forms with our senses, for instance, at *Republic* VI 507b9–10: "And we say that the many beautiful things and the rest are visible but not intelligible, while the forms are intelligible but not visible;" and at *Symposium* 211a5–7: "Nor will the beautiful appear to him in the guise of a face or hands or anything else that belongs to the body." Thus this claim that the Good (or One) would not be able to be perceived is consistent with Plato's general claims about the Forms, as some of the earlier conclusions of the First Hypothesis were.

137 I agree with the following interpreters that the Plotinian One cannot be known, in some sense, even though Plotinus does say we can know the Good: A. H. Armstrong (1945, p. 142; 1974, p. 182); cf. Hardie (1936, pp. 122, 130), that the experience is supra-intellectual, beyond thought, or transcends knowledge: Bréhier (1958, p. 154); Findlay (1974, p. 370); Stace (1967, pp. 372–3); and even that the knowledge of the One is different from other knowledge (Merlan 1960, p. 1n. 1), because this is a way of allowing Plotinus to say that the knowledge of the Good is the most important thing to learn, and yet that it is not knowledge as the term is usually used. Whitby (1909, p. 121) is one of the few who argues that Plato and Plotinus have the same view that "God" cannot be known; assuming that "God" refers to the One or the Good for both thinkers, I concur with Whitby. Lastly, A. H. Armstrong (1974, p. 182) correctly notes that the One does not think; see VI.7.40.1–2. But see Gerson (1994, p. 20) for some passages to the contrary, as well as Rist (1973, p. 77).

138 For further passages that state that the Good or One is not knowable, see VI.9.4.1–11, V.3.13–14, VI.7.35.

139 The following commentators take a different view on the unknowability of the Plotinian One versus the Good of Plato: Gadamer (1986, pp. 28–9) says

Plotinus takes a new step from Plato when he says that the One is beyond all thinking, but Plato gives sufficient indication that the Good is not knowable, so it is not clear that Plotinus takes a new step. Harris (1976, p. 8) notes that Neo-Platonism holds that the first principle is indefinable and knowable; he is not accounting for Plotinus' many statements that the One is unknowable. Lynch (1959, pp. 88–9) argues first: "The Good is above all our knowing and there can be no scientific knowledge of it", but then (after noting that Neo-Platonists even today identify the First Hypothesis One with the Good): "They still fail to recognize that similar phrasing is discoverable in a number of dialogues dealing with altogether different subjects. This similarity is always due to the presence of a common epistemological principle. There can be no scientific knowledge of strict unity and no such knowledge of strict multiplicity." Whatever dialogues Lynch has in mind that have similar phrasing (besides perhaps *Symposium* 211a–b on the "no knowledge" point), Plato does not claim that anything other than the Good is the source or cause of the Forms and knowledge (and is beyond knowledge), and not being but beyond being. Thus, without seeing what passages Lynch is thinking about, we do not have a reason to think that the First Hypothesis One is not the Good. Meijer (1992, p. 37) says that the One is thinkable (for mind) contrary to what Plotinus says, though Meijer says that the One is unaffected by being the object of thought. Rist (1973, p. 77) claims that Plotinus alludes to the One's ability to think, but his cited passages refer either to Intellect (V.4.2.17) or to a context where Plotinus simultaneously seems both to conclude that the One is an active actuality that transcends—and causes—intellect, thought and life (VI.8.16.35–7) and also that the One is an ever-existing thought that transcends thought (VI.8.16.32–3). The problem, as Rist (1967a, pp. 39–52) acknowledges, is that it is far from clear what cognition, knowledge or (self) consciousness Plotinus is attributing to the One (at, say, VI.8.16.12–19, V.1.7.12, V.4.2.12–26, VI.7.39.1–2, VI.8.18.26), especially given his more frequent denials of these attributes (III.9.7, III.9.9, V.6.5–6, III.8.10, VI.7.38–40, V.3.13, I.7.1, VI.9.6.42–55). (6) Ross (1951, p. 97) argues that we can legitimately ask if Plato meant to set up an unknowable One, but that evidence from the *Republic* and the *Parmenides* points that he did not; namely, when Plato says that the Good is more exalted than knowledge, that is not enough evidence that the Good is unknowable, and that the First Hypothesis One is unqualified so this One cannot be the Good. Runciman (1959, p. 104) states without argument that the First Hypothesis One, qua "beyond knowledge, opinion, or perception … cannot be equated with the Good of the *Republic*." Shorey acknowledges that the First Hypothesis One is unknowable (1938, p. 49) and that the Neo-Platonic theology of the Unknowable goes back to Plato's *Parmenides* (pp. 53–4), but he clearly does not endorse my view that the First Hypothesis One is Plato's Good, let alone that these are interpretively equivalent to the Plotinian One.

140 The group of thinkers includes at least D. Jackson (1967, p. 322) and Rochel (1971, pp. 502–3; cf. pp. 500–1), though I am certain that there are others.

141 Hitchcock, 1985, p. 90n. 56.

142 Plotinus apparently avers that the First, Second and Third Hypotheses of the *Parmenides* refer, respectively, to the One, Intellect and the World-Soul, at V.1.8.23–7. I use the word "apparently," because Gurtler (1992, pp. 443, 455, 457) argues that this passage does not commit Plotinus to claiming that the entire First Hypothesis, for example, is to be interpreted as the One, the entire Second as Intellect and the Third as the All-Soul, but that: "Plotinus is giving a brief parallel between his three Hypostases and characteristics of unity found at specific junctures in the argument of Plato's great dialogue. He is not, however, making the claim that Plato was actually talking about his metaphysical hierarchy. To substantiate that charge, one should at least find a text where Plotinus explicitly analyzes the *Parmenides* with the ideas Cornford mentions in full view. There is, in fact, no such text. Plotinus does analyze the *Parmenides*, as I will demonstrate, but never in the naive way that Cornford suggests" (p. 443). For more on this, see Cornford (1939: introduction); Dillon (1973, pp. 387–8); Hardie (1936, p. 130). I do not need to take a stand on this issue, but also note that Findlay (1974, p. 185) alone seems to support the idea that one can find Plotinus' Three Hypostases in the first three Hypotheses of the *Parmenides*. As evidence that the connection is weak, Atkinson (1983, p. 197) points out that Plotinus only twice refers to the *Parmenides* after 157b5; but Gurtler's hypothesis seems to explain this lack of Plotinian explanation of every hypothesis. I suggest that Plotinus could be referring to more of the second section than just those mentioned by Henry-Schweitzer in the OCT. (See also the Appendix for more on my overall view of the second section of the *Parmenides*.)

143 To my knowledge, Robert Price first proposed the intriguing and plausible idea that the One is the Good as seen or experienced by the Intellect, a reaction after becoming one with the One, just as one comes to have knowledge as a result of the experience (but see VI.7.16.10–24 for a closely related passage). I will not pursue this idea here, however.

144 See also especially II.9.1.12–16 and VI.2.11.27–9. For further passages that state that the Good is the First and/or the One, see III.8.9–10, V.1.1, V.1.6, V.3.15, VI.7.33, VI.8.10, VI.8.16, VI.8.20–1. Similar to a claim that the Good or One is First is the claim that the Good or One is *prior* to everything else, which Plotinus also avers: see V.1.7, V.3.12, V.4.1, V.5.9, V.9.2, VI.7.22, VI.7.39, VI.8.8–9, V.5.4.

145 A. H. Armstrong, 1947, p. 153. I am sympathetic with the following commentators: Dodds (1928, p. 133) says: "Read the second part of the

*Parmenides* as Plotinus read it, with the single eye of faith; do not look for satire on the Megarians or on anybody else; and you will find in the first hypothesis a lucid exposition of the famous 'negative theology.'" Schroeder (1996, p. 344; cf. p. 353n. 21) states: "Negative theology is not an expression of mystical silence, but is always a function of speech used in the service of philosophy." And Dodds (1928, p. 134) points out an inconsistency in Taylor's analysis – he apparently accepts Proclus' negative theology "seriously as a necessary and salutary 'moment' of religious experience, but when he meets it in the *Parmenides*, describes it as 'a highly-enjoyable philosophical jest.'" Cf. Bechtle (1999, p. 76) and Merlan (1960, p. 1n. 1).

146 Bussanich (1987; 1996, p. 59.) Bussanich (1996, p. 50) and Gerson (1994, p. 18) both point out that the Plotinian One is everywhere and nowhere (see, for example, VI.8.16); I interpret Plotinus' claim as saying that the One is everywhere because it sustains Being, Life and everything that is good, but also because it is accessible somehow to living things (or at least human beings); for example, soul is anywhere where there is life, and the whole universe is a living being imitating the Living Being, and all soul has some kind of access to the One or Good. On the other hand, the One is nowhere because it is not a being, it is immaterial, has no place (see Plato's *Parmenides* 139a) and is not in time (cf. Plato's *Parmenides* 141d). Both of these claims are plainly Platonic. Moreover, Gerson rightly states that the Plotinian One is good (1994, p. 18) and presumably, though not explicitly, eternal (1994, pp. 17, 117; but see VI.9.9 where Plotinus says that the eternals – Forms – spring from an eternal principle), and again, these attributions of the Good are entirely Platonic. Cf. Blumenthal (1993, p. 3).

147 Findlay (1974, p. 370) and perhaps O'Meara (1993, p. 52).

148 Many commentators have negative things to say about this interpretation: Allen (1983, p. 190), it is an "honored misinterpretation"; A. H. Armstrong (1940, p. 116), "there is no reason why we should take the Neo-Platonic interpretations of Plato's *Parmenides* seriously"; A. H. Armstrong (1947, p. 181), it is a "quite illegitimate interpretation"; Brumbaugh (1961, pp. 10–11), "one must reject, as not being Plato's, the mystical interpretation of the first hypothesis"; Cornford (1939, p. vi), it is "the mirage of Neoplatonic mysticism"; Hardie (1936, p. 112), "most modern students, from Stallbaum to Shorey, have found little good to say of the Neoplatonic elucidations, or obfuscations, of Plato"; D. Jackson (1967, p. 321; cf. p. 322), "Plotinus goes beyond anything that can be found in the *Parmenides*"; Merlan (1967, p. 353), "following what are at best hints in Plato, Plotinus developed a full-fledged theory of the One as the highest principle, or cause"; M. Miller (1986, p. 236, and p. 237n. 4), "for appreciative accounts that, nonetheless, rightly reject the neo-Platonic reading, see [Cornford, Allen, and Speiser]"; Pistorius (1952, p. 20), "[The One of Plotinus] is a universal concept

robbed of all its qualities. It is more universal than the highest idea in the scheme of Plato, because the ideas of Plato are reasonable and open to human understanding"; Rist (1962a, p. 1), "All these ingenious interpretations [Wahl and Wundt, in favor of the Neo-Platonic theory] need no further comment; Runcimann's rejection of them adequately summarizes the difficulties in them that have frequently been pointed out"; Rist (1964, p. 43), it is an "obvious fact that Plotinus derived many of his own views on the One from the writings of Plato – albeit from a misinterpretation of those writings"; Scoon (1942, p. 128), "These concepts are so vague that contradictory consequences can be drawn from them, and that all kinds of meanings can be read into them by Neo-Platonists and other interpreters"; A. E. Taylor, implied (1896, p. 297), it is a less "accredited view"; A. E. Taylor (1896, p. 299), "It will hardly be necessary for me to offer a formal disproof of that ancient view which sees in our dialogue a treatise of mystical theology. For it would be generally admitted now that Plato, like Hegel, has no secret doctrine, no esoteric sense, though unwise persons have often sought to discover one in both. It is most significant of the difference between the genuine philosopher and the charlatan that the abstract logic of the *Parmenides* is all we find when we look for a *disciplina arcani* in Plato's writings"; de Vogel (1953, p. 59; see also p. 58), "May we then say that it is the Plotinian One? I repeat: it was not the author's intention to give a description of anything; it was his intention to make logical deductions"; Walker (1938, p. 489), "The conclusion to which we are forced is that Plato in this most careful of dialogues was a jester, a mystic, an Hegelian, or a logician… . None of these interpretations does justice to the full significance and importance of the dialectic." Cornford (1939, p. 133) states: "The Neoplatonists make the further assumption that the Good of the *Republic* is the supreme god of Plato's theology, superior to the divine [*Nous*], which they locate in Hyp. II." I can only state that Plotinus most definitely does not fall into this group of interpreters. Cf. Cornford (1939, p. ix); Gadamer (1986, p. 137); Hampton (1990, p. 87); Shorey (1938, p. 49).

149 Cornford (1939, p. 133) makes a similar criticism.

150 Allen, 1983, pp. 194–5; cf. pp. 192–3.

151 A. H. Armstrong, 1947, p. 181.

152 Runciman (1959, p. 105) makes the same criticism in his point (d), but my reply is similar and must be addressed.

153 Chen, 1944, p. 101.

154 Cornford, 1939, p. 131.

155 Ibid., pp. 131–2.

156 Rochel (1971, p. 502) makes the same point: "It is incomplete and therefore impossible to characterize 'beyond' by a simple 'not.'" My reply is identical;

namely, he fails to acknowledge that Plato says that the Good is "not being" and combines this with the "beyond being" claim at *Republic* VI 509a.

157 Gerson (1994, p. 19). He also argues: "there is very little to be said for the identification of the subject of the first hypothesis with the Form of the Good. I do not wish thus so cavalierly to dismiss an entire tradition's interpretation of Plato. I wish merely to set it aside, for to say that Plotinus was inclined to identify the Form of the Good and 'the one' of the first hypothesis of the second part of the *Parmenides* is ancillary to the analysis of his own arguments for his own principle. Even if Plotinus thought that Plato meant what he himself meant, we cannot go to Plato to find out what Plotinus meant, for this would be circular reasoning on behalf of establishing what Plotinus means" (1994, p. 19). Contra Gerson, I believe we can go to Plato to make the case that he believed that the First Hypothesis One is the Good, and that there are many other parallels between their philosophies on the One, Good, let alone the myriad entities and claims argued for in this work.

158 It is clear that the Good is eternal, just as any other Form; it could not be in time and be the cause of eternal Forms, even as it is not being but beyond being: the Platonic One or Good is unlimited; Plotinus' claims that the One is everywhere and nowhere are Platonic as well.

159 Consider three objections: (1) The fact that Plato seemingly attributes willing or wishing to God here guarantees that he cannot be referring to the Good, especially because Socrates says that he will not discuss the nature of the Good in *Republic* VI. However, one needs to address the implication that, since Plato states that the Good causes the Forms to exist (*Republic* VI) and states that God creates the Bed Itself, we need to interpret "God" here as the Good; and my interpretation of ineffability has accounted for Plato's saying *something* about the Good, just as Plotinus makes similar ineffability claims and yet discusses the One. (2) From the Plotinian side, Plotinus states that the way in which the Good is the source of the Forms—the Good is the source of and contains everything—is not the same way in which the Demiurge is the source of the Forms—Nous is the instrument of the One and creates by reflecting back upon the One. The different types of sourcing do not necessarily bear on the way in which the Demiurge is the source of Forms, if I am right that "God" here refers to the Good (also, see Gerson [1994, pp. 45–7] for the related issue of the ontological priority of Forms to intellect).

160 Robin, 1928, pp. 372–3.

161 Rochel, 1971, p. 503.

162 See also Shorey (1938: 53–4), who, after claiming that the Neo-Platonists got their theology of the One from the *Parmenides*, claims that they stripped the One of affirmations until only negations remained. See my response to Rochel, in the text immediately following.

163 Runciman (1959, p. 104) makes the same claim in his point (a); but the same reply holds against his view.

164 Stace, 1967, pp. 372–3.

## Chapter 2

1 Unfortunately I cannot also discuss these related issues, here: (1) perceptibly beautiful things partake of Beauty Itself; (2) beauty causes everything that is beautiful to be beautiful; (3) those who do not recognize that the Form of Beauty exists are dreamers and not awake.

2 Here is a reasonably complete list of where Plato refers to Beauty as a Form: *Cratylus* 416d–e, 439c–40b, *Euthydemus* 300e–1a, *Greater Hippias* 286d–e, 287b–d, 289c–d, 292c–d, 295a–c, *Phaedo* 65d, 75d, 76d–7a, 78d–9a, 100b–e, *Symposium* 206e, 210e–11c, *Republic* V 475e–6d, 479a–b, 479e–80a, VI 493e–4a, 501b–c, 507b, *Parmenides* 130b–c, 131a, 134c, 135c–d, *Theaetetus* 186a, *Phaedrus* 249d–e, *Sophist* 258c, *Philebus* 15a.

3 Few commentators contest the claim that Beauty is a Form; Morrison's (1977, p. 215) description of Beauty Itself in *Symposium* 211a–b is especially astute; Findlay (1976, p. 30), on the other hand, claims that Plato claims that Beauty is "Unity itself." I disagree with the latter account because Plato definitely states that every Form is one, but not that any Form (other than the Form of Oneness) *is* Unity itself.

4 For more on Beauty as a Form, see VI.3.11.21–7 (the monkey quotation is from Heraclitus, Fragment B 82 DK, quoted by Plato in *Greater Hippias* 289a); see also VI.3.12.17–9. For more on bodily beauty versus Beauty Itself, see V.9.2, I.6.1 and II.9.17.

One might think that Beauty is identical to all the Forms and not a specific Form, given I.6.9.35–6 (intelligible beauty is the place of the Forms) and V.8.9.40–2; however, my reading of V.8.9 is that the Intelligible Region is beautiful, but Plato believes that as well; and a claim that every Form is beautiful, or that intelligible beauty is the place of the Forms, is compatible with the claim that there is, in addition, Beautiful Itself.

5 I address another relevant objection from Wallis in note 8 below.

6 Anton (1964, p. 234; see also pp. 236–7) attempts to argue that Plotinus is attempting to refute the theory of beauty as symmetry; Plato does not believe that the Form of Beauty is identical to symmetry, and everything that Anton mentions that Plotinus believes (the world is a blessed god, a perfect being, an offspring of supreme beauty) are all Platonic, so Anton fails to convince me.

7 Rist, 1967a, p. 183.

8 First, Wallis (1972, p. 87) makes the same argument that, for Plotinus, Beauty is not Form but Life (and that Life is the essence of beauty); the reply I gave to Rist's argument applies. Second, Wallis also charges: "More radically still, he argues that even the beauty of the Forms would fail to stir us were they not quickened to life by the radiance cast upon them by the Good" (1972, p. 87). However, Plotinus is clearly discussing there the beauty of the Forms in general, and Intellect or Nous, and not Beauty Itself. He is poetically arguing that the Good causes Beauty (and the Forms and Intellect), and the beauty of the Forms and Intellect, and that the Good is what makes these things good – all of which is implied by Plato's Cave Allegory. Lastly, Wallis claims that: "Plotinus goes as far as to declare that Primary Beauty is formless (VI.7.33.37–8), so breaking completely with traditional Platonism" (1972, p. 87); however, VI.7.34 contains a denial of "intellectual shape" as a property of beauty, which is telling. Plato nowhere states that the Forms have intellectual shape, so we do not have a contradiction. Put another way, there is no problem if Plotinus is claiming that Beauty is formless in the sense of its not possessing Aristotelian form qua function; for this may be merely denying that Forms contain within them functions in the literal sense (for instance, Beauty Itself causes beautiful things, but not what beautiful things are for, or the value of beauty; this is caused by, or due to, Goodness Itself).

9 Findlay (1976, p. 30) interprets *Symposium* 211a–b as saying that Beauty is Unity itself; from the perspective that the Good is the One, and that Plato seems to say that the Good is beautiful or similar to Beauty, this is a fitting interpretation; however, it seems pretty clear that Beauty is not Unity Itself in Plato's view. In other comments related to the *Symposium*, Sayre (1983, p. 173) claims: "In the speech of Diotima in the *Symposium*, on the other hand, there are strong intimations that the Good is the Beautiful." A. E. Taylor argues: "The place assigned to both [the Good in the *Republic* and Beauty in the *Symposium*] in the ascent to 'being and reality' is identical, and in both cases the stress is laid on the point that when the supreme 'form' is descried, its apprehension comes as a sudden 'revelation,' though it is not to be had without the long preliminary process of travail of thought, and that it is apprehended by 'direct acquaintance,' not by discursive 'knowledge about' it" (1956, p. 231). My only caveat is that Plato does not make the same claims about Beauty's being beyond being and the source of all that exists, and/or of all knowledge and truth.

10 Plato reveals a difference between ugly and beauty elsewhere: "ugliness is out of harmony with all that is godly. Beauty, however, is in harmony with the divine" (*Symposium* 206d1–2).

11 One might argue that Plotinus does not believe that the Good stands to many goods as Beauty stands to many beauties, because a horse is good by being a horse and nothing else, for example, and something is beautiful by being an instance of

*any* Form. However, first, Plotinus says that many beautifuls partake of Beauty. Second, a perceptible horse is not technically the nature of a horse, so to speak, for either philosopher; it is a copy of Horse Itself; a perceptible horse is good by fulfilling the function of a horse (see *Republic* I). Third, Plotinus and Plato can assert that something is beautiful by partaking in Forms in general (speaking loosely)—because all the Forms (and Intellect or Nous) are beautiful—while *still* maintaining that Beauty is also a Form, as well as that all Forms partake in Beauty just as they partake in Being, Sameness and so on.

12 Plotinus also believes, along with Plato (from *Republic* V 476a), that Beauty and ugly (or Ugly, depending on whether Ugly is a Form) are each one; see I.6.6.21–5. Ultimately, Plotinus and Plato align evil and ugliness with Matter. Note though that Plotinus is focusing on the aspect of Beauty and Good that makes them similar: when opposed to Ugliness and Evil, Beauty and Good are practically the same thing.

13 Plotinus claims that the Intellect is beautiful as well at III.7.6.1–4; see also V.8.13.

14 For more on possessing Beauty, see VI.5.10.

15 Indeed, Plotinus explicitly states that in his writing he is using "beauty" in more than one sense, or referring to different kinds of beauty; see VI.2.18.1–8; and see I.6.9.37–40, where Plotinus says that the Good is the primary beauty, but only when one speaks in a loose and general way.

16 Gerson's (1994, p. 212) insightful comments are helpful as well: the One or Good is Beauty "as [an] object of a desire that has been satisfied," adducing I.6.7.14–8 in support. Harris (1976, p. 3) claims that the *Enneads* as a whole affirm, among other things, "the tendency to identify the beautiful, the good, and the true as one and the same"; I agree with the tendency, but hurry to note that both philosophers do not identify these entities with one another in the end. Allen (1983, p. 194) argues that "[The Good] is also on the same level as the Beautiful (507b, cf. 532b), which Plotinus acknowledged to be a thing which is and an object of knowledge." I disagree that the Good and Beauty are precisely on the same level according to Plotinus, and acknowledge the paradox of the possibility that the Good might not be knowable.

17 Other objections include The Alexandrian Press' (1985, p. 14; see also p. 19) claim that, in Plotinus' view, "The Supreme One is the Beautiful Itself." Cf. Anton (2010, p. 13), who intimates this as well of Plato. As we have seen, however, neither Plato nor Plotinus ultimately identifies the Good with Beauty. Inge (1929b, pp. 126–7) seems to claim that Plotinus (although he exalts Good to a more inaccessible altitude than Plato does) insists that the "Absolute" is not Beauty but the Good; but out of loyalty to Plato, he retains the name Good instead of referring to it more accurately as the One. I have argued thus far, however, that Plato and Plotinus have similar views of the One, Good and Beauty, so I have addressed this criticism.

18 Rist (1964, pp. 187–8) also argues that *Symposium* 211 "describes the advance to an intuitive knowing or seeing of the Good or the Beautiful. All the other Platonic passages which speak of the 'flash' of insight, the 'vision' of the eye of the soul, do likewise. This is not the Plotinian ecstasy; there is nothing in the *Symposium* passage to suggest 'becoming Beauty'; all the talk is of seeing the beautiful aura of knowing it." First, I deny that Plato in the *Symposium* is describing the vision of knowledge of the Good *or* the Beautiful, but only that of the latter. Second, Plotinus does not claim that we can become identical with Forms such as Beauty, Goodness, Tallness, although our souls can certainly become good, beautiful and just—all of which we read in Plato. Indeed, Plato states that one's soul can be beautiful (see, for example, *Symposium* 210b–c, *Republic* X 611b–c), so that, if one knows what Beauty is, it is plausible that one's soul is more beautiful than a soul that is ignorant thereof; and if one is mainly one's soul, as both philosophers believe, then we can infer that one can become more, if not truly, beautiful.

19 Rist, 1967a, p. 64.

20 Ibid., p. 184.

21 A. E. Taylor (1956, pp. 230–1) has a nice rendition of the passage right before this one, and of Diotima's speech in general, except for his unfortunate translation "one single science" instead of "one single knowledge," which seems clear from the context. Moreover, he claims (1956, p. 231) that the experience of the Good in the *Republic* is about the same as the experience of Beauty in the *Symposium*.

22 See also *Phaedrus* 250c–d, where Plato states that vision is the keenest way to perceive beauty, and 250e–1a for another way of describing the lover of sights and sounds that does not admit the reality of Beauty and engages in the life of pleasure.

23 I especially agree with A. H. Armstrong (1974, p. 182) when he says that, in Plotinus' *Enneads*: "There can surely be no doubt that we are confronted with a claim to repeated first-hand, direct and comprehensive experiences of divine reality. And I can see no reason why the claim should be disallowed, however we may explain the experiences." And: "We must see Plotinus as a man driven to philosophize by what he believed to be a direct awareness of divine reality and saying what he had to say under the pressure of that direct experience, although determined to make what he said as rationally convincing as possible, and to show that it was in accordance with the real thought of Plato." I also agree with the comments made by Edwards (1993, p. 486) that the soul is transformed by the vision of Beauty; Miles (1999, p. 170) that one needs to be committed to the refinement "of one's own beauty in preparation for recognizing the great beauty characteristic of the One"; Rist (1967a, p. 56) that: "Plotinus is tremendously indebted to the terminology of Plato's *Symposium* and that here the Beautiful is the aim of the philosopher's quest."

24 See also I.6.9.1–6. For a passage on how a musician can become a philosopher by seeing the beauty of harmonies and continuing to study them in the abstract, see I.3.1. Also, for Plato's claim that the vision of Beauty Itself quickens one with the true or perfect virtue, as Plotinus implies in this passage, see *Symposium* 212a; cf. Findlay (1978, pp. 101–2). Concerning *Phaedrus* 254b–c, Mohr (2005, p. 251) rightly argues: "the Form of beauty suggests to the mind that perceives it the Form of self-control or temperance," but that "Beauty is not analytically entailed by temperance or vice versa." I only hasten to point out the *Symposium* 212a passage, where Plato implies that the vision of Beauty entails one's being truly or perfectly virtuous, which in turn implies Temperance, Justice and the rest.

25 At V.8.11, Plotinus also states that we can be lifted to a better beauty in this process and that we must become divine in order to be truly beautiful.

26 For another passage where Plotinus states that the vision of Beauty implies that one also understands the First (or Transcendent of that Divine Being), see V.8.1.1–6; see also V.5.8.

27 See III.5.1.30–8 and III.5.1.55–6, which is reminiscent of *Phaedrus* 251a1–2b1.

28 There are three other notable objections: (1) Louth (1981, p. 41) claims that Plotinus' view on Beauty "feels" differently than what Plato says; however, they have a similar view of Beauty. (2) Rist (1964, pp. 187–8), who argues that the Platonic Ladder of Love gives no support to a doctrine of ecstasy or of the ecstatic knowledge of God in the Plotinian sense. However, (i) I read Plato's *Symposium* and *Phaedrus*, for instance, as giving us plenty of reason to believe that the experience of Beauty is ecstatic (see quotations in this section), and (ii) nowhere does Plotinus state that if one has a vision of Beauty she therefore knows God. Also, (iii) Rist there says that the *Symposium* is also describing the ascent to the Good as much as it is the Beautiful, so, given that Plotinus refers to the One as God, perhaps the Platonic passage *can* be so read. (3) Sinnige (1999, p. 19): "What we find in Plato's dialogues is descriptions of an intellectual process of ascent. There is no reference, as in Plotinus, to the personal experience of being caught up into another form of existence. What Plotinus describes is a movement of transformation in which the existence of the whole individual person is implied, not simply a development of philosophical knowledge. Plato's philosophical system and Plotinus' description of mystical surrender move in different worlds. The stress on getting away from the senses is found in both, but it has a different meaning. In Plato the way out is through knowledge and philosophy. It is a rational process. In Plotinus is an existential process, which has its roots in the deepest of human emotions, not in theoretical distinctions." It is clear that the vision of beauty for Plato is equally as life-transforming as it is in Plotinus, because such a vision implies true virtue, that one will never be attracted in a real way to any perceptibly beautiful thing. Moreover, they both claim that you can have knowledge of Beauty,

and that dialectic and philosophy are the ways out of ignorance and unhappiness. Thus, Sinnige's argument that Plato and Plotinus differ on this score rings hollow.

29 Hadot quotes VI.9.7.21–3, 26–7; Hadot, 1993, p. 56.

30 Compare what Plato says in the *Sophist*: "So don't those craftsmen say goodbye to truth, and produce in their images the proportions that seem to be beautiful instead of the real ones? [Absolutely.]" (236a4–7).

31 In the *Philebus*, the following claims are relevant: (1) Socrates is concerned to make a distinction between what most people understand about beauty, such as that of a living thing or a picture, as opposed to things like straight and round that are not relatively beautiful but absolutely beautiful (51b–d); (2) the human good takes refuge in the beautiful (due to measure and proportion) (64e); (3) the human good is not a single form, but a mixture of beauty, proportion and truth (65a); (4) smooth, clear, audible sounds are absolutely beautiful (51d–e). Note that claims (1) and (2) can be confirmed in Plotinus (these confirmations will not be made here), while, though claims (3) and 4) seem Platonic to me, they cannot be confirmed explicitly in Plotinus.

32 Plotinus also argues that living beauty is more glorious than dead beauty, and even that the living ugly are more attractive than the sculptured handsome ones, at VI.7.22.24–36.

33 Gerson, 1994, p. 213.

34 See also V.9.5.36–48.

35 Fuller, 1938, p. 310.

## Chapter 3

1 Menn (1992, p. 554) is dissatisfied with the translation of *nous* as either "mind" or "intellect," calling both seriously misleading. If the reader agrees with Menn, she can substitute *nous* (or her favorite translation thereof) for each occurrence in Plato or Plotinus in the translations. I am only translating it in the same convention as A. H. Armstrong and MacKenna in terms of the *Enneads*, and seeing what characteristics Nous has in Plato.

2 I cannot additionally verify, due to lack of space, that they also agree that Nous: (1) is the ordering or containing principle of causation in the universe; (2) is good and beautiful; (3) is also named Kronos (where "Zeus" is the name of the World-Soul); (4) is the One-Many.

3 I agree with the following commentators: A. H. Armstrong (1945, p. 139), that Plotinus conceives Nous in the true Platonic tradition; Dodds (1960, p. 4), that Plotinus makes Nous intensely real and even more real than Plato, except that we can find most of what Plotinus says about Nous in Plato (arguments to follow);

Findlay (1978, p. 215), that Plotinus carries Plato's notions slightly further in his systematization of Nous. I disagree with Gurtler (1988, p. 12), that Plotinus developed Plato's thought by "showing how the Intellect and its content form a living unity," because this is Plato's view; Pistorius (1952, p. 29), that the "Platonic ideas have no mutual unity," because Plato says that there is a realm of Being, which is precisely the realm of Forms. Pistorius (1952, p. 29) also claims that Plotinian ideas do not form a hierarchy (but are unity), as in Plato; however, we have seen that both thinkers place Good above being as the cause of the Forms, that Beauty seems to be a rather important Form due to their accounts of the vision thereof, and we will see that they agree on the Five Greatest Kinds.

4 Cf. Menn, 1995, p. 11.

5 See, for example, Shorey (1938, p. 49); cf. Louth (1981, p. 2). I disagree with de Vogel (1986, p. 77), who renders Plato as saying that the Divine Mind does not contain the Ideas as its objects, but is eternally related to them; the fact that Nous is a Divine Mind presumes that there are intellectual objects there, whether or not they are exactly contained by Nous. Lastly, Menn (1995, p. 45) raises the issue of whether Nous is a Form (since it is a virtue), which I hesitate to believe; instead, I believe that when Mind is said to be a positive quality of the human soul in, say, the *Timaeus* 51d–2a, it is not the same Nous that I am discussing here.

6 See Findlay, 1974, p. 154; Gerson, 2005, p. 267 (who takes *Sophist* 248e6–9a2 as asserting that knowledge is present in "the realm of the really real," which I take to be Nous); and Menn, 1992, p. 572; cf. de Vogel, 1986, p. 74.

7 Louth (1981, p. 2) rightly mentions "a place above the heavens" as the dwelling-place of the gods, but does not claim that this realm of the Forms is Nous, which is what I am claiming.

8 I do not believe that Plato changed his mind later about this region described in the *Phaedrus* that I am referring to as Nous; thus Carone's (2005, pp. 5, 19) claim that mind cannot exist independently of the body is not Plato's view.

9 See, for instance, *Timaeus* 39e, and I argue that Nous in Plato is best interpreted as God (usually but not always) and the Demiurge, so those Platonic passages are relevant here as well. Also see, for example, the *Republic*'s Sun Simile ("What the good itself is in the intelligible realm, in relation to understanding and intelligible things, the sun is in the visible realm, in relation to sight and visible things" at (508b13–c2); cf. 508d, the upper sections, understanding and intellect, of the Divided Line Analogy, and the area outside of the cave in the Cave Allegory (and see 517b).

10 I agree with the following commentators: A. H. Armstrong (1945, p. 139), that Plotinus conceives Nous in the true Platonic tradition; Dodds (1960, p. 4), that Plotinus makes Nous intensely real and even more real than Plato, except that we can find most of what Plotinus says about Nous in Plato; Findlay (1978, p. 215),

that Plotinus carries Plato's notions slightly further in his systematization of Nous. I disagree with Gurtler (1988, p. 12), that Plotinus developed Plato's thought by "showing how the Intellect and its content form a living unity," because this is Plato's view; Pistorius (1952, p. 29), that the "Platonic ideas have no mutual unity," because Plato says that there is a realm of Being, which is precisely the realm of Forms. Pistorius claims on the same page that Plotinian ideas do not form a hierarchy (but are unity), as in Plato. However, both thinkers place Good above being as the cause of the Forms, and Beauty seems to be a rather important Form due to their accounts of the vision thereof, and they agree on the Five Greatest Kinds.

11 I agree with A. H. Armstrong (1947, p. 190; 1954; 1955, pp. 50–1, 53); Findlay (1976, p. 31); Lloyd (1990, p. 166); Sumi (1997, pp. 413, 416, 418–19); de Vogel (1970, p. 194; 1986, p. 86).

12 See also V.1.6.38–49.

13 Here I agree with Menn (2001, pp. 245–6) and More (1923, p. 246).

14 See also V.3.13.

15 I agree with Gerson (1994, p. 98); Inge (1929b, pp. 40–1); Rist (1964, pp. 42–3). I take issue with Katz (1950b, p. 21), who argues that Nous unites past, present and future, because if Nous is eternal, as I believe these thinkers take it to be, it is only eternal Being; it is not everlasting—that is, existing throughout time.

16 For further Plotinian passages on Nous as Being, see I.4.3, I.8.2, II.3.13, II.9.1, 17: III.3.1, III.6.17, III.7.3–4, III.8.8–10, III.9.1, IV.3.11, 18; IV.4.32, V.3.5–9, 16; V.4.2, V.8.4–5, 9; VI.2.7–8, 11, 21; VI.3.1, VI.6.6, 18; VI.7.10, 16, 35; VI.9.2, 5.

17 Here I agree with Rappe's (2000, p. xiii) general statement about Neo-Platonists' believing that Intellect is its objects, even though she does not say that Plato has the same view.

18 Cf. V.9.8, and see Gerson (1994, p. 47) for more Plotinian passages that show he believes that Intellect is eternal.

19 There is a controversy as to whether the "it" here refers to the One or Intellect; see A. H. Armstrong (1984b, pp. 34, and 35n. 1) and Atkinson (1983, pp. 157–60 with 135–40); however, the main intent of my using this passage is to point out that Plotinus holds with Plato that Intellect is an image of the Good, and not that the One or Good creates Intellect.

20 Compare VI.9.2.32–44 and II.9.1.46–54.

21 See, for example, the conversion of the soul passages at *Republic* VII 518, 521c, 525a–35a (where the context is converting the soul to be able to see the Good), and cf. *Laws* XII 957d–e; for a passage that one possesses "mind" when one is in contact with Being, see, for example, the *Timaeus* 51d–2a.

22 I admit confusion as to whether Plotinus is saying that it is the Good's returning to see itself that causes Intellect. If that is Plotinus' contention, I do not see Plato making that claim anywhere in his corpus.

23 I will briefly address eight other objections: (1) Anton (1992, pp. 7–9) argues that one of the reasons that Plotinus is Neo-Platonic and not Platonic is "the conception of *Nous* as the realm and structure of the Forms ensuring the intelligibility of the world" (pp. 8–9); however, at least this conception is entirely Platonic. (2) A. H. Armstrong (1960, p. 395) argues: "I think that Plotinian scholars would generally agree that it would be an inadequate and unsatisfactory description of this relation to say that for Plotinus the Ideas are the thoughts of Intellect. If we are to summarize his doctrine more or less in his own language and according to his own mind we must say rather 'The Ideas are Intellect and Intellect is the Ideas' or 'Real Being is Ideas and Intellect; they are one reality described from different points of view.' " He then adds that he cannot find these views in Plato's dialogues. There is more in, or as part of, or equivalent to, Nous for both philosophers—God, Demiurge, Five Greatest Kinds—if they are something other than Forms; we certainly find all of these entities in the dialogues; and if God is wise, God must have knowledge; if God has knowledge, God must know the Forms (in Plato's view if not in Plotinus' view); then the only question is whether God is at the level of or equivalent to Nous. (3) Bréhier (1958, pp. 101–2) claims that Plotinus holds that the "intelligible world, with all its richness and its diversity, is reabsorbed into a universal and undifferentiated being," but that this is "no longer the world of articulated notions of which Plato speaks." Contra Bréhier, it stands to reason that the Platonic Nous is one-many; and if Plotinus claims that Intellect contains, or just *is,* the Forms, that, whatever "undifferentiated" means here, it has to include the idea that Intellect is, or possesses, many things along with its being one. (4) Bréhier (1958, pp. 141–2) also argues that, for Plotinus, Intellect is no longer an active seeker of knowledge, but is perfect and complete intelligence with nothing to seek. But if Nous is the realm of knowledge, as we have seen both thinkers state, then Nous does not actively seek knowledge, but has it or contains it. (5) Louth (1981, p. 38) argues that, in Plato's Intellect, knower and known are one, and knowledge is intuitive and infallible, but that, in Plotinus' Intellect, knower and known are not identical, even if they are united. Plato does not state that knower and known are one or that knowledge is intuitive at the level of Nous (the exceptions being the visions of the Good and Beauty); therefore, knowledge of Forms in general remains dual even if Nous is one and the Forms are somehow united. (6) Pistorius (1952, p. 2) claims that the Plotinian Nous far excels the Platonic world of Ideas; however, many of the main claims that Plotinus makes about Nous can also be found in Plato. (7) Rist (1964, pp. 67–8) avers that Platonism is dualistic, composed of the unchanging world of Forms and the moving world of souls, but that Plotinus' world is monistic, as a direct result of putting the Forms into the Divine Mind. However, Plato has many more levels than Rist mentions—we

should add the Good beyond being, Nous as living thing, World-Soul, guardian spirits (which are halfway in between gods and humans) and matter. But then all of these entities exist in Plotinus' world as well, coming from a common source, so is Plato's view not monist as well? In short, I fail to see how it follows from the claim that Nous contains Forms that Plotinus has a monistic view. Finally, (8) Rist (1964, p. 94) also argues that there is barrier between the Platonic Forms and Gods—lifelessness; not so for the One-Nous-Forms (in Nous) of Plotinus, which are part of a single system. I believe that these latter entities are equivalent to the Platonic ones, and that they are part of a single system in Plato as well.

24 Others who seem persuaded by Rist are Kenney (1991, p. 93); Mayhall (2004, pp. 25–6); Merlan (1967, p. 353).

25 Rist, 1964, p. 61.

26 Rist, 1967a, p. 185; cf. 1964, p. 67.

27 Sumi (1997, p. 409) especially makes the point that Plotinus' view is obviously incongruent with Plato's own insistence that the Form is not a thought. In *Parmenides* 132b–c, Plato was only arguing that humans do not create the Forms by thinking about them, and Forms do not "disappear" or fail to exist if we are not thinking of them—he is denying some version of what we now refer to as conceptualism. But this does not imply that Nous or God or human souls cannot contemplate the Forms, as in fact, in the *Phaedrus,* Plato implies that they can—God and gods have clearer access thereto. Cf. A. H. Armstrong (1960, p. 399).

28 Here I agree with de Vogel (1970, p. 208); cf. Ambuel (2007, p. 121), who argues against the view that Plato is revising his theory of Forms here—I take it that Plato is discussing Nous here and not the Forms themselves; and Benitez (1995, pp. 132–3).

29 I basically agree with the following commentators on the following points of interpretation: Findlay (1978, p. 163) on the *Sophist* interpretation here; Menn (1995, p. 23): "Read in its full context, the *Sophist* passage not only permits but *requires* that *nous* should be a separate intelligible being"; de Vogel (1970, p. 197), that Forms are not living, thinking and moving, and that the *Timaeus* (30b–c; see 30c–31b and 37c–d as well) has the same view of an absolute Living Being with a soul that thinks (pp. 198–9).

30 *tōi pantelōs onti* (see the quotation) is also translated "that which wholly is," "what completely is," "perfect Being," or "absolute Being." Note that Plato is in general addressing the "friends of the Forms" in this passage, which starts at 248a. Mohr (2005, p. 191) *tōi pantelōs onti* "what completely is;" de Vogel (1970, p. 197) argues against that translation in favor of "perfect Being" or "absolute Being," because *on* "to be taken as '*existential* being'" and *pantelōs* means "in an absolute way"; White translates it "that which wholly is" (Cooper 1997, p. 270). On any of

these renderings, however, we can only interpret this phrase as denoting Plato's intelligible region.

31 See also: "So He [that is, God or Nous], then, having given all these commands, was living in His own proper and usual state" (*Timaeus* 42e5–6; adapted from Bury), which Plotinus quotes in V.4.2. I disagree with Rist (1964, p. 43) who argues that Plotinus misinterprets "*Sophist* 248D*ff.*" as saying that the Forms are active powers and that Being is a Form: Forms are active powers according to Plato—they cause everything of their kind to be that kind of thing. Moreover, contra Rist, who charges that "*Sophist* 248D*ff.*" is the *locus classicus* for those who find a Form of Being in Plato, I believe that Plato is committed to that Form in all of the following passages: *Phaedrus* 247c–e, *Theaetetus* 185c–d, 186a, *Timaeus* 27e–8a, 35a–b, *Sophist* 249d, 250b–e, 254a, 254c–d, 256d, 257a–b, 258a–b, 259a–b; cf. *Cratylus* 439c–d.

32 I agree with Findlay (1975, p. 674–5), who argues that Mind is "Intelligence itself" and has knowledge; he also claims that Aristotle borrowed much from Plato on the subject of the Divine Intelligence thinking itself [when it thinks of everything—de Vogel (1970, pp. 208–9)] seems to agree with Findlay on the Aristotelian view. Moreover, I agree with de Vogel on these two points: the idea (in reference to *Sophist* 248e–9a) that thinking cannot be denied of "intelligible Being itself" (1969a, p. 228; cf. 1970, pp. 207–8 and 1986, p. 74), and that the Forms do not themselves think (1970, p. 197). I take issue with Carone (2005, p. 4), who conceives of an intelligent living being (as God) for Plato, but claims that this God just *is* the universe. This issue is a bit beyond the scope of this section, but Carone argues that there is no intelligent being beyond the perceptible universe. My reply is that Plato states in the *Sophist* that we cannot deny intelligence of the absolutely real, and we know that in his view the perceptible universe is but a copy of the intelligible region, the realm of the absolutely real.

33 Cf. *Laws* X 892b.

34 See de Vogel (1970, pp. 198–9).

35 See also Findlay (1978, pp. 176–7), who argues that Mind, and Life itself, are the cause referred to in *Philebus* 28d–30d; I agree with Keyt (1971, pp. 233), who states that that the Absolute Living Creature in the *Timaeus* is eternal; I also agree with de Vogel (1969, p. 228; 1970, pp. 196–9, 208) on this issue (that Plato is best interpreted as saying that Nous is living); and, with J. Whittaker (1968, p. 143), that the Living Creature (qua Form) is not itself alive. Cf. Mohr (2005, pp. 35, 183) on this issue generally.

36 The way in which I have construed the *Sophist* passage allows me to agree with Menn (1995, p. 21): "Hackforth is right to say that Plato is here requiring a soul 'of that which *has nous*, not of that which *is nous*.'" I believe Plato is arguing

that if something has intelligence (and other characteristics), it must have a soul, but I also believe that, in the larger context (especially at *Sophist* 248e–9a), Plato is claiming that we must attribute soul to the intelligible region in some way. I realize that this solution may not please Menn, however. Cf. Carone (2005, p. 44), who argues that the Demiurge (which I identify with Nous and God—in general) has a soul. I disagree with her conception, however, that God just *is* the universe (4); see note 53 below.

37 I agree with Cornford (1957, pp. 244–5) and Gerson (2005, p. 267) that the *Forms* do not necessarily change, according to Plato's argument at *Sophist* 248e–9a. However, Gerson (1994, p. 251n. 74; cf. p. 99 and Carone 2005, p. 212n. 75) argues that *Phaedrus* 245c4 and *Laws* X 896a5–b1 state that soul is the source of all motion, but that *Laws* X 897c5–6, d3 mentions the motion of *nous* (I will leave it ambiguous between human *nous* and Nous), which "would seem to contradict what the *Phaedrus* says unless [*kinēsis*] is being used equivocally or intellect and soul are actually more closely connected than Plato explicitly indicates." Without taking a hard line against Gerson, I merely want to note that this motion of reason may just be that of the All-Soul, which governs the universe just as the Intelligible Region governs the universe, in the sense that the Forms cause everything of their kind to be that kind of thing. Moreover, Motion Itself exists at the level of Nous in Plato's view. I also appreciate Hackforth's (1965, p. 446) explanation that the activity of Nous is motion as well as Menn's (1995, p. 23) explanation of the *Sophist* argument. I agree with de Vogel (1969, p. 228; 1970, pp. 197, 207–9) on the issue of the necessity of Nous' having motion. See also Findlay (1978, p. 164), who gives an account of the Forms' possibly changing; and Mohr (2005, p. 192) for an interesting rendition of the *Sophist* passage. Cf. Keyt (1969, 1), who argues that if the Forms are known, they are acted upon; Being is a Form, so Being (when known) changes; on this point, see also Ambuel (2007, pp. 119–21).

38 For Motion Itself references, see *Parmenides* 129e, *Sophist* 252d, 254d; cf. *Parmenides* 130b, *Timaeus* 57d–8a.

39 Carone 2005, p. 44–5; see also p. 49.

40 I agree with the following commentators that Plotinus may be reading Plato correctly in his interpretation: Ciapolo (1997, p. 489); Deck (1967, p. 48n. 7); Inge (1929b, p. 40–1); Sumi (1997, pp. 410–12). I disagree with A. H. Armstrong (1947, p. 187; see also 1971, pp. 68, 74), who argues: "The World of Forms as Plotinus describes it differs a good deal from Plato's. Its organic character as a single living reality is greatly stressed, probably as the result of Stoic influence." Whether or not Armstrong is correct about the Stoic influence, Plato himself was committed to the view that there was an eternal living being, that the Demiurge modeled the universe after (*Timaeus*) and that the perfectly real must have life (*Sophist*). Cf. Corrigan (2005, p. 229) and Rist (1964, pp. 61, 94).

41 I agree with Findlay (1974, pp. 315, 372; 1976, p. 31) and Inge (1929b, pp. 40–1) that Plotinus believes that Intellect has intelligence. I disagree with A. H. Armstrong on several points: (1) That Plotinus' Nous is self-contemplating and contemplating the One, but Plato's Nous is the Demiurge, which is concerned with the world of sense (1940, pp. 88–9). I have shown that *Sophist* 248e7–9b4 passage commits Plato to Nous' cognitive capability, and I will deal with the Demiurge later. But there is no prohibition in Nous' working through its creation (the All-Soul) in governing the universe, so I can answer Armstrong's concern that only Plato's Nous is concerned with the world of sense, even if I am wrong that Nous is the Demiurge. (2) That the Plotinian Forms are living intelligences in Nous (1947, pp. 187–8); this is not an implausible view of Plato, given his claims that the whole intelligible region is an Absolute Living Thing, and that Nous has intelligence, and given that both philosophers believe that Forms are causes of their likenesses—so Forms are not merely "static objects of contemplation," as Armstrong presumably says of the Platonic Forms. (3) That Platonic Forms are not a divine Mind's thoughts (1960, p. 399). However, given that Platonic Nous is intelligent and wise, it stands to reason that the objects of Its thought would be the Forms, including the Form to the Good. (4) That Albinus' identification of the Peripatetic divine *noēton* [mind] with the *noēta* [thoughts] of the "thoughts of God" interpretation of Platonism, the Forms of Ideas was the principal stimulus of Plotinus' similar identification: "This identification is extremely important, because it is only through it that the doctrine of the self-thinking intellect can be brought into a Platonic system" (1960, pp. 411–12). However, if we do see Plato arguing that the perfectly real—that which I am interpreting as Nous or Intellect—possesses intelligence, then the idea that the Forms are its thoughts is consistent with this reading, and I need not look to Aristotle or any other Middle Platonist or Peripatetic in order to find this doctrine in Plato. Lastly, I disagree with Bréhier (1958, pp. 100–1), who argues: "If the intelligible must exist in Intelligence, we must indeed understand the counterpart of this thesis, namely, that the intelligible is fused with Intelligence itself. 'Essential truth is not agreement with another thing, but agreement with itself. Truth affirms nothing but itself. It is, and it affirms its being.' Intelligence is then an immediate passage from thought to being, but to the very being of thought. To affirm the immanence of the intelligible in this sense is not to denote a simple difference with traditional Platonism. It is its exact opposite. It is denying any diversity in the intelligible world." Plato says that the intelligible is infused with intelligence, and it makes Platonic sense for Nous to confirm its truth, since every member of Nous would be true and a being. Further, if thought is part of the perfectly real (as Plato says it is in *Sophist* 248d–9b), then, while it is not necessarily true that it is an immediate passage from thought to being, it would be true that thought and

being are at the same level, so to speak, in the Intelligible Region (cf. Sumi 1997, pp. 406–7).

42 On the motion or change of Nous in particular, I agree with A. H. Armstrong (1967b, p. 246) that Plotinus can find his position in Plato, but disagree with him that for Plato the intelligible world is one of "statuesque immobility," thanks in part to *Sophist* 248d–9b. On all these traits in general, I agree with de Vogel (1953, p. 56–7), who says that Plotinus and Plato have the same view on these traits of Nous. I disagree with Anton (2010, p. 9), who claims that Plotinus recasts the role of Nous (my reply is my coverage of Nous in this project), and with A. E. Taylor (1934, pp. 154–6), who holds that the Mind of Plotinus might be equivalent to the one in the *Timaeus,* but denies Plotinus' interpretation of Nous overall.

43 See, for example, *Timaeus* 39e1, e8. For more on Plotinus' reading of the "living being" passage in the *Timaeus*, see III.9.1.

44 Cf. IV.8.3.14–21.

45 See also III.2.4.

46 For further Plotinian passages that discuss Nous' intelligence, wisdom and understanding, see V.4.2, V.5.1, VI.7.35, 37, VI.9.5; cf. V.8.5, V.9.5, VI.2.8.

47 See also VI.2.20.16–23, where Plotinus discusses Nous' intellect as well as individual souls' intellects.

48 See also V.9.14.20–2.

49 For further Plotinian passages that discuss the changeability (or lack thereof) of Nous, see II.2.3, II.9.1–2, III.7.3, VI.7.13, VI.9.5; cf. II.1.4, and Gerson (1994, p. 47) adds I.1.8.4–6 and III.7.5.25–8 to my list. I concur with Gerson's (2005b, p. 268) explanation of the Neo-Platonists' supposition that Intellect must have something that changes in it. I disagree with McGroarty (2006, p. 169), who argues—in the context of pleasure's being possibly attributed to Plotinian Nous, since pleasure implies replenishment of a lack—that the Platonic Nous has no movement of any kind. However, not all pleasures are replenishments from lacks; pleasures of knowledge and good odors imply no such prior lacks.

50 See also VI.7.39 for a passage where Plotinus refers to the movement of Intellection.

51 Note that Corrigan (2005, p. 185) and Rist (1967a, p. 215) both correctly argue that Plotinus' view is not pantheistic, contra Zeller (1931, p. 294).

52 Nonetheless, I agree with J. Armstrong (2004, p. 175), that God is the creator in Plato's view; Morrow (1950, p. 151), that the true cause in the *Phaedo* is a craftsman, which is equivalent to the God or Demiurge of the *Timaeus*; and Mohr (2005: ix), who reminds us that God does not strictly make the world "*out of* anything," even though he is described as a craftsman or maker. I disagree with Pistorius (1952, pp. 23–4), who argues that there is nothing in the nature of the

Good (qua God) to make it a creator. That may be so in Pistorius' view, and Plato may not have told us precisely the way in which either the Good or Nous (God) creates, but nonetheless Plato says it, which is all my project requires. It does not make much sense that the Good should be the first principle, but then Plotinus comes along and agrees with Plato—this just makes it more probable that there is some vision one can have of the Good which "tells" one that this is the way things are, versus the option that Plotinus merely liked or deferred to Plato's arguments to come to have that view.

53 I agree with the following commentators on this issue: J. Armstrong (2004, pp. 171, 174), God is Nous in the *Timaeus*, the *Philebus* and the *Laws*; Findlay (1974, p. 204), God is "eternal Thinkingness", but not where he says that the God of *Phaedrus* 249c is "Mind as Such" (1974, p. 154); Hackforth (1946, p. 123), God is Nous in the *Timaeus*; Joseph (1948, p. 22), God is Nous in general; Menn (1992, p. 546), God is Nous in the *Timaeus*, the *Philebus* and *Laws* XII; Menn (1992, p. 571), the highest Platonic God is the Good, beyond Nous; Menn (1995, p. 5), God-Divine Cause in the *Timaeus* and the *Statesman* is Nous—see also pp. 7–8; Menn (ibid., p. 6), God is Nous in the *Timaeus*); Mohr (2005, p. 20) the Platonic God does not resemble the God of the ontological argument. I disagree with the following commentators: Bechtle (1999, p. 86), that the "mainstream" Platonic tradition identifies the One or Good with the first God and mind; Plato usually refers to God as Nous and only in one prominent place as the Good. Benitez (1995, p. 118), who argues that the Good (of *Republic* VI) equals the Demiurge (of the *Timaeus*), equals God (of *Laws* IV). The Good of *Republic* VI is beyond being, the Demiurge is an eternal being that creates the All-Soul and looks to the Forms to create the perceptible universe. Benitez (1995, pp. 132–3), that Divine Reason in the *Philebus* is the Good; on the contrary, I believe Socrates is stating that Nous is very good, but that our human reason is not the ultimate good, implying as other dialogues do that if we wish to be good, we must be godlike, which is also consistent with the claim that Nous is God. Carone (2005, p. 42), that God must have a body; if Nous is God, an eternal being, and the realm of the Forms, it is not in need of a body any more than the Form of Bed "needs" a perceptible bed to exist in order for it to exist. Carone (2005, p. 4), that "there is for Plato no god over and above the universe itself" (where "god" is an intelligent living being); we have seen that Nous is best read as being living in some sense, and that Nous is at the level of eternal beings (the Forms), and thus cannot be the perceptible, ever-becoming universe. Inge (1948a, p. 38), that God equals Soul for Platonists. If Inge is referring to either Plato or Plotinus, I disagree, from the evidence adduced. Joseph (1948, p. 67; cf. de Vogel 1969, p. 236), that God does not refer to the Good in *Republic* X—he seems to note the passage, but not state that this "God" must be different from other occurrences

thereof. Mohr (2005, pp. xxi–xxii, p. 20; cf. pp. 149–50), that God in *Laws* X (apparently at 894e–5b) is different than the God of the *Timaeus* because the former is proved to exist cosmologically; my reply is that *Laws* X 894e–895b only intends to establish a soul qua first-mover, or All-Soul, or perhaps even the Form of Motion—as a first mover that is not moved by something else—but does not prove that God, the Demiurge, Nous, or the Good exists; in fact, "God" does not appear in the passage. Rist (1964, p. 182), that for Plato, God does not equal the Good; Rist is right in general, except for *Republic* X. Strong (1895, p. 106), that the Good of the *Republic* is equivalent to the *Timaeus*' creator and the *Philebus*' cause; the Good is beyond being and the cause of Intellect or Nous; the latter two (creator and cause) are Nous. A. E. Taylor (1956, p. 232, cf. pp. 491–2), that Plato portrays God as soul in the *Laws* but as immutable and eternal everywhere else, and not as equivalent to the Good, such that his view is incoherent; while he does refer to different entities when he uses "God," we can usually figure out to which he is referring. I again disagree with A. E. Taylor (1934, pp. 152–4), who considers many options as to what God could refer to, usually siding with Nous, but sometimes with soul, and he asks whether God could refer to the Good, without noting the *Republic* X passage. Taylor is making more of the problem than is there, and is not proving that, in most cases, "God" refers to Nous in Plato. And de Vogel (1969, pp. 225–6): "God-the-Demiurge in the *Timaeus* and God-the-good-World-Soul in *Laws* X might actually have taken the place of the Ideas and the Good"; just because the Demiurge and All-Soul are good does not imply that they are *the* Good; they are not said to be beyond being, the source of knowledge, truth, and the Forms, as the Good is. There is no reason to believe that Plato gave up, or changed, his view of the Form of the Good in later dialogues.

54 This assumes that when Socrates uses the word God in the *Apology* and *Crito*, those references are meant to be interpreted as the views of Socrates and not Plato. However, Socrates only makes statements such as these—all of which are perfectly compatible with what we read in the middle and late dialogues concerning God and the gods: "when God ordered me, as I thought and believed, to live the life of a philosopher, to examine myself and others" (*Apology* 28e4–6; adapted from Grube); "I do know, however, that it is wicked and shameful to do wrong, to disobey one's superior, be he God or man" (29b6–7); "I will obey God rather than you" (d3–4); a good man's "affairs are not neglected by the gods" (41d2–3); "let us act in this way, since this is the way God is leading us" (*Crito* 54e1–2; adapted from Grube).

55 Here I disagree with Murdoch (1993, p. 38), who states that "Plato never identified his Form of the Good with God (the use of *theos* at *Republic* 597B is a *façon de parler*), and this separation is for him an essential one. Religion is

above the level of the 'gods'. There are no gods and no God either. Neo-Platonic thinkers made the *identification* (of God with Good) possible." First, no one should assume that, when Plato uses *theos*, he has in mind any of the standard Western monotheistic conceptions, including a personal God. It is a simple and justified interpretation to make from Plato's claiming in Books VI and VII that the Good is the creator or source of the Forms, to Book X, where he claims that God creates the Forms. If this is only a manner of speaking, then is what Plato says about the Form of the Good a *façon de parler* as well? Second, Plato not only does not deny God's (or the gods') existence, he affirms it many times, and is concerned about the atheist's views and how to convert him in the *Laws*; thus Murdoch is over-reaching in her claim that there are no gods and no God in Plato. Lastly, echoing the first point, we do not need to credit the Neo-Platonists with making it possible to identify God with the Good, at least in this passage, for the reasons given already.

56 Thus, I should not be taken to have Doherty's (1956, p. 459) view that it is more probable that Plato identifies God with the Good in general.

57 Also, in the *Phaedo*, Plato claims that the deathless is eternal [*aidion*] (106d3), and that God (and anything that is deathless) is never destroyed (106d5–6), which implies that God is eternal. If God is eternal, however, since the All-Soul is in time, then "God" cannot refer to the All-Soul.

58 Both Plato and Plotinus think that the created, visible, universe is the fairest and best of all possible worlds. For Platonic passages, see: *Gorgias* 507e–508a, *Republic* VII 530a, *Timaeus* 28a–9c, 29d–31b, 41a–d, 53b, 68e–9a, 92c and *Philebus* 28d–9a, 30a–c; cf. *Timaeus* 47e–8a and *Statesman* 269c–70b. For Plotinian passages, see: IV.8.1, V.8.12, II.9.4, III.2.1, 3, 17; cf. IV.4.36, II.9.9, II.9.17, III.2.2, 4, 6; III.2.11, 14; III.3.7. I agree with A. H. Armstrong (1967b: 231) when he says that Plotinus "maintains, in a genuinely Platonic way, that it is neither a perfect world nor a wholly bad world, but the best world which divinity could produce in the difficult conditions of this lower level."

59 Not surprisingly, in a gibe against Protagoras, Plato argues that God is preeminently the measure of all things, and not man, as Protagoras says; the moderate man is God's friend, being like him; the immoderate, unjust (and other vices) man is unlike God and God's enemy (*Laws* IV 716c–d). This is completely consistent with Plato's philosophy, given that Nous is the level of Forms, which are eternal standards to which the Demiurge looks to create the universe, and which the perceptible realm imitates.

60 Note that Plato refers to the "king of all" in *Letter* II 312e1–2, which is best interpreted as referring to the One or Good. This merely shows, however, that Plato himself uses "God" and "king" in different ways in different dialogues; it does not show that Plotinus' view of God is not the same as Plato's.

61 I concur with Shorey's (1938, p. 49) description that, according to Plotinus, Nous is the Demiurge or God of Plato; the only caveat is that I think Shorey denies this claim.

62 See, for instance VI.9.6.10–13; see also III.4.2.12–15, V.5.3 (Nous is God, a "great" and "second" God), and Sleeman et al. (1980, pp. 497–8) for further references. In my view, the occurrences of "God" in V.1.11 and V.5.9.30–5 do not clearly refer to either Nous or the One.

63 The following commentators note that "God" refers to the One or Good in Plotinus and/or Plato: Leftow (1990, pp. 585, 592) and Mayhall (2004, p. 1–2) note that both philosophers identify God with the One (I add that I have Plato only using "God" for the Good once); Stace (1967, pp. 372–3; for Plotinus and not for Plato); Rist (1962b, pp. 172–3, 179). Inge puzzlingly denies that Plotinus refers to God as the One (1948a, p. 45; Plotinus does not use the word God of the "Absolute" which is "the One" or "the Good;" cf. 1948b, p. 153).

64 See also V.1.11, VI.8.15, 17, 19–21; and see Sleeman et al. (1980, p. 498) and Rist (1962b, pp. 172–3, 179) for more references.

65 See *Timaeus* 53b, for the statement that God created the fairest and best possible world, thus anticipating Leibniz's view hundreds of years later.

66 Plato mentions all of the following gods and discusses their genealogy: Oceanus, Tethys, Earth, Heaven, Phorcys, Kronos, Rhea, Zeus and Hera (*Timaeus* 40e5–41a1), "all the gods in that generation" and their "siblings" (41a1-3).

67 See also: "['God' at 69b3] himself fashioned those that were divine, but assigned his own progeny the task of fashioning the generation of those that were mortal" (*Timaeus* 69c3–5). Cf. 46c–e.

68 For references where Plotinus says: "Intellect makes the world of sense through parts of soul," see Majumdar (2007a, p. 118).

69 See also II.1.5.1–5.

70 See also I.2.7.3–4; cf. III.2.1.18.

71 Also, if humans can be wise and should be godlike, and if God just *is* Intellect or Nous and has knowledge, then how could God not also be wise?

72 De Vogel (1970, p. 206) reminds us that in the *Timaeus* the Forms are referred to as eternal gods as well.

73 For Plato's arguments to support the proposition that gods exist, see *Laws* X 887c–8d, 899c–d, and 905b–d; for passages that the gods care about humans, see *Republic* X 613a–b and *Laws* X 907a–b, and see the Athenian's arguments directed in opposition to the polytheists (those who believe in many gods who do not interact with humans), at *Laws* X 899d–903e, and 905b–d. For a statement that theology is the most important study, see *Laws* XII 966c; that we should always begin every significant undertaking with a prayer to the gods, see *Timaeus* 27c–d.

74 See also, further in the passage, where Plotinus says that the gods continually contemplate the things in that higher heaven, which are said to be the Forms in Intellect (V.8.3.27–34).

75 So O'Meara (2003, p. 38), who says Plotinus held that there were more gods, and more differentiated ones.

76 This paragraph is my response to A. H. Armstrong (1938, p. 194–5), who argues that Plotinus and Plato have very different views on the gods' caring for humans, and that Plotinus believes that the gods cannot be bothered to help vicious humans. Moreover, Plato nowhere states that the gods aid bad souls in the sense that their aid will actually benefit them later; such aid will actually harm a vicious, undeserving recipient.

77 Cf. III.2.9 and III.5.6.9–10.

78 Here I concur with Mohr (2005, pp. xxi, 54) and Doherty (1961, p. 513), but I note that I arrived at this judgment before reading their view on this issue. Reale (1997, pp. 308–15) actually claims that the Demiurge is in the *Phaedo* in principle because Plato says Nous or Mind is the cause of all things, cf. 98b–9b.

79 Cf. *Republic* X 596b–7d, where Plato alludes that God is the master craftsman, producing the Forms and everything else, such as animals; however, I hold that God in that passage is best construed as being the Good, since it is claimed there that God creates the Forms.

80 The following commentators hold or argue that the Platonic Demiurge is God: Benitez (1995, pp. 128–9); Carone (2005, p. 54); Findlay (1974, p. 304); Joseph (1948, p. 22); Menn (1992, p. 546; 1995, p. 6); Mohr (2005, pp. ix, xxi—but not the God of *Laws* X). The Demiurge is Nous: Carone (2005, p. 35); Findlay (1974, p. 304; 1975, pp. 674–5; 1978, pp. 52, 185–6); Hackforth (1965, p. 439); Menn (1992, pp. 546, 557; 1995, pp. 6–8, 10, 48, 67n. 3; 2001, pp. 245–6); de Vogel (1969, pp. 226, 228–9; 1970, pp. 202, 205; 1986, p. 40). The Demiurge is not the Good: More (1923, pp. 218–19), or just the Forms: Carone (2005, p. 45). Reale (1997, p. 326) gives five parallels between the Demiurge of the *Statesman* and the *Timaeus*. I disagree with the following commentators' views that: (1) The Demiurge is the Good: Benitez (1995, pp. 118–19, 126–9); Doherty (1961, p. 515; "the Demiurge is not a being distinct from the Good, not an inferior subagent, but rather an epiphany of the Good in its relation to the visible cosmos"); Shorey (1895, pp. 65–6; he seems open to this possibility); Strong (1895, p. 106); de Vogel (1969, pp. 225–6; "God-the-Demiurge in the *Timaeus* and God-the-good-World-Soul in *Laws* X might actually have taken the place of the Ideas in the Good. Or what else can we think?"); (2) The Demiurge is not God: de Vogel (1953, p. 52; "I do not think that Plato himself gives us reason to make this identification"); (3) The Demiurge is the World-Soul or soul of the universe: Carone (2005, pp. 19, 43–5); Cornford (1937, p. 197; 1939, pp. v–vi);

(4) The Demiurge is illogical or mad: Keyt (1971, p. 232; "mad craftsman"); Pistorius (1952, p. 58; "illogical God"); see Mohr's (2005, pp. 12–13) convincing argument against this view; (5) The Demiurge is Eros: Murdoch (1993, p. 146; "The *Timaeus* Demiurge, a high but not highest being, is also Eros"); I disagree, because Timaeus states that the Demiurge is eternal (and I view the Demiurge as God for Plato), and Eros is said to be a demi-god and not either eternal or (a) God; (6) There is no ontology in the *Timaeus*: Sayre (1983, p. 241); cf. Dillon (1989, p. 72). I like Mohr's (2005, p. 37) point that, since the Demiurge (for instance) appears in mythical (*Timaeus*, *Statesman*) and non-mythical (*Republic*, *Sophist*, *Philebus*) settings, we cannot easily excise him from Platonic metaphysics. I am not sure if I agree with Mohr (2005, p. xxii; and Ch. 11, esp. pp. 198–9) that the God of the *Laws* X is not the *Timaeus* God, but we do not need to settle that issue for our present purposes. Lastly, see Mohr (2005, pp. 36–7) for other interesting—but in my view mistaken—interpretations of the Demiurge.

81 There are several general interpretive issues for the *Timaeus*: (1) Whether or not to take the *Timaeus* literally in general; see Cherniss (1944, pp. 421–32); Dillon (1989, p. 72); Johansen (2004, pp. 51–2); Mohr (2005, pp. 213–14); Morrow (1950, p. 151); Shorey (1938, p. 49); Silverman (2002, p. 257). Karamanolis (2006, p. 241) and Schroeder (1996, p. 339) claim that Plotinus takes the *Timaeus* non-literally in general—I do not agree. (2) Whether the world's creation took place in time or not. (3) Whether we should take the Demiurge literally or whether we can rid our interpretation of the *Timaeus* of the Demiurge period; see Johansen (2004, p. 79–83), with whom I agree in his assessment that we need the Demiurge to explain how the Forms, Receptacle and appearances were "regimented in the creation of an ordered cosmos" (p. 83). I will simply examine the texts and show that Plato and Plotinus make similar claims concerning the Demiurge and the creation of the universe.

82 The Greek for Demiurge (*ho dēmiourgos*) first appears at *Timaeus* 28a6, but it is used generally and hypothetically there for a creator of any object, and not this universe, as at 28c.

83 Cf. *Timaeus* 38b.

84 I agree with these commentators that the Demiurge or God creates the World-Soul: Findlay (1974, p. 304; 1978, pp. 52, 185–6; cf. 1975, p. 675); Menn (1992, p. 557; 1995, pp. 47, 52); Mohr (2005, pp. 165, 182–4); de Vogel (1970, p. 205); cf. Wilberding (2006, pp. 6–7). And that the Demiurge is not identical to the World-Soul: Hackforth (1965, p. 439); Menn (1995, p. 12), "nothing authorizes us to override Plato's contrast between the [World-Soul], 'which has become the best of the generated things,' and the god who has made it such, 'the best of the intelligible and eternally existing things' (*Timaeus* 37a1–2)"; cf.

p. 67n. 3); de Vogel (1970, p. 202); cf. Mohr (2005, pp. 189–90, 194–5). Moreover, Menn (1995, p. 9) rightly claims that the Demiurge carries out the plan when he harmonizes the World-Soul.

85 See Mohr (2005, p. 52–3); but see Wilberding (2006, pp. 6–7), who argues that there is not a temporal beginning to Plato's creation of the universe.

86 For further Platonic evidence that the World-Soul is in time, see p. 202, n. 28

87 Carone (2005, p. 44). See also: "We have shown that *nous* cannot exist without motion, motion presupposes space, and space presupposes body". (p. 49; and see, pp. 44–5). An additional proponent of this view is McEvilley (2002, p. 162); my objections apply to his view as well.

88 Wilberding (2006, p. 21), for instance, notes that the Demiurge is in motion as well. Also, "motion" translates *kinēsin*, which can also be translated as "change."

89 Carone (2005, pp. 44–5, 49).

90 This soul is also the soul that Nous somehow has, in the *Sophist*.

91 It is interesting to note that Gerson (1994, p. 63) raises this possibility for Plotinus, saying that it is not explicitly stated in the *Enneads*, but implied in these spots: II.3.18.15, II.9.8.2–5, III.9.1.2, IV.4.10.2–3, IV.8.1.43–50, V.1.8.6–7, V.8.2.4.

92 As Carone (2005, p. 36) reminds us, the Demiurge does not create the matter, but Plato says that the soul is placed in the body of the universe (*Timaeus* 34b), even though the soul is prior to body.

93 I concur with Inge (1929a, pp. 76–7) and Phillips (1997, pp. 195–7) here. Gerson (1994, pp. 56–7) says that Plotinus has an inconsistent view of the Demiurge.

94 See Gerson (1994, p. 105) for a list of references where Plotinus states that the sensible world is an image of the intelligible world.

95 See also II.1.5.5–8. Shorey (1888, p. 407) says that the *Timaeus* was a sacred Neo-Platonist text, "every letter of which was charged with mystic meanings." If one merely reads what Plato says there, however, it is pretty clear that this is his creation story, parts of which are confirmed outside the *Timaeus*.

96 See II.1.5.5–8, II.9.6 (where he admonishes the Gnostics for misreading into their Plato the view that Soul is the creator and not Mind; cf. II.9.10), II.3.18, III.9.1, IV.8.1, V.1.8, V.1.10, V.8.7, V.8.8, V.9.3 (cf. II.4.7). I am in good company in this assessment that Intellect (Nous) is the Demiurge in Plotinus' view: A. H. Armstrong (1967b, p. 252); Blumenthal (1971, p. 58; citing "II.3.18.9*ff*."); Rist (1964, pp. 61–2); Shorey (1938, p. 49); Wilberding (2006, pp. 58, 174; even though he seems to hint that our thinkers differ on this issue—see pp. 68–70). This makes it highly improbable that the assessments of A. E. Taylor (1934, pp. 158–9), and A. H. Armstrong, made earlier in his work that the Demiurge is the World-Soul (1940, pp. 87–9; 189; 1960, p. 411: "Plotinus knew, and wished to respect at least verbally, the tradition which made the Forms in the *Timaeus* the plan in the mind of the divine architect") are correct.

97 Gerson (1993, pp. 567–8) notes that the Demiurge is good as well. Technically, the passage is hypothetical—if the craftsman is good, then he modeled the universe on the eternal model, but elsewhere says that the Demiurge did model the universe after the eternal (*Timaeus* 28a–b, 29e–31a, 37c–d).

98 Gerson (1994, p. 40) correctly points out that necessity for Plato and Plotinus is "whatever happens outside the control of [*nous*] or intellect," contra More (1923, pp. 221, 221n. 19).

99 I will briefly address these commentators' objections: Anton (2010, p. 14) argues that Plotinus "altered the independence of the Forms" in the *Timaeus* (14n. 11), using it beyond its original setting, to hold that the Forms were in the Nous or the Divine Intellect, which is "clearly a non-Platonic stance." Plato unequivocally states that the Demiurge uses the Forms as paradigms to create the perceptible universe, at *Timaeus* 28a–31b, and, since God desires (30a), reflects (30b) and is wise, it stands to reason that God-Demiurge-Nous can contemplate the Forms, as Sumi (1997, pp. 407–8) says. Atkinson (1983, pp. 22–3, 189); and see Wilberding (2006, p. 180) for a similar line—he objects that Plato's Demiurge is similar to Plotinus' but creates the body of the sun, moon and planets, unlike Plotinus' Demiurge; see V.8.7.8–10, however, where it is pretty clear that Plotinus has in mind a Demiurge who has the Forms in mind before creating the earth, water, the heavens and the rest. Bréhier (1958, p. 4) believes that Plotinus no longer has the view that the Demiurge brings about the creation of the sensible world according to an ideal model; but see V.8.7.8–10, for which Bréhier must account. Rist (1973, p. 83) charges that, in Plotinus' creation story, "there is no pre-existent material substrate, the *Timaeus* notwithstanding. Or, rather, the *Timaeus* is re-interpreted." However, Plotinus directly refers at V.8.7.6–7 to Plato's view about matter, that evil comes from the "ancient nature," where matter is not yet set in order, but does not claim that matter came into existence, keeping in mind that Plato and Plotinus both agree that soul is prior to body. See also *Statesman* 273b, d, which A. H. Armstrong (1966a, p. 296) cites in reference to this passage) for Plato, and III.6.11, I.8.3, V.8.7, III.6.8, for Plotinus.

100 Corrigan (1996, p. 112). See also Majumdar (2007a, pp. 98–9), who refers to Bréhier as her source.

101 Following Emilsson (1988, p. 17), who says they are Forms or Kinds, because Plato is committed to the existence of these entities as Forms elsewhere. Inge (1929b, p. 57) argues that the Five Greatest Kinds cannot be identical with the Ideas because: "There is no place among them for Truth, Beauty, or the Good." Aside from the point that the Five Greatest Kinds are said elsewhere to be Forms, if all the Ideas partake in each other and "blend" (*Republic* V 475e6–6a7, *Sophist* 259e4–7, and *Timaeus* 35a1–6; Plotinus: IV.2.2.42–55, II.3.11.10–13, II.4.11, III.3.4, III.6.19, IV.7.8[1], V.8.7, VI.2.19, VI.3.10, 20, 25, VI.9.8) then Beauty, and

Truth, if it is a Form, can partake of Being, as well as Sameness—being the same as itself—and Difference (being different from other Forms). The Good is said to be both a being and not a being, so it is difficult to conclusively state if it partakes in Being or not. The Good would presumably be the source of the Five Greatest Kinds. Pistorius (1952, p. 31) claims that the Forms of Plotinus do not, as they do in Plato, form a hierarchy, but are unity. My evidence, including what is said about the Good and Beauty, seems to undermine this claim, as well as that the Platonic Intelligible Region (Nous) seems as unified as Plotinus'.

102 Cf. *Timaeus* 35a–b, where Timaeus discusses Being, Sameness, and Difference.

103 The Greek is *megista mēn tōn genōn* at *Sophist* 254d4.

104 Chen (1944, p. 114) hints and Pistorius (1952, p. 37) asserts that Not-Being is also one of the supposed "Six" Greatest Kinds. Based on my analysis of *Sophist* 257d–8b, that denies bad Forms, I admit this theoretical possibility, but deny it based on what Plato actually says.

105 A. E. Taylor (1956, p. 389) more assertively claims that Plotinus follows Plato on this issue. See Gerson (1994: 57, 100, 261n. 58); Inge (1929b, p. 60); Rist (1964, pp. 42–3), for further detail as to how closely Plotinus follows Plato on this issue. Corrigan (1996, p. 115) describes Plotinus' view of the Five Greatest Kinds, and I merely want to emphasize that this is Plato's view as well, especially since Corrigan (1996, p. 106) states that Plotinus "adapts" Plato's view of the Five Greatest Kinds from the *Sophist* without describing what the alleged adaptation is. Puzzlingly, Inge (1929a, p. 192) claims that Plotinus is hampered because he has to accept the Five Greatest Kinds, though it is just an "impression." I fail to see why Plotinus, any more than Plato, is hampered by having such a view.

106 See also V.1.4, V.8.4, VI.2.7, 15, 18; VI.3.27, VI.6.9, 13.

# Chapter 4

1 Plotinus also refers to the All-Soul as the Cosmic Soul (*tēs psychēs kosmou*) at III.4.6.23; Plato alludes to the Cosmos' having a soul at *Timaeus* 30b, and *Philebus* 30a (cf. *Philebus* 30b–d; and see *Timaeus* 32c and *Philebus* 29e for the body of the world).

2 Unfortunately, I cannot also show, due to space limitations, that the All-Soul: (1) is immaterial; (2) is good and not evil; (3) is in the center of the universe and is itself one; (4) has intelligence, forethought, consciousness, and discursive reasoning; (5) envelops the body of the universe; (6) is prior to body; (7) controls heaven itself; (8) governs, is sovereign over and cares for the universe; (9) contains love; (10) is beautiful.

3 I agree here with Menn (1995, pp. 34–5; cf. p. 45) who makes this very point. Also, Mohr (2005, pp. 181, 186) makes some interesting points about the World-Soul. I disagree with Sayre (1983, p. 241), who claims that we find no ontology in the *Timaeus* because it is a "figurative exploration."

4 The Greek for "of the universe" is *tou pantos*, which can be translated "of the All" or "of everything" as well, which justifies the expression "All-Soul" for the Platonic name of the soul of the universe. For another use of this phrase, see, for example, *Timaeus* 41d. Note also that the *Enneads* are replete with Plotinus' phrase "the All," by which he usually refers to the universe, but sometimes it refers to Nous.

5 Compare this passage from the *Phaedrus*, where Plato states that the universe would collapse if the All-Soul did not exist: "A self-mover is a source of motion. And *that* is incapable of being destroyed or starting up; otherwise all heaven and everything that has been started up would collapse, come to a stop, and never have cause to start moving again" (*Phaedrus* 245d7–e2). For further references to the All-Soul, see *Timaeus* 30b–c, 34b–35b, 36d–37c and 41d; *Laws* X 896a–897d, 898c–d, 899b; cf. *Timaeus* 90d and *Laws* XII 966d–e.

6 I agree with these commentators who claim that the two philosophers have the same basic view, even if Plotinus might give more details about the All-Soul: A. H. Armstrong (1947, p. 189); Deck (1967, pp. 51–2; the All-Soul does not fall, according to both thinkers); Findlay (1975, p. 675); K. S. Guthrie (1896, p. 33; Plotinus took his view from Plato, not the Stoics); Inge (1929a, pp. 76–7); D. Jackson (1967, pp. 317, 325–7; *Parmenides* 155e–157b refers to World-Soul); Tripolis (1978, p. 51); de Vogel (1970, p. 205; visible realm governed by World-Soul); de Vogel (1986, p. 44; soul is metaphysically in between the ideal and sensible realms); and de Vogel (1986, p. 225; same basic view).

7 See also, for example, IV.3.1–7, 9 for many references to the Soul of the All. Cf. III.5.4.2–3, where Plotinus mentions "universal soul" and "the soul of the All," where these may be two entities—Soul, the Third Hypostasis and the All-Soul—or he may be referring to the same entity. Somewhat correspondingly, Plotinus makes some pretty direct arguments against materialism; see IV.7.5, 6, 8–12.

8 In using "eternal God," Plato most likely intends to refer to Nous.

9 I agree with the following commentators: Hackforth (1965, pp. 439, 442); Menn (1992, p. 557; 1995, pp. 37, 52; cf. 1995, pp. 24, 34); Mohr (2005, pp. 182–3, 189); de Vogel (1986, p. 223). I also agree with those who explicitly and correspondingly state that Nous creates souls: Menn (1995, p. 47) and de Vogel (1969, p. 229). I disagree with Carone (2005, pp. 43–4, 168, 212n. 75), who argues that Nous *is* the World-Soul. Contra Carone, see Hackforth (1965, p. 442) and Menn (1995, p. 12: "nothing authorizes us to override Plato's contrast between the World-Soul, "which has become the best of the generated things," and the god who has made it

such, "the best of the intelligible and eternally existing things" (*Timaeus* 37a1–2)"; Carone does not address their points.

10 Another affirmation that Nous is the source of the All-Soul: "Because it shares in reason and harmony, the soul came to be as the most excellent of all the things begotten by him who is himself most excellent of all that is intelligible and eternal" (*Timaeus* 36e6–37a2). See also 30b–c, where Plato claims that God created the universe as a living creature, endowed with soul and intelligence. I argue that the Demiurge is Nous, and Mohr (2005, pp. 182–3) reminds me that, "In the *Statesman* myth the Demiurge is said to make the World-Soul, to make it rational (269d1), and to form the ordered World-Body (269d7–9, 273b6–7, 273e3)", and of *Philebus* 30c–d (2005, p. 189).

11 I concur with the following commentators: Blumenthal (1971, p. 58); K. S. Guthrie (1896, p. 33); Wilberding (2006, p. 58); Witt (1931, p. 105).

12 See also, for example, II.1.4 and II.9.3; cf. IV.7.8 and V.1.10. Plotinus states that the All-Soul makes the universe a god at V.1.2. III.5.3.24 and refers to a "heavenly soul."

13 The following passage seems to claim that the soul indeed came to be: "Because it shares in reason and harmony, the soul came to be as the most excellent of all the things begotten by him who is himself most excellent of all that is intelligible and eternal" (*Timaeus* 36e6–37a2; see also 34c). However, per Gerson (1994: 122), perhaps time is created when soul is created, so there was no time when soul was not. Moreover, since Plato (*Phaedrus* 245c9–d4) and Plotinus (III.9.3.1–2) seem to state that it is impossible that the All-Soul can come into being, but also seem to indicate that it does come to being (*Timaeus* 34a8–b9 and III.5.3, IV.8.1.41–50, respectively), both philosophers appear to be equally inconsistent on this issue.

14 Menn (1995: 74n. 1) notes that circular motion "specially belongs to reason and intelligence" (*peri noun kai phronēsin malista ousan*) at *Timaeus* 34a2, and the World-Soul likewise has circular motion; Menn (2001, pp. 245–6) also states that souls have their home in the intelligible world, which is compatible with their contemplating Nous. Ignoring differences across dialogues that Mohr (2005, pp. 149–50) raises, I agree with the general point that the World-Soul is maintainer of orderly motion and Nous or God (which is not a soul) is a source of motion; and Mohr (2005, p. 151), where the World-Soul orders the universe to have circular motion as well. However, Carone (2005, p. 45) argues that, since the World-Soul "revolves upon itself" (*Timaeus* 36e3–4) and Nous revolves as well, the Demiurge is the World-Soul. As Menn (1995, p. 12) states, Nous is eternal and the World-Soul is generated, despite the fact that both in some way move or revolve; this does not show that Nous is the World-Soul. Silverman (2002, pp. 256-7) is agnostic on whether the Demiurge is "over and above the world-soul."

15 Cf. *Timaeus* 34a–b and *Philebus* 62a–b, where Plato discusses the divine circle and the divine sphere.

16 I also agree with Blumenthal (1971, p. 58) that the World-Soul and the individual souls have direct access to Nous (on their views).

17 For further passages on the All-Soul's following Nous, see I.7.2—soul is directed to the Good via intellect—and IV.3.11.

18 See also II.3.9.

19 Cf. Menn, 1995, p. 53.

20 Compare also what Plato says later: "When he had finished this speech, he turned again to the mixing bowl he had used before, the one in which he had blended and mixed the soul of the universe. He began to pour into it what remained of the previous ingredients and to mix them in somewhat the same way, though these were no longer invariably and constantly pure, but of a second and third grade of purity" (*Timaeus* 41d4–7).

21 De Vogel (1986, p. 72) argues against this possibility, based on *Timaeus* 41c–d, but I fail to see how she accounts for the passages I cite here.

22 I agree with Corrigan (1996, p. 113) that Plato and Plotinus basically have the same view here; Majumdar (2007a, p. 56), that Plotinus follows Plato at *Timaeus* 41d7; Majumdar (2007a, p. 117), that higher soul contemplates while a lower soul descends to deal with body (but this could refer to either a lower phase of World-Soul, star-souls or gods, or other individual souls—human, animal, or plant); Rist (1967b, p. 421), that both thinkers have the same view of the upper Soul; de Vogel (1986, p. 217), that "Soul is undivided, but it seems to divide itself to the benefit of the beings that receive it [VI.4.14.13–14]." I disagree with A. H. Armstrong (1947, p. 189; cf. pp. 190–3), that Plotinian upper Soul is Plato's God or Demiurge, and lower soul is Nature; as Armstrong himself notes, Plotinus himself denies that these phases (World-Soul and Nature) are really distinct. I also disagree with Helleman-Elgersma (1980, p. 136), who states that Plotinus says that the lower World-Soul is nature, but not only nature. Keeping in mind that Plato refers to nature as well, we have no incompatibility here. She bases her claim that lower World-Soul is nature on III.4.2, but this is compatible with Plato's view and does not explicitly state that the lower World-Soul is nature. I disagree with with Helleman-Elgersma (1980, p. 457), that Plotinus (but not Plato) says that our souls and the World-Soul are each derived from the same source; this is exactly what Plato implies at *Timaeus* 41d, where God is said to pour the remainder of the ingredients from which he made the World-Soul into a cup, whereupon he creates three kinds of mortal creatures (41b); Finally, I disagree with Pistorius (1952, p. 58), that Plotinian World-Soul (with its two phases) is "a logical substitute for the illogical God in the [*Timaeus*] of Plato"; we need not take Plotinus' passages in this manner, as we've seen.

23 See also especially V.3.7.26–7, but also II.2.2, III.4.4, III.9.3, IV.4.32, IV.8.7, V.3.7, VI.3.1. Not surprisingly, Plotinus states that the All-Soul knows no desire, distress, or fear, and is unaffected by furnishing power to bodily existence (IV.8.2; cf. II.1.4). For Plotinus' interpretation of Plato's *Phaedrus*: "All soul looks after all that lacks a soul" (246b6), see III.4.2.

24 Plotinus says in IV.3.4 that the Soul of the All is transcendent, but then says it has a lower part (presumably the World-Soul), just as we have lower and upper parts to our human souls. As Plotinus mentions at IV.3.7.18, Plato mentions at *Phaedrus* 246b7 a soul that is "perfect" (*telea*), which can be the equivalent of Plotinus' All-Soul that remains above and never "falls" (see, for instance, IV.3.7). See especially Blumenthal (1971, pp. 51–2, 57–8) and Emilsson (1988, p. 23) on this issue.

25 For further Plotinian passages that analyze or mention the *Timaeus* 34c–35b passage, see I.1.8 and IV.3.5, 7, 9.

26 Plotinus claims that all souls are one in at least nine places: see III.1.8, III.5.4, III.7.13, IV.3.1, 7; IV.8.2, VI.4.4, 14, VI.9.1 (cf. IV.3.3); for a passage where Plotinus argues that we should not understand "part" in the context of soul to refer to quantity, see IV.3.2; and Plotinus argues that the existence of compassion in humans implies the unity of all souls, at IV.9.3. Plotinus also states that if souls had the same body, they would have the same feelings, at IV.9.2. Cf. Blumenthal (1971, pp. 51–2, 57–8) and Helleman-Elgersma (1980, pp. 458–9) on this issue.

27 Using Mohr's (2005, p. 53) correct assessment that "time is the product of the Demiurge," I can also infer that the All-Soul is in time because it is created by the Demiurge and is associated with human souls, which are definitely in time. To my knowledge, only Inge (1929a, pp. 76–7) questions the doctrine of time's coming into existence with the world-order because of the disorderly motion before the Demiurge ordered it.

28 See also *Phaedo* 95b–d, especially 107c–d and 108a–c; *Meno* 81a–c, *Phaedrus* 246b–d, 248c–9c, and *Timaeus* 44a–d. Cf. *Gorgias* 496e, *Phaedrus* 253e–4e and *Timaeus* 43a–b.

29 I agree with Blumenthal (1972, p. 343; soul is linked with time, citing III.7.11.20), Findlay (1978, p. 216; both thinkers hold that the World-Soul is in time); Gerson (1994, p. 121; time is life of soul, citing III.7.11.43–5; 122: there is no time apart from soul); de Vogel (1986, p. 225), "Time, then, is essentially connected with Soul, just as eternity belongs to the realm of intelligible Being [III.7.11.59–60]." I disagree with Inge's (1929a, p. 205) unsubstantiated interpretation that the World-Soul is exalted above Time.

30 See also III.7.12, especially lines 21–3.

# Chapter 5

1 The Greek for Hypostasis is *hē hypostasis*, which Plato never uses.

2 On the issue in general, as to whether there are Three Hypostases in Plato's view at all (let alone in the *Parmenides*), I agree with the following commentators who argue in the affirmative: Findlay (1974, pp. 35, 296–7: they are found in *Letter* II, *Republic*, *Sophist* and *Philebus*; 368–9: in *Letters* II and VI, *Timaeus*, *Republic* and *Parmenides*; 1975, pp. 661; 665–70: they can be adduced to Plato from Aristotle as well; 1976, pp. 23–4: they are in *Letters* II and VI, *Timaeus*, *Republic*, and *Parmenides*; 1978, p. 52: in *Phaedrus*, *Phaedo*, *Timaeus* and *Letter* II; p. 171: *Letter* II has all three, *Timaeus* has the Second and Third Hypostases; pp. 214–15); Hardie (1936, p. 128: A. E. Taylor might be right that the God, model, and world are not members of the Triad in the *Timaeus*); Mayhall (2004, pp. 1–2: matter and evil are not part of the Three Hypostases, which is true in Plato's view as well); Rist (1964, p. 80; Soul is in Nous, Nous is in the One, which is consistent with Plato's view); Robin (1928: 373); de Vogel (1953, p. 43: generally follows Plato on the Three Hypostases view; pp. 55–6); de Vogel (1970, pp. 183, 188–91; 1986, p. 85); cf. Blumenthal (1996, pp. 82–3: Plotinus' view *may* be found in Plato; I more positively assert this of Plotinus' view); Gatti (1996, pp. 17–18); Shorey (1938, p. 49).

3 See Inge (1929a, p. 214) for an example.

4 Here I include, for example, Allen (1983, p. 195); Atkinson (1983, p. 197); Cornford (1939, pp. v–vi); Dillon (1973, pp. 387–8); Dombrowski (1981, pp. 107–9); Ross (1951, p. 97); Shorey (1938, pp. 45–6); A. E. Taylor (1934, pp. 146–9); cf. Anton (2000, p. 76); Gurtler (1992, p. 457); Hardie (1936, p. 126). We have good reason to believe that the Three Hypostases are referred to in the *Parmenides*, and consider that no one has rebutted in English-language the idea that the Third Hypostasis can represent Soul, the All-Soul or individual souls. See also the Appendix.

5 I arrived at this view independently of Hardie (1936, p. 130), but this is precisely his view as well.

6 Gerson, 1994, p. 63. For references to the Form of Soul in Plotinus, see III.6.18.24–6, where Plotinus indeed claims that soul is itself a Form (*eidos*); V.9.14.20–2, and cf. IV.3.2.54–8.

7 See Gerson (1994, pp. 63, 250n. 57, 250n. 65, and 252n. 84) for references to $\text{Soul}_{3H}$ in the *Enneads*; see, for example, I.8.2, III.9.1, IV.4.16, IV.9.4.6–8, V.1.6–8, V.2.1, V.3.9, V.9.4.

8 Incidentally, Gerson's account of $\text{Soul}_{3H}$ includes the idea that, while $\text{Soul}_{3H}$ is eternal, the World-Soul and individual souls are in time (1994, p. 63). According to Plato (and Plotinus), the All-Soul is in time, and we can readily assume that

individual souls are in time as well, in part, since all souls (individual souls and the World-Soul) are one.

9 It should be kept in mind too, that Plato sometimes says "soul" in general, when referring to more than one soul or the soul of the universe (*Phaedrus* 246b–c, for instance).

10 Plato also implies that there is a Form of Soul, given that he says in the *Phaedrus*, "All soul looks after all that lacks a soul" (246b6); with the *Republic*, "We customarily hypothesize a single Form in connection with each of the many things to which we apply the same name" (X 596a6–7; adapted from Grube and Reeve). Thus, all souls, individual souls, and the All-Soul must have something in common, and whatever that is (or those things are), that is Soul Itself.

11 For additional passages on the Three Hypostases, see I.7.2, I.8.2, II.3.18, V.3.15, and especially VI.7.42.8–24.

12 For other "circle passages," where a circle metaphor is described in general for the relation between the Three Hypostases, see II.2.1–2; III.8.8, IV.2.1–2, IV.3.17, IV.4.16, V.1.7, 11; VI.2.12, VI.4.2, VI.5.5, VI.8.18, VI.9.8.

13 For passages in II.9 relevant to the Three Hypostases, see II.9.1, II.9.9 and II.9.6, the latter of which contains an admonition that the Gnostics would do best to adopt Plato's metaphysics (after a brief run-down of the Three Hypostases).

14 Cf. II.9.9.29–35.

15 I disagree with: Anton (1992, pp. 7–9), that Plotinus is a Neo-Platonist in part because he believes in the Three Hypostases (whereas Plato does not), however, we find them in Plato if we read the dialogues carefully and review the implications and subtleties of Plato's statements therein, thus they are Platonic; Cornford (1939, pp. v–vi), that the Third Hypostasis is the Demiurge of Plato; Dillon (1992, p. 189); cf. Merlan (1967, p. 353), that the Three Hypostases do not occur in Plato; Dombrowski (1981, pp. 107–9), that Findlay is wrong to find the Three Hypostases in Plato because the Good is not beyond being for Plato, he and the Neo-Platonists need to assume that the First is God for Plato but the "gods" are clearly "self-moving souls" in the *Phaedrus*, the *Timaeus* and the *Laws* ("God" does in one passage refer to the First on my reading of *Republic* X), and that emanation denies free will; Gerson (1994, p. 196), that Plotinus holds that the One is the cause of being of absolutely everything but Plato does not account for the source of matter: Plato claims that the Good is the cause in some sort of all the things that the released prisoner saw in his journey from the cave; Gerson (1997, pp. 295–6), that each of the Plotinian Three Hypostases have internal and external *energeiai*, but Plato does not (because Plotinus used the term from Aristotle): this may be a development of Plato's Three Hypostases, but it is still true that there are activities that the Good, Nous-God-Demiurge, and the All-Soul or World-Soul do in Plato's view: causing, creating, ordering, governing, thinking, moving, living,

and ordering, governing, and caring for the perceptible universe; D. Jackson (1967, p. 316), that the Three Hypostases are an original idea of Plotinus': they each occurred first in Plato, even if Plotinus gives us more detail concerning them and even if Plotinus does not document this finding in Plato well, as Jackson says (1967, p. 316); Lee (2004, p. 79); cf. Sambursky (1965, pp. 6–7), who declares that Plotinus has a "complex ladder of levels of reality," that Plotinus qua Neo-Platonist has an "elaborate" metaphysical hierarchy: his hierarchy occurs in Plato as well; Lloyd (1990, p. 126), that the Three Hypostases are experiences, and not non-phenomenological entities: why not both, for each thinker? Continuing, I fail to concur with: Majumdar (2007b, p. 145), that Plotinus has a radical monism that differentiates his view from Plato: Plato has the same Three Hypostases, plus the rest of the Plotinian ontology, so either they are both radical monists, or not; Rist (1967a, p. 181), that the Three Hypostases are not in Plato, but that Plotinus' "tendency rather is to state his own principle *ad nauseam* till, as he hopes, they are inculcated in the reader by some kind of osmosis": again, we can find the Three Hypostases in Plato; Mohr (2005, p. 49), that Plato is not a Neo-Platonist because by examining any two grades of being does not produce some third intermediary: this statement does not apply to Plotinus, at any rate; Schroeder (1996, p. 342), that Plotinus reshapes the architecture in Plato's intelligible universe: I fail to feel the force of this charge; A. E. Taylor (1934, pp. 153–4), that *Letter* VI is sportive and it is difficult to see what Plato intends to refer to by "captain" and "father" there, so *Letter* VI cannot be taken seriously to imply the Three Hypostases: though I can neither prove Plato's sincerity or deny the "sportive" charge without begging the question, I can only state that, since God or captain is Nous, then the Father of the captain on Plato's view must be the Good, also, Taylor's questions do nothing to dissuade us from thinking that (in general) God is Nous for Plato; lastly, de Vogel (1986, p. 47), that Plotinian Nous was a development of Plato's philosophy (even though she agrees that the Three Hypostases are found in Plato's work).

16 A. E. Taylor (1934, pp. 150–1; cf. pp. 148–9, 154–6). In 1934, pp. 152–3, Taylor claims that the "King" in *Letter* II would refer to the Good in the *Republic*, but it would refer to Soul or Mind in the *Laws* X; Taylor seems to assume that Plato has given up his belief in the Good by the time of *Laws* X, but we have no reason to believe such a thing: Plato is merely describing the rest of the hierarchy in more detail without mentioning the highest principle, having already made clear the Forms' and Being's source in the *Republic*. He also claims that it is uncertain what the seconds and thirds are; if the Good is the First, or King, then the seconds must refer to the Forms-Being-God-Nous-Demiurge, and the thirds must refer to All-Soul or souls; it is nowhere near as confusing as Taylor makes it appear.

17 Per *Letter* VII 341a–e and 345a–c.

18 A. E. Taylor, 1934, pp. 154–5.

19 A. E. Taylor, 1963, pp. 12–13.

20 The following sources explicitly or implicitly express the idea that emanation is the major difference between Plato's and Plotinus' views, or at least one of a very few: Anton (2010, p. 13), Plotinus' One outshines Plato's Good in part because it emanates and sustains the cosmic hierarchies, the progenitor of all (with the exception of evil); Gatti (1996, p. 27), emanation—"procession"—one of the "two main axes in a whole Plotinian system"; *Microsoft Encarta* (1999; "Plotinus" entry); Shorey (1938, p. 48); Sinnige (1999, pp. 6–8), for the most part, but see p. 111–12 for more comment on, and objections against, Sinnige's view; cf. Santayana (1913, pp. 595–6); Mayhall (2004, pp. 1–2) seems to follow him on this, saying that it is Plotinus' mystical experience that leads him to posit emanation: this is curious, at least on my reading of Plato; Zeller (1931, p. 294), who claims that Plotinus is a dynamic pantheist rather than an emanationist.

21 The following commentators actually note that emanation is just a metaphor, for Plotinus: A. H. Armstrong (1937, p. 61), it is easy to discover what emanation means in his view; (cf. Merlan [1967, p. 354], who says that emanation in Plotinus is "strangely ambiguous"); Clark (1949, p. 138) the emanation "illustration" should not be pressed to imply geographical or astronomical distinctions between the Three Hypostases; Robin (1928, p. 372), "Between emanation and immanence there is no preference; it is only a difference of image"; A. E. Taylor (1918, p. 612), but in later works he seems to take it more literally. The following sources describe emanation as a feature of Plotinus' thought without mentioning that it is a metaphor: Kenney (1991, p. 91), many philosophers of religion take Plotinus as an emanationist—not necessarily Kenney; *Microsoft Encarta* (1999; "Plotinus" entry); Sells (1994, p. 27–31); cf. Inge, 1929a, p. 221.

22 For further passages on the emanation of Nous from the One, see III.8.10, V.1.6, V.2.1, V.3.12, V.3.15, V.4.2, VI.8.18. Sinnige (1999, p. 5) mentions V.4.1.28–35 as well; cf. Emilsson (2007, p. 62), who mentions I.9.1.41; I.7.1.15; VI.7.23.21 as passages of the "One's productive activity."

23 See also VI.9.5.5–7, where Plotinus says that $\text{Soul}_{3H}$ "derives from Intellect"; cf. III.5.3, IV.3.17, and V.1.3; cf. I.1.8, III.5.2, III.8.8–9.

24 See, for example, V.1.3 and V.1.8.

25 See V.1.3, VI.4.10, VI.9.9; cf. V.5.9 and VI.8.14.

26 For a passage where the universe is said to emanate from the All-Soul, which emanates from Nous, see II.3.18; where matter emanates from the All-Soul, and Being emanates from the One, see V.5.5; where the Forms emanate from Nous, see V.3.7; for where matter emanates from Nous, and reason emanates from Nous, see III.2.2.

27 Cf. Walker (1938, p. 488), who mentions that one reading of the *Parmenides*' second section is "the mystical emanation theory of the Neo-Platonists."

28 The following commentators find this option appealing to some extent or other: Emilsson (2007, p. 62), in *Republic* VI and *Phaedrus* 245c–d; Gerson (1993, pp. 567–8), implied, but not full-blown emanation, for Gerson believes that Plotinus is not an emanationist—but perhaps some version of creationist—at 574; Harris (1976, pp. 5–6), "logical" not "chronological" emanation seems to come from Plato's *Republic* VI; cf. Kolb (1974, p. 139), who claims Plotinus *himself* warns not to take emanation chronologically; Rist (1964, pp. 32, 34, 66), the *Timaeus* to some extent foreshadows emanation, and, following Trouillard, that a germ of emanation is in the *Symposium*; de Vogel (1953, pp. 52–3), though I do not endorse every detail of her view.

29 Of course, Plotinus mentions often that the Good or One in no way diminishes itself in causing Intellect and the rest (VI.9.5.35–8, VI.7.36–7; cf. VI.5.3, I.7.1), thus remaining unlimited in power (VI.9.6.10–12, V.5.10); we have no reason to believe that Plato believes any differently.

30 I agree with Notopoulos (1944, p. 240) that the "light as outflow" metaphor originates at least as far back as Plato; cf. Rist (1967a, p. 197), who claims that it was a Platonic doctrine and, in addition, found it "in orthodox Platonism and probably in the writings of Posidonius"; Sinnige (1999, p. 7), who claims that there are no references to emanation in Plato: but if we find the light metaphor in Plato, contra Dodds (1928, p. 131), we should claim that Plotinus found it in Plato and not necessarily in Middle Platonists.

31 I will briefly respond to five additional objections: Dombrowski (1981, pp. 107–9) argues that Plotinian necessary emanation implies no human freedom, except in a Hegelian sense, however, Dombrowski ignores the fact that emanation is a metaphor, and overlooks passages where Plotinus does claim that humans have ("Plotinian") freedom, something that Dombrowski needs to explain in the context of Plotinus' philosophy; Gerson (1994, p. 4) claims, "Plotinus' paradigmatism is more complex than Plato's. For Plato, Forms alone are paradigms. For Plotinus, however, although Intellect is the locus of Forms, the One and Soul also serve a paradigmatic function. Thus, the notion of image or copy is expanded beyond its basic Platonic reference to the instances of Forms." I disagree, because the Good is the ultimate source and desired by all souls, and as such is a paradigm for ethics and for the ideal state. The All-Soul is a paradigm because it is perfect, and Plato says in *Phaedrus* 246b–c that we human souls can be perfect too, at least to the extent that we can see Nous (*Phaedrus*) and ultimately the Good (*Republic*). Everything that the Demiurge creates in the *Timaeus* is supposed to be imitating the region that is eternal and never changes (28c–9a, 37c–8b), so we can infer that the All-Soul is an image of Nous-God-Demiurge (also, see 69c3–7: "[God] himself fashioned those that were divine, but assigned his own progeny the task of fashioning the generation of those that were mortal. They imitated him: having taken the immortal

origin of the soul, they proceeded next to encase it within a round mortal body [the head], and to give it the entire body as its vehicle"); Hackforth (1946, p. 123) philosophically objects that neither Plato nor Plotinus (except through emanation or radiation, which does not work) explains how Nous is derived from the Good, but I do not have to justify emanation or precisely the way in which each entity or hypostasis proceeds from the Good or One: I merely need to show that Plato and Plotinus hold that the same kinds of entities exist and cause others to exist; Hardie (1936, p. 128) claims that, in the *Timaeus*, God, the model and the world are not related by emanation, so Taylor's (1934, pp. 154–5) contention that there is no Neo-Platonism in the *Timaeus* or the *Laws* is warranted: however, see *Timaeus* 69c, and it is not Plotinus' contention that the Three Hypostases occur in the *Timaeus* or the *Laws* (two, however, do—Nous-Demiurge-God and the World-Soul); A. E. Taylor (1963, pp. 12–13) argues that Plotinus tries to fill the "imperfectly filled gap [in Plato] between the doctrine of the Forms, the basis of the Platonic theory of science, and the doctrine of God and the soul which is the foundation of his theory of nature and human life. Plotinus tries to bridge the gap, relying mainly on the great passage of the *Republic* about that ineffable Good which is at once the source of all things and itself 'on the further side of Being.' He and his followers elaborated the famous conception of the scale, or ladder, of successive 'emanations' or 'progressions' which connect this supreme Good with the whole hierarchy of its increasingly blurred and imperfect 'images.' Wherever in later philosophy or theology we come upon the 'scale of being' or 'ladder of perfection' we may be sure that we are dealing with the influence of Plato transmitted through Plotinus." However, I (and apparently Plotinus) deny any such gap. Plato says that the Good causes the Forms' and Nous' existence; Nous is God (usually) and the Demiurge; the Demiurge causes the World-Soul to exist, and soul is prior to body. Furthermore, Taylor ignores here, though he noted it much earlier in his career (1918, p. 612), that emanation is only a metaphor for Plotinus.

32 Dodds, 1960, p. 3.

33 Sinnige, 1999, p. 8. Majumdar (2007a, p. 77) agrees with this criticism, so take my rebuttal to apply to her view as well. See also Sinnige (1999, pp. 6–7).

## Chapter 6

1 See Mohr (2005, p. 93n. 23) for a list of scholars who take the Receptacle to be matter. Cherniss (1945, p. 22) believes that the Receptacle is not matter. Reale (1997, pp. 381–4) seems to think that the Receptacle has two distinguishable aspects of being space and unregulated matter. For more on the Receptacle, see Kolb (1974, p. 137).

2 The Greek for "the matter in which" (Jowett, in Hamilton et al. 1961) at *Timaeus* 50d5–6 is *tout' auto en hōi*, which also is translated "that substance wherein" by Bury; this lends a little credence to the view that the Receptacle is matter.

3 D. Miller 2003.

4 Mohr, 2005, pp. 90–1, 93–4, 105, 109–10. Silverman (2002) states both that the Receptacle "provide[s] space ... for these logically distinct attributes [Form-copies]" (p. 264) and that "There is only space and Forms" in Plato's view (p. 283). However, if there is only space and Forms in Plato's view, then there are not technically Form-copies, but the Receptacle does exist as space.

5 Zeyl, 2000, p. lxiii.

6 Breaking my general rule of ignoring Aristotle, I note, as Fleet (1995, p. 166) did, that Aristotle states: "Plato in the *Timaeus* says that matter and space are the same" (*Physics* IV.209b11–12), realizing that this may do little to convince some that this is the proper interpretation of the *Timaeus* (cf. Mohr 2005, p. xxiv).

7 I agree with Emilsson (1988, p. 16), who argues that Plotinian "matter is responsible for the dispersion of things in space"; with Fuller (1912, p. 282) and Miles (1999, p. 94), that they have the same basic view of the Receptacle; with Rist (1967a, p. 104; cf. p. 111), that "Plotinus is in some sense a Platonist" in terms of his theory of matter or sense objects. I disagree with Findlay (1976, p. 36), when he reasons that, since Plotinus denies bulk and size of prime matter, he goes "beyond Plato's treatment of *Chora* in the *Timaeus*": Plato states that the Receptacle is formless and invisible (*Timaeus* 51a), so it is plausible, and size and bulk are not a part of Platonic matter either (cf. Findlay, 1978, p. 192). Gerson (1994, p. 110), citing II.5.5.12–13 and II.9.3.15, argues that Plotinian matter is generated and not in time, but Plato believes matter is in time, so they have different views on matter: however, it is not the case that II.5.5.12–13 shows that matter is not in time; the example is based on a conditional: "For instance, 'the bronze is potentially a statue;' for if nothing was going to come out of a thing or come upon it, and it was not going to be anything subsequent to what it was and there was no possibility of its becoming anything, it would be what it was alone" (II.5.1.12–15). But Form-copies go in and out of matter, so the conditional is not satisfied. And the text of II.9.3.12–15 is: "Things that are said to have come into being did not just come into being [at a particular moment] but always were and always will be in process of becoming." Both Plato and Plotinus believe paradoxically (in my view) that time and "body" were created, but also that the Receptacle and matter always existed. Lastly, Robin (1928, p. 372–3) argues that the One, like Plato's Receptacle, is formless; this is an awkward idea, hopefully misleading no one, that there may be some strong connection or identity between the One and the Receptacle.

8 See *Timaeus* 52a8 for a Platonic use of *chōras*; see 52b1 and 53a2 for some uses of *hedran*.

9 See also III.6.17 and III.6.19; Gerson (1994, p. 109) adds II.4.1.1–2 and III.6.14.29–32.

10 Plotinus sums up practically every quality that Plato states that the Receptacle possesses or lacks in the *Timaeus*, at III.6.7.5–43.

11 Plotinus also states that matter is apprehended by spurious reasoning at II.4.10. For further passages where Plotinus discusses matter as the Receptacle or receiver of Form-copies, see II.4.1, III.6.14, 17, 19; for another passage that matter remains what it is despite Form-copies entering and leaving, see VI.9.7; for further passages where Plotinus discusses space, see IV.3.20 and VI.1.28.

12 See II.4.13, II.5.4–5, III.6.7, 9, 13, 17; and VI.9.7; for a similar Platonic passage, see *Theaetetus* 157a–c.

13 See I.8.10, II.4.8, 12, 13, 15; and III.6.7–8, 15.

14 See II.5.5, II.9.3 and III.6.9–12, 14, 19.

15 See II.4.1, 7, 12, 16; III.6.7, 11–13, 15, 18; IV.4.13, VI.3.4, VI.4.10, VI.5.8.

16 See II.4.9, III.6.6–7, 16, 18; VI.1.26.

17 See especially O'Brien (1971, pp. 144–5); but also Rist (1996, p. 391).

18 See Findlay (1978, p. 192–3); Gerson (1997, p. 298); O'Brien (1991, p. 75); Rist (1973, p. 83).

19 It is even more puzzling for them to claim that *eternal* Forms are *created* by the Good, at least if Platonic or Plotinian creation occurs temporally.

20 See, for instance, III.6.13.13–15, for the claims that matter and the Receptacle exist before becoming and alteration if the Receptacle is not identical with becoming, which is true for Plotinus; and III.6.14.1–4, for the claim that if matter did not exist, then nothing would come into existence (cf. II.4.12.20–6).

21 Cf. I.1.12, I.8.3, III.6.8, 11, V.8.7.

22 Compare: "There must always be something opposed to the good" (*Theaetetus* 176a6–7). See Cherniss (1954, pp. 246, 257) for his conception of negative evil (which is a privation of reality) and positive evil (caused by the soul). I disagree with McGinley (1977, p. 49) and Shorey (1895, p. 38) that Plato does not have the privation view of evil, or that we have to "read into Plato the Neo-Platonic or modern fancy that evil is purely negative and that things exist only insofar as they are good," respectively. Given the passage just cited and my brief defense of the claim that there are no "negative" Forms (see note 46, Ch. 1), it seems clear that Plato has the privation view of evil. Cf. Sprague (1951, p. 565), who states, "Plotinus, on the other hand, is hopelessly confused on this point. He would like to account for evil by identifying it with matter, but cannot bring himself to make the identification, because of the positive effect he supposed this would have on the furthest limit of the emanative process. Had he realized that the matter which is a contradictory to form is not the same as the matter which exists in nature, he could have avoided this difficulty." First, Plotinus does so identify matter as

evil and as the furthest thing from the Good (both of which we have seen); and second, Plotinus realizes the distinction between matter and sensible thing (that is, the compound of form and matter).

23 I agree with Findlay (1974, pp. 374–5); Mayhall (2004, pp. 1–2); Rist (1961, p. 159); Zeller (1931, p. 296) on this issue.

24 See also I.8.7, 9; cf. VI.7.15. Interestingly, Plotinus states in one place that Ugly is the primal evil, which again implies that it is a lack (in this case, of beauty).

25 See Cherniss (1954, p. 246; cf. pp. 254, 257) on this point; Mohr (2005, pp. 200–1), for evil in the *Timaeus*, and for the idea that Plato has to explain the problem of evil in *Laws* X but not in the *Timaeus* (pp. xxii, 197–8, 201).

26 See Cottingham (2000, p. 263).

27 See Gerson (1994, p. 205) for four principles of evil. If I understand Santayana (1913, pp. 595–6) correctly (that Plotinus does not have the same view as Plato on the "ineradicable evil" issue), I disagree. Sharples (1994, pp. 171, 178, 181) argues that Plotinus does a better job of explaining the problem of evil, basing his decision on Plato's *Timaeus*, but it is unclear on what evidence Sharples bases this judgment.

28 See also I.8.6–7.

29 I agree with Carone (2005, pp. 178–9) and Mohr (2005, p. 200): preservation of free will in Plato explains why evil souls are permitted. I disagree with Majumdar (2007b, p. 156) that the Good causes the ignorance in the cave (by aiding in producing shadows), because she is ignoring the passages where the soul gets what it deserves due to past habits and behavior, and chooses its life, for which God is blameless, though I agree that the Good's "light" somehow does aid in casting the cave shadows.

30 Cf. when Plato states that God is not the cause of evil (*Republic* II 379c). Plato also states that we talk idly if we deem anything else ridiculous but evil (V 452d–e), and: "Movement that is irrational, disorderly, unseemly, unrhythmical and inharmonious is wholly lacking in number, as is everything that shares in any evil. This is how anyone who is going to die happy must think" (*Epinomis* 978a6–b2). Plotinus claims that all evil is alien to the soul and an accretion to it (IV.7.10) and that soul is not an evil Kind because not every soul is evil (I.8.4).

31 See also III.2.5 and I.8.6–7.

## Conclusion

1 For other comments that I hope I have at least supported, if not proven, see: A. H. Armstrong (1974, pp. 181, 192–3); Blumenthal (1993, pp. 1–3); Dodds (1960, pp. 1–2, 7); Edman (1925, p. 54); Findlay (1970, p. 258; 1974, pp. x, 29, 377,

407, 412; 1978, pp. 213, 216, 241); Fuller (1938, p. 284); Gatti (1996, pp. 10, 19–21, 34); Gerson (1997, p. 297; 2005, p. 264); Gregory (1991, p. 12); Hardie (1936, p. 8); Inge (1929a, p. 21; 1929b, p. 145); Rist (1967b, p. 422); de Vogel (1986, p. 84). Cf. Gerson (1996b, pp. 3–4, 6), who raises some legitimate Plato-Plotinus connection issues.

2 Bechtle, 1999, p. 132.

3 Emilsson, 1988, p. 3.

4 For other comments that show that we can at least seriously question, see: Anton (2000, p. 125; 2006, pp. 1–2, 9); A. H. Armstrong (1973, p. 22; Plato did not have a system); Clark (1949, p. 137); Dillon (1992, p. 189); Hare (1982, p. 25); Katz (1950b, pp. 2, 23–4); Mayhall (2004, p. 9); McGinley (1977, p. 46 and see p. 49n. 1); Merlan (1960, p. 2); Natorp (2004, p. 10); Organ (1991, p. 22); Rist (1964, pp. 7, 104–5; 1967a, pp. 185–6); Robinson (1953a, p. 4); Shorey (1938, pp. 36, 46–7, 49–51); A. Smith (1996, pp. 196–7); A. E. Taylor (1960, pp. 94–5); Tigerstedt (1974, p. 53; 1977, pp. 65–6); Tripolis (1978, p. 141); Turnbull (1948, p. ii); Wallis (1972, pp. 17–18, 93); Zeller (1931, pp. 290–1).

5 Anton, 2010, p. 15.

6 Katz, 1950a, p. xii.

7 Organ, 1991, pp. 45–6.

8 Rist, 1964, p. 57.

9 Stace, 1967, p. 372.

10 Tigerstedt, 1977, p. 57. This view might be Hoffmann's; it is not clear from the context.

11 The main objectors here are Harris (1976, p. 3; see also p. 4), "The Platonism of the *Enneads* is actually a hybrid resulting from the blending of Platonism and Aristotelianism, and at times it is difficult to determine which one is dominant," and More (1923, p. 213), "Neoplatonism is undoubtedly more Aristotelian than Platonic at the core." The other, similar, objection is that Neo-Platonism *simply* tries to reconcile Plato and Aristotle: Harris (1976, p. 8); Fuller (1938, p. 279); More (1923, pp. 178–9), Plotinus mixed Aristotelian and Stoic metaphysics, Plotinus used Aristotle's method of reasoning (pp. 204–5); Wallis (1972, pp. 17–18). For additional comments on the Aristotelian side of the issue, see More (1923, pp. 204–5), Plotinus used Aristotle's method of reasoning. The following commentators mention these Stoic elements of Plotinus' thought, but they do not imply that he is therefore more of a Stoic than a Platonist: A. H. Armstrong (1947), Stoic universal sympathy is the basis of magic, but the reason the sage is immune therefrom is Platonic (p. 194), and Plotinus is closer to the Stoics on the order and harmony of the universe (pp. 194–5): everything he mentions here seems to be Platonic to me, however; Bréhier (1958, p. 168), Plotinus took over the Stoics' theory of destiny, Logos as the dispenser of fate, sympathy of the parts, providence

and theodicy, and then adjusted these doctrines; Graeser (1972, p. 69), "There can be no doubt that the underlying ideas for which the doctrine of sympathy is employed must be related to Plato himself"; Katz (1950a, pp. xii–xiii), Plotinus used Aristotelian and Stoic logic to prove his assertions; Wilberding (2006, p. 213), Plotinus takes the Stoic view of cosmic sympathy. I give my response here in the conclusion.

12 The following commentators raise this point as a major point of difference between Plotinus and Plato: Anton (1992, pp. 7–9); A. H. Armstrong (1947, pp. 187–8); Fuller (1938, pp. 288–9); Gerson (1994, p. 72): "Nowhere in the dialogues does Plato even hint that Forms of individuals make the slightest bit of sense"; Mayhall (2004, pp. 25–6); Merlan (1967, p. 353); Rist (1963, p. 229; cf. p. 223; 1967a, pp. 182–3); Robin (1928, pp. 373–4).

13 See Anton (1992, p. 5), "Obviously there would be no ground for claiming modern indebtedness to a thinker like Plotinus if his views only repeat what Plato had already stated and faithfully adopted as the model of philosophical method," and Anton (2010, p. 8), "What kind of footnote do Plotinus' *Enneads* project? … By calling him either a Platonic or Neoplatonic footnote, the result would be to scale him down to an intellectual imitator, if not to an operatic singer of a philosophical opus." I suppose I would answer that Plotinus does not leave a footnote, but some significant philosophical commentary that is worthy of study (see the rest of my response on pp. 126–7).

14 Note that I was unable to cover mysticism in this work, so this objection is an allusion to my additional work that will hopefully be published in the future. The following commentators either simply mention this feature of Plotinian thought, or claim that this is a unique feature of Plotinus' thought that we do not find in Plato: Anton (2000, pp. 6, 53, 161–2; cf. 142–3, 146–7); D. Jackson (1967, p. 322); Loy (1988, p. 1), Plotinus is the epitome of a philosopher who describes the non-dual experience; Majercik (1995, p. 48); Meijer (1992, p. 263); More (1923, p. 184); T. Whittaker (1961, p. 103). The following commentators claim that Plotinus holds that we can become the Good (but Plato does not): Majumdar (2007b, p. 145), who implies this in Plotinus with a "radical monism" interpretation, and Plato does not believe that one can become the Good (p. 158); Organ (1991, p. 22).

15 For instance, Majumdar 2007b, pp. 145–6, 155–8.

16 The following either mention this issue as a problem or merely mention it: A. H. Armstrong (1967b, pp. 213–4), but: "This does not mean that the Platonism of Plotinus has nothing to do with the Platonism of Plato" (p. 214); Atkinson (1983, pp. 185–6); Gatti (1996, pp. 26–7); Hathaway (1969, pp. esp. 19n. 4, 20, 22, 24, 26); Rist (1967a, pp. 181–2; 1996: 389); Wallis (1972, pp. 20–3, 93).

17 For Plato's (and Plotinus') claims that the individual soul is a part of the All-Soul, see Ch. 4.4 above; for Plato's argument that individual souls exist, see *Alcibiades*

I 129b1-130c7; for their agreement in passages that life is like a play, see the next note.

18 Plato and Plotinus both hold that we are created as a toy for God, and that we need to play our role well. For Plato, see *Laws* VII 803c2–8; see also *Laws* I 644d–5c and X 902b8–9. For Plotinus, see IV.4.45.24–6, III.2.15.21–30, III.2.15.43–50. And then we see that Epictetus states: "Remember that you are an actor in a play, the character of which is determined by the Playwright: if He wishes the play to be short, it is short; if long, it is long; if He wishes you to play the part of a beggar, remember to act even this role adroitly; and so if your role be that of a cripple, an official, or a layman. For this is your business, to play admirably the role assigned you; but the selection of that role is Another's." *Encheiridion*, Ch. 17, Oldfather 1928, p. 497. Cf. Graeser, 1972, pp. 82–4.

19 Thus I do not deny the existence of Aristotelian or Stoic elements in Plotinus, for which see Emilsson (1988, pp. 4–5); Gerson (1993, pp. 566–7), Plotinus does not use *energeia* as Aristotle did; Gurtler (1988, p. 92), Plotinus adapts Stoicism to suit his Platonism; K. S. Guthrie (1896, p. 20), Aristotelian and Stoic elements in Plotinus; Karamanolis (2006, pp. 239–40; cf. p. 241): "Plotinus finds the Aristotelian distinction between *kinesis* and *energeia* questionable"; Rist (1964, p. 56; 1967a, p. 178), Plotinus uses *dunamis* differently from Aristotle, Aristotelian influence on Plotinus even if Plotinus uses him as he sees fit (pp. 178–9); Sinnige (1999, p. 91), followed Stoics to an extent, but decidedly a Platonist in several ways; Witt (1931, p. 109), Plotinus uses Stoic logos, but this does not imply Stoic determinism. Cf. Mohr (2005, p. 260). But de Vogel (1970, pp. 208–9) argues rightly, I think, that Plato, and not Aristotle, is the first to say that God is a Mind that thinks itself.

20 Gerson, 2005.

21 Wilberding, 2006, p. 213.

22 See also Zeller (1931, pp. 297–8).

23 Here I strongly disagree with More (in More et al. [1925, p. 136]), who actually claims—after acknowledging that Plotinus chiefly names Aristotle only to refute him—that Plotinus' "system in the last analysis must be judged to have more affinity with the Aristotelian metaphysics than with Platonic philosophy." The reasons for my disagreement should be apparent. Moreover, to my knowledge, no commentator in English suggests that Plotinus' thought is more Stoic than Platonic.

24 See A. H. Armstrong (1940, p. 112; 1947, pp. 179, 195; 1971, p. 68); Findlay (1978, pp. 206–7), Plotinus is not an Aristotelian; Gerson (1994, p. 225): "As a critic of Aristotle, Plotinus deserves at least as much attention as does Aristotle as a critic of Plato"; and: "If, however, one still longs to know what a Platonist could or should say to an Aristotelian, there is one outstanding remedy. Read Plotinus" (p. 226);

Harris (1976, p. 4), Plotinus rejects Aristotle's "world view, his conception of the range of philosophy, and the adequacy of his logic as a basis for dialectics," keeping in mind that Harris cannot decide if Plotinus is more Platonic or Aristotelian (p. 3), and that Plotinus argued against the Stoics (p. 5); Inge (1929a, pp. 112–13), Plotinus was mainly hostile toward the Stoics; Karamanolis (2006, p. 216), Plotinus refers to Stoics and Aristotle, but criticizes them throughout; O'Meara (1993, p. 15), Plotinus "argues [in IV.7] for Plato's position by disproving the theories of Aristotle, of the Stoics, and of the Epicureans", see also pp. 18–19, 34; Rist (1967a, p. 173), a list of anti-Stoic elements in the *Enneads*, a list of anti-Aristotelian points in the *Enneads* (p. 179), and see also (1973, pp. 73, 82).

25 For instance, Plotinus implicitly criticizes Aristotle's view that plants cannot be happy in I.4.1–3, and defends Plato's "number of infinity" view against Aristotle's, in VI.6.2–3 (see Slaveva-Griffin, 2009, pp. 19–20).

26 See A. H. Armstrong (1977, p. 50); Blumenthal (1966, p. 61); Gerson (1994, pp. 76–7).

27 Gerson, 1994, p. 76.

28 The following additional points can be made: Plato says that we can know ourselves and that knowledge is of Being or Forms, so we are beings, which implies there would be Forms of Individuals, or at least that this is a plausible possibility given Plato's views. Also, both thinkers agree that all souls are one, so how can Plotinus assert this, and that there are Forms of individuals? Assuming he does, as I am for the sake of argument, this principle does not disqualify Plato from holding Forms of individuals.

29 The qualification Gerson adds is that a "reductionism" must accompany the Platonic principle, that, for example, this does not entail that there is a Form of my house (1994, p. 76). I add that I endorse Gerson's reading of Plotinus' passages on Forms of individuals (pp. 74–8). He also states that Forms of individuals do not repudiate Plato's reason for holding that Forms exist, but are an extension of Plato's theory (p. 78).

30 See, for example, V.9.5, VI.6.11–14, VI.6.4, VI.7.16, VI.5.6.

31 Cf. *Timaeus* 30c6–d1: "Let us lay it down that the universe resembles more closely than anything else that Living Thing of which all other living things are parts, both individually and by kinds. For that Living Thing comprehends within itself all intelligible living things, just as our world is made up of us and all the other visible creatures." If all living creatures are "individually and by kinds" parts of Nous, the Living Creature after which we are crafted, which itself is eternal and at the level of Forms (indeed containing them), then it is plausible to suggest that this passage *may* (not that it must) imply that there are Forms of individuals.

32 Gerson, 1994, pp. 72–8.

33 Cf. A. H. Armstrong, 1945, p. 131.

34 See, for example, Findlay (1976, p. 40; cf. 1978, pp. 214–15): "Plato and Plotinus should be studied together: the second provides an essential commentary on the first."

35 Though I tried to address this objection on my own, I certainly appreciate these commentators' thoughts on this issue: Dodds (1928, p. 140): "To say that the *Enneads* were not the starting-point of Neoplatonism but its intellectual culmination is no disparagement of Plotinus' originality"; Dodds (1960, p. 2): "[The Plotinian system's] true originality is not in the materials but in the design"; Emilsson (1988, p. 148) implies that Plotinus is original because he is the founder of the mind-body problem; Gatti (1996, pp. 17–18, 26–7) says in different ways that Plotinus is an innovator who followed tradition; Gerson (1996b, p. 7; cf. 1997, pp. 295–6) rightly states: "Plotinus is rethinking the grounds for the claims he has inherited"; D. Jackson (1967, p. 316) says that Plotinus used ideas that were already in circulation but he is still original.

36 Cf. *Symposium* 204e and 202c.

37 Majumdar (2007, p. 158) states that, for Plato, the released prisoner of the Cave Allegory "cannot become the Good." But Plotinus does not state that someone can become the Good in the sense that, from that point forward, that person is beyond being, eternal, immaterial (only) and the cause of the Forms. Thus, the interpretation of what becoming the Good means is important here and we should not overstate what Plotinus is claiming.

38 Plato: Vision of the Good: *Phaedrus* 277d–e, and *Republic* VII 516b–c, 516e–17c, 518a–b, 518d–19b, 519c8–10, 520c, 526d–e, 532a–d, 533a, 540a–c; cf. *Republic* VI 500d, VII 508b–c, 533b–d, X 615a; *Letter* VIII 357a–d; *Epinomis* 986c–d, 988e–989a; *Alcibiades* I 134d. Touching or grasping the Good: *Republic* VI 490a8–b6; compare *Phaedo* 79d1–7, *Phaedrus* 249d4–e4, *Letter* VII 344d4–5 with 344e1–2; *Cratylus* 404d1–3 and 412b–c. Plotinus: Vision: IV4.4.1, I.4.13, I.4.15, III.5.3, III.8.10, V.1.5, V.2.1, V.5.10, V.6.5, VI.9.3. Cf. de Vogel (1986, p. 215). Touching: VI.7.36.3–4 and VI.9.9.17–19; cf. VI.9.7.16–26.

39 See Findlay (1974, p. 370): "It will be plain that almost everything that Plotinus says of the First Hypostasis simply dots the *i*'s and crosses the *t*'s of what Plato said of the Good or One in *Republic*, VI and in the First Hypothesis of the *Parmenides*. The only apparent exception lies in the mention of a self-transcendent, self-simplifying mode of direct touch with the Supreme Point of Unity, but this is surely implicit in what Plato says in the *Republic*. What transcends Being, which is the object of Knowledge, must surely be reached in a manner which transcends Knowledge."

40 Loy (1988, p. 2) notes that Plato (and others—Pythagoras, Heraclitus, Parmenides), according to how we interpret him, was more sympathetic than Aristotle to the non-dual claim.

41 *Republic* VI 505d7-e4, *Meno* 78b3-8, *Philebus* 61a1-2 with 20d1-6, *Euthydemus* 282a-c; cf. *Laws* III 687d.

42 *Symposium* 206a.

43 *Theaetetus* 176a5-b2 and b8-c5; *Republic* VI 500c9-d2 with *Republic* I 353d–4a, IV 441d-e, 442c-d, 443c-444a; *Laws* V 726a2-3 and 728b.

44 Henry et al. (1982, p. 348) cite Plotinus as referring to the *Apology* once.

45 Henry et al. (1982, p. 348) cite Plotinus as referring to the *Alcibiades* I 13 times.

46 Henry et al. (1982, p. 349) cite Plotinus as referring to the *Greater Hippias* four times.

47 First, note that I used the Brandwood chart as a rough guide. Second, in an expanded version of this work, which in addition to metaphysics includes Plato and Plotinus on mysticism, epistemology and ethics, I also cited passages from these early dialogues that parallel Plotinus' view: *Euthyphro*, *Charmides*, *Lesser Hippias*, *Ion*, *Laches*, *Protagoras*, and *Menexenus*. This leaves, on my count, the *Lysis* and its account of friendship, where it is difficult to fathom exactly what Plato is trying to express, and the *Crito*, which nonetheless is consistent with the *Republic*'s argument that the state is more important than the individual. In short, the themes in these dialogues are not, arguably, un-Plotinian. (See the Index Locorum for the passages adduced from these dialogues.)

48 They did not cite the *Euthydemus* or the *Meno*. And see the third point of "Replies to (6)" (p. 130), concerning Henry et al."s OCT citations.

49 In an expanded version of the present project, that includes mysticism, epistemology, and ethics, I also cited a passage from the *Critias* that is parallel to Plotinus, to which Henry et al."s OCT citations do not refer.

50 Tigerstedt, 1977, p. 13.

# Bibliography

## Primary Sources

**Aristotle**

Barnes, Jonathan (ed.) (1984), *The Complete Works of Aristotle: The Revised Oxford Translation*. Bollingen Series LXXI. 2 vols. Princeton: Princeton University Press

**Epictetus**

Oldfather, W. A. trans. (1928), *Epictetus*. Encheiridion. Loeb Classical Library. Vol. II. Cambridge: Harvard University Press

**Plato**

Adam, James (ed.) (1902), *The* Republic *of Plato*. Vol. II. (repr. 1929) Cambridge: Cambridge University Press

Burnet, J. (1900–7), *Platonis Opera*. 5 vols. Oxford: Clarendon Press

Cooper, J. M. and D. S. Hutchinson (eds) (1997). *Plato's Complete Dialogues*. Indianapolis: Hackett Publishing Company, Inc.

Denyer, Nicholas (ed.) (2001), *Plato*: Alcibiades. New York: Cambridge University Press

Hamilton, Edith, and Huntington Cairns (eds) (1961), *The Collected Dialogues of Plato*, (repr. 1996). New York: Pantheon

Gould, G. P. (ed.) (1914–35), *Plato*. Loeb Classical Library. 12 vols [v. 1, trans. H. N. Fowler, 1914 (repr. 1982); v. 2, trans. W. R. M. Lamb, 1924 (repr. 1977); v. 3, trans. W. R. M. Lamb, 1925 (repr. 1983); v. 4, trans. H. N. Fowler, 1926 (repr. 1977); v. 5, trans. Paul Shorey, 1930 (repr. 1982); v. 6, trans. Paul Shorey, 1935 (repr. 1987); v. 7, trans. H. N. Fowler, 1921 (repr. 1987); v. 8, trans. H. N. Fowler and W. R. M. Lamb, 1925 (repr. 1975); v. 9, trans. R. G. Bury, 1929 (repr. 1989); v. 10, trans. R. G. Bury, 1926 (repr. 1984); v. 11, trans. R. G. Bury, 1926 (repr. 1984); v. 12, trans. W. R. M. Lamb, 1927 (repr. 1986)]. Cambridge: Harvard University Press

Jowett, Benjamin (1953), *Plato: Dialogues; translated into English with analyses and introductions*, 4 vols, 4th edn. Oxford: Clarendon Press

Reeve, C. D. C. (2004), *Plato*: Republic. Indianapolis: Hackett Publishing Company, Inc.

Zeyl, Donald J. (2000), *Timaeus*. Indianapolis: Hackett Publishing Company, Inc.

**Plotinus**

Armstrong, A. H. trans. (1966a), *Plotinus*. Loeb Classical Library. Vol. I. 2nd edn. (repr. 1995). Cambridge: Harvard University Press

—trans. (1984a), *Plotinus*. Loeb Classical Library. Vol. IV. Cambridge: Harvard University Press

—trans. (1984b), *Plotinus*. Loeb Classical Library. Vol. V. Cambridge: Harvard University Press

—trans. (1988a), *Plotinus*. Loeb Classical Library. Vol. VI. Cambridge: Harvard University Press

—trans. (1988b), *Plotinus*. Loeb Classical Library. Vol. VII. Cambridge: Harvard University Press

Henry, Paul, and Hans-Rudolf Schwyzer (eds) (1964, 1976, 1982), *Plotini Opera*. 3 vols (*editio minor* = H-$S_2$). Oxford: Clarendon Press. (v. 1, *Enneads* I–III); (v. 2, *Enneads* IV–V); (v. 3, *Ennead* VI)

MacKenna, Stephen trans. (1992), *Plotinus:* The Enneads. Burdett: Larson Publications

MacKenna, Stephen trans. and John Dillon (ed.) (1991), *Plotinus:* The Enneads. New York: Penguin Books

O'Brien, Elmer ed. and trans. (1986), *The Essential Plotinus*. 2nd edn. Indianapolis: Hackett Publishing Company, Inc.

Turnbull, Grace H. comp. (1948), *The Essence of Plotinus: Extracts from the Six* Enneads *and Porphyry's Life of Plotinus*. Stephen MacKenna trans. New York: Oxford University Press

## Secondary Sources

Alexandrian Press (1985), *The System of Plotinus*. Edmonds: The Alexandrian Press

Allen, R. E. (1983), *Plato's* Parmenides. *Translation and Analysis*. Minneapolis: University of Minnesota Press

Ambuel, David (2007), *Image and Paradigm in Plato's* Sophist. Las Vegas: Parmenides Publishing

Anderson, Albert (2004), "Plato's heritage in the arts: form as essence", in *Neoplatonic Aesthetics: Music, Literature, and the Visual Arts*. Liana Cheney and John Hendrix (eds). New York: Peter Lang, 67–77

Annas, Julia (1999), *Platonic Ethics: Old and New*. Ithaca: Cornell University Press

—(2000), *Ancient Philosophy: A Very Short Introduction*. New York: Oxford University Press

Anton, John P. (1964), "Plotinus' refutation of beauty as symmetry," *The Journal of Aesthetics and Art Criticism*. Vol. 23, No. 2 (Winter), 233–7

—(1992), "Plotinus and the Neoplatonic conception of dialectic," *The Journal of Neoplatonic Studies*. Vol. 1, No. 1 (Fall), 3–30.

—(2000), *Archetypal Principles and Hierarchies: Essays on Neoplatonic Themes*. Binghamton: Global Publications

—(2010), "Is Plotinus a Platonist?" *Philosophein*. Issue 2 (June), 6–15

Armstrong, A. Hilary (1937), "'Emanation' in Plotinus," in A. H. Armstrong (1979: 61–6)

—(1938), "The gods in Plato, Plotinus, Epicurus," *The Classical Quarterly*. Vol. 32, No. 3–4 (July–October), 190–6

—(1940), *The Architecture of the Intelligible Universe in the Philosophy of Plotinus: An Analytical and Historical Study*. Cambridge: Cambridge University Press

—(1945), "Platonic mysticism," *The Dublin Review*. Vol. 216, 130–143

—(1947), *An Introduction to Ancient Philosophy* (repr. 1983). Totowa, NJ: Littlefield, Adams & Company

—(1954–5), "Plotinus's doctrine of the infinite and Christian thought," in A. H. Armstrong (1979: 47–58)

—(1960), "The background of the doctrine 'that the intelligibles are not outside the Intellect,' " in A. H. Armstrong (1979: 393–413)

—(1967b), *The Cambridge History of Later Greek and Early Medieval Philosophy*. Cambridge: Cambridge University Press

—(1971), "Eternity, life and movement in Plotinus' accounts of *Nous*," in A. H. Armstrong (1979: 67–74)

—(1973), "Elements in the thought of Plotinus at variance with classical intellectualism," *The Journal of Hellenic Studies*. Vol. 93, 13–22

—(1974), "Tradition, reason and experience in the thought of Plotinus," in A. H. Armstrong (1979: 171–94)

—(1977), "Form, individual and person in Plotinus," in A. H. Armstrong (1979: 49–68)

—(ed.) (1979), *Plotinian and Christian Studies*, London: Variorum Reprints

Armstrong, John M. (2004), "After the ascent: Plato on becoming like God," *Oxford Studies in Ancient Philosophy*. Vol. 26, 171–83

Atkinson, Michael (1983), *Plotinus:* Ennead *V.1: On the Three Principal Hypostases*. Michael Atkinson trans. New York: Oxford University Press

Bechtle, Gerald (1999), *The Anonymous Commentary on Plato's* Parmenides. Bern: Paul Haupt Berne

Benitez, Eugenio E. (1989), *Forms in Plato's* Philebus. Assen: Van Gorcum

—(1995), "The Good or the demiurge: causation and the unity of good in Plato," *Apeiron*. Vol. 28, No. 2 (June), 113–40

Blumenthal, Henry J. (1966), "Did Plotinus believe in Ideas of individuals?" in Blumenthal (1993: 61–80)

—(1971), "Soul, World-Soul and individual soul in Plotinus," in *Le Néoplatonisme: Royaumont: 9–13 Juin 1969. Colloques Internationaux du Centre National de la Recherche Scientifique*. Paris: Centre National de la Recherche Scientifique, 55–66

—(1972), "Plotinus' psychology: Aristotle in the service of Platonism," in *Soul and Intellect: Studies in Plotinus and Later Neoplatonism*. Brookfield: Variorum, 340–64

—(1993), *Soul and Intellect: Studies in Plotinus and Later Neoplatonism*. Brookfield: Variorum.

—(1996), "On soul and Intellect," in Gerson (1996a: 82–104)

Bowe, G. S. (2003), *Plotinus and the Platonic Metaphysical Hierarchy*. New York: Global Scholarly Publications

Brandwood, Leonard (1976), *A Word Index to Plato*. Leeds: W. S. Maney and Son

—(1992), "Stylometry and chronology," in *The Cambridge Companion to Plato*. Richard Kraut (ed.). New York: Cambridge University Press, 90–120

Bréhier, Émile (1958), *The Philosophy of Plotinus*. Joseph Thomas trans. Chicago: The University of Chicago Press

Brisson, Luc (1995), "Premises, consequences, and legacy of an Esotericist interpretation of Plato," *Ancient Philosophy*. Vol. 15, 117–34

—(2002), "'Is the world one?' A new interpretation of Plato's *Parmenides*," *Oxford Studies in Ancient Philosophy*. Vol. XXII (Summer). New York: Oxford University Press, 1–20

—(2005), "*Republic* VI 509a9–c10 and its interpretation in antiquity: dialogical or dogmatic reading," in *History of Platonism: Plato Redivivus*. Robert Berchman and John Finamore (eds). New Orleans: University Press of the South, 1–15

Britannica (1991), *The New Encyclopædia Britannica*. 15th edn. Chicago: Encyclopædia Britannica

Brumbaugh, Robert S. (1961), *Plato on the One: The Hypotheses in the* Parmenides. New Haven: Yale University Press

Bussanich, John (1987), "Plotinus on the inner life of the One," *Ancient Philosophy*. Vol. 7, 163–89

—(1988), *The One and Its Relation to Intellect in Plotinus: A Commentary on Selected Texts*, Philosophia Antiqua: A Series of Studies on Ancient Philosophy. W. J. Verdenius and J. C. M. Van Winden (eds). Vol. XLIX. New York: E. J. Brill

—(1996), "Plotinus's metaphysics of the One," in Gerson (1996a: 38–65)

Carone, Gabriela Roxana (2005), *Plato's Cosmology and Its Ethical Dimensions*. New York: Cambridge University Press

Carter, Robert Edgar (1975), "Plato and mysticism," *Idealistic Studies*. Vol. 5, No. 4 (September), 255–68.

Chen, Chung-hwan (1944), "On the *Parmenides* of Plato," *The Classical Quarterly*. Vol. 38, No. 3 and 4 (July–October), 101–14

Cherniss, Harold F. (1932), "Parmenides and the *Parmenides* of Plato," *The American Journal of Philology*. Vol. 53, No. 2, 122–38

—(1944), *Aristotle's Criticism of Plato and the Academy*. Vol. I. Baltimore: The Johns Hopkins Press

—(1945), *The Riddle of the Early Academy*. New York: Russell & Russell (reissued 1962)

—(1954), "The sources of evil according to Plato," in Vlastos (1978b: 244–58)

—(1957), "The relation of the *Timaeus* to Plato's later dialogues," *American Journal of Philology*. Vol. 78, 225–66. Reprinted in *Harold Cherniss: Selected Papers*. Leonardo Tarán (ed.) Leiden: E. J. Brill, 1977, 298–339

Ciapolo, Roman T. (1997), "The relation of Plotinian *eudaimonia* to the life of the serious man in treatise I.4 (46)," *American Catholic Philosophical Quarterly*. Vol. 71, No. 3 (Summer), 489–98

Clark, Gordon H. (1949), "Plotinus on the eternity of the world," *The Philosophical Review*. Vol. 58, No. 2 (March), 130–40

Cornford, Francis MacDonald (1937), *Plato's Cosmology* (repr. 1952). London: Routledge & Kegan Paul Ltd.

—(1939), *Plato and Parmenides* (repr. 1950). London: Kegan, Paul, Trench, Trubner & Co., Ltd.

—(1957), *Plato's Theory of Knowledge* (repr. 1983). Indianapolis: The Bobbs-Merrill Company, Inc.

Corrigan, Kevin (1996), "Essence and existence in the *Enneads*," in Gerson (1996a: 105–29).

—(2005), *Reading Plotinus: A Practical Introduction to Neoplatonism*. West Lafayette: Purdue University Press

Cottingham, John (2000), *Western Philosophy: An Anthology*. Malden: Blackwell Publishers

Curd, Patricia K. (1989), "Some problems of unity in the First Hypothesis of the *Parmenides*," *The Southern Journal of Philosophy*. Vol. 27, No. 3 (Fall), 347–59

Deck, John (1967), *Nature, Contemplation, and the One: A Study in the Philosophy of Plotinus* (repr. 1991). Burdett: Larson Publications

Denyer, Nicholas (2007), "Sun and line: the role of the Good," in *The Cambridge Companion to Plato*, G. R. F. Ferrari (ed.). New York: Cambridge University Press, 284–309

Desjardin, Rosemary (2004), *Plato and the Good: Illuminating the Darkling Vision*. Boston: Brill

Dillon, John (1973) ed. and trans. *Iamblichi Chalcidensis: In Platonis Dialogos Commentariorum Fragmenta. Philosophia Antiqua: A Series of Monographs on Ancient Philosophy*. W. J. Verdenius and J. H. Waszink (eds). Vol. XXIII; Leiden: E. J. Brill

—(1989), "Tampering with the *Timaeus:* ideological emendations in Plato, with special reference to the *Timaeus*," *The American Journal of Philology*. Vol. 110, No. 1 (Spring), 50–72

—(1992), "Plotinus at work on Platonism," *Greece & Rome*. 2nd Ser., Vol. 39, No. 2 (October), 189–204.

Dillon, John and Lloyd P. Gerson (2004), *Neoplatonic Philosophy: Introductory Readings*. Indianapolis: Hackett Publishing Company, Inc.

Dodds, E. R. (1928), "The *Parmenides* of Plato and the origin of the Neoplatonic 'One'," *The Classical Quarterly*. Vol. 22, No. 3 and 4 (July–October), 129–42

—(1960), "Tradition and personal achievement in the philosophy of Plotinus," *The Journal of Roman Studies*. Vol. 50, Parts 1 and 2, 1–7

Doherty, Kevin F. (1956), "God and the Good in Plato," *The New Scholasticism*. Vol. 30, No. 4, 441–60

—(1961), "The demiurge and the Good in Plato," *The New Scholasticism*. Vol. 35, No. 4, 510–24

Dombrowski, Daniel A. (1981), *Plato's Philosophy of History*. Washington, DC: University Press of America

Duncan, Patrick (1940), "Socrates and Plato," *Philosophy*. Vol. 15, No. 60 (October), 339–62

Edelstein, Ludwig (1962), "Platonic anonymity," *The American Journal of Philology*. Vol. 83, No. 1 (January), 1–22

—(1966), *Plato's Seventh Letter*. Leiden: E. J. Brill

Edman, Irwin (1925), "The logic of mysticism and Plotinus," *Studies in the History of Ideas*. Vol. II. New York: Columbia University Press, 51–81

Edwards, Mark J. (1993), "A portrait of Plotinus," *The Classical Quarterly*. New Series, Vol. 43, No. 2, 480–90.

—trans. (2000), *Neoplatonic Saints: The Lives of Plotinus and Proclus by their Students*. Liverpool: Liverpool University Press.

Emilsson, Eyjólfur Kjalar (1988), *Plotinus on Sense-Perception: A Philosophical Study*. New York: Cambridge University Press

—(2007), *Plotinus on Intellect*. Oxford: Clarendon Press

Ferguson, John (1963), "Sun, line, and cave again," *The Classical Quarterly*. New Series, Vol. 13, 188–193

Findlay, John N. (1970), *Ascent to the Absolute: Metaphysical Papers and Lectures*. New York: Humanities Press

—(1974), *Plato: The Written and Unwritten Doctrines*. New York: Humanities Press

—(1975), "The three hypostases of Platonism," *The Review of Metaphysics*. Vol. 28, No. 4 (June), 660–80

—(1976), "The Neoplatonism of Plato," in R. Baine Harris (ed.), *The Significance of Neoplatonism*. Norfolk: International Society for Neoplatonic Studies, 23–4

—(1978), *Plato and Platonism: An Introduction*. New York: Times Books

Fleet, Barrie trans. (1995), *Plotinus:* Ennead *III.6: On the Impassivity of the Bodiless*. Oxford: Clarendon Press

Frank, Erich (1940), "The fundamental opposition of Plato and Aristotle," *The American Journal of Philology*. Vol. 61, No. 1 (1940), 34–53

Friedländer, Paul (1969), *Plato: Volume 1: An Introduction*. Hans Meyerhoff trans. 2nd edn. Princeton: Princeton University Press, 1969. (Originally published by Bollingen Foundation, New York, New York, 59th in a Bollingen Foundation series.)

Fuller, B. A. G. (1912), *The Problem of Evil in Plotinus*. Cambridge: Cambridge University Press

—(1938), *A History of Ancient and Medieval Philosophy*. New York: Henry Holt and Company

Gadamer, Hans-Georg (1986), *The Idea of the Good in Platonic-Aristotelian Philosophy*. P. Christopher Smith trans. New Haven: Yale University Press.

Gaiser, Konrad (1980), "Plato's enigmatic lecture 'on the Good,'" *Phronesis*. Vol. 25, No. 1, 5–35.

Gatti, Maria Luisa (1996), "Plotinus: the Platonic tradition and the foundation of Neoplatonism," in Gerson (1996a: 10–37)

Gerson, Lloyd P. (1989), "Plato on virtue, knowledge, and the unity of goodness," *Essays in Ancient Greek Philosophy III: Plato*. J. P. Anton and A. Preus (eds). Albany: State University of New York Press, 85–100

—(1993), "Plotinus's metaphysics: emanation or creation?" *Review of Metaphysics*. Vol. 46 (March), 559–74

—(1994), *Plotinus: The Arguments of the Philosophers*. Ted Honderich (ed.). New York: Routledge

—(ed.) (1996a), *The Cambridge Companion to Plotinus*. New York: Cambridge University Press

—(1996b), "Introduction," in *The Cambridge Companion to Plotinus*. Lloyd Gerson (ed.). New York: Cambridge University Press, 1–9

—(1997), "The study of Plotinus today," *American Catholic Philosophical Quarterly*. Vol. 71, No. 3 (Summer), 293–300

—(2005), "What is Platonism?" *Journal of the History of Philosophy*. Vol. 43, No. 3 (July), 253–76

Gonzalez, Francisco J. (1998), *Dialectic and Dialogue: Plato's Practice of Philosophical Inquiry*. Evanston: Northwestern University Press

Graeser, Andreas (1972), *Plotinus and the Stoics: A Preliminary Study*. Leiden: E. J. Brill

Gregory, John trans. (1991), *The Neoplatonists*. London: Kyle Cathie Limited

Grote, George (1875), *Plato and the Other Companions of Sokrates*. Vol. 3, 3rd edn. London: John Murray Press

Gurtler, Gary M. (1988), *Plotinus: The Experience of Unity*. New York: Peter Lang

—(1992), "Plotinus and the Platonic *Parmenides*," *International Philosophical Quarterly*. Vol. 32, No. 4, Issue No. 128 (December), 443–57

Guthrie, Kenneth Sylvan (1896), *The Philosophy of Plotinus*. Philadelphia: Dunlap Printing Company

Hackforth, Reginald (1946), "Moral evil and ignorance in Plato's Ethics," *The Classical Quarterly*. Vol. 40, No. 3 and 4 (July–October), 118–20

—(1965), "Plato's theism," in *Studies in Plato's Metaphysics*. R. E. Allen (ed.). London: Routledge and Kegan Paul

Hadot, Pierre (1993), *Plotinus or The Simplicity of Vision*. Michael Chase trans., Introduction by Arnold I. Davidson. Chicago: The University of Chicago Press

Hampton, Cynthia (1990), *Pleasure, Knowledge, and Being*. Albany: State University of New York Press

Hardie, W. F. R. (1936), *A Study in Plato*. New York: Oxford University Press

Hare, R. M. (1982), *Plato*. Past Masters Series. New York: Oxford University Press

Harris, R. Baine (1976), "A brief description of Neoplatonism," in *The Significance of Neoplatonism*, R. Baine Harris (ed.). Norfolk: International Society for Neoplatonic Studies, 1–20

Harward, J. (1928), "The seventh and eighth Platonic epistles," *The Classical Quarterly*. Vol. 22, No. 3 and 4 (July–October), 143–54

Hathaway, R. F. (1969), "The Neoplatonist interpretation of Plato: remarks on its decisive characteristics," *Journal of the History of Philosophy*. Vol. III, No. 1 (January), 16–26

Helleman-Elgersma, Wypkje (1980), *Soul-Sisters: A Commentary on* Enneads *IV 3 (27), 1–8 of Plotinus*. Amsterdam: Rodopi N.V.

Henry, Paul (1917–30), "Introduction: The place of Plotinus in the history of thought," in *The Enneads*, Stephen MacKenna trans., B. S. Page (ed.). 3rd edn (repr. 1961). London: Faber and Faber, xxxv-lxx

Hermann, Arnold (2010), *Plato's* Parmenides*: Text, Translation and Introductory Essay*. Arnold Hermann and Sylvana Chrysakopoulou trans. Las Vegas: Parmenides Publishing

Hitchcock, David (1985), "The Good in Plato's *Republic*," *Apeiron*. Vol. 17, 65–92

Inge, W. R. (1929a), *The Philosophy of Plotinus: The Gifford Lectures at St. Andrews, 1917–18*. 3rd edn, Vol. I. New York: Longmans, Green and Co.

—(1929b), *The Philosophy of Plotinus: The Gifford Lectures at St. Andrews, 1917–18*. 3rd edn, Vol. II. New York: Longmans, Green and Co.

—(1935), "Great thinkers: (IV) Plotinus," *Philosophy*. Vol. 10, No. 38 (April), 144–53

—(1948a), "Theism," *Philosophy*. Vol. 23, No. 84 (January), 38–59

—(1948b), *Mysticism and Religion* (repr. 1976). Westport: Greenwood Press, Publishers

Irwin, Terence H. (1992), "Plato: the intellectual background," in *The Cambridge Companion to Plato*. Richard Kraut (ed.). New York: Cambridge University Press, 51–89

Jackson, B. Darrell (1967), "Plotinus and the *Parmenides*," *The Journal of the History of Philosophy*. Volume V, 315–27

Jessop, T. E. (1930), "The metaphysics of Plato," *Journal of Philosophical Studies*. Vol. 5, No. 17 (January), 36–50

Johansen, Thomas Kjeller (2004), *Plato's Natural Philosophy: A Study of the* Timaeus-Critias. New York: Cambridge University Press

Jordan, Robert William (1983), *Plato's Arguments for Forms*. Cambridge: The Cambridge Philological Society

Joseph, H. W. B. (1948), *Knowledge and the Good in Plato's* Republic. London: Geoffrey Cumberlege, Oxford University Press

Karamanolis, George E. (2006), *Plato and Aristotle in Agreement? Platonists on Aristotle from Antiochus to Porphyry*. New York: Clarendon Press

Katz, Joseph (1950a), *The Philosophy of Plotinus*. New York: Appleton-Century-Crofts, Inc.

—(1950b), *Plotinus' Search for the Good*. New York: King Crown's Press

Kenney, John Peter (1991), *Mystical Monotheism: A Study in Ancient Platonic Theology*. London: Brown University Press

Keyt, David (1969), "Plato's paradox that the immutable is unknowable," *The Philosophical Quarterly*. Vol. 19, No. 74 (January), 1–14

—(1971), "The mad craftsman of the *Timaeus*," *The Philosophical Review*. Vol. 80, No. 2 (April), 230–5

Knox, Bernard (1993), *The Oldest Dead White European Males*. New York: W. W. Norton & Company

Kolb, David A. (1974), "Time and the timeless in Greek thought," *Philosophy East and West*. Vol. 24, No. 2, Time and Temporality (April), 137–43

Kraut, Richard (ed.) (1992), *The Cambridge Companion to Plato*. New York: Cambridge University Press

Lachterman, David (1989–90), "What is 'the Good' of Plato's *Republic*?" *St. John's Review*. Vol. 39, 139–71

Laguna, Theodore de (1934), "Notes on the theory of Ideas," *The Philosophical Review*. Vol. 43, No. 5 (September), 443–70

Ledger, Gerald R. (1989), *Re-counting Plato: A Computer Analysis of Plato's Style*. New York: Clarendon Press

Lee, Jonathan Scott (2004), "'... If one had the power to look at the God in oneself' – metaphysics as hermeneutics in the aesthetics of Plotinus," in *Neoplatonic Aesthetics: Music, Literature, and the Visual Arts*. Liana Cheney and John Hendrix (eds). New York: Peter Lang, 79–87

Leftow, Brian (1990), "Is God an abstract object?" *Nous*. Vol. 24, No. 4 (September), 581–98

Lewy, Hans (1978), *Chaldean Oracles and Theurgy: Mysticism Magic and Platonism in the Later Roman Empire*. Paris: Études Augustiniennes

Lloyd, A. C. (1990), *The Anatomy of Neoplatonism*. Oxford: Clarendon Press

Louth, Andrew (1981), *The Origins of the Christian Mystical Tradition: From Plato to Denys*. Oxford: Clarendon Press

Loy, David (1988), *Nonduality: A Study in Comparative Philosophy*. Amherst: Humanity Books

Luban, David (1978), "The form of the Good in the *Republic*," *The Journal of Value Inquiry*. Vol. 12, 161–8

Lynch, William F. (1959), *An Approach to the Metaphysics of Plato through the* Parmenides (repr. 1969). Westport: Greenwood Press, Publishers

Majercik, Ruth (1995), "Plotinus and Greek Mysticism," in Donald H. Bishop (ed.), *Mysticism and the Mystical Experience: East and West*. Selinsgrove: Susquehanna University Press, 38–61

Majumdar, Deepa (2007a), *Plotinus on the Appearance of Time and the World of Sense: A Pantomime*. Burlington: Ashgate Publishing

—(2007b), "Mysticism and the political: stairway to the Good in Plato's allegory of the cave: two models of numinous politics (part I)," *Philotheos: International Journal of Philosophy and Theology*. Vol. 7, 144–59

Mayhall, C. Wayne (2004), *On Plotinus*. Belmont: Thomson-Wadsworth

McCabe, Mary Margaret (1994), *Plato's Individuals*. Princeton: Princeton University Press

McEvilley, Thomas (2002), *The Shape of Ancient Thought*. New York: Allworth Press

McGinley, John (1977), "The doctrine of the Good in *Philebus*," *Apeiron*. Vol. 11, No. 2 (December), 27–57

McGroarty, Kieran trans. (2006), *Plotinus on* eudaimonia: *A Commentary on* Ennead *I.4*. New York: Oxford University Press

Meijer, P. A. (1992), *Plotinus on that Good or the One* (Enneads *VI, 9): An Analytical Commentary*. Amsterdam: J. C. Geiben

Meinwald, Constance C. (1991), *Plato's* Parmenides. New York: Oxford University Press

Menn, Stephen (1992), "Aristotle and Plato on God as Nous and as the Good," *Review of Metaphysics*. Vol. 45 (March), 543–73

—(1995), *Plato on God as Nous*. Carbondale and Edwardsville: Southern Illinois University Press

—(2001), "Plotinus on the identity of knowledge with its object," *Apeiron*. Vol. 34, No. 3 (September), 233–46

Merlan, Phillip (1960), *From Platonism to Neoplatonism*. 2nd edn. The Hague: Martinus Nijhoff

—(1967), "Plotinus," in *The Encyclopedia of Philosophy*. Paul Edwards (ed.). Vol. 6. New York: Macmillan Publishing Co., Inc.

Microsoft Encarta (1999), *Microsoft® Encarta® Encyclopedia 99*. © 1993–8 Microsoft Corporation

Miles, Margaret R. (1999), *Plotinus on Body and Beauty: Society, Philosophy and Religion in Third-Century Rome*. Malden: Blackwell Publishers, Inc.

Miller, Dana (2003), *The Third Kind in Plato's* Timaeus. Göttingen: Vandenhoeck & Ruprecht

Miller, Mitchell (1986), *Plato's* Parmenides*: The Conversion of the Soul*. University Park: The University of Pennsylvania Press

Mohr, Richard D. (2005), *God and Forms in Plato*. Las Vegas: Parmenides Publishing

More, Paul E. (1916), "The *Parmenides* of Plato," *The Philosophical Review*. Vol. 25, No. 2 (March), 121–42

—(1923), *Hellenistic Philosophies*. Princeton: Princeton University Press

More, Paul E., W. D. Ross, and G. Dawes Hicks (1925), "Symposium: Platonic philosophy and Aristotelian metaphysics," *Proceeding of the Aristotelian Society. Supplementary Volumes. Philosophy and Metaphysics*. Vol. 5, 135–72

Morrison, J. S. (1977), "Two unresolved difficulties in the line and cave," *Phronesis*. Vol. 22, 212–31

Morrow, Glenn R. (1929), "The theory of knowledge in Plato's seventh epistle," *The Philosophical Review*. Vol. 38, No. 4 (July), 326–49

—(1950), "Necessity and persuasion in Plato's *Timaeus*," *The Philosophical Review*. Vol. 59, No. 2. (April), 147–63

Morrow, Glenn R., and John M. Dillon trans. (1987), *Proclus' Commentary on Plato's* Parmenides. Princeton: Princeton University Press

Murdoch, Iris (1993), *Metaphysics as a Guide to Morals*. New York: Penguin Books

Murphy, N. R. (1951), *The Interpretation of Plato's* Republic. Oxford: Clarendon Press

Nails, Debra (2002), *The People of Plato: A Prosopography of Plato and Other Socratics*. Indianapolis: Hackett Publishing Company, Inc.

Natorp, Paul (2004), *Plato's Theory of Ideas: An Introduction to Idealism*. Vasilis Politis (ed.), Vasilis Politis and John Connolly trans. International Plato Studies. Vol. 18. Sankt Augustin: Academia Verlag

Notopoulos, James A. (1944), "The Symbolism of the Sun and Light in the *Republic* of Plato II," *Classical Philology*. Vol. 39, No. 4 (October), 223–40

O'Brien, Denis (1971), "Plotinus on evil: a study of matter and the soul in Plotinus' conception of human evil," in *Le Néoplatonisme: Royaumont: 9–13 Juin 1969. Colloques Internationaux du Centre National de la Recherche Scientifique*. Paris: Centre National de la Recherche Scientifique, 55–66.

—(1991), *Plotinus on the Origin of Matter: An Exercise in the Interpretation of the* Enneads. Napoli: Bibliopolis

O'Grady, Patricia (2005), *Meet the Philosophers of Ancient Greece*. Burlington: Ashgate

O'Meara, Dominic J. (1993), *Plotinus: An Introduction to the* Enneads. Oxford: Clarendon Press

—(2003), *Platonopolis: Platonic Political Philosophy in Late Antiquity*. New York: Oxford University Press

Organ, Troy Wilson (1991), *The One: East and West*. New York: University Press of America

Owen, G. E. L. (1953), "The place of the *Timaeus* in Plato's dialogues," *The Classical Quarterly*. New Series, Vol. 3, No. 1 and 2 (January–April), 79–95

Pater, Walter (1893), *Plato and Platonism* (repr. 2005). New York: Barnes and Noble Books

Peck, A. L. (1953) "Plato's *Parmenides*: some suggestions for its interpretation," *The Classical Quarterly*. New Series, Vol. 3, No. 3 and 4 (July–October). 126–50

—(1954) "Plato's *Parmenides*: some suggestions for its interpretation. II," *The Classical Quarterly*. New Series, Vol. 4, No. 1 and 2 (January–April), 31–45

Penner, Terry (1987), *The Ascent From Nominalism: Some Existence Arguments in Plato's Middle Dialogues*. Boston: D. Reidel Publishing Company

—(1992), "Socrates and the early dialogues," in *The Cambridge Companion to Plato*. Richard Kraut (ed.). New York: Cambridge University Press, 121–69

—(2003), "The forms, the form of the Good, and the desire for Good in Plato's *Republic*," *The Modern Schoolman*. Vol. 80, 191–233

Phillips, John F. (1997), "Neoplatonic exegeses of Plato's cosmogony (*Timaeus* 27c–28c)," *The Journal of the History of Philosophy*. Vol. 35, No. 2 (April), 173–97

Pistorius, Philippus Villiers (1952), *Plotinus and Neoplatonism: An Introductory Study*. Cambridge: Bowes and Bowes Publishers Limited

Pond, Enoch (1856), *Plato: His Life, Works, Opinions, and Influence*. Boston: G. W. Cottrell

Post. L. A. (1927), "Thirteen epistles of Plato," *Mind*. New Series, Vol. 36, No. 141 (January), 121–3

Press, Gerald (2007), *Plato: A Guide for the Perplexed*. New York: Continuum

Prior, William J. (1985), *Unity and Development in Plato's Metaphysics*. La Salle: Open Court Publishing Company

Rappe, Sara (2000), *Reading Neoplatonism: Non-discursive Thinking in the Texts of Plotinus, Proclus, and Damascius*. Cambridge: Cambridge University Press

Rawson, Glenn (1996), "Knowledge and desire of the Good in Plato's *Republic*," *Southwest Philosophy Review*. Vol. 12, No. 1 (January), 103–15

Reale, Giovanni (1997), *Toward the New Interpretation of Plato*. 10th edition. John R. Catan and Richard Davies trans. and eds. Washington, DC: The Catholic University of America Press

Reeve, C. D. C. (1988), *Philosopher-Kings: The Argument of Plato's* Republic. Princeton: Princeton University Press

—(2003), "Plato's metaphysics of morals," *Oxford Studies in Ancient Philosophy*. Vol. 25 (Winter), 39–58

Richards, Herbert (1900), "The Platonic letters: II. (Continued)," *The Classical Review*. Vol. 14, No. 7 (October), 335–44

Rist, John M. (1962a), "The *Parmenides* again," *Phoenix*. Vol. 16, 1–14

—(1962b), "Theos and the One in some texts of Plotinus," *Medieval Studies*. Vol. 24, 169–80

—(1963), "Forms of individuals in Plotinus," *The Classical Quarterly*. New Series, Vol. 13, No. 2 (November), 223–31

—(1964), *Eros and Psyche: Studies in Plato, Plotinus, and Origen*. Phoenix: Supplementary Volume VI. (repr. 1991). Ann Arbor: UMI Out-of-Print Books on Demand

—(1967a), *Plotinus: The Road to Reality*. Cambridge: Cambridge University Press

—(1967b), "Integration and the undescended soul in Plotinus," *The American Journal of Philology*. Vol. 88, No. 4 (October), 410–22

—(1973), "The One of Plotinus and the God of Aristotle," *Review of Metaphysics*. Vol. 27, 75–87

—(1996), "Plotinus and Christian Philosophy," in Gerson (1996a, 386–413)

—(1999), "Moral motivation in Plato, Plotinus, Augustine, and ourselves," in *Plato and Platonism*, Johannes M. Van Ophuijsen (ed.). *Studies in Philosophy and the History of Philosophy*, Vol. 33, Ch. 12. Washington, DC: The Catholic University of America Press, 261–77

Robin, Léon (1928), *Greek Thought and the Origins of the Scientific Spirit*. New York: Alfred A. Knopf

Robinson, Richard (1942a), "Plato's *Parmenides*. I." *Classical Philology*. Vol. 37, No. 1 (January), 51–76

—(1942b), "Plato's *Parmenides*. II." *Classical Philology*. Vol. 37, No. 2 (April), 159–86

—(1953a), *Plato's Earlier Dialectic*. Oxford: Clarendon Press

—(1953b), "Hypothesis in the *Republic*," in Vlastos (1978a: 97–131)

Rochel, Hans (1971), "The dialogue *Parmenides*: insoluble enigma in Platonism?" *International Philosophical Quarterly*. Vol. XI, No. 4 (December), 496–520

Ross, Sir David (1951), *Plato's Theory of Ideas* (repr. 1963). Oxford: Oxford University Press

Runciman, Walter Garrison (1959), "Plato's *Parmenides*," *Harvard Studies in Classical Philology*. Vol. 64, 89–120

Ryle, Gilbert (1939a), "Plato's "'*Parmenides*,'" *Mind*. New Series, Vol. 48, No. 190 (April), 129–47

—(1939b), "Plato's '*Parmenides*' (II)," *Mind*. New Series, Vol. 48, No. 191 (July), 302–25

Sambursky, S. (1965), "Plato, Proclus, and the limitations of science," *The Journal of History of Philosophy*. Vol. 3, 1–12

Santas, Gerasimos (1985), "Two theories of Good in Plato's *Republic*," *Archiv für Geschichte der Philosophie*. Vol. 67, No. 3, 223–45

Santayana, George (1913), "Dr. Fuller, Plotinus, and the nature of evil," *The Journal of Philosophy, Psychology and Scientific Methods*. Vol. 10, No. 22 (October), 589–99

Sayre, Kenneth M. (1983), *Plato's Late Ontology: A Riddle Resolved*. Princeton: Princeton University Press

—(1987), "The *Philebus* and the Good: the unity of the dialogue in which the Good is unity," in John Cleary (ed.). *Proceedings of the Boston Area Colloquium in Ancient Philosophy*. Vol. 2. Lanham: University Press of America, 45–78

Schleiermacher, Friedrich (1973), *Schleiermacher's Introductions to the Dialogues of Plato*. William Dobson trans. New York: Arno Press

Schofield, Malcolm (1977), "The antinomies of Plato's *Parmenides*," *The Classical Quarterly*. New Series, Vol. 27, No. 1, 139–58

Schroeder, Frederic M. (1996), "Plotinus and language," in Gerson (1996a) 336–55

Scolnicov, Samuel (2003), *Plato's* Parmenides. Los Angeles: University of California Press.

Scoon, Robert (1942), "Plato's *Parmenides*," *Mind*. New Series, Vol. 51, No. 202 (April), 115–33

Sells, Michael A. (1994), *Mystical Languages of Unsaying*. Chicago: The University of Chicago Press

Sharples, R. W. (1994), "Plato Plotinus, and evil," *Bulletin of the Institute of Classical Studies*. Vol. 39 (New Series, Vol. 1), 171–81

Sheppard, Anne (2005), "Philosophy and philosophical schools," in Iorwerth Eiddon and Stephen Edwards (eds), *The Cambridge Ancient History: XIV: Late Antiquity: Empire and Successors: A.D. 425-600*. Cambridge: Cambridge University Press, 835–54

Shorey, Paul (1888), "The interpretation of the *Timaeus*," *The American Journal of Philology*. Vol. 9, No. 4, 395–418

—(1903a), *The Unity of Plato's Thought*. Chicago: The University of Chicago Press

—(1903b), "Plato's ethics," in Vlastos (1978b: 7–34)

—(1933), *What Plato Said*. Chicago: The University of Chicago Press

—(1938), *Platonism: Ancient and Modern*. Berkeley: University of California Press

Sinnige, Th. G. (1999), *Six Lectures on Plotinus and Gnosticism*. Boston: Kluwer Academic Publishers

Silverman, Allan (2002), *The Dialectic of Essence: A Study of Plato's Metaphysics*. Princeton: Princeton University Press

Slaveva-Griffin, Svetla (2009), *Plotinus on Number*. New York: Oxford University Press

Sleeman, J. H. and Gilbert Pollet (eds) (1980), *Lexicon Plotinianum*. Leiden: E. J. Brill, 1980

Smith, Andrew (1996), "Eternity and time," in Gerson (1996a: 196–216)

Smith, Nicholas D. (2004), "Did Plato write the *Alcibiades* I?" *Apeiron*. Vol. 37, 93–108

Sprague, Rosamond Kent (1951), "Negation and evil," *Philosophy and Phenomenological Research*. Vol. 11, No. 4 (June), 561–7

Stace, W. T. (1967), *A Critical History of Greek Philosophy*. New York: St. Martin's Press

Strong, Thomas B. (1895), *Platonism*. London: Richard Clay and Sons, Limited

Sumi, Atsushi (1997), "Plotinus on *Phaedrus* 247d7–e1: the Platonic *locus classicus* of the identity of Intellect with the intelligible objects," *American Catholic Philosophical Quarterly*. Vol. 71, No. 3 (Summer), 404–20

Szlezák, Thomas A. (1999), *Reading Plato*. Graham Zanker trans. New York: Routledge

Taylor, A. E. (1896), "On the interpretation of Plato's *Parmenides* (I)," *Mind*. New Series, Vol. 5, No. 19 (July), 297–326

—(1918), "The philosophy of Proclus," *Proceedings of the Aristotelian Society*. New Series. Vol. 18, 600–35

—(1934), *The* Parmenides *of Plato*. Oxford: Clarendon Press

—(1956), *Plato: The Man and his Work*. New York: Meridian Books

—(1960), *The Mind of Plato* (Originally *Plato*). (2nd Printing, 1964.) Ann Arbor: University of Michigan Press

Tigerstedt, E. N. (1974), *The Decline and Fall of the Neoplatonic Interpretation of Plato: An Outline and Some Observations*. Helsinki: Societas Scientiarum Fennica

—(1977), *Interpreting Plato*. Uppsala: Almqvist & Wiksell

Tripolis, Antonia (1978), *The Doctrine of the Soul in the Thought of Plotinus and Origen*. New York: Libra Publishers, Inc.

Turnbull, Grace H. (1948), *The Essence of Plotinus*. New York: Oxford University Press

Underhill, Evelyn (1974), *Mysticism*. New York: New American Library

Vlastos, Gregory (ed.) (1978a), *Plato: A Collection of Critical Essays. Vol. I: Metaphysics and Epistemology*. Notre Dame: University of Notre Dame Press

—(ed.) (1978b), *Plato: A Collection of Critical Essays. Vol. II: Ethics, Politics, and Philosophy of Art and Religion*. Notre Dame: University of Notre Dame Press

Voegelin, Eric (2000), *The Collected Works of Eric Voegelin. Vol. 16: Order and History. Vol. III: Plato and Aristotle*. Dante Germino (ed.). Columbia: University of Missouri Press

Vogel, C. J. de (1953), "On the Neoplatonic character of Platonism and the Platonic character of Neoplatonism," *Mind*. New Series, Vol. 62, No. 245 (January), 43–64

—(1959), "La théorie de l" ἄπειρον chez Platon et dans la tradition platonicienne," *Revue Philosophique de la France et de 'Etranger*. Vol. 49, 21–39

—(1969), "What was God for Plato?" in *Philosophia: Part I: Studies in Greek Philosophy*. Assen: Van Gorcum, 210–42

—1970), "Some controversial points of Plato interpretation reconsidered," in

*Philosophia: Part 1: Studies in Greek Philosophy*. Assen: Royal Van Gorcum Ltd., 183–209

—(1986), *Rethinking Plato and Platonism,* in *Mnemosyne*, Su, v. 92. Leiden: E. J. Brill

Walker, Merle G. (1938), "The one and many in Plato's *Parmenides*," *The Philosophical Review*, Vol. 47, No. 5 (September), 488–516

Wallis, R. T. (1972), *Neoplatonism*. London: Duckworth

Whitby, Charles J. (1909), *The Wisdom of Plotinus: A Metaphysical Study*. London: William Rider and Son Ltd.

White, Nicholas P. (1976), *Plato On Knowledge and Reality* (repr. 1980). Indianapolis: Hackett Publishing Company

—(1979), *A Companion to Plato's* Republic. Indianapolis: Hackett Publishing Company

Whittaker, John (1968), "The 'eternity' of the Platonic forms," *Phronesis*. Vol. 13, 131–44

Whittaker, Thomas (1961), *The Neo-Platonists: A Study in the History of Hellenism*. 4th edn. Hildesheim: Georg Olms Verlagsbuchhandlung

Wilberding, James (2006), *Plotinus' Cosmology: A Study of* Ennead *II.1 (40): Text, Translation, and Commentary*. James Wilberding trans. Oxford: Oxford University Press

Witt, R. E. (1931), "The Plotinian logos and its Stoic basis," *The Classical Quarterly*. Vol. 25, No. 2 (April), 103–11

Wolfson, H. A. (1952), "Albinus and Plotinus on divine attributes," *The Harvard Theological Review*. Vol. 45, No. 2 (April), 115–30

Zeller, Eduard (1931), *Outlines of the History of Greek Philosophy*. (13th edn) (repr. 1980). Revised by Wilhelm Nestle, L. R. Palmer trans. New York: Dover Publications, Inc.

# Index Locorum

# General Index

Lightning Source UK Ltd.
Milton Keynes UK
UKHW02f0659070618
323877UK00005B/950/P

9 781474 283687